149

# Distinctive HOME PLANS

200 Designs from 3,400 to 7,700 sq. ft.

CREATIVE HOMEOWNER PRESS®

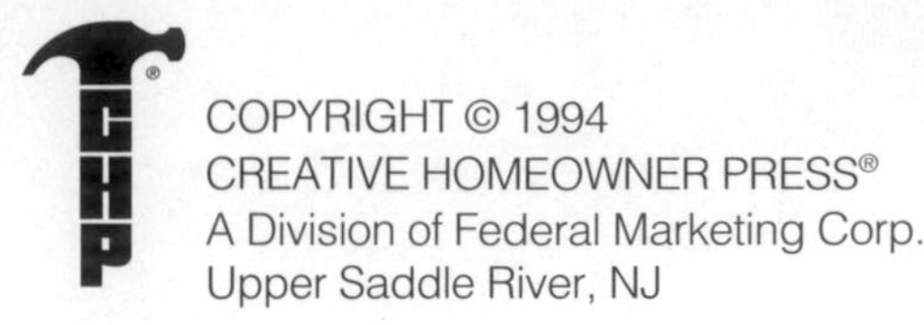



Manufactured in the United States of America

Cover Photographs: Home Planners, Inc.
House by Kellett & Saylor
Photographer: Laszlo Regos

Printed at Webcrafters, Inc.

Current Printing (last digit)
10 9 8 7 6 5 4 3 2 1

Distinctive Home Plans
LC: 93-074839
ISBN: 1-880029-32-4

CREATIVE HOMEOWNER PRESS®
A Division of Federal Marketing Corp.
24 Park Way
Upper Saddle River, NJ 07458

## Photography Credits

Creative Homeowner Press® would like to thank the following photographers and organizations for their kind permission to reproduce their photographs in the book:

**American Olean**: 8 (middle)

**James Brett**: 14 (bottom)

**California Spa**: 15 (bottom)

**Phillip H. Ennis Photography**: 6, 7, 9, 10, 11 (bottom right & left), 13

**Home Planners Inc./Laszlo Regos**: 1,3

**Melabee M. Miller**: 4, 5, 8 (top), 11 (top), 12 (top)

**Perma Built**: 15 (top)

**Rutt**: 12 (bottom)

**Cookie Samuels**: 8 (bottom)

**Everett Short**: 14 (top)

**Stockpile Inc./Jerry Demoney**: 16 (bottom)

*Building a distinctive home is not an everyday event, and finding a plan for the home of your dreams can be intimidating. This book has been specially designed to assist you in your search for the finest home plans available. They have been carefully chosen and we are certain that you will find a house that fulfills your dreams.*

## CONTENTS

# *the magnificent* **Entry**

Every fine home welcomes the public with an intriguing entry. Not only is an entry aesthetically pleasing, it is also the link between the exterior and interior of the home.

A successful entry embraces its guests, drawing them from the street into the home. Exterior elements assist in this task. As a focal point, the entry is emphasized by the landscaping, lighting arrangement and a semi-circular driveway. A stone path is helpful in assisting the guest directly to the front door.

A considerate homeowner provides a covered entry, such as a portico, for those days when the weather is less than agreeable. Iron benches and a pleasing overhead lamp are welcome touches. Decorative trim previews the quality furnishings that are found inside the home.

Whatever the style, the entry is the introduction of the home and it should welcome guests as warmly as the homeowner.

# *the grand* Foyer

As the introduction to your home, a grand foyer should leave your guests with a welcoming first impression.

Reveal the family personality with displays of artwork, paintings or photographs, a colorful gallery extending up the stairs. Mirrors serve a dual purpose, both as a practical piece for those tidying up on the way in and also as space creators. A small desk with an array of candlesticks or a vignette of collectibles provides an interesting focal point.

Splurge on a marble floor, or paint a faux finish. On the practical side, a table is perfect for placing keys and dropping off packages while a coat closet or brass rack is a must. Waiting guests will appreciate a comfortable chair or bench.

To top it off, install a skylight, hang a sparkling chandelier or create a stir with a ceiling fan. With a few unique touches, your foyer can become a glamorous transition to the rest of the home.

From *Choosing a Color Scheme* (Creative Homeowner Press®)

# *the formal*
# Living Room

Opulence is reborn in an elaborately decorated formal living room. With a family room to handle casual affairs, the living room is free to explore the depths of extravagance.

This is the perfect place for luxurious French doors and ornamental parquet floors. A massive fireplace with a marble mantel is sure to be the focal point, while antiques add style and sophistication. For those who prefer a contemporary look over the traditional design, there are a multitude of plush couches and armchairs that are simple yet elegant.

Floorcoverings range from lush wall-to-wall carpeting to fine Oriental throws. A sunken floor and a high ceiling distinguish a formal living room from the others. Cover the chair rail with a relief wallcovering for a classy touch or add texture by creating a border. Vases, artwork and statuettes tie the room scheme together in a personal way.

From *Home Decorating with Paint, Tile, Wallcovering* (Creative Homeowner Press®)

# *the stately* Dining Room

The art of fine dining is being rediscoverd. Taking the time for leisurely meals and conversation with groups of friends or business associates requires sufficient space and suitable furnishings.

When it comes to furniture, the traditional set is not your only option. Take note of the ambience that permeates your favorite restaurants. Then, adapt this feeling in your own home. Mix-and-match a table with uphostered chairs. Unique storage pieces, such as a painted armoire or a fancy set of bookshelves can add a savory twist.

Lighting should be functional and appealing. Although candlelight may be perfect for a romantic evening, a stronger light is better for larger gatherings. A combination of chandelier, recessed lights and floor lamps provides for a broad range of possibilities.

# the extravagant Kitchen

From *Planning the Perfect Kitchen* (Creative Homeowner Press®)

Today's kitchen is served up with good, old-fashioned friendliness. Once again the heart of the home, the kitchen is a place not only for cooking, but for living as well.

No matter what the style: traditional, contemporary, country, high-tech, or classic; modern appliances are crafted to ease the work load. A built-in refrigerator, innovative cooktop, restaurant-style range, handy ice maker, dishwasher, and garbage disposer provide all you need for cooking and cleanup. these items, are coupled with an island for food preparation, a space for eating, and plenty of extra room for those who would like to sit and chat with the busy cook.

The use of rich materials and attention to details convey a desirable ambience. Extra touches such as a fireplace, walk-in pantry, a parquet wood floor, and granite countertops contribute to an extravagnt yet user-friendly environment.

From *Kitchens: Design, Remodel, Build* (Creative Homeowner Press®)

From *Dream Kitchens* (Creative Homeowner Press®)

# *the lavish* Bathroom

From *Designing and Planning Bathrooms* (Creative Homeowner Press®)

No distinctive home would be complete without a lavish bathroom to serve as a peaceful retreat to indulge in "self-pampering."

Consider the following: a contoured whirlpool bath, stepped tub, or a new multiple-head shower for all-over body massage; a spacious His and Her double vanity; exercise equipment and a stereo system to get the blood moving; a steam room or sauna to rejuvenate; and a fireplace and sitting area for quiet relaxation. The options are endless. From remote-controlled fixtures to automatic shampoo dispensers, there is a flow of bathroom innovations from which to choose.

As for decor, use your imagination to create a beautiful and tranquil oasis. Seek out storage-rich furnishings and items that evoke personal style such as a colorful mural or stone countertop. The modern elements available today help your bathroom to become a timeless, serene getaway.

From *Designing and Planning Bathrooms* (Creative Homeowner Press®)

From *Designing and Planning Bathrooms* (Creative Homeowner Press®)

# *the sumptuous* Master Bedroom

Creating a haven means surrounding yourself with the things you love. This is most evident in the bedroom where personal preference takes the reins. Furnishings, decorative pieces, color and pattern should be chosen for physical as well as psychological comforts.

Although the bed is the most important piece of furniture in the room, a small sitting area consisting of a table and love seat is a luxurious addition. After all, it is not unusual for one to watch television, listen to music, catch up on reading or enjoy a light meal in the bedroom.

Create an intimate atmosphere with plush carpeting, comfy couches, and an abundance of soft furnishings and pillows. Don't be afraid to add unconventional touches such as a small art gallery on the wall, or family treasures displayed in unexpected places. Concentrate on the things that relax and refresh you.

From *Designing and Planning Bedrooms* (Creative Homeowner Press®)

From *Designing and Planning Bedrooms* (Creative Homeowner Press®)

From *Designing and Planning Bedrooms* (Creative Homeowner Press®)

# *the precious* Child's Bedroom

A child's room must be as versatile as its growing occupant. The needs and desires of the child will place new demands on the bedroom as the youngster advances in age.

Use your imagination when it comes to decor. A fantasy mural or colorful theme can create a playful paradise filled with sensory stimulation. The simplest room can be transformed with paint, wallcovering and the appropriate toys.

A child will use his or her room for a myriad of activity; storage utilities and furnishings should be chosen accordingly. For instance, a trundle bed or bunk is a handy convenience when guests slumber overnight, a small desk is a must for creative work and an accessible closet may promote neatness at an early age. Scrubbable paint or wallcovering is a lifesaver when a creative child gets the urge to do his or her own decorating. Furnishings and materials used in the room must be safe, non-toxic and durable.

From *Designing and Planning Bedrooms* (Creative Homeowner Press®)

From *Designing and Planning Bedrooms* (Creative Homeowner Press®)

From *Designing and Planning Bedrooms* (Creative Homeowner Press®)

# *the congenial*
# Great Room

For centuries, castles, palaces and villas contained a multi-purpose space where family and friends gathered for casual meals and entertainment. Today, a large, open living area, called the Great Room, fulfills this function.

The key to a successful Great Room is to evoke a feeling of welcome. Even with elegant and formal furnishings, a friendly, casual mood should shine through.

Entertaining is a priority in this room and therefore seating should be arranged in a way that encourages conversation. The television set or entertainment center is likely to be the focal point in today's living arrangement. However, with the trend turning towards tradition, a new energy-efficient fireplace is an option that provides a heartwarming place fo the family to gather.

Express the family's personality to achieve a unique style. Create a gallery of family art or memorable photographs. Cherished mementoes and travel finds make wonderfdul accent pieces and a library, filled with your favorite books, is a personal addition.

From *Planning the Perfect Living Room* (Creative Homeowner Press®)

From *Planning the Perfect Living Room* (Creative Homeowner Press®)

# *the sophisticated* Media Room

The best listening and viewing is done without the distractions of everyday home living. For those tuned into the high-tech world, a media room is an oasis where you can appreciate a projection television, video cassettes, laser discs and CD's.

The arrangement of seating in relation to speakers and video screen is of the utmost importance. Place the speakers in such a way that sound fills the room. Be sure the video screen is kept out of the sun; a large projection screen can be installed in the ceiling to be dropped down when ready for use.

Today, high-tech equipment itself is sleekly designed and you may opt to leave it out in the open. However, built-in units or cabinets can stow equipment for a neat look. A dimmer switch, track lighting or recessed spotlights guide light away from the video screen and accentuate artwork.

For the room devoted to sound and vision, an art deco or Hollywood-style theme provides a classic look.

# *the opulent*
# Swimming Pool

With some inventive thinking, a pool can be much more than a body of water wallowing in the backyard. The latest wave is the lap pool and compact lap pool. Of course, pools can be custom designed and built to unique shapes and size.

A pool is enhanced by its surroundings. Popular today are natural scenes, with carefully placed boulders, an abundance of plantings and picturesque waterfalls. Indoor pools, although a challenge to maintain, can be decorated with the same design and architectural elements used inside the home, creating a unified look.

A lengthy but narrow lap pool is perfect for the swimming enthusiast. However, those who lack space can enjoy the same benefits of swimming in compact lap pools that are equipped with jets that push water into a streaming motion. A cabana sited nearby provides changing areas, showers, a kitchen and space for entertaining.

From *Swimming Pools* (Creative Homeowner Press®)

From *Swimming Pools* (Creative Homeowner Press®)

*the indulgent*

# Spa & Hot Tub

The steaming water and bursting bubbles of a spa or hot tub is a welcome sight at the end of the day. Tensions and stress are soothed away while the mind and body is rejuvenated with this age-old practice.

In the past, having a hot tub or spa at one's home was a rare convenience, but today they are common household additions that add beauty and entertainment to the home. Depending upon personal preference, choose a natural redwood hot tub, a shapely thermoplastic spa or a custom-built ceramic tile spa.

No matter where you put it, inside or out, the spa or hot tub will become the center of attention. To enhance its impact, thoughtful architectural design and landscaping can create a unique, intimate environment. A small enclosed garden is a relaxing oasis that provides a peaceful place to soak.

From *Spas & Hot Tubs, Saunas & Home Gyms* (Creative Homeowner Press®)

From *Spas & Hot Tubs, Saunas & Home Gyms* (Creative Homeowner Press®)

# *the expansive*
# Deck & Patio

Everyone enjoys a day or evening spent outdoors. For relaxing after hours or on the weekend, dining alfresco or entertaining formally, a deck or patio will add a new dimension to your life and home.

High-style decks are custom-built to fit any architectural style. There are many basic styles to choose from: low-level garden floors, twin or multi-level decks, or even a hillside deck. Options range from building a sun deck over the garage to surrounding a glamorous pool.

A well-planned patio will combine the beauty of nature with the comforts of indoor living. As the stepping stone between home and garden, the materials used for the patio will determine its ambience. Irregular flagstone, mossy bricks laid in sand, adobe tile and poured concrete provide different colors and textures.

An arbor or trellis provides shade and adds romantic appeal. Careful placement of spacious benches and tables, curved handrails, planters filled with shrubs and flowers and a stimulating hot tub will further enhance the visual beauty and utility of the outdoor space. Add to this the luxury of an open-air kitchen with dining area, barbecue and storage.

The best designs echo the contours of the surrounding and and harmonize with the environment.

From *Decks & Patios* (Creative Homeowner Press®)

From *Decks* (Creative Homeowner Press®)

# *Distinctive Homes* PORTFOLIO

A distinctive home means different things to different people. Hence, we have selected 200 elegant plans from our own collection to give you the opportunity to make your own distinctive choice. Although each design in this book is unique, all the plans share some special amenities. Regardless of their particular size or style, each home is designed to provide an abundance of comfortable, convenient, living space. By definition, a distinctive home must also include some special, or distinguishing characteristics. These homes have all been custom-designed to complement your particular lifestyle. We realize that those who are interested in building a custom home are looking for more than just a house; they are looking for something special, a stunning representation of their own distinctive personality.

## Space

Distinctive homes tend to be quite expansive simply because it takes a larger space to include all of the special amenities. Each plan in this book is at least 3,400 sq. ft. Inside you'll find vast kitchens with walk-in pantries, workable islands and an abundance of storage; master suites with lavish bathrooms, walk-in closets and beautiful balconies; grand entrances with high ceilings and magnificent staircases; and a variety of outdoor living spaces such as patios, pools and decks.

## Amenities

The amenities chosen for your home will distinguish its character. Depending on your family, certain options will be chosen while others are excluded. For instance, a physically fit family may dedicate a large space to a home gym, enhanced with a whirlpool. On the other hand, if there are artistically inclined members in the family, an art studio would be more appropriate.

## Architectural Details

Just as the inside of the home demands a great deal of thought and planning, the outside is of equal importance. Careful attention to detail will result in a home that adds drama to the surrounding property. A stunning portico, tall entry doors, French windows and chimneys not only serve a purpose, but they are pleasing to the eye as well. Exterior ornamentation such as windows, cornices and entry details provide the finishing touches.

**Design CP2993**

# Columbia

This home, with its dramatic columns, is beautifully proportioned and offers impressive livability on two levels. A gathering room, with massive fireplace, is flanked by the library and formal dining area. The gourmet kitchen is joined by a breakfast room and family room with fireplace. Upstairs, the master bedroom suite features a whirlpool tub and through-fireplace. Two bedrooms on the second floor share a full bath. A fourth bedroom is the perfect guest bedroom with its own private bath.

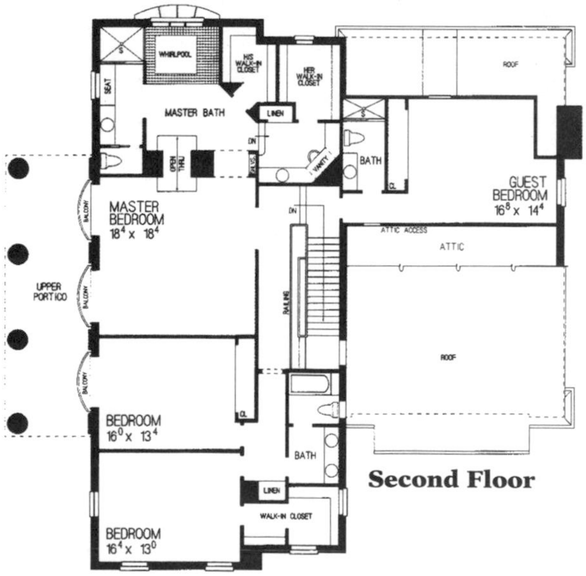

**Second Floor**

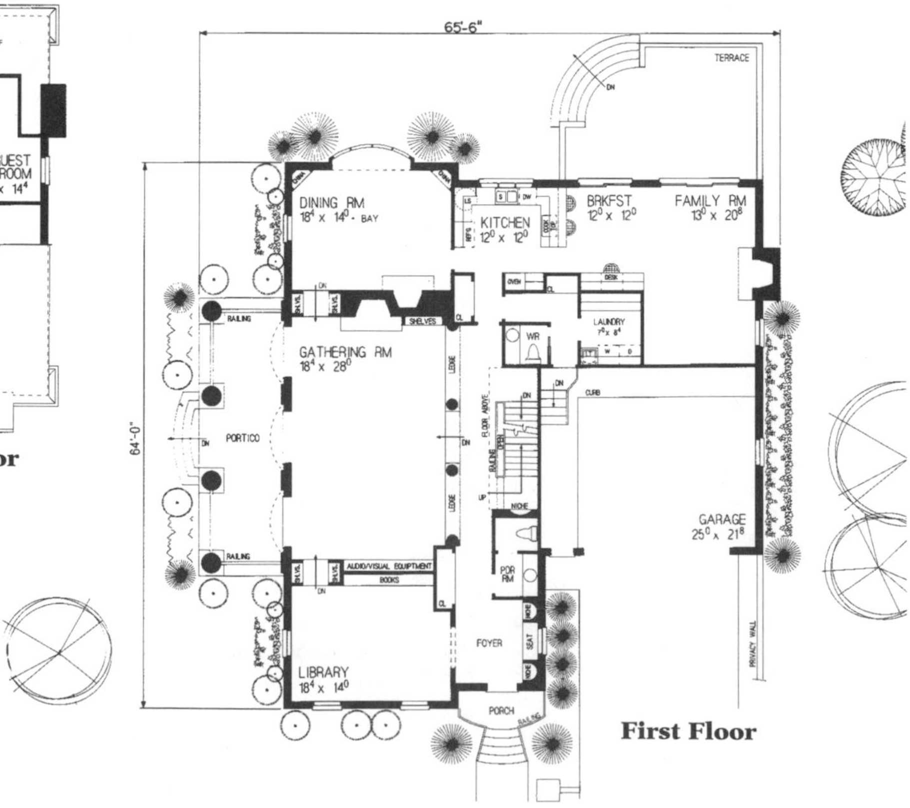

**First Floor**

| | |
|---|---|
| *First Floor:* | *2,440 sq. ft.* |
| *Second Floor:* | *2,250 sq. ft.* |
| *Total:* | *4,690 sq. ft.* |

*(Foundation Type: Basement)*

# Dearborn

**Design CP2192**

This is a fine adaptation from the 18th Century. The authentic detailing centers around the fine proportions, the dentils, the window symmetry, the front door and entranceway, the massive chimneys and the masonry work. Inside, the formal living room and sunken family room feature fireplaces. Built-in amenities include a wall of bookshelves and cabinets in the library, corner china cabinets in the formal dining room, cabinets in both passages to the family room and a china cabinet in the breakfast room.

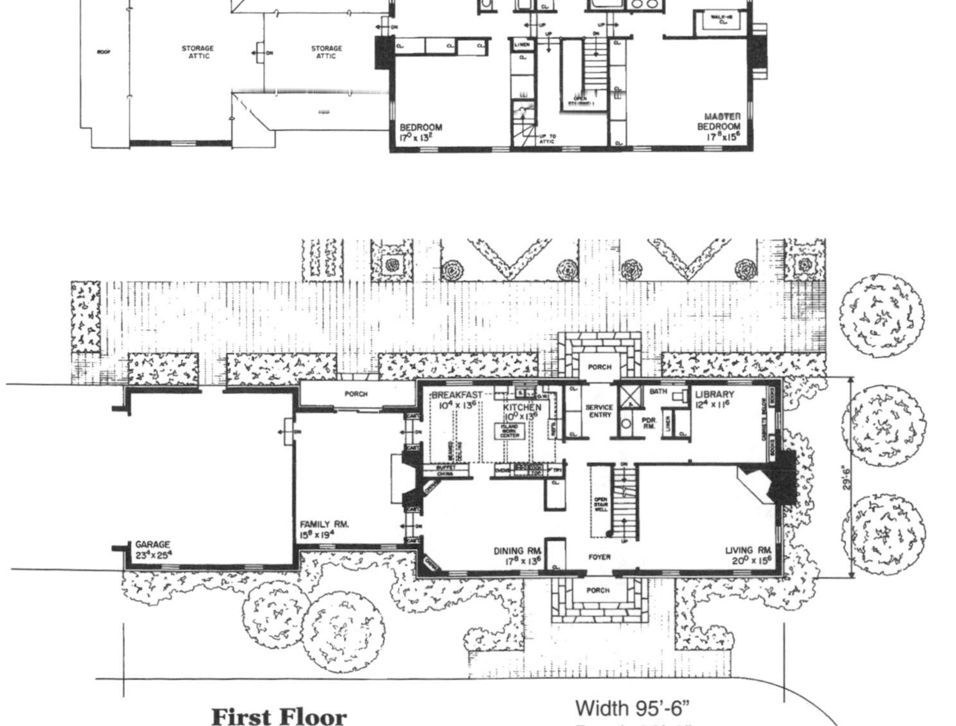


**Second Floor**

**First Floor**

Width 95'-6"
Depth 29'-6"

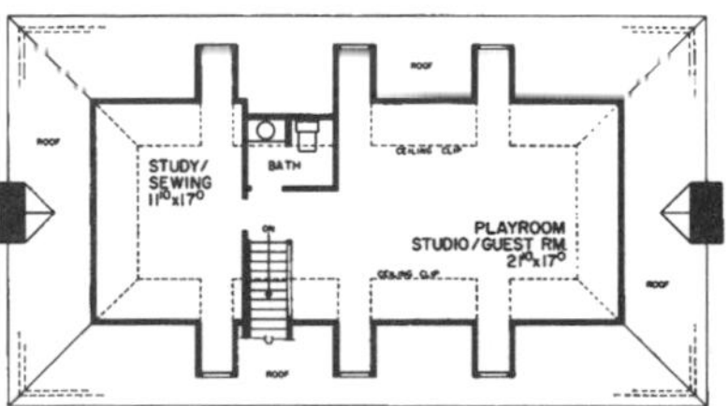


**Third Floor**

| | |
|---|---|
| *First Floor:* | *1,884 sq. ft.* |
| *Second Floor:* | *1,521 sq. ft.* |
| *Total:* | *3,405 sq. ft.* |

*(Foundation Type: Basement)*

## Design CP2975

# Faribault

Three wonderful floors of living space include a useful guest bedroom and study or hobby room on the top floor. The second-floor master suite has a pampering bath. Two family bedrooms share a full bath on this floor as well. Living areas include the formal living and dining rooms, country kitchen and library. Notice the six fireplaces, including two in the master bedroom! A full-width terrace adds special appeal for outdoor enjoyment.

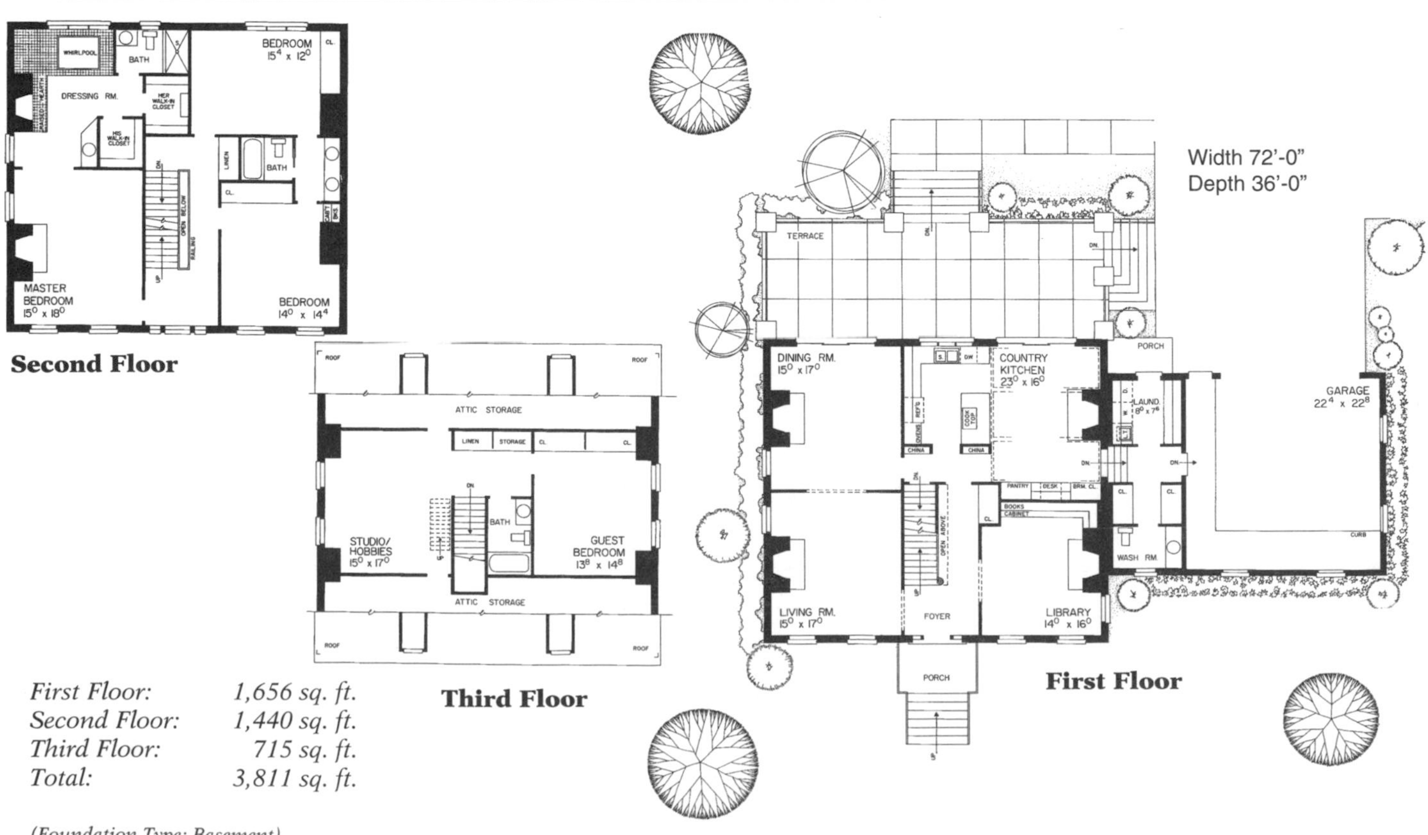


**Second Floor**

**Third Floor**

**First Floor**

| | |
|---|---|
| *First Floor:* | *1,656 sq. ft.* |
| *Second Floor:* | *1,440 sq. ft.* |
| *Third Floor:* | *715 sq. ft.* |
| *Total:* | *3,811 sq. ft.* |

*(Foundation Type: Basement)*

# Gaylord

## Design CP2662

Influences from both Georgian and Federal architecture are apparent in the design of this home. First-floor features include fireplaces in the gathering room, breakfast room, and study, as well as a built-in barbecue in the U-shaped kitchen. The second floor is dominated by a sumptuous master suite and two family bedrooms that share a full bath. A third floor holds two additional bedrooms that might serve well as guest rooms or as studio or study space.

**First Floor**

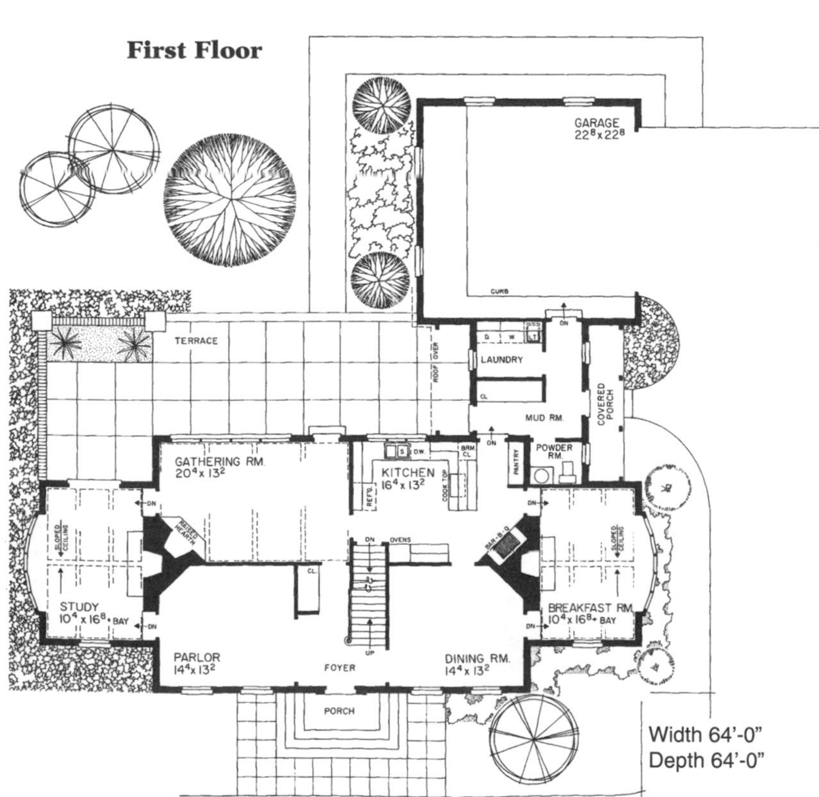


**Second Floor**

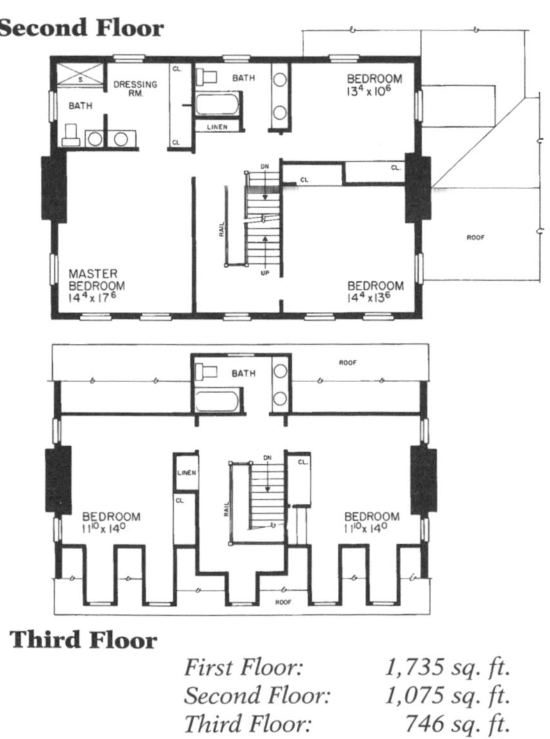


**Third Floor**

| | |
|---|---|
| *First Floor:* | *1,735 sq. ft.* |
| *Second Floor:* | *1,075 sq. ft.* |
| *Third Floor:* | *746 sq. ft.* |
| *Total:* | *3,556 sq. ft.* |

*(Foundation Type: Basement)*

## Design CP2990

# Winona

Designed to resemble the St. George Tucker house in Williamsburg, this stately home offers a floor plan for today's family. First-floor rooms include a family room with informal dining space at one end of the plan and a formal living room at the other end. In between are the media room, guest powder room, dining room and kitchen. Three second-floor bedrooms include a luxurious master suite with sitting room. There is also a guest room with private bath over the garage.

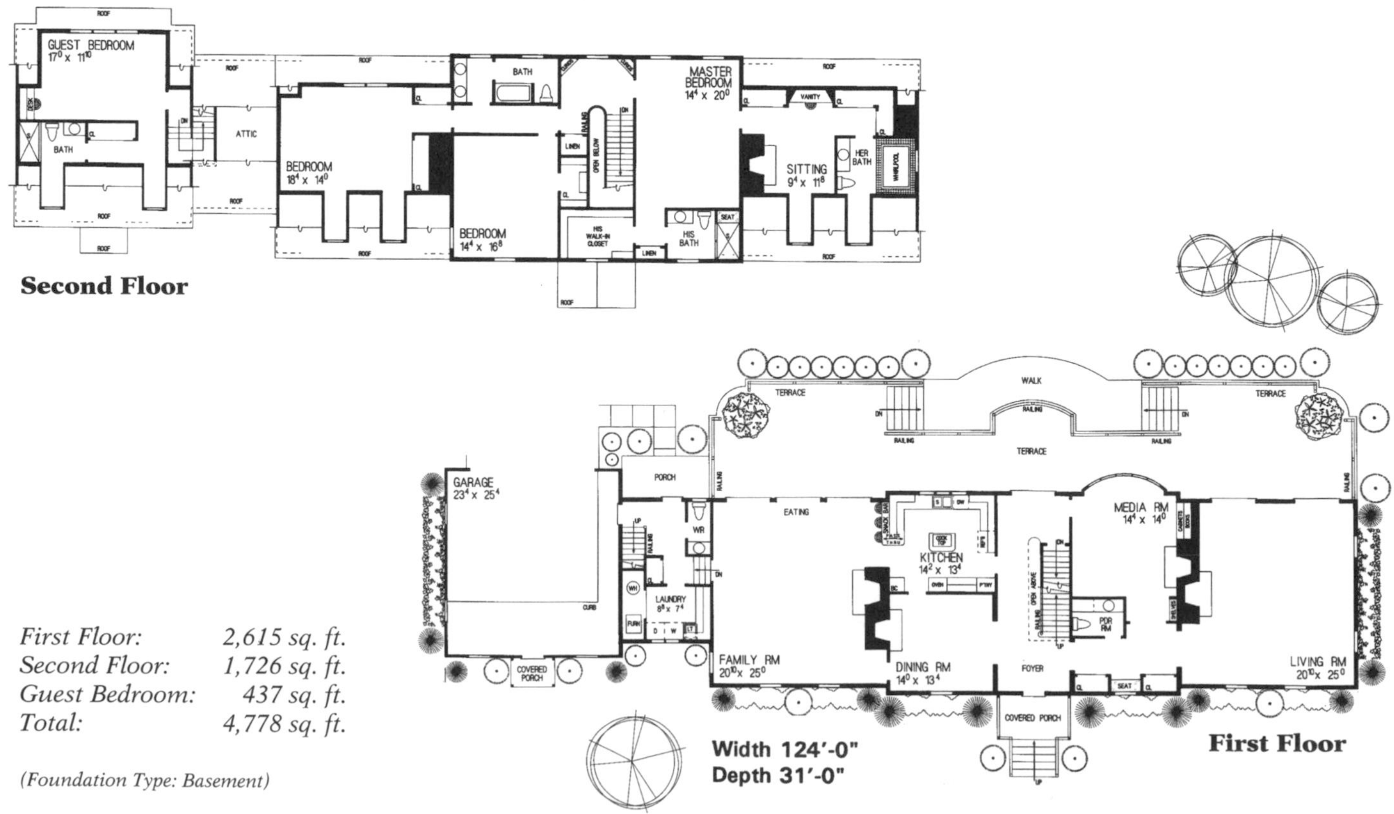


**Second Floor**

**First Floor**

*First Floor:* *2,615 sq. ft.*
*Second Floor:* *1,726 sq. ft.*
*Guest Bedroom:* *437 sq. ft.*
*Total:* *4,778 sq. ft.*

*(Foundation Type: Basement)*

# Rochester

**Design CP2996**

The porches on the first and second floors define this gracious New York farmhouse. Fireplaces are found in the living room, formal dining area, study and spacious family room. An island kitchen with snack bar is flanked by the dining and family rooms. The terrace is accessible through the family room. A master bedroom suite, with His and Her walk-in closets, a dressing room and whirlpool bath, is joined by three bedrooms to complete the second floor.

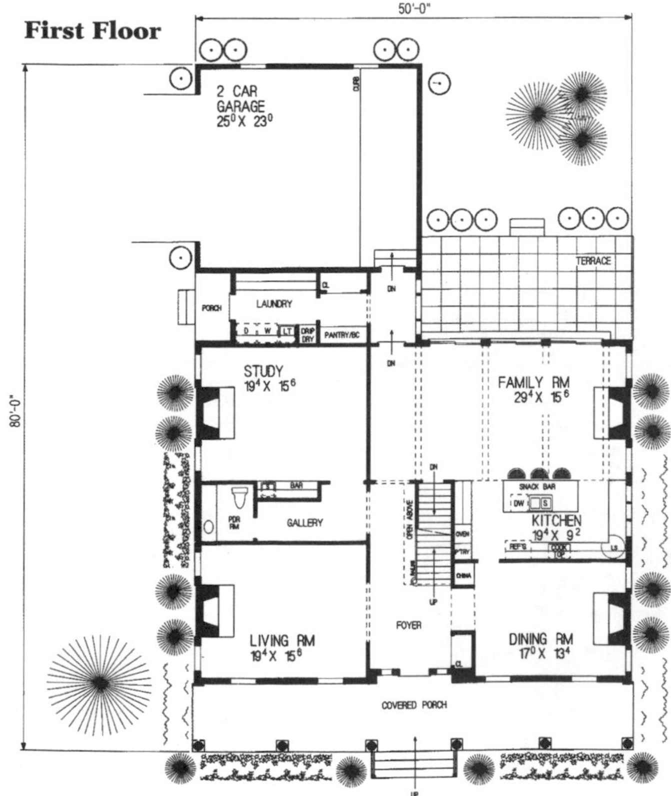


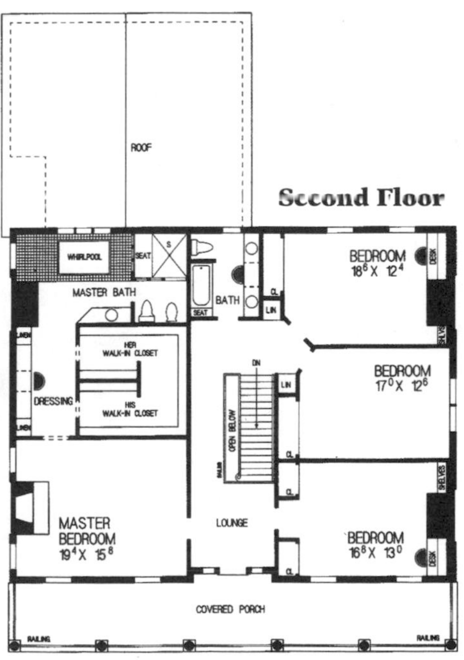


| | |
|---|---|
| *First Floor:* | *2,191 sq. ft.* |
| *Second Floor:* | *1,928 sq. ft.* |
| *Total:* | *4,119 sq. ft.* |

*(Foundation Type: Basement)*

## Design CP2133

# Krista

This is a country-estate home which will command all the attention it deserves. The projecting pediment gable supported by the finely proportioned columns lends an aura of elegance. The window treatment, the massive capped chimney, the cupola, and the varying roof planes complete the characterization of this impressive home. Inside is a 3,024-square-foot first floor and a two-bedroom second floor. Don't overlook the compartmented baths, the sauna, the laundry and the many built-ins available.

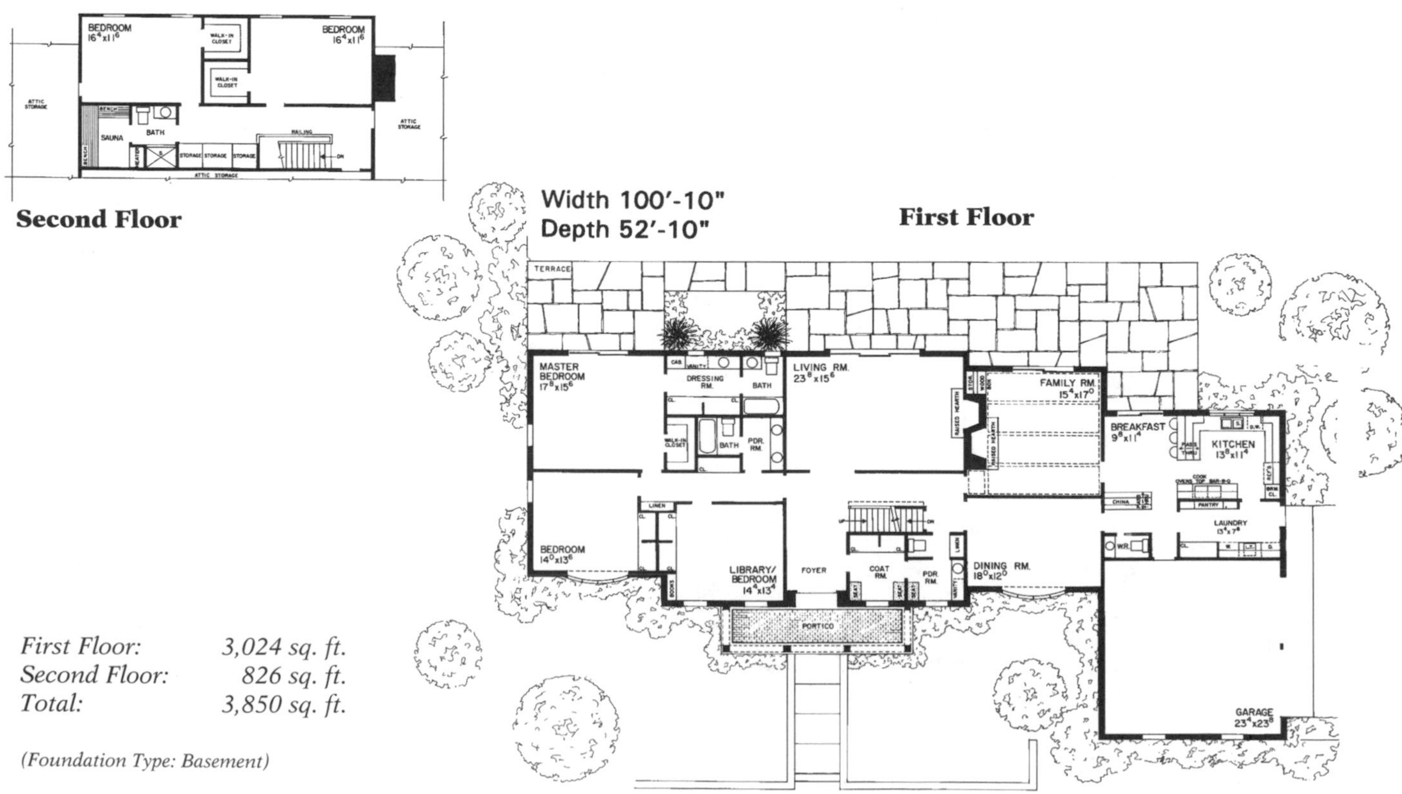


**Second Floor**

Width 100'-10"
Depth 52'-10"

**First Floor**

*First Floor:* *3,024 sq. ft.*
*Second Floor:* *826 sq. ft.*
*Total:* *3,850 sq. ft.*

*(Foundation Type: Basement)*

# Homestead

## Design CP9095

If you are looking for a plan that delivers a wealth of fine features, this one should appeal to you. Fireplaces in the dining room, living room and study keep everyone warm and snug. A window-surrounded breakfast nook starts the day with sunshine. Built-ins abound: bookcases in the library loft, study and gallery, wine rack in the family room, niche in the hall and bookcases and cabinets in two upstairs bedrooms. The family room has a vaulted ceiling and is overlooked by the balcony from above.

**First Floor**

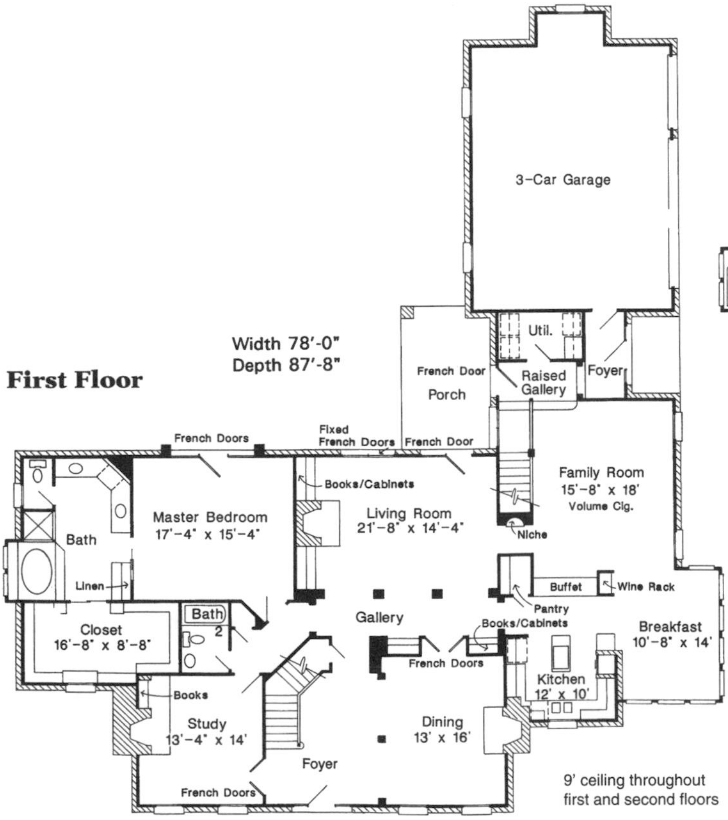

Width 78'-0"
Depth 87'-8"

3-Car Garage
Util.
Raised Gallery
Foyer
French Door
Porch
French Doors
Fixed French Doors
French Door
Books/Cabinets
Family Room 15'-8" x 18' Volume Clg.
Master Bedroom 17'-4" x 15'-4"
Living Room 21'-8" x 14'-4"
Niche
Bath
Linen
Gallery
Buffet
Wine Rack
Pantry
Books/Cabinets
Breakfast 10'-8" x 14'
Closet 16'-8" x 8'-8"
Bath 2
French Doors
Kitchen 12' x 10'
Books
Study 13'-4" x 14'
Dining 13' x 16'
Foyer
French Doors

9' ceiling throughout first and second floors

**Second Floor**

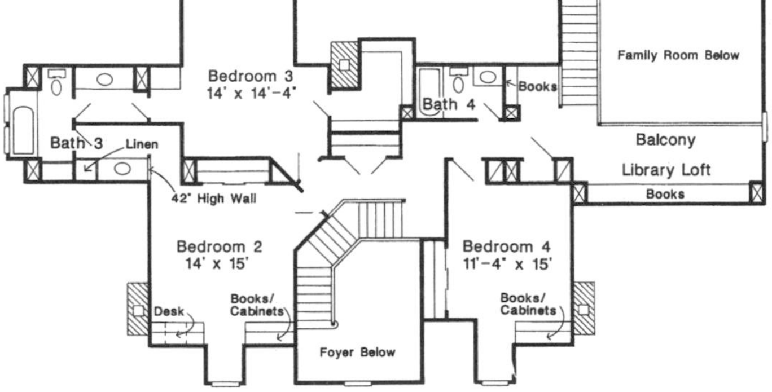

Bedroom 3 14' x 14'-4"
Bath 3
Linen
Bath 4
Books
Family Room Below
Balcony
Library Loft
Books
42" High Wall
Bedroom 2 14' x 15'
Bedroom 4 11'-4" x 15'
Desk
Books/Cabinets
Books/Cabinets
Foyer Below

| | |
|---|---|
| *First Floor:* | *2,824 sq. ft.* |
| *Second Floor:* | *1,334 sq. ft.* |
| *Total:* | *4,158 sq. ft.* |

*(Foundation Type: Slab)*

## Design CP9910 **Broadwings**

A symmetrical facade with twin chimneys makes a grand statement. A covered porch welcomes visitors and provides a pleasant place to spend cool evenings. The entry foyer is flanked by formal living areas: a dining room and a living room, each with a fireplace. A third fireplace is the highlight of the expansive great room to the rear. The deck is accessible through the great room, the sun room or the master bedroom. The second floor offers three bedrooms, two full baths and plenty of storage space.

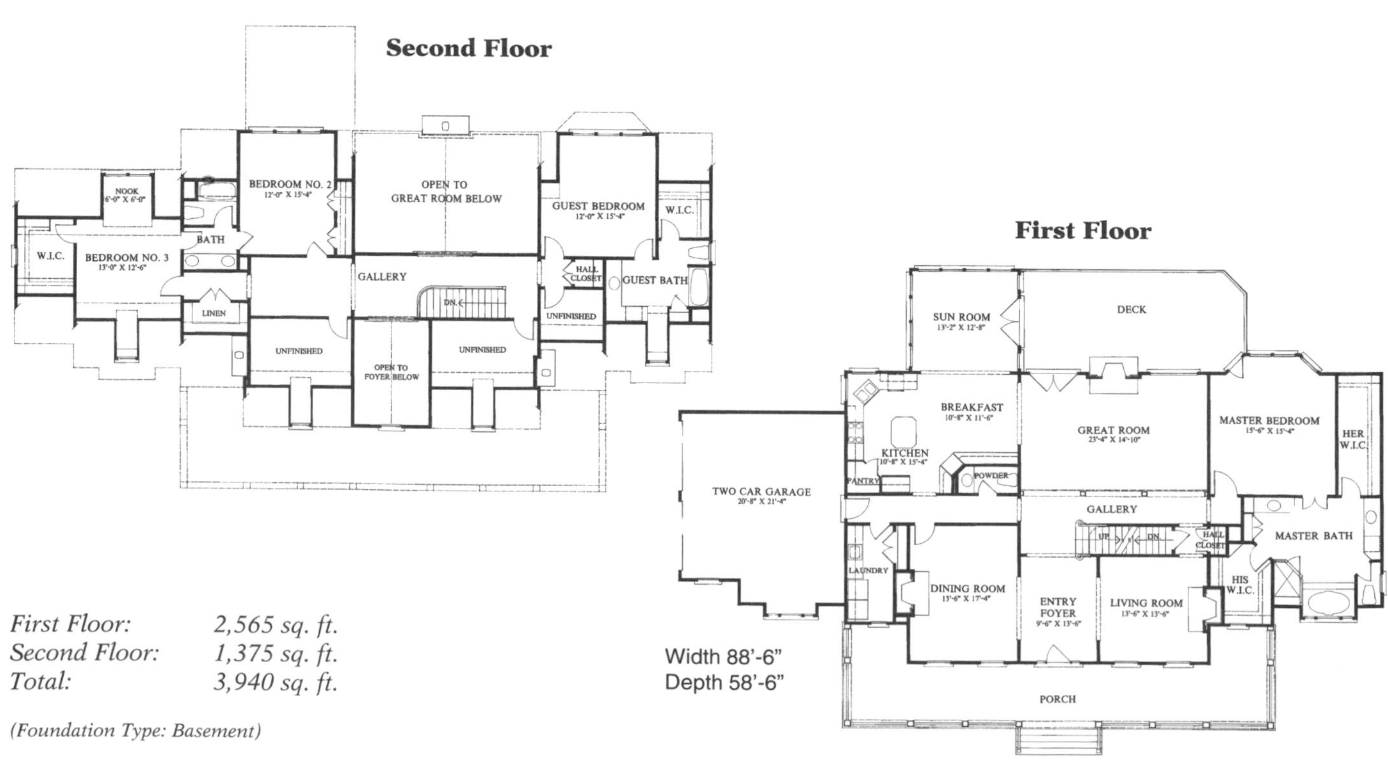


| | |
|---|---|
| *First Floor:* | *2,565 sq. ft.* |
| *Second Floor:* | *1,375 sq. ft.* |
| *Total:* | *3,940 sq. ft.* |

*(Foundation Type: Basement)*

# *Hallmark* **Design CP9911**

An elegant floor plan offers living space for every activity. Formal living and dining rooms flank the foyer. The informal family room and keeping room with breakfast bay are to the rear. Note the four fireplaces! A powder room is placed conveniently in the center of the plan. Four bedrooms, including a master suite with yet another fireplace and a deluxe bath, occupy the second floor. Covered porches enhance the front and rear of the plan.

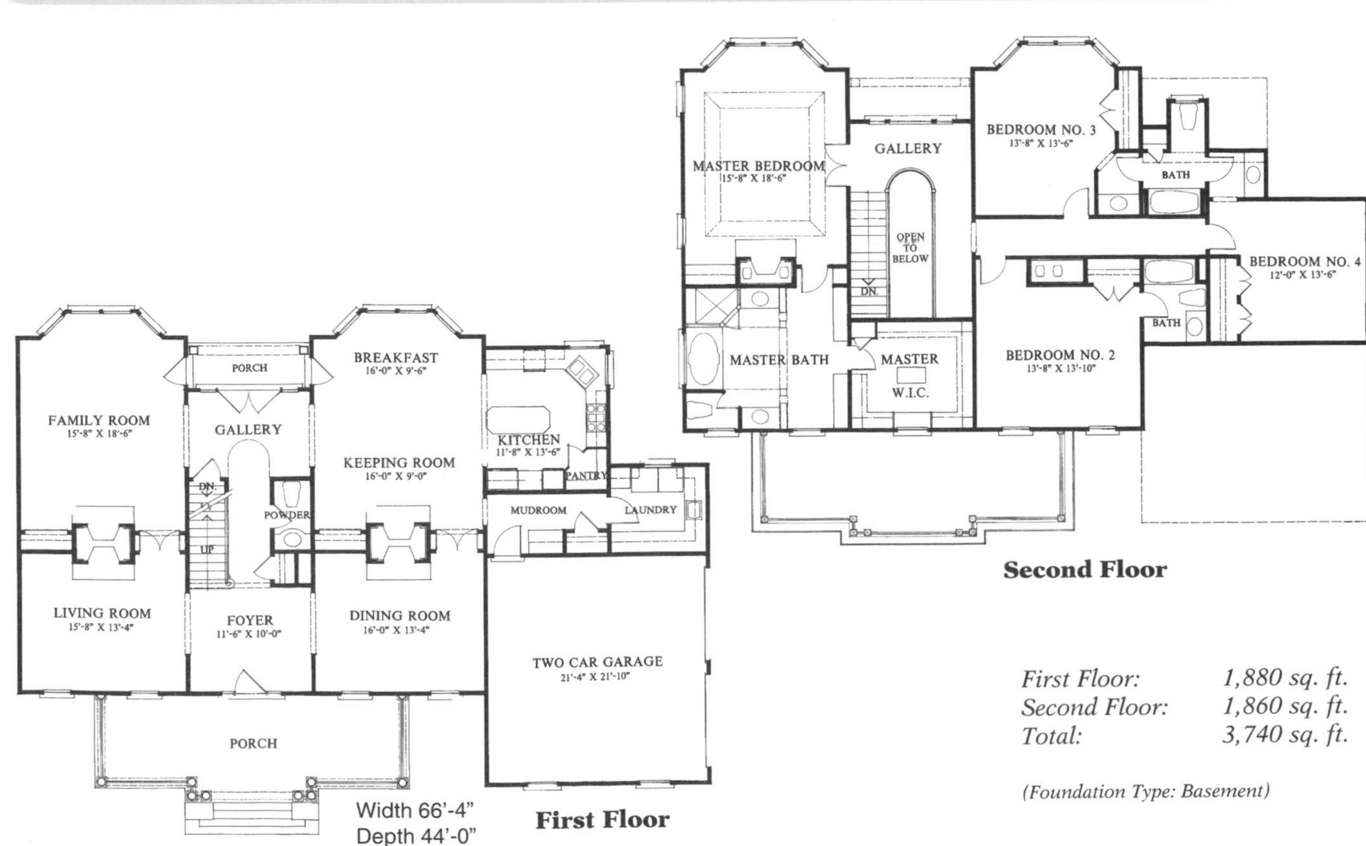


| | |
|---|---|
| *First Floor:* | *1,880 sq. ft.* |
| *Second Floor:* | *1,860 sq. ft.* |
| *Total:* | *3,740 sq. ft.* |

*(Foundation Type: Basement)*

# Design CP2998 Cottonwood

This gambrel-roofed two-story is a fine example of historical homes. The classic floor plan includes formal living and dining rooms flanking the entry hall. The living room has a fireplace and the dining room a bay window. A media room/study also sports a fireplace and has access to a rear terrace. The family room with yet another fireplace connects to the kitchen via a snack bar. On the second floor are three bedrooms and two full baths. The third floor contains unfinished space which acts as superb storage.

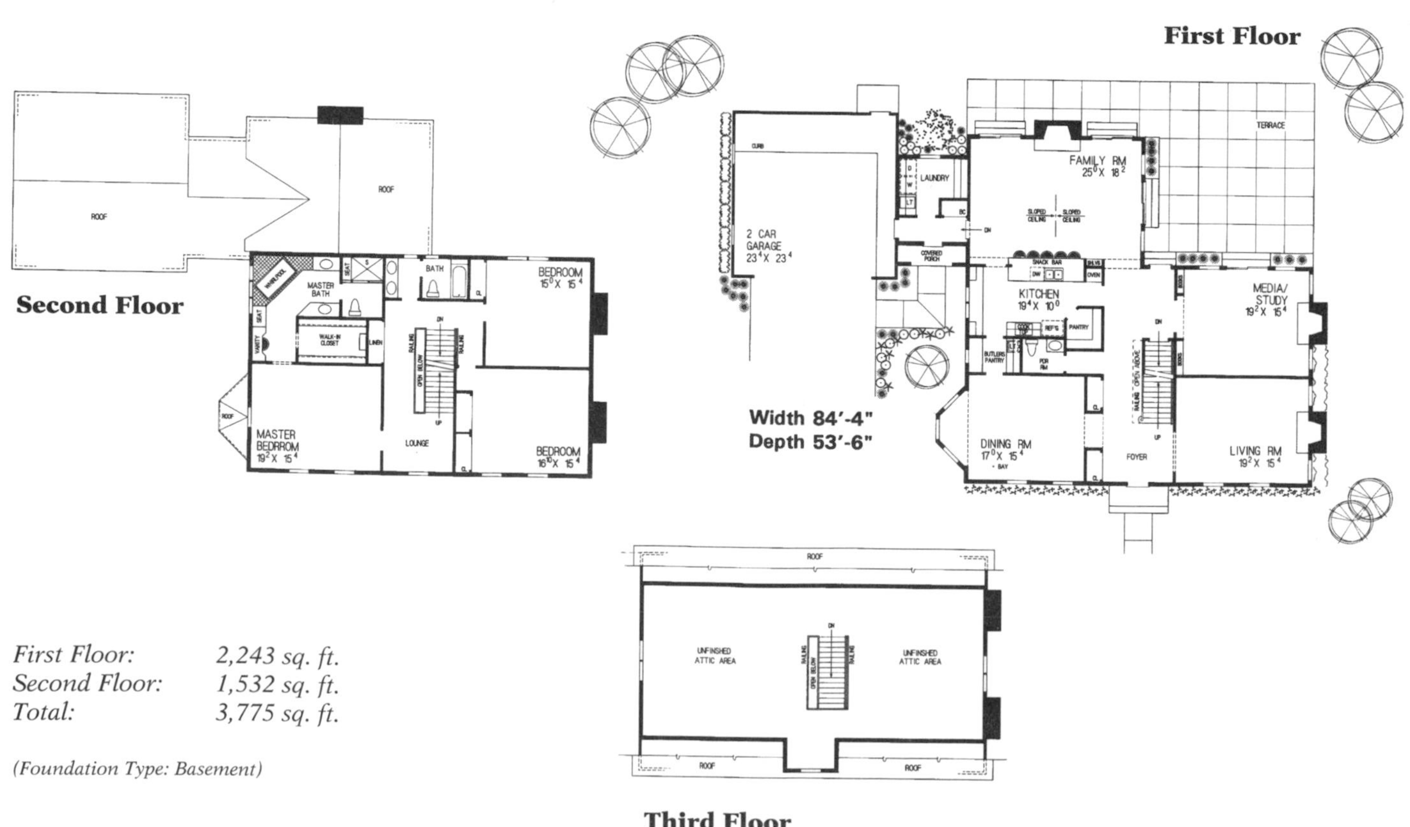


*First Floor:* *2,243 sq. ft.*
*Second Floor:* *1,532 sq. ft.*
*Total:* *3,775 sq. ft.*

*(Foundation Type: Basement)*

# *Mayfair*

**Design CP2981**

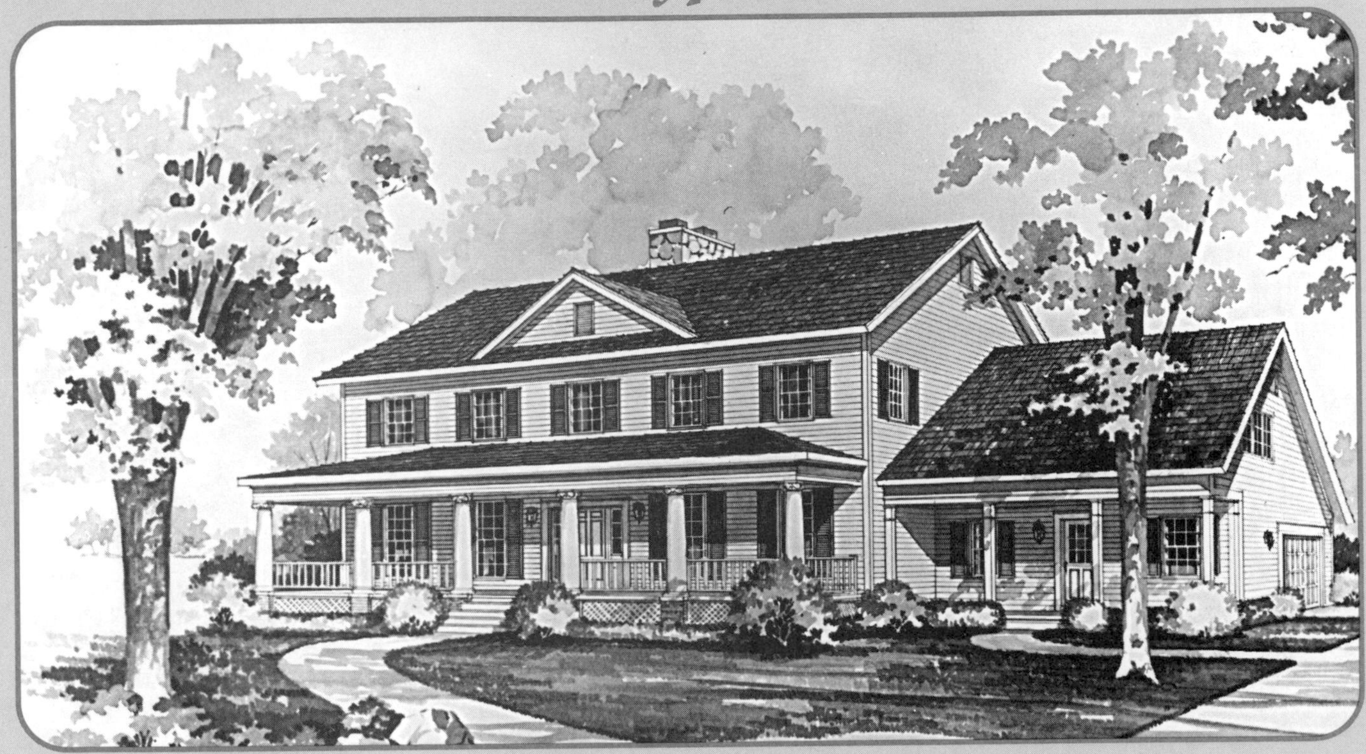

This formal two-story recalls a Louisiana plantation house, Land's End, built in 1857. The Ionic columns of the front porch and the pediment gable echo the Greek Revival style. Highlighting the interior is the bright and cheerful spaciousness of the informal family room area. It features a wall of glass stretching to the second-story, sloping ceiling. Enhancing the drama of this area is the adjacent glass area of the breakfast room. Note the His/Hers areas of the master bedroom.

**First Floor**

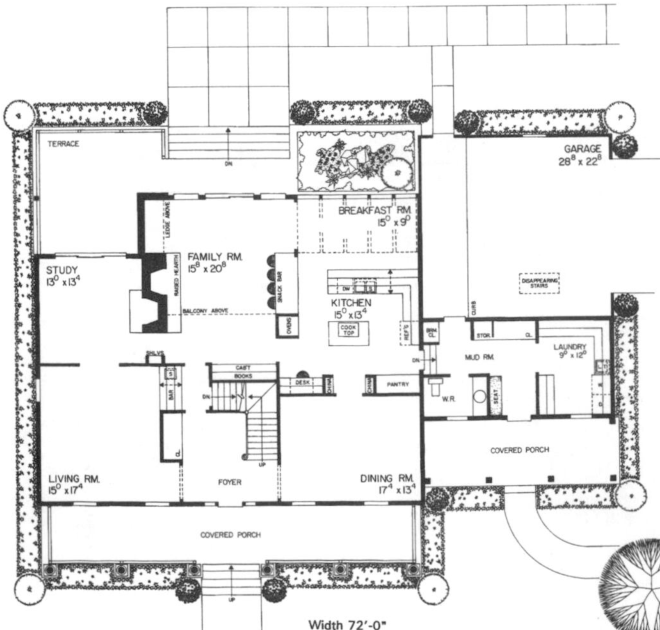

TERRACE
GARAGE
28⁸ x 22⁸
BREAKFAST RM.
15⁰ x 9⁰
FAMILY RM.
15⁸ x 20⁸
STUDY
13⁰ x 13⁴
KITCHEN
15⁰ x 13⁴
MUD RM.
LAUNDRY
9⁰ x 12⁸
COVERED PORCH
LIVING RM.
15⁰ x 17⁴
FOYER
DINING RM.
17⁴ x 13⁴
COVERED PORCH


Width 72'-0"
Depth 57'-0"

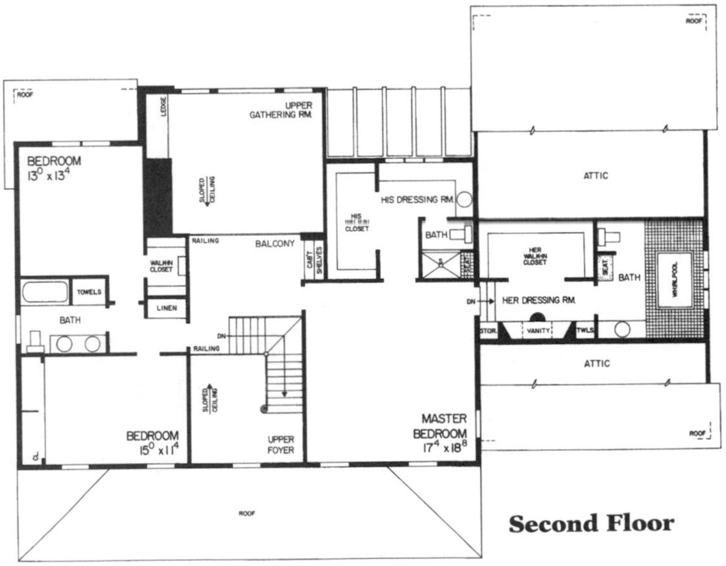

ROOF
UPPER GATHERING RM.
BEDROOM
13⁰ x 13⁴
HIS DRESSING RM.
HIS CLOSET
ATTIC
BALCONY
RAILING
BATH
HER WALK-IN CLOSET
TOWELS
LINEN
HER DRESSING RM.
BATH
ATTIC
BEDROOM
15⁰ x 11⁴
UPPER FOYER
MASTER BEDROOM
17⁴ x 18⁸
ROOF


**Second Floor**

| | |
|---|---|
| *First Floor:* | *2,104 sq. ft.* |
| *Second Floor:* | *2,015 sq. ft.* |
| *Total:* | *4,119 sq. ft.* |

*(Foundation Type: Basement)*

## Design CP4560 — Jeffersonian

This handsome Georgian exterior features a great facade and magnificent interior floor plan. The living room opens to the den through a short, shelf-lined passage. The den has one full wall of built-in cabinets and bookshelves. Upstairs, the master bedroom has a bath with stall shower and separate tub. There are three additional bedrooms and two baths on the second floor. The lower level contains a fifth bedroom and a playroom..

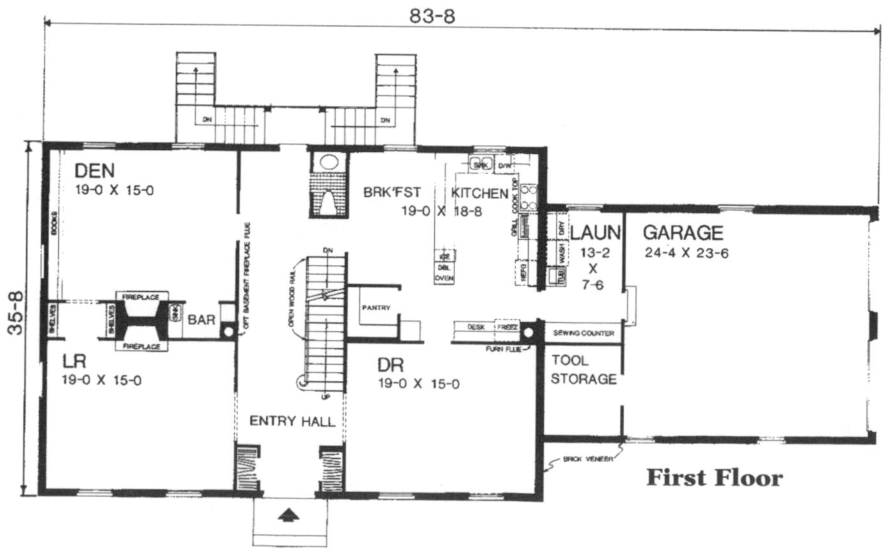


**First Floor**

**Second Floor**

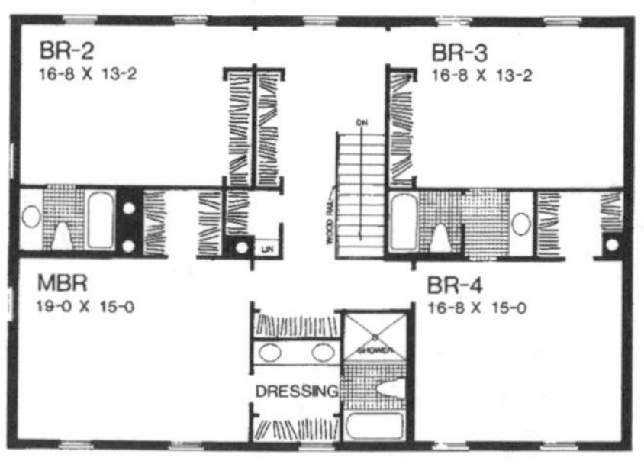


**Third Floor**

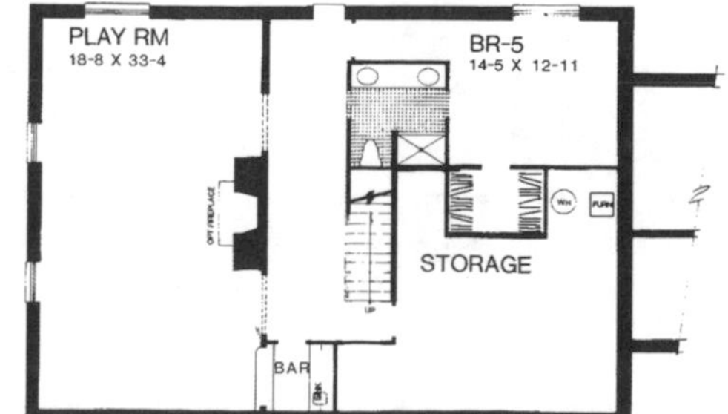


| | |
|---|---|
| *First Floor:* | *1,914 sq. ft.* |
| *Second Floor:* | *1,807 sq. ft.* |
| *Lower Level:* | *1,425 sq. ft.* |
| *Total:* | *5,146 sq. ft.* |

*(Foundation Type: Basement)*

# Dalton

**Design CP2992**

This home was inspired by the Dalton house, which was built between 1750 and 1760. The formal living and dining areas flank a foyer highlighted by a grand staircase. An island kitchen is enhanced by a useful snack bar and easily accessed by the family room and sunny breakfast area. The master suite, found on the second floor, is joined by two bedrooms and a shared bath. The third floor is occupied by a guest bedroom with private bath and spacious studio.

**First Floor**

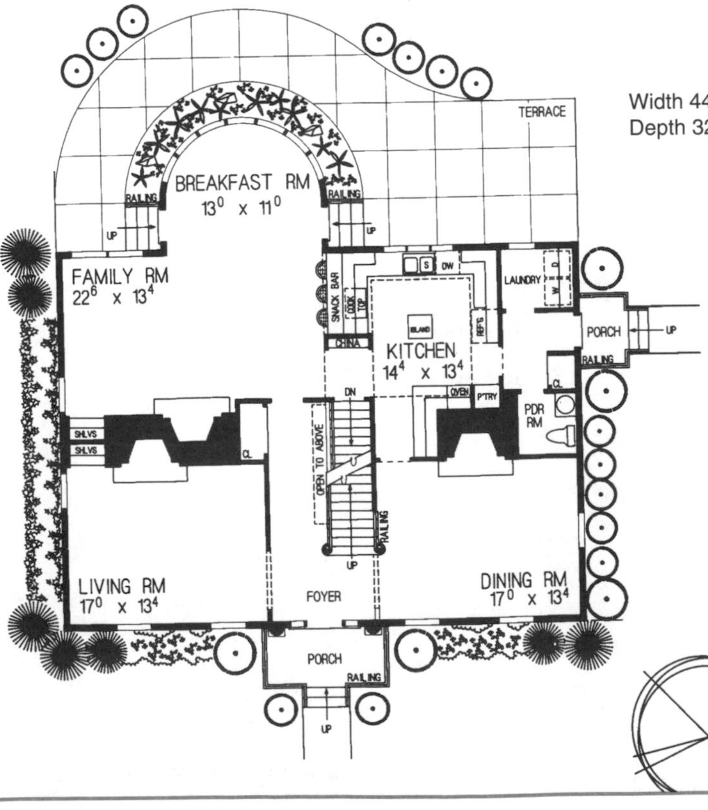

Width 44'-0"
Depth 32'-0"

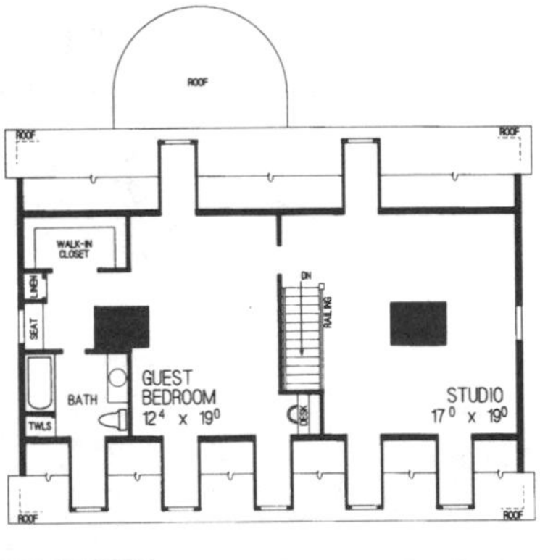

**Second Floor**

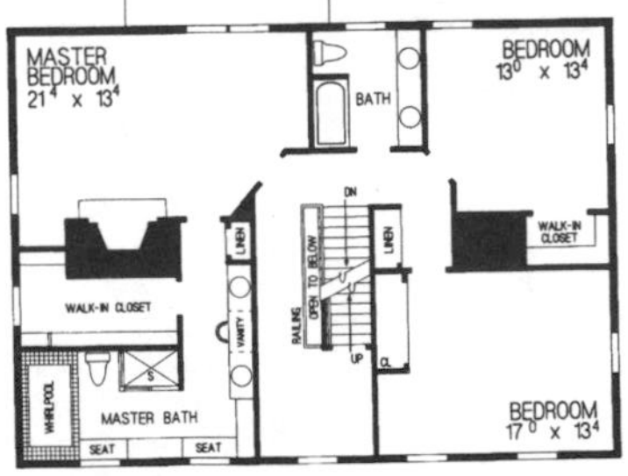

**Third Floor**

| | |
|---|---|
| *First Floor:* | *1,541 sq. ft.* |
| *Second Floor:* | *1,541 sq. ft.* |
| *Third Floor:* | *1,016 sq. ft.* |
| *Total:* | *4,098 sq. ft.* |

*(Foundation Type: Basement)*

## Design CP4527 **Hamilton**

This Georgian exterior encloses a thoroughly modern floor plan. The foyer is flanked by library and dining room. The Great Room, with massive fireplace and built-in bookshelves, has access to a large patio. The first-floor master bedroom features its own deck and private bath. Three bedrooms and two full baths occupy the second floor. The basement is made up of a massive recreation room, a bedroom and two storage areas.

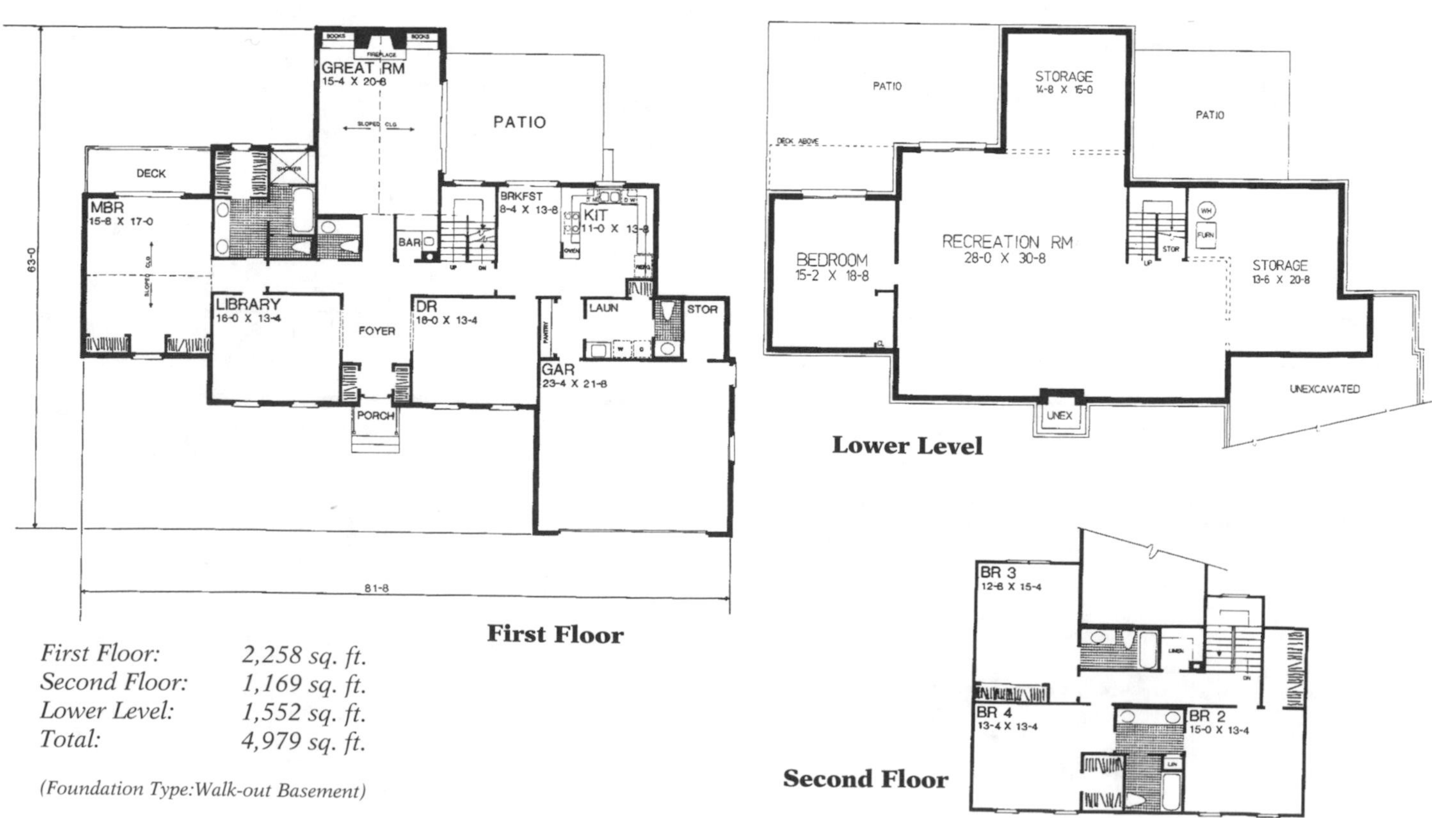


**First Floor**

**Lower Level**

**Second Floor**

| | |
|---|---|
| *First Floor:* | *2,258 sq. ft.* |
| *Second Floor:* | *1,169 sq. ft.* |
| *Lower Level:* | *1,552 sq. ft.* |
| *Total:* | *4,979 sq. ft.* |

*(Foundation Type:Walk-out Basement)*

# Huntington Park **Design CP4290**

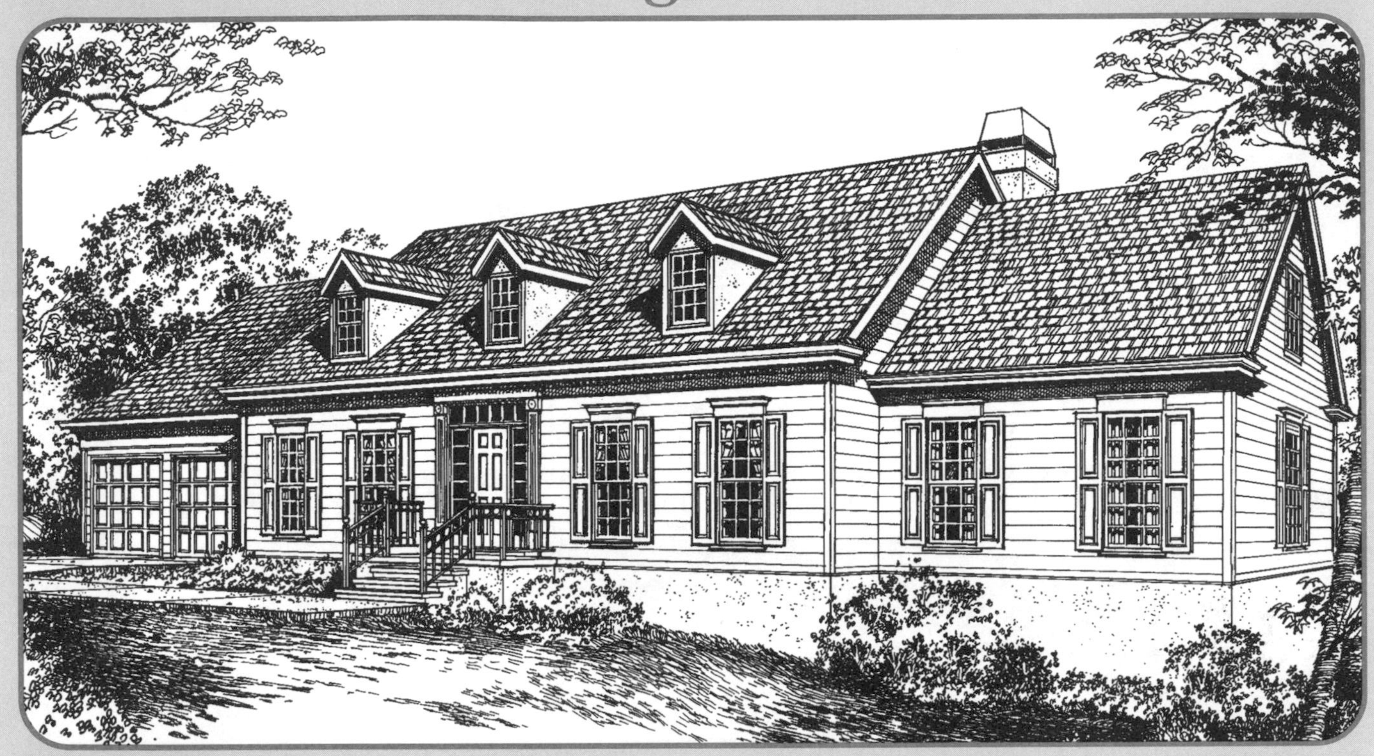

This home is distinguished by its long, low Colonial facade. The foyer is flanked by the formal dining and living areas. The breakfast area and family room with fireplace have access to a spacious screened porch at the rear of the home. The master bedroom features a cozy fireplace, double vanity and walk-in closet. Upstairs, bedrooms are accented with dormer windows and each has access to attic storage. The basement level provides a huge recreation room and additional storage.

**Width 85'-0"**
**Depth 41'-8"**

**First Floor**

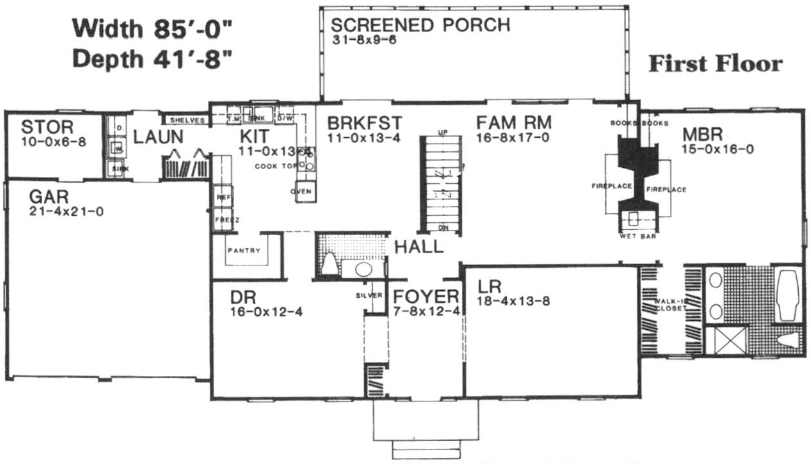

SCREENED PORCH
31-8x9-6
STOR
10-0x6-8
LAUN
SHELVES
KIT
11-0x13-8
COOK TOP
OVEN
PANTRY
BRKFST
11-0x13-4
FAM RM
16-8x17-0
BOOKS
BOOKS
MBR
15-0x16-0
FIREPLACE
FIREPLACE
WET BAR
GAR
21-4x21-0
HALL
DR
16-0x12-4
SILVER
FOYER
7-8x12-4
LR
18-4x13-8
WALK-IN CLOSET


**Second Floor**

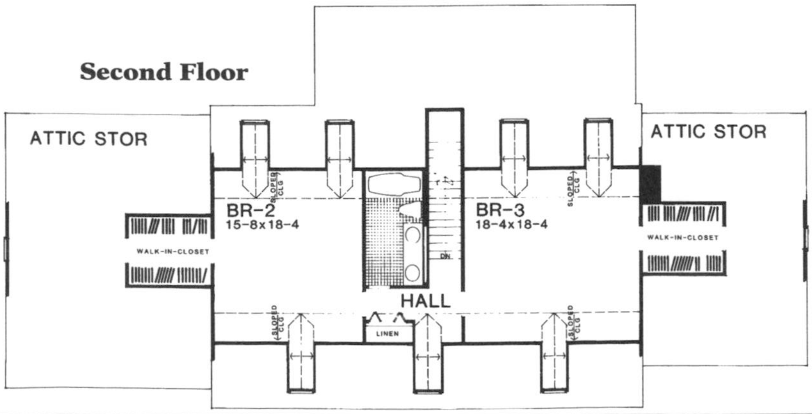

ATTIC STOR
ATTIC STOR
BR-2
15-8x18-4
BR-3
18-4x18-4
WALK-IN-CLOSET
WALK-IN-CLOSET
HALL
LINEN


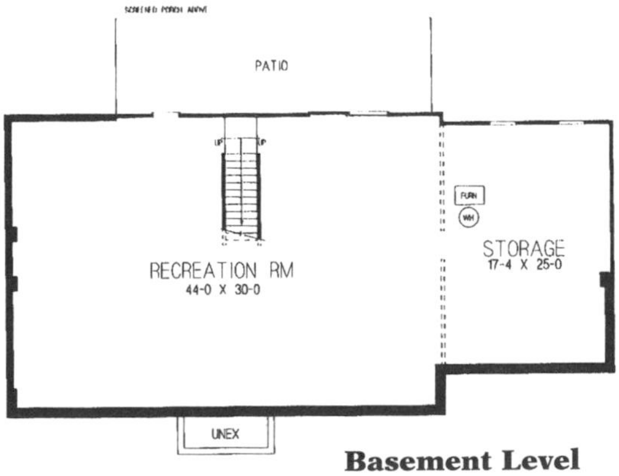

PATIO
RECREATION RM
44-0 X 30-0
STORAGE
17-4 X 25-0
UNEX


**Basement Level**

| | |
|---|---|
| *First Floor:* | *2,104 sq. ft.* |
| *Second Floor:* | *1,147 sq. ft.* |
| *Basement Level:* | *1,911 sq. ft.* |
| *Total:* | *5,162 sq. ft.* |

*(Foundation Type: Basement)*

## Design CP4525 — Newport

Unlike its historical exterior, this New England Colonial abounds in modern amenities. The foyer is flanked by the library and formal dining area. The Great Room features built-in shelves, a fireplace and access to the large patio. The kitchen is accessed by the dining area and patio for easy entertaining. The master suite sports a private deck. Three bedrooms occupy the second floor, while the lower level provides a spacious recreation room and an extra bedroom.

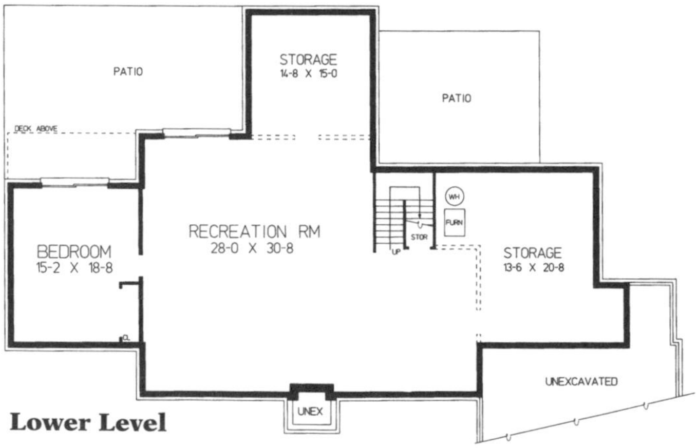

**Lower Level**

PATIO
STORAGE 14-8 X 15-0
PATIO
DECK ABOVE
BEDROOM 15-2 X 18-8
RECREATION RM 28-0 X 30-8
STORAGE 13-6 X 20-8
UNEXCAVATED
UNEX

**Second Floor**

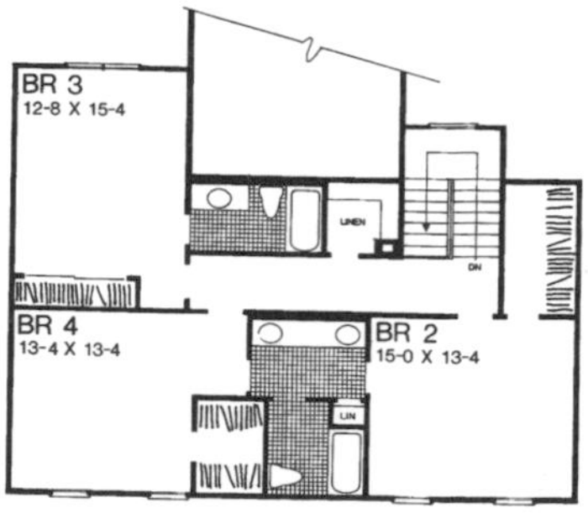

BR 3 12-8 X 15-4
BR 4 13-4 X 13-4
BR 2 15-0 X 13-4

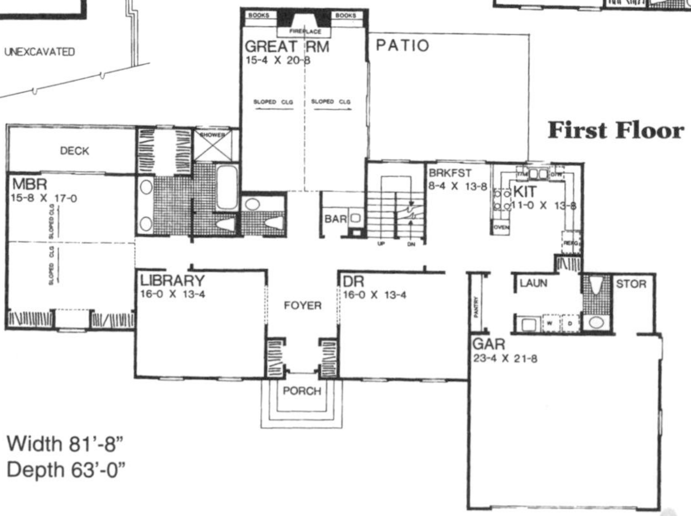

**First Floor**

GREAT RM 15-4 X 20-8
PATIO
DECK
MBR 15-8 X 17-0
BRKFST 8-4 X 13-8
KIT 11-0 X 13-8
LIBRARY 16-0 X 13-4
FOYER
DR 16-0 X 13-4
LAUN
STOR
GAR 23-4 X 21-8
PORCH

Width 81'-8"
Depth 63'-0"

| | |
|---|---|
| *First Floor:* | *2,258 sq. ft.* |
| *Second Floor:* | *1,169 sq. ft.* |
| *Lower Level:* | *1,552 sq. ft.* |
| *Total:* | *4,979 sq. ft.* |

*(Foundation Type: Basement)*

# Raleigh

**Design CP4397**

Simple lines and style dominate the exterior of this Colonial home. An entry foyer, highlighted by a double staircase, leads to the Great Room with fireplace. The adjoined dining area has a decorative window seat and accesses the deck and screened porch. The full kitchen has a special greenhouse window. The master bedroom is joined by a bedroom and bath and a bonus room on the second floor. A private bedroom suite, including family and recreation rooms, occupies the basement level.

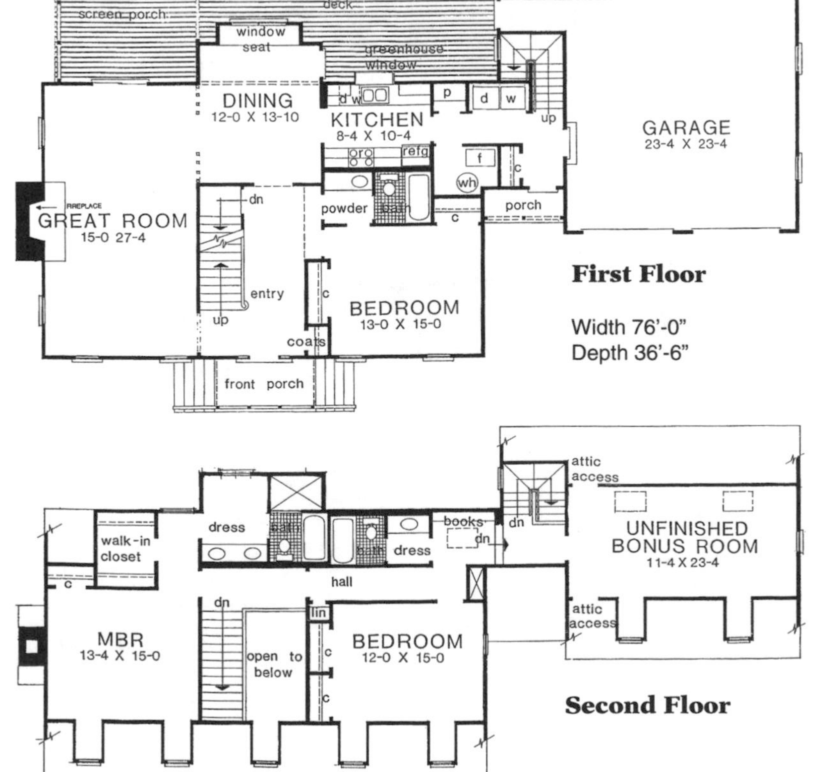


**First Floor**

Width 76'-0"
Depth 36'-6"

**Second Floor**

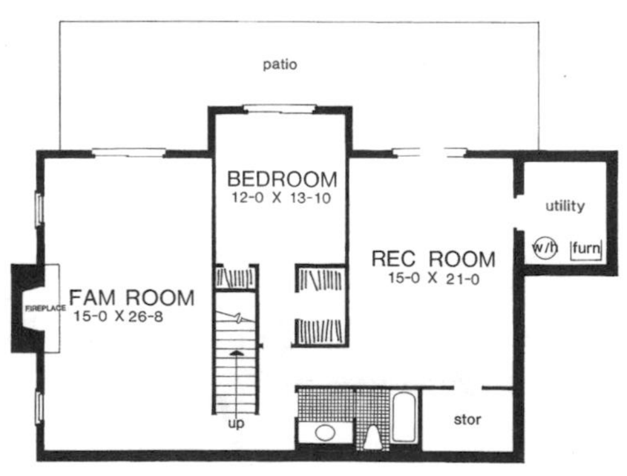


**Basement Level**

| | |
|---|---|
| *First Floor:* | *1,421 sq. ft.* |
| *Second Floor:* | *967 sq. ft.* |
| *Basement Level:* | *1,380 sq. ft.* |
| *Total:* | *3,768 sq. ft.* |

*(Foundation Type: Basement)*

## Design CP3399 **Wheatridge**

This is the ultimate in farmhouse living—six dormer windows and a porch that stretches essentially around the entire house. Inside, the plan is open and inviting. Besides the large country kitchen with fireplace, there is a small game room with attached tavern, a library with built-in bookshelves and a fireplace, and a formal living room. The second floor has four bedrooms and three full baths.

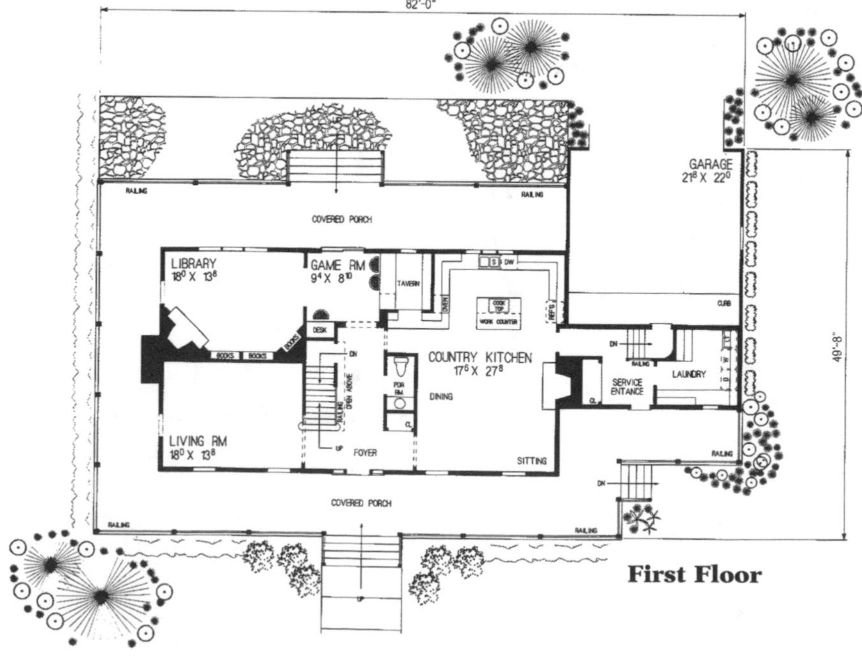


**First Floor**

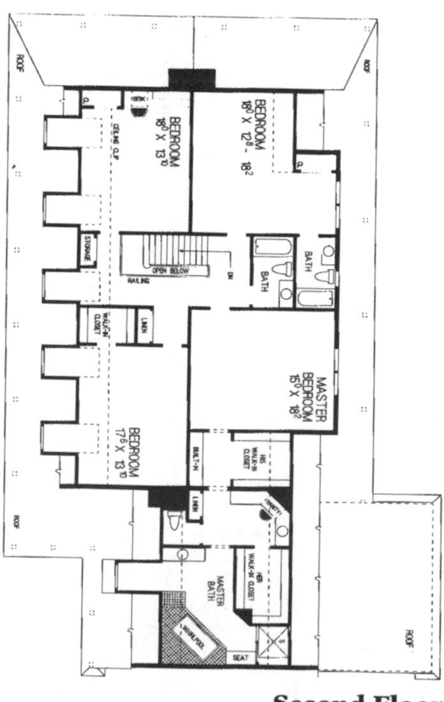


**Second Floor**

*First Floor:* *1,716 sq. ft.*
*Second Floor:* *2,102 sq. ft.*
*Total:* *3,818 sq. ft.*

*(Foundation Type: Basement)*

# Dumont

## Design CP4501

A simple, yet elegant brick facade and gracious central portico highlight the exterior of this home. The living room features a formal fireplace surrounded with paneling and built-in cabinetry. The elegant, oval-shaped dining room boasts luxury with walk-in cupboards for fine china and silver. A spacious family room with large windows is warmed by a massive fireplace. The master suite includes a private lounge and complete bath. Each of the three bedrooms on the second floor has access to two full baths.

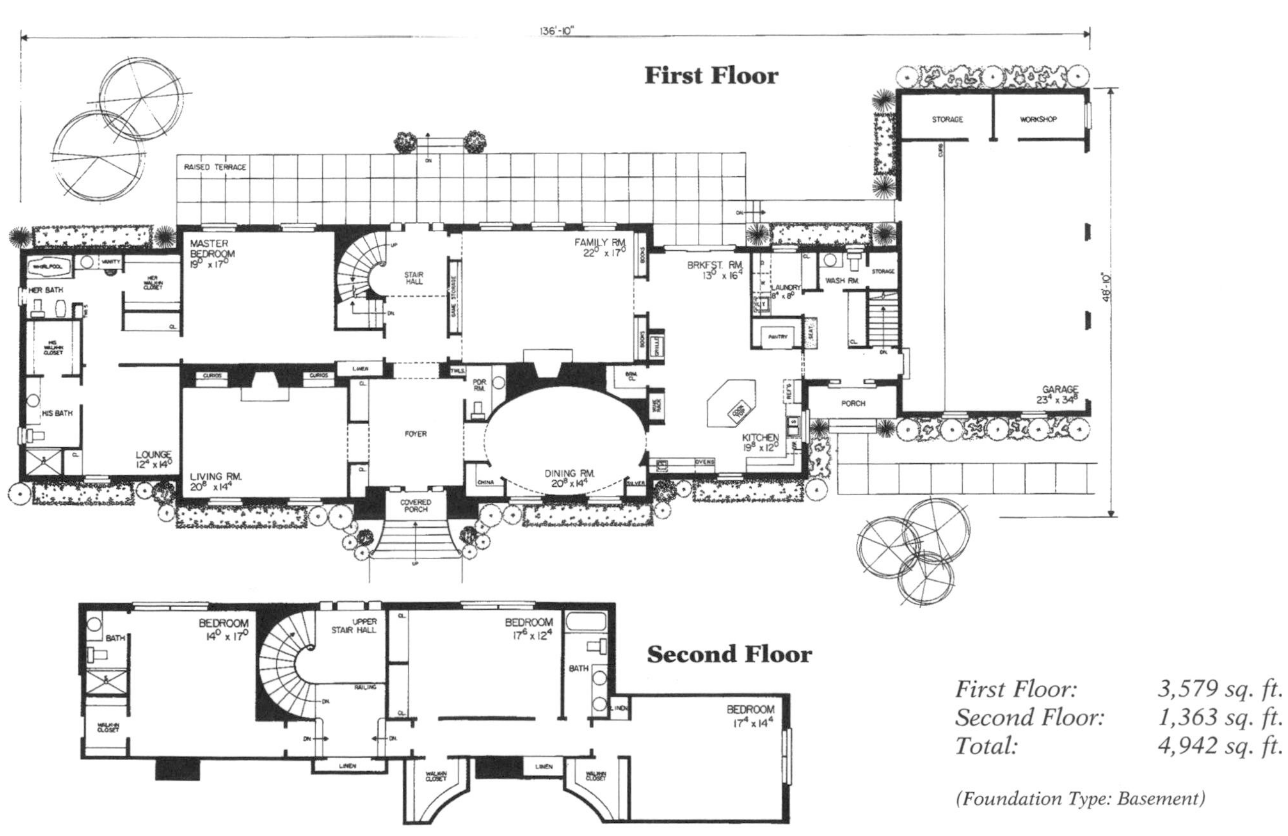


| | |
|---|---|
| *First Floor:* | *3,579 sq. ft.* |
| *Second Floor:* | *1,363 sq. ft.* |
| *Total:* | *4,942 sq. ft.* |

*(Foundation Type: Basement)*

## Design CP2212

# Cannes

This elegant French country house highlights spacious living and family rooms with fireplaces and sliding glass doors. A U-shaped kitchen and nook overlook the front courtyard. Two bedrooms with private baths open to the terrace. The master suite has His and Her baths with dressing rooms that are secluded from the bedroom. A study, with entrances from the main hall and master suite, provides a quiet place to read or relax.

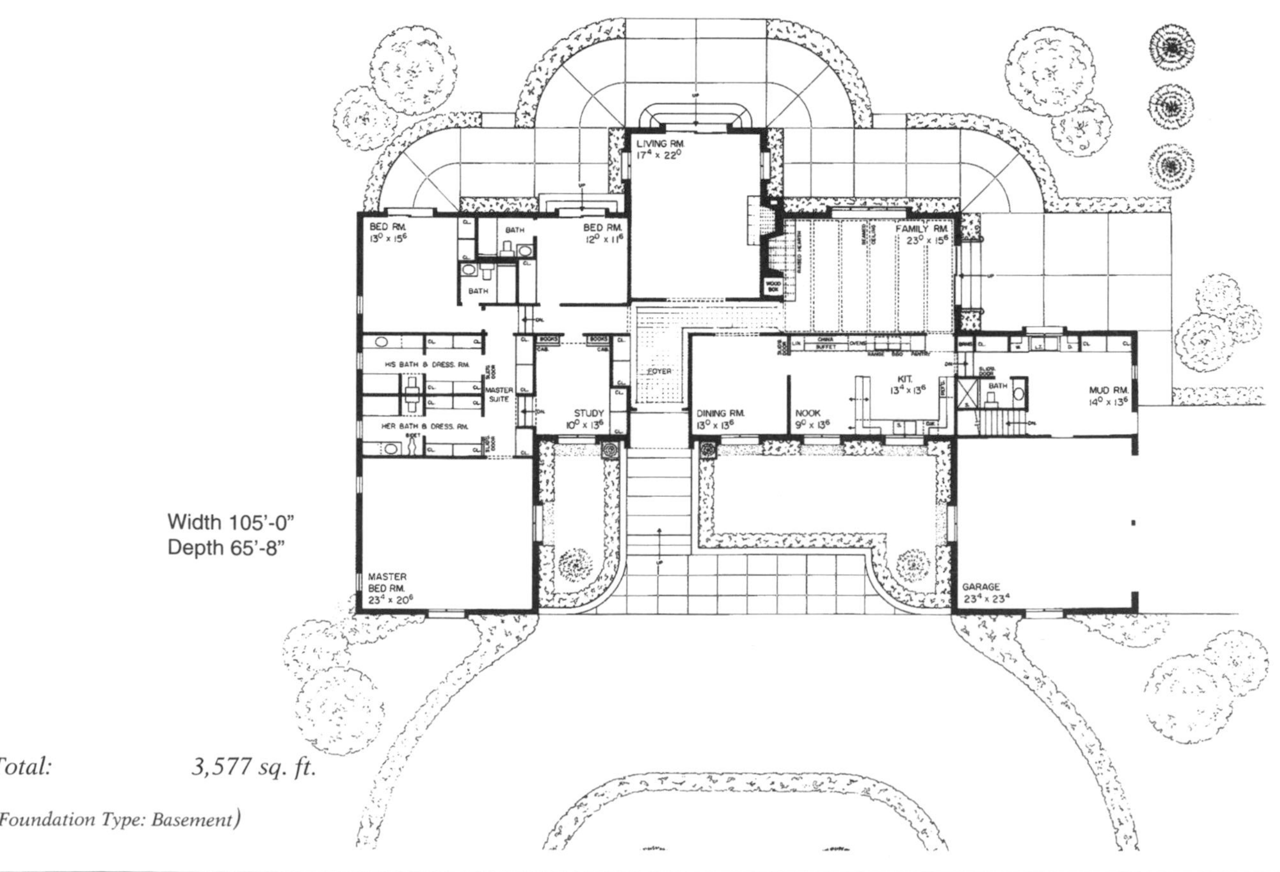


Width 105'-0"
Depth 65'-8"

*Total:* *3,577 sq. ft.*

*(Foundation Type: Basement)*

# Williamsburg

## Design CP2237

A formal entrance hall draws guests into the elegant living room, anchored by a fireplace. The adjoined dining room shares a view of the back terrace. The kitchen and breakfast nook are conveniently accessed by the nearby family room, accented by a beamed ceiling and decorative, massive fireplace. The library with built-in shelves is a cozy retreat. Two bedrooms share a large bathroom. Upstairs, the private master suite sports His and Her baths, a built-in desk and plenty of storage space.

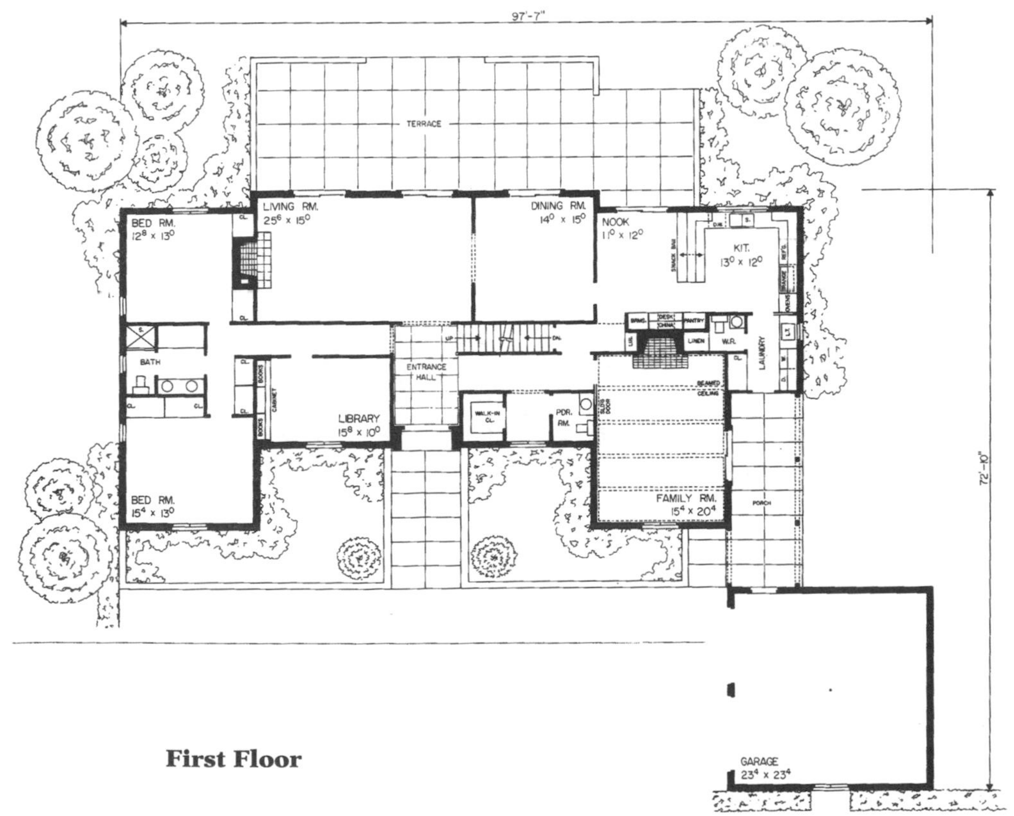


First Floor

Second Floor

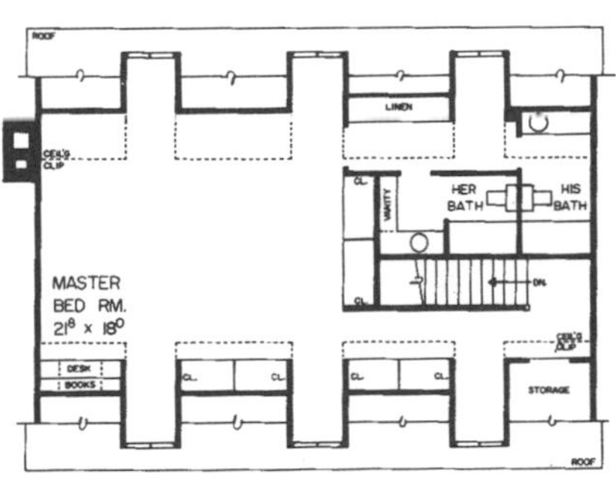


| | |
|---|---|
| *First Floor:* | *2,714 sq. ft.* |
| *Second Floor:* | *1,010 sq. ft.* |
| *Total:* | *3,724 sq. ft.* |

*(Foundation Type: Basement)*

**Design CP2245**

# Katherine

The exterior of this country home is marked by a drive court and stone path to the entrance. Inside, the living and dining rooms overlook the back terrace. A massive fireplace in the living area warms the two adjoined rooms. A country kitchen has an island cooktop and a brick hearth. The family room is conveniently adjoined to the kitchen snack bar. The master suite occupies the entire second floor. His and Her baths and dressing rooms and built-in storage and bookshelves are highlights.

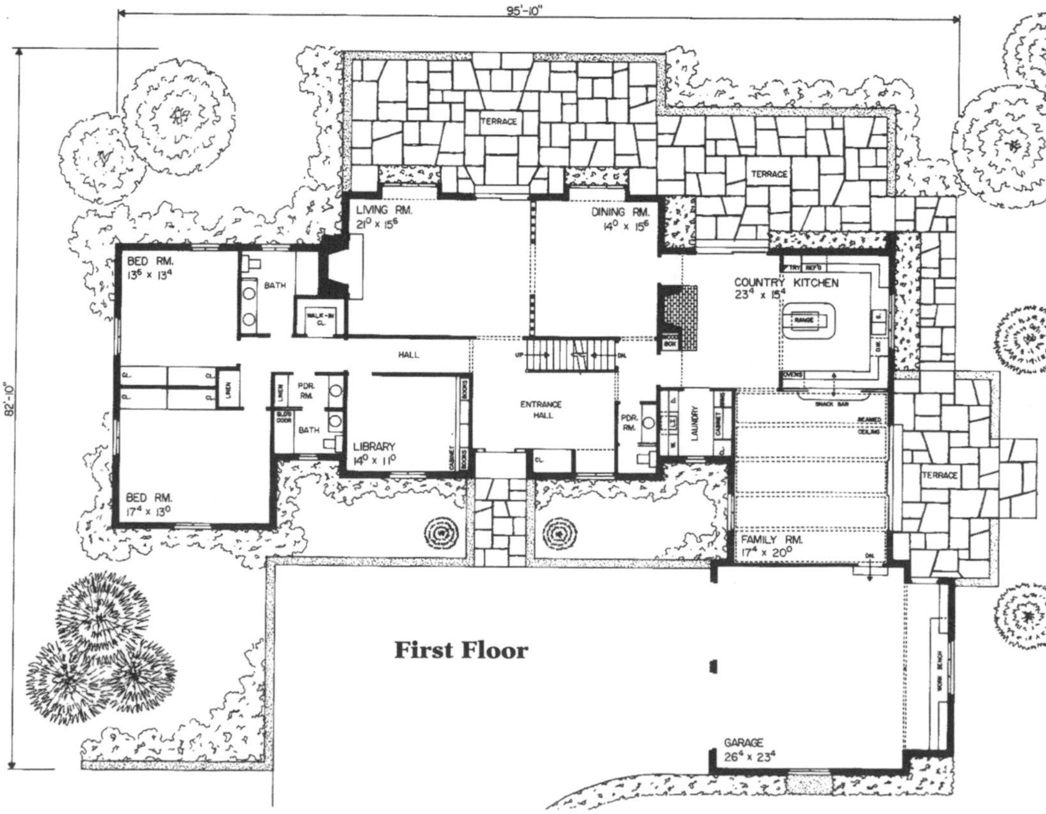

**First Floor**

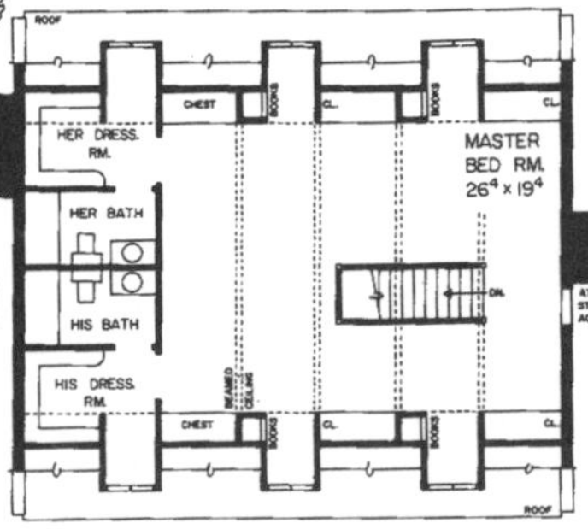

**Second Floor**

| | |
|---|---|
| *First Floor:* | *2,855 sq. ft.* |
| *Second Floor:* | *955 sq. ft.* |
| *Total:* | *3,810 sq. ft.* |

*(Foundation Type: Basement)*

# Bellwood

**Design CP3367**

This unique plan requires a lot that is narrow and quite deep. A porch entrance leads to the foyer with U-shaped stair. The media center with massive fireplace and a formal dining room can be found to either side. The large gathering room is warmed by a fireplace. The island kitchen adjoins a keeping room with bay window and fireplace. The master bedroom has a sloped ceiling and roomy His and Her closets. Upstairs, three bedrooms and two complete baths are complemented by a balcony.

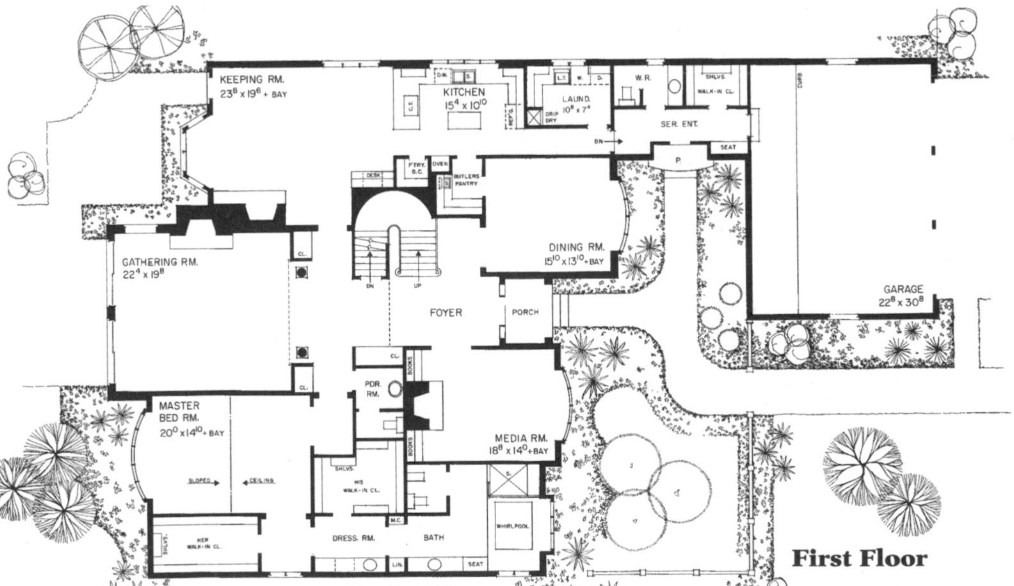

**Second Floor**

**First Floor**

Width 104'-4"
Depth 64'-0"

| | |
|---|---|
| *First Floor:* | *3,634 sq. ft.* |
| *Second Floor:* | *1,450 sq. ft.* |
| *Total:* | *5,084 sq. ft.* |

*(Foundation Type: Basement)*

**Design CP2963** 

# *Fitzgerald*

The rambling proportions of this house reflect Colonial precedents. Both the dining and living rooms boast large fireplaces. Family meals are likely to be served in the cozy breakfast room attached to the kitchen. The study is tucked away behind the living room. Upstairs, four bedrooms provide a comfortable retreat for each family member. The master bedroom includes a bay window and His and Hers walk-in closets.

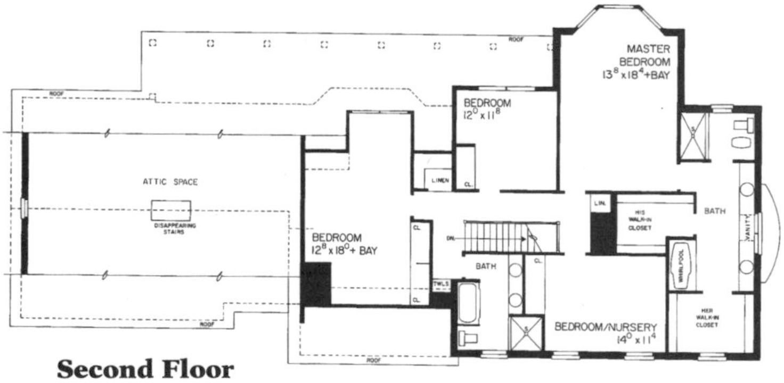

**Second Floor**

Width 87' 4"
Depth 42'

**First Floor**

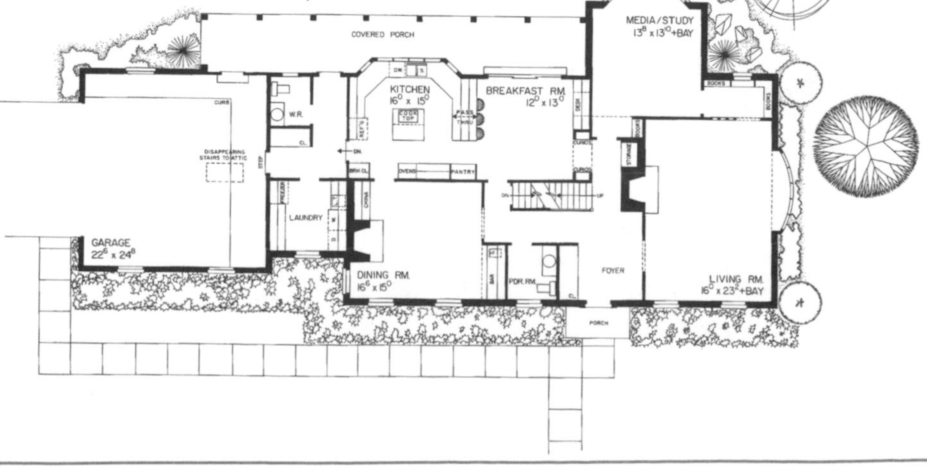

| | |
|---|---|
| *First Floor:* | *2,046 sq. ft.* |
| *Second Floor:* | *1,644 sq. ft.* |
| *Total:* | *3,690 sq. ft.* |

*(Foundation Type: Basement)*

# Coatsworth

**Design CP3504**

This Colonial home exudes a feeling of comfort and simple elegance. Formal living areas include the dining room, the living room with fireplace and columns and the library with a bay window. A large family room with a fireplace and a bar accommodates informal activities. The kitchen offers an island cooktop, a snack bar and an attached breakfast area. A curving staircase leads to the sleeping area on the second floor. The expansive master suite with His and Hers walk-in closets is joined by two family bedrooms.

**First Floor**

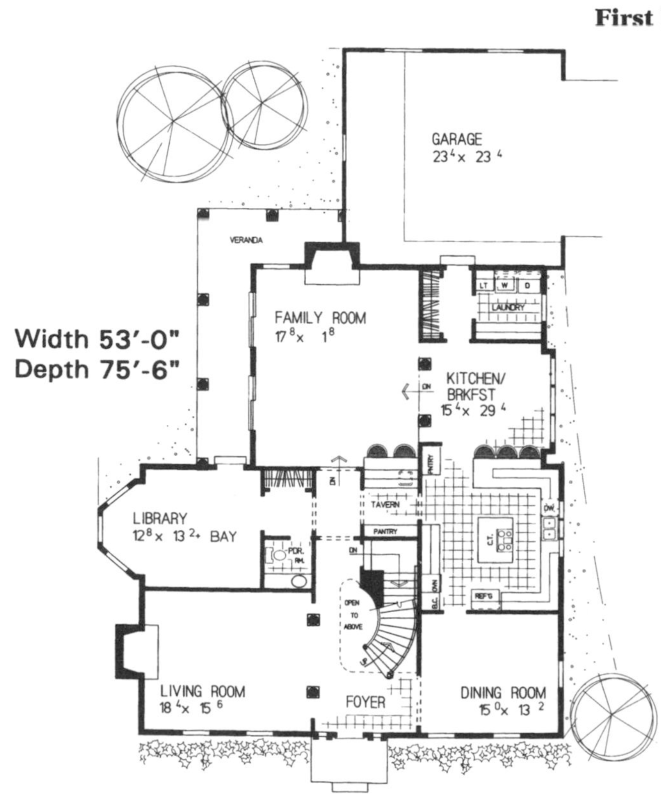


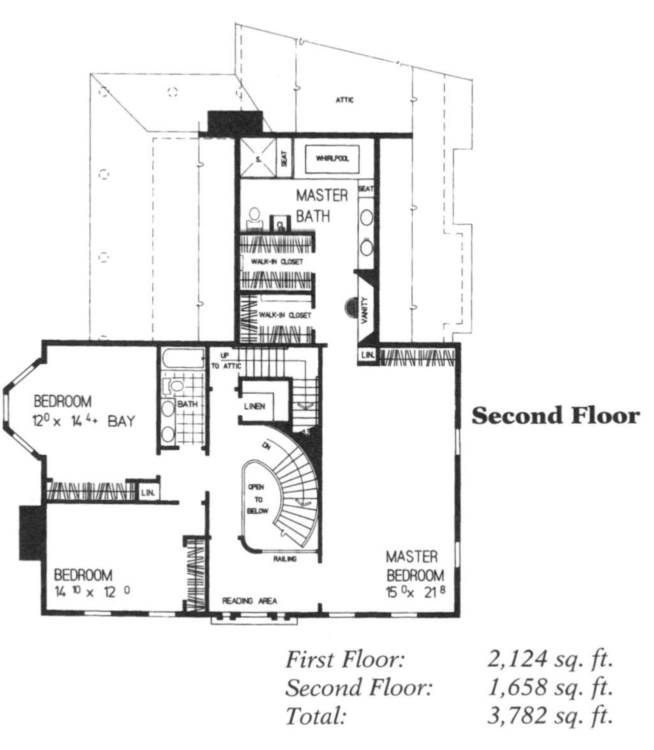


**Second Floor**

| | |
|---|---|
| *First Floor:* | *2,124 sq. ft.* |
| *Second Floor:* | *1,658 sq. ft.* |
| *Total:* | *3,782 sq. ft.* |

*(Foundation Type: Basement)*

## Design CP2687

# Napoleon

The exterior styling of this home is reminiscent of the past, but its floor plan is as up-to-date as it can get. Its many unique features include: a greenhouse, a huge country kitchen, a media room and a hobby/laundry room. Four bedrooms, including a master bedroom with deluxe bath, are on the second floor. Fireplaces highlight the living room and the country kitchen.

**Second Floor**

**First Floor**

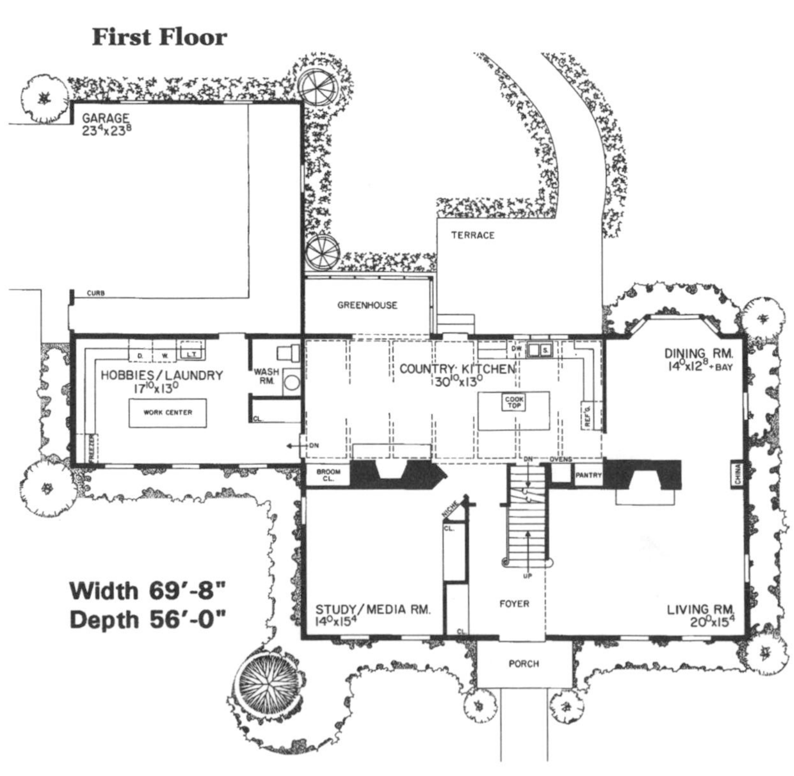


| | |
|---|---|
| *First Floor:* | *1,819 sq. ft.* |
| *Second Floor:* | *1,431 sq. ft.* |
| *Total:* | *3,250 sq. ft.* |

*(Foundation Type: Basement)*

# Renfroe

## Design CP2653

Livability and special features are absolutely outstanding in this Colonial design. Imagine a living room, with beamed ceiling and fireplace, that measures more than 20 x 27 feet. The second fireplace in the luxurious master suite makes it a very special retreat. The kitchen is placed between the informal family room with snack bar and the formal dining room, which includes several built-in china cabinets. The library offers a special retreat.

**First Floor**

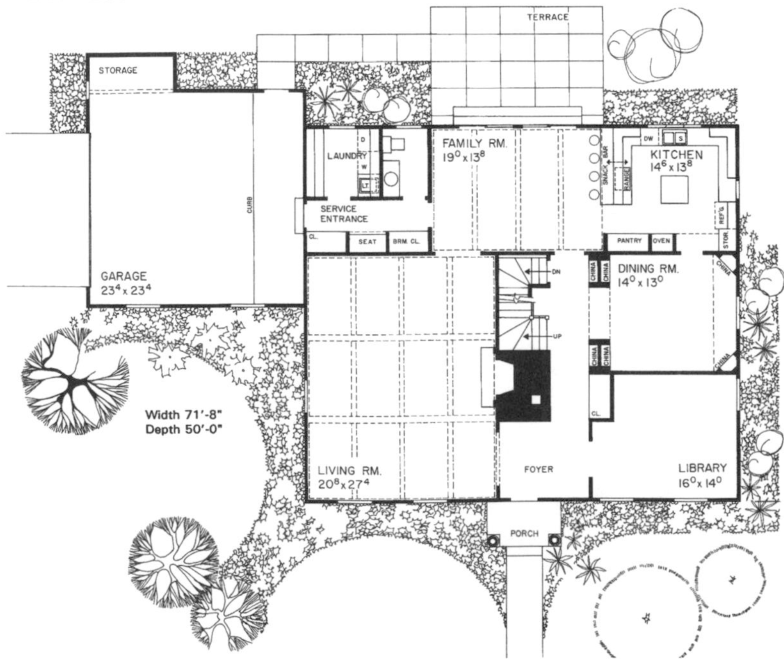

**Second Floor**

| | |
|---|---|
| *First Floor:* | *2,016 sq. ft.* |
| *Second Floor:* | *1,656 sq. ft.* |
| *Total:* | *3,672 sq. ft.* |

*(Foundation Type: Basement)*

## Design CP2100 — Northfield

This gambrel-roofed Colonial features a charming widow's walk and chimney pots. Bonus space resides on the third floor which can be used for a play room, guest room or study. Four second-floor bedrooms include a fine master with full bath and dressing area. The first-floor features include a dining room with corner china cabinets, a cozy study and two fireplaces. The U-shaped kitchen serves a handy breakfast room. Note the formal living room and casual family room.

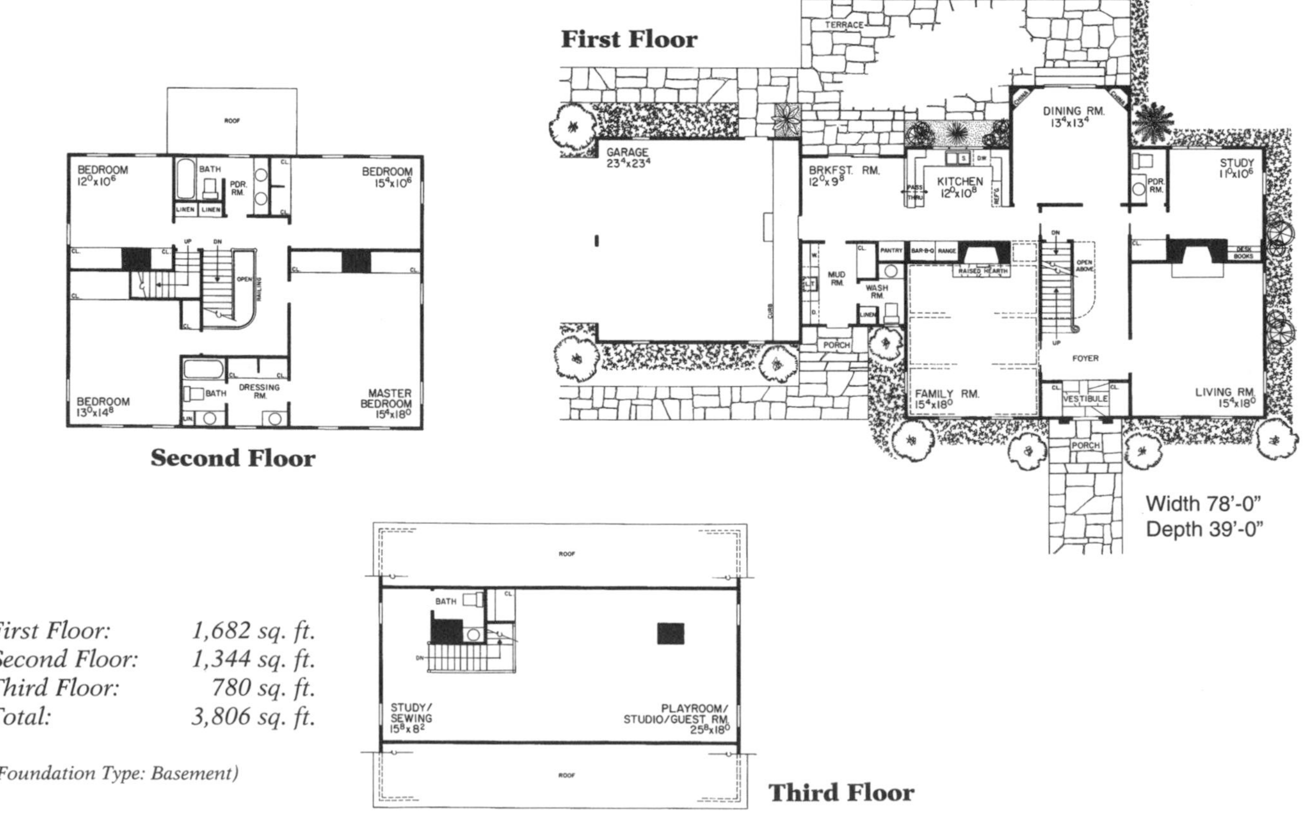


| | |
|---|---|
| *First Floor:* | *1,682 sq. ft.* |
| *Second Floor:* | *1,344 sq. ft.* |
| *Third Floor:* | *780 sq. ft.* |
| *Total:* | *3,806 sq. ft.* |

*(Foundation Type: Basement)*

# Candlewood **Design CP2978**

The Nathaniel Hawthorne house, constructed in Salem, Massachusetts around 1730, was the inspiration for this two-story gambrel. This modern version shows off its interior living space in a family-pleasing country kitchen with island and built-in desk, library and formal living and dining rooms. The highlight of the second floor is the luxurious master bedroom with His and Hers closets and a heavenly whirlpool spa.

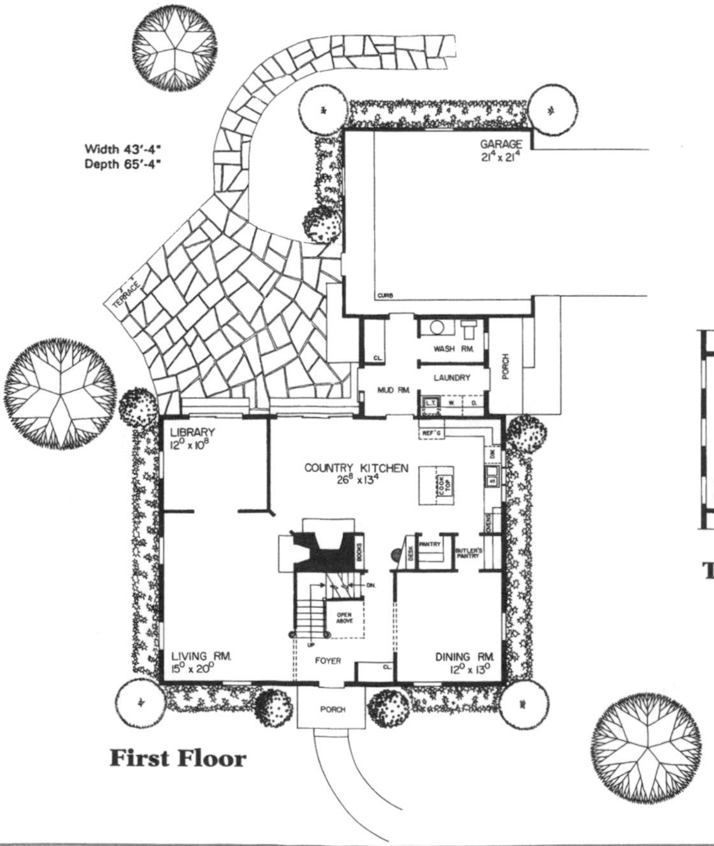

Width 43'-4"
Depth 65'-4"

**First Floor**

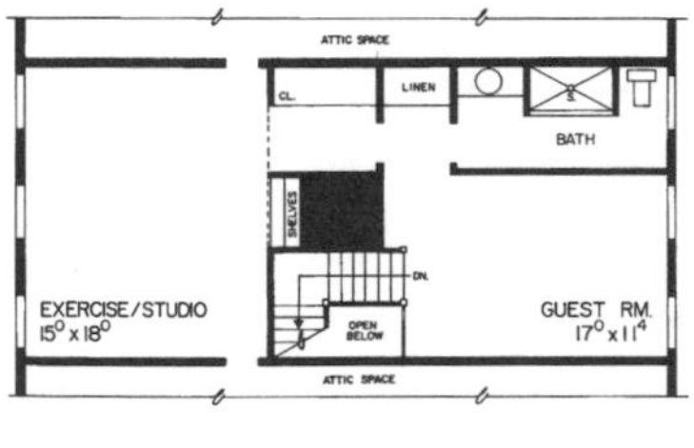

**Third Floor**

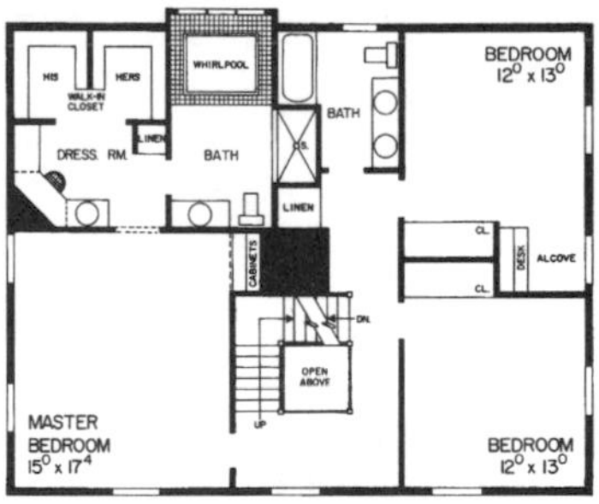

**Second Floor**

| | |
|---|---|
| *First Floor:* | *1,451 sq. ft.* |
| *Second Floor:* | *1,268 sq. ft.* |
| *Third Floor:* | *746 sq. ft.* |
| *Total:* | *3,465 sq. ft.* |

*(Foundation Type: Basement)*

## Design CP2980 — Eleanor

This late Georgian adaptation is reminiscent of the Cowles house built in Farmington, Connecticut around 1786. The formal symmetry and rich ornamentation are typical of houses of this period. Ionic columns, a Palladian window and a pedimented gable are among the details that set the character of this historic house. Inside are three floors of livability. Note the through fireplace separating the living room and dining room.

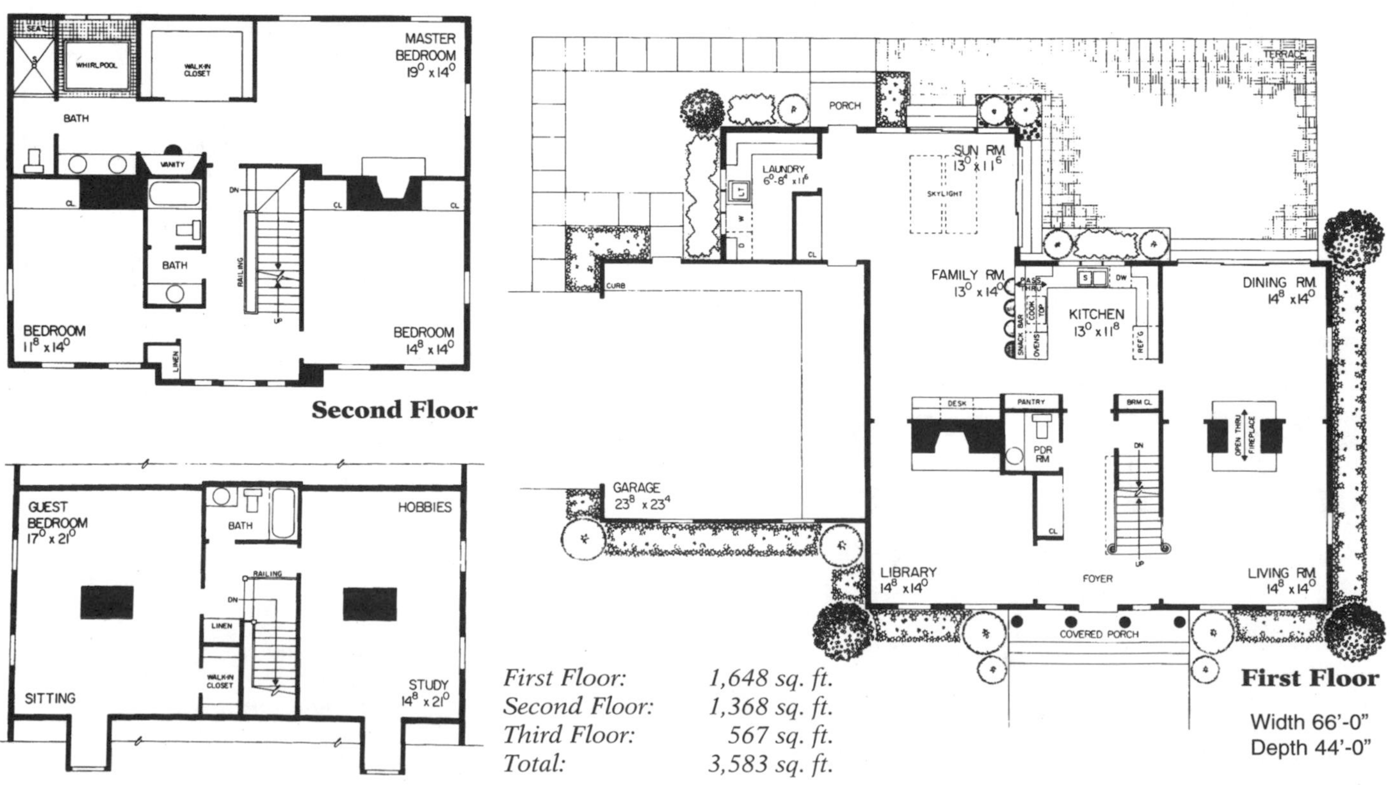


| | |
|---|---|
| *First Floor:* | *1,648 sq. ft.* |
| *Second Floor:* | *1,368 sq. ft.* |
| *Third Floor:* | *567 sq. ft.* |
| *Total:* | *3,583 sq. ft.* |

*(Foundation Type: Basement)*

# Mankato

**Design CP2989**

This dramatic residence, patterned after one built in 1759 by Major John Vassall in Cambridge, offers a floor plan that is intriguing in its wealth of amenities. On the first floor are the formal living and dining rooms, each with a fireplace. A front study connects to the family room with built-ins and another fireplace. Upstairs are three bedrooms, including a master suite with sitting room and deluxe bath. Family bedrooms share a large bath.

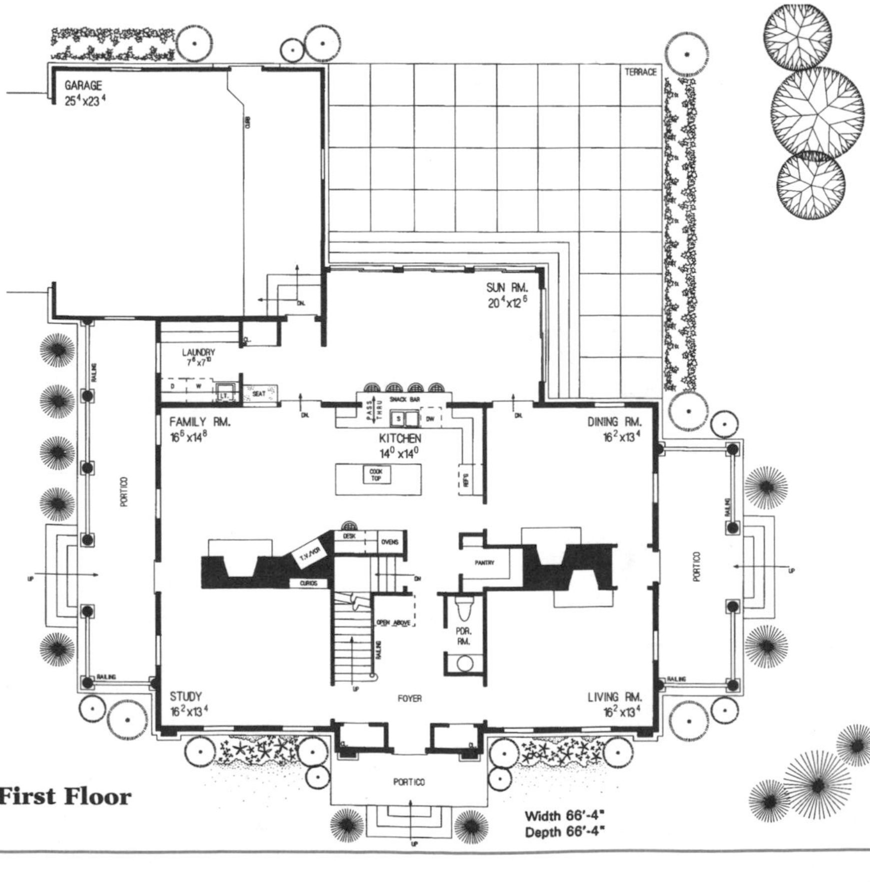

**Second Floor**

**First Floor**

Width 66'-4"
Depth 66'-4"

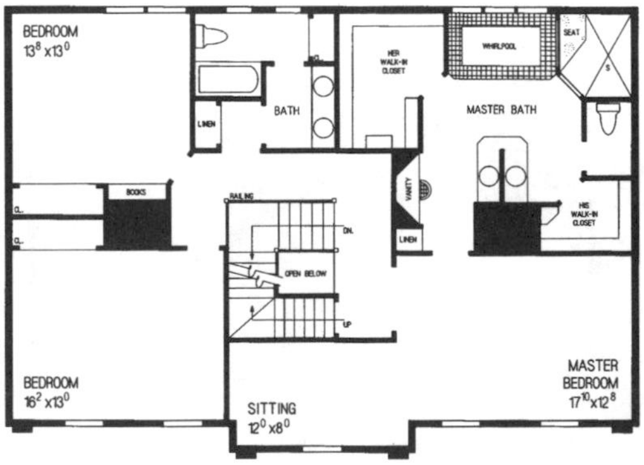

| | |
|---|---|
| *First Floor:* | *1,972 sq. ft.* |
| *Second Floor:* | *1,533 sq. ft.* |
| *Total:* | *3,505 sq. ft.* |

*(Foundation Type: Basement)*

## Design CP9126

# Goldwater

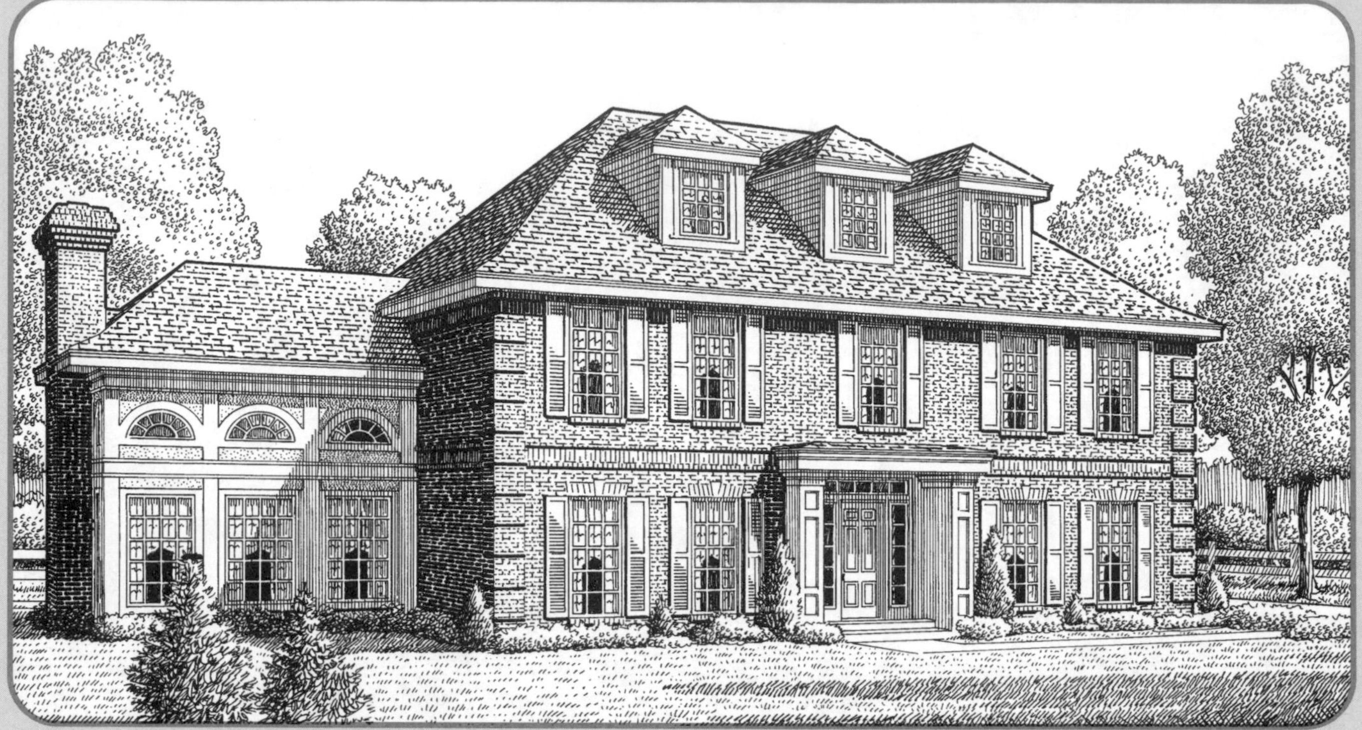

This plan is a true work of art. The entry foyer contains a curved staircase to the second floor and is open to the formal dining room. The living room has a fireplace, as does the family room. A quiet study features built-in shelves and is tucked away to the rear of the plan. Note the master bedroom on the first floor. It boasts a double walk-in closet, corner shower and large tub. Four bedrooms upstairs revolve around a game room with vaulted ceiling.

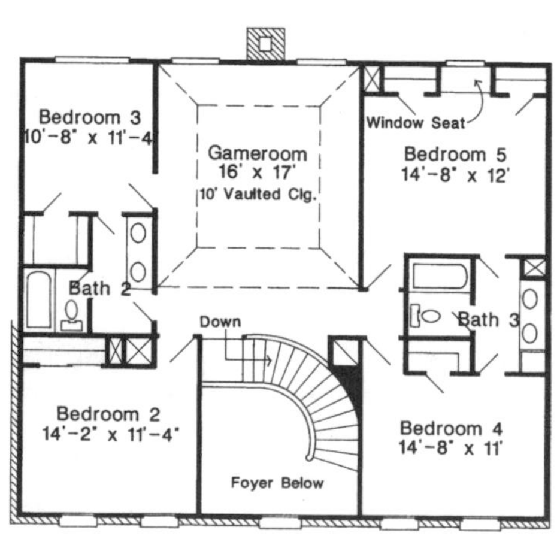


**Second Floor**

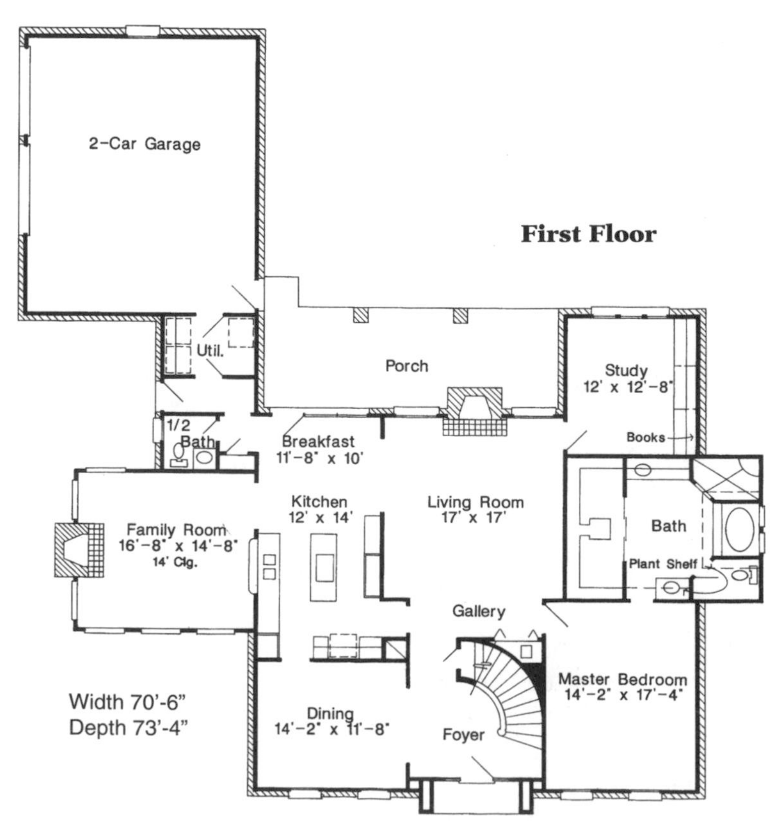


*First Floor:* *2,157 sq. ft.*
*Second Floor:* *1,346 sq. ft.*
*Total:* *3,503 sq. ft.*

*(Foundation Type: Slab)*

# *Silverspring* **Design CP2999**

Recalling the grandeur of its Maryland ancestors, this manor house is replete with exterior details: keystoned lintels, fluted pilasters, a dormered attic and pedimented doorway. The centerhall floor plan allows formal living and dining areas to the front of the plan. Complementing these are the cozy library and large family room/breakfast room area. Upstairs bedrooms allow more than adequate space. Over the garage is a complete guest apartment with living area, office, bedroom, bath and kitchen.

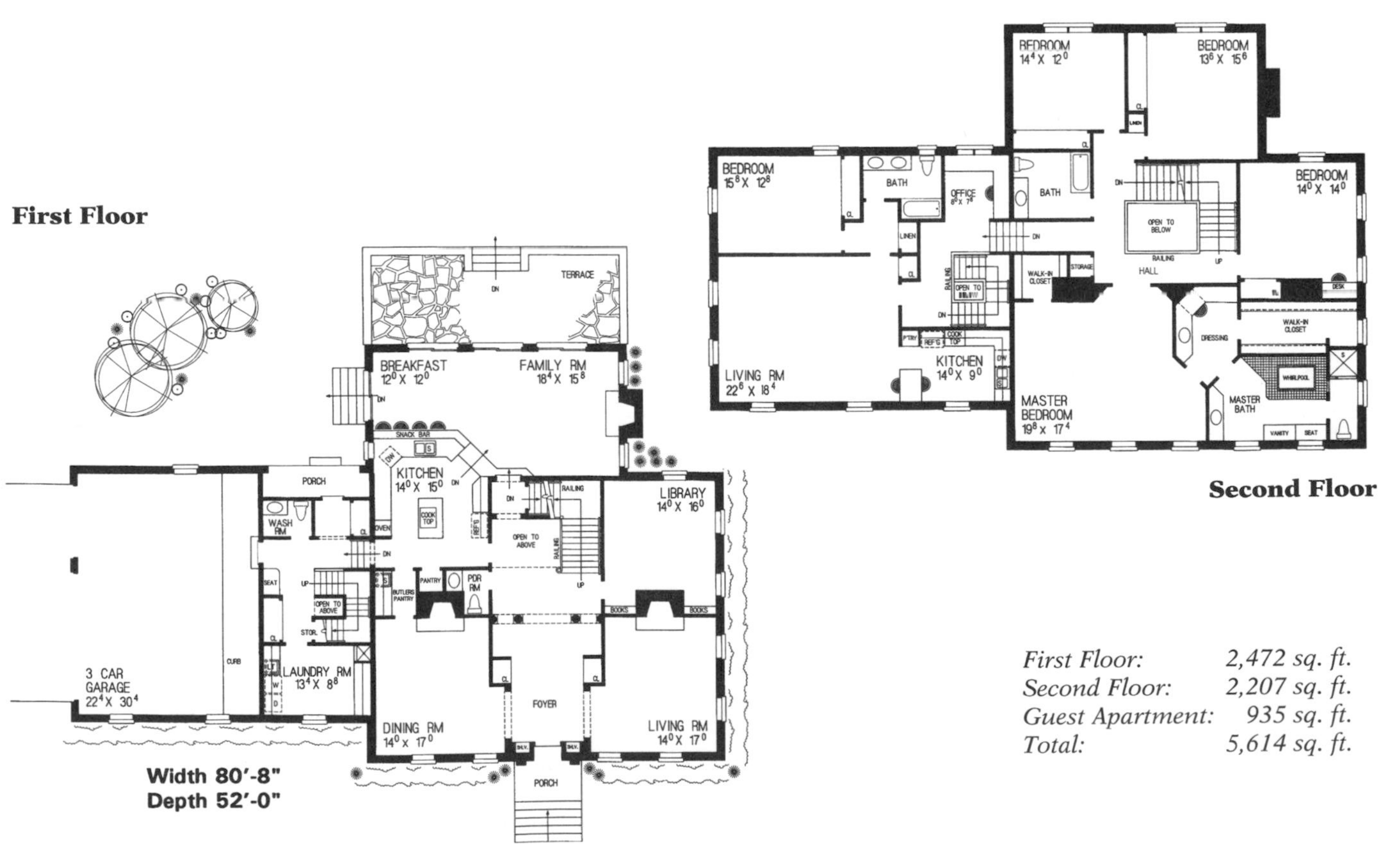


| | |
|---|---|
| *First Floor:* | *2,472 sq. ft.* |
| *Second Floor:* | *2,207 sq. ft.* |
| *Guest Apartment:* | *935 sq. ft.* |
| *Total:* | *5,614 sq. ft.* |

# Design CP9802 Fontana

The exterior of this home is decidedly European-inspired. Surrounding the arched entry are windows with arched transoms, which admit outside light to enhance the magnificence of the two-story foyer. The formal atmosphere of the living and dining room is enhanced by a central, dual-opening fireplace. The master suite features an expansive master bath with His and Hers closet space.

**Second Floor**

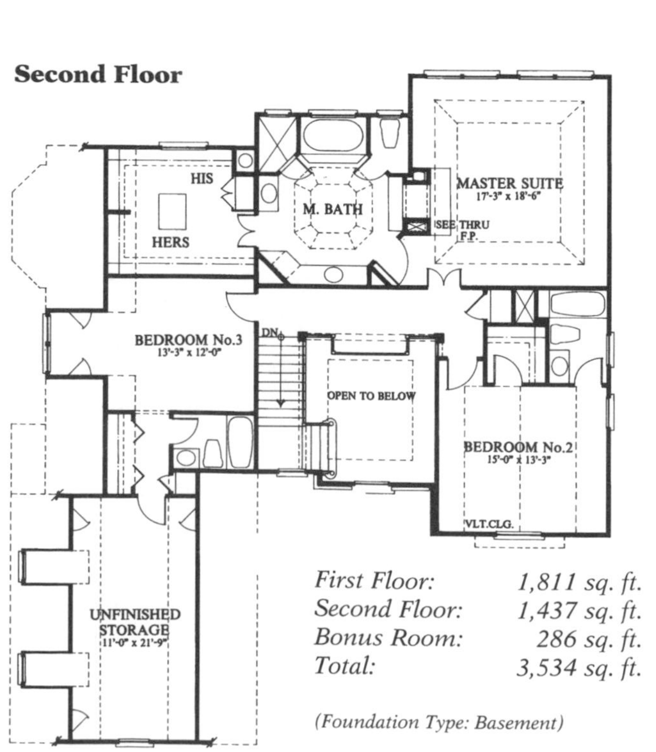


| | |
|---|---|
| *First Floor:* | *1,811 sq. ft.* |
| *Second Floor:* | *1,437 sq. ft.* |
| *Bonus Room:* | *286 sq. ft.* |
| *Total:* | *3,534 sq. ft.* |

*(Foundation Type: Basement)*

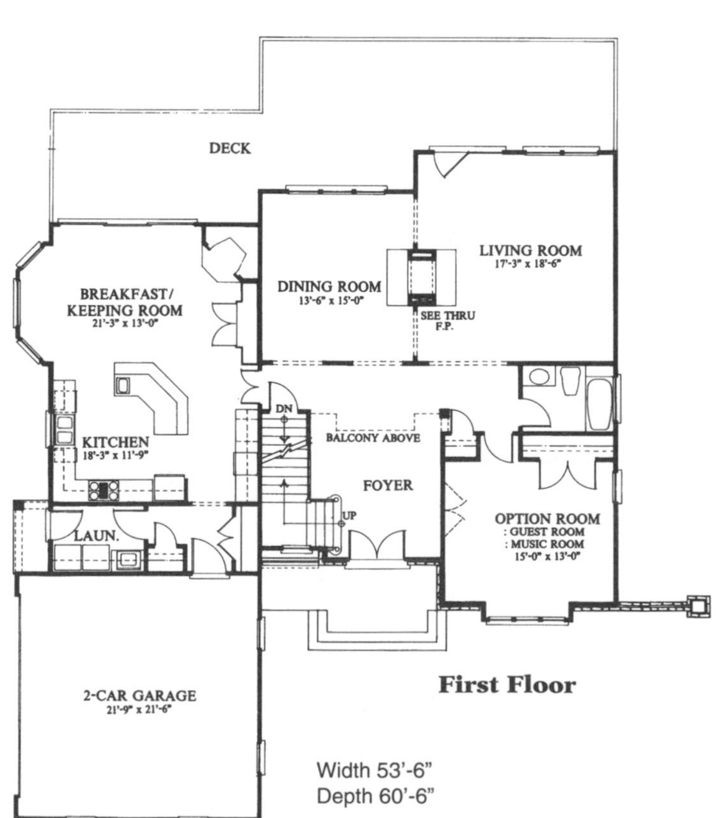


**First Floor**

Width 53'-6"
Depth 60'-6"

# Sullivan

## Design CP3386

This beautiful folk Victorian is decorated with a handful of elegant windows. Living areas include a formal parlor, a private study and a large gathering room. The formal dining room has its more casual counterpart in a breakfast room with bay windows. The master suite, found on the second floor, sports a bathroom with whirlpool, dressing room and walk-in closets. Two bedrooms a bathroom and a balcony complete the space. A useful third floor contains two additional bedrooms and a bath.

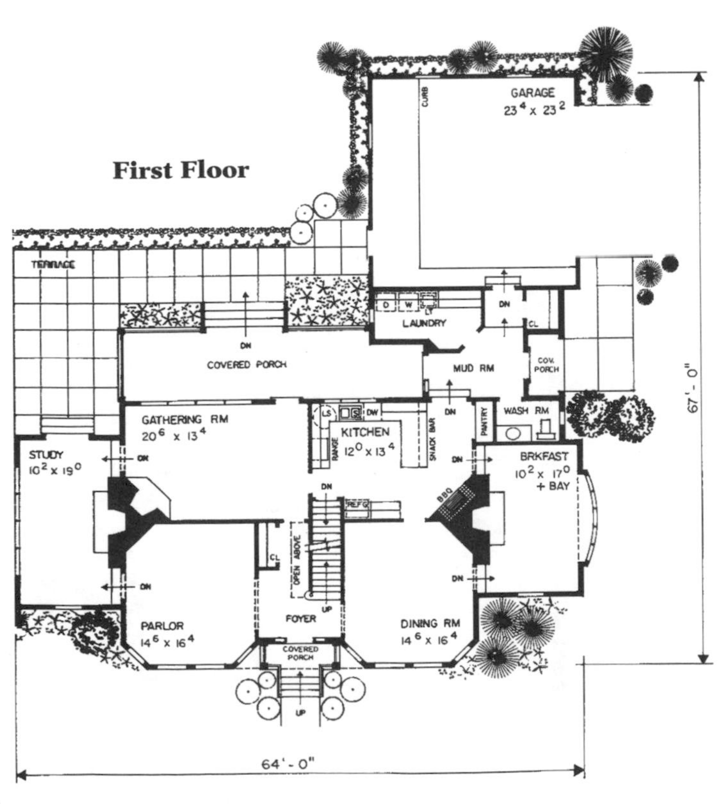


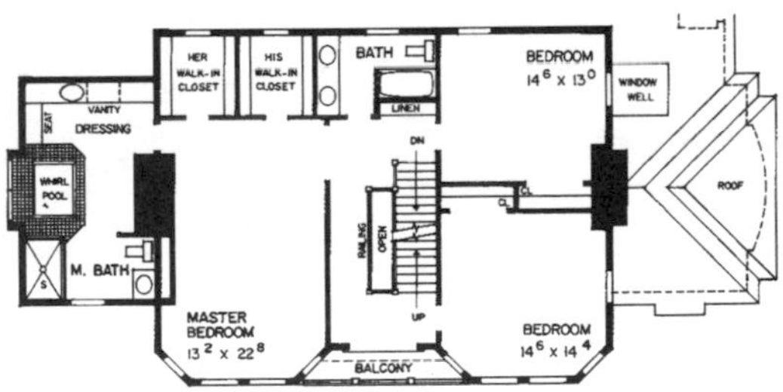


**Second Floor**

**Third Floor**

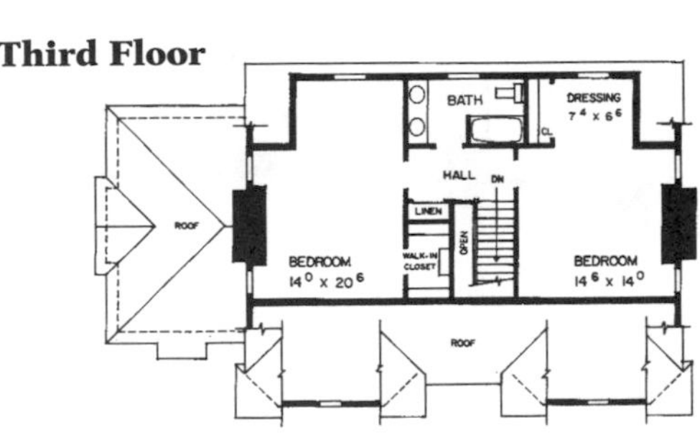


| | |
|---|---|
| *First Floor:* | *1,683 sq. ft.* |
| *Second Floor:* | *1,388 sq. ft.* |
| *Third Floor:* | *808 sq. ft.* |
| *Total:* | *3,879 sq. ft.* |

*(Foundation Type: Basement)*

**Design CP3387**

# Pleasant View

Borrowing from the bold style of Henry Hobson Richardson, this sprawling Victorian features a distinguished round turret. Along with the formal living and dining rooms and a casual family room, there is a study with corner fireplace. The kitchen is joined by a breakfast room and easily accessed by the dining area. The master suite, with whirlpool bath and walk-in closet, is located on the second floor. The third floor is occupied by a bedroom, a private bath and an alcove.

## First Floor

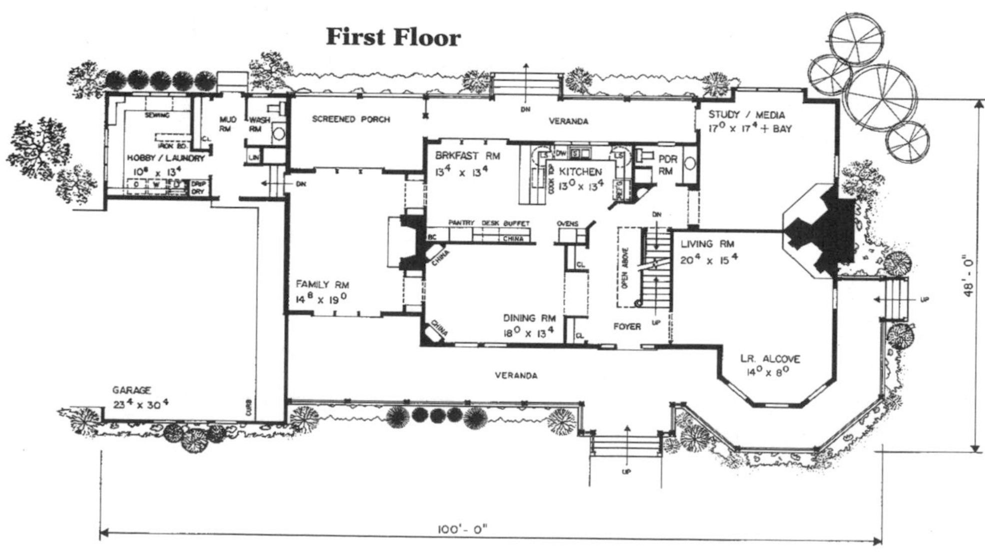


## Third Floor

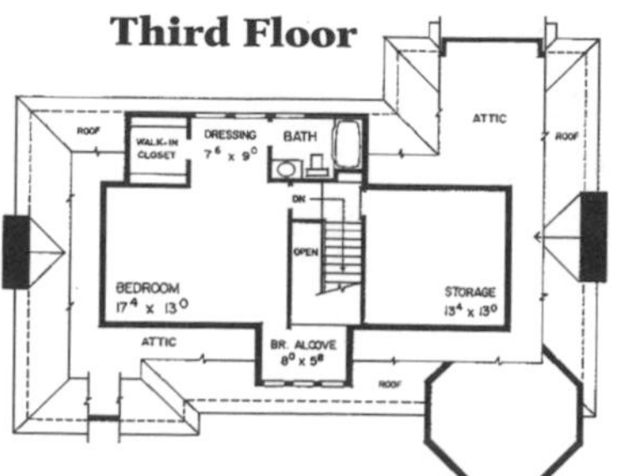


## Second Floor

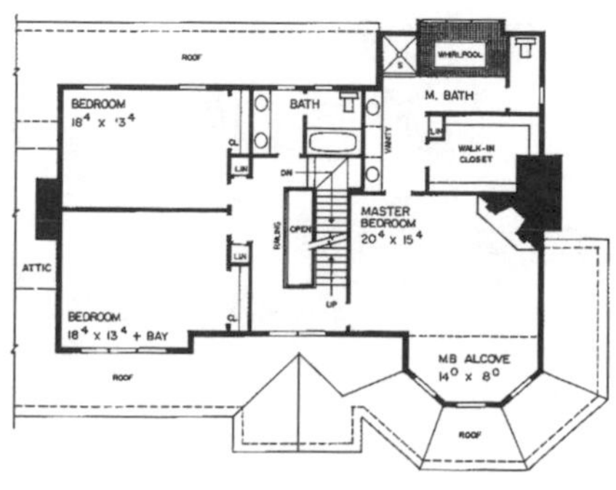


| | |
|---|---|
| *First Floor:* | *2,393 sq. ft.* |
| *Second Floor:* | *1,703 sq. ft.* |
| *Third Floor:* | *716 sq. ft.* |
| *Total:* | *4,812 sq. ft.* |

*(Foundation Type: Basement)*

# Westminster

**Design CP3304**

The most exquisite proportions are displayed within this Victorian home. Along with the large living room, formal dining room and two-story family room, there is a cozy study for private time. The gourmet kitchen has a pass-through counter to the breakfast room. The master suite, found on the second floor, includes an exercise room and whirlpool bath. Two additional bedrooms with private baths share second-floor space with the master suite.

**First Floor**

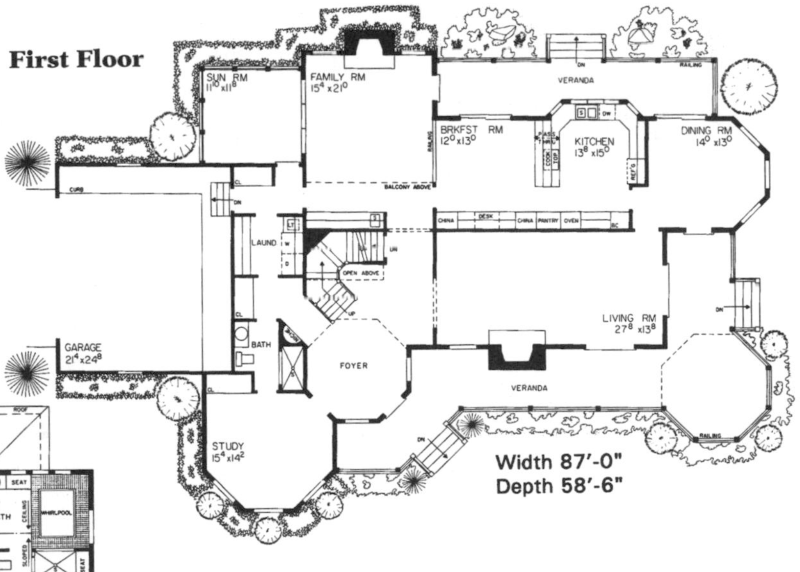

Width 87'-0"
Depth 58'-6"

**Second Floor**

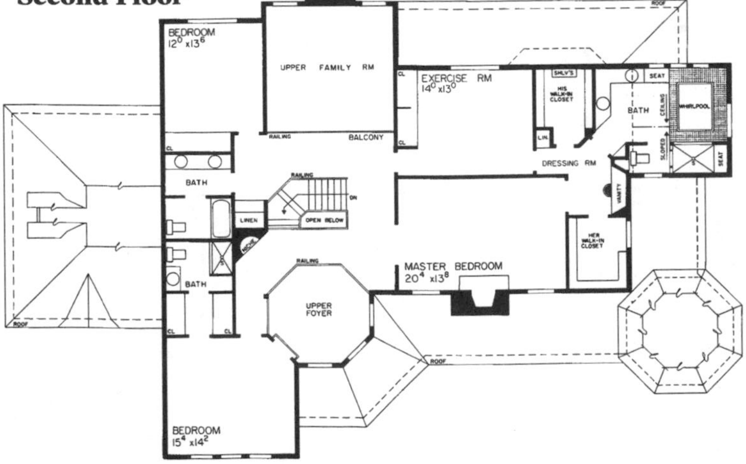

| | |
|---|---|
| *First Floor:* | *2,102 sq. ft.* |
| *Second Floor:* | *1,971 sq. ft.* |
| *Total:* | *4,073 sq. ft.* |

*(Foundation Type: Basement)*

**Design CP3395**

# Galveston

This home is a lovely example of classic Queen Anne architecture. The main level includes an island kitchen with breakfast room, formal dining area, unusually shaped study, and gathering room. A utility center, including laundry room and butler's pantry, is a convenient addition. The master suite is found on the second floor, along with three bedrooms and a bath. The third floor provides space for a guest room, a library and a game room. There are verandas on the front and rear of the house.

**Second Floor**

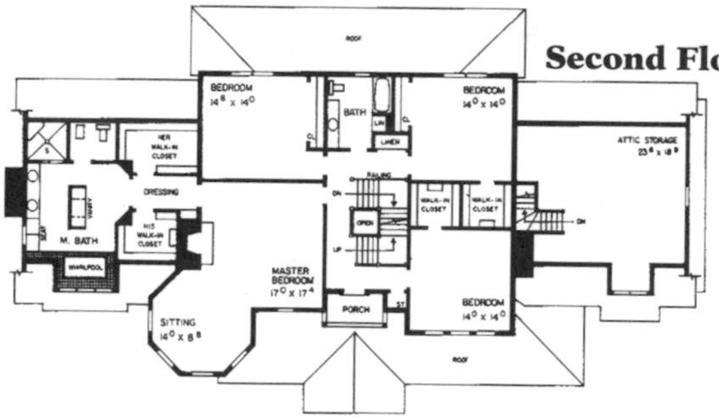

**Third Floor**

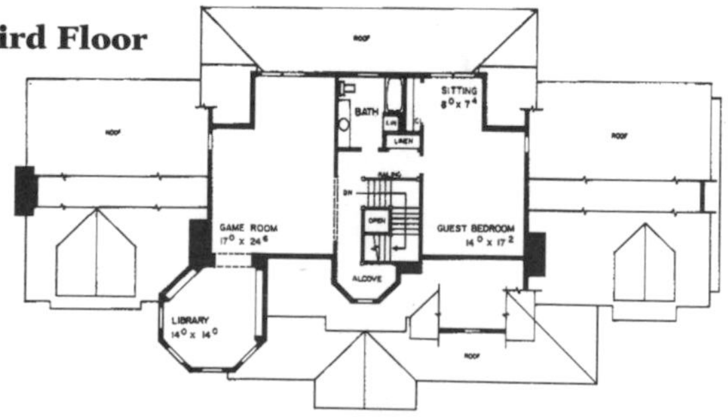

**First Floor**

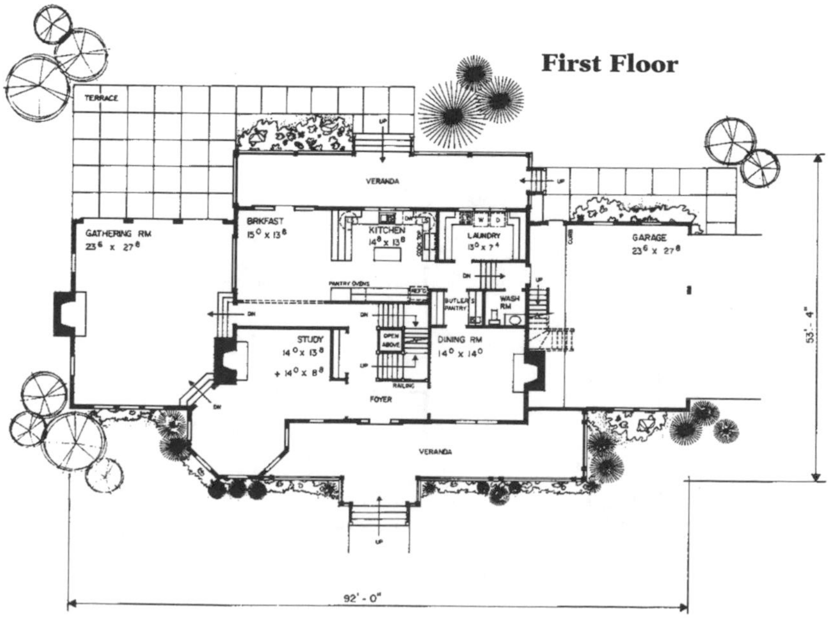

| | |
|---|---|
| *First Floor:* | *2,248 sq. ft.* |
| *Second Floor:* | *2,020 sq. ft.* |
| *Third Floor:* | *1,117 sq. ft.* |
| *Total:* | *5,385 sq. ft.* |

*(Foundation Type: Basement)*

# Sommerset

**Design CP3308**

Uniquely shaped rooms and a cache of amenities define this beautiful three-story home. The foyer is flanked by the formal dining area and living room. An island kitchen is joined by a breakfast room. The family room and study finish off the main floor. The second floor has two family bedrooms with a full bath plus a master suite with His and Her closets and whirlpool. The third floor includes a guest bedroom and exercise room with its own sauna and bath.

**Second Floor**

**First Floor**

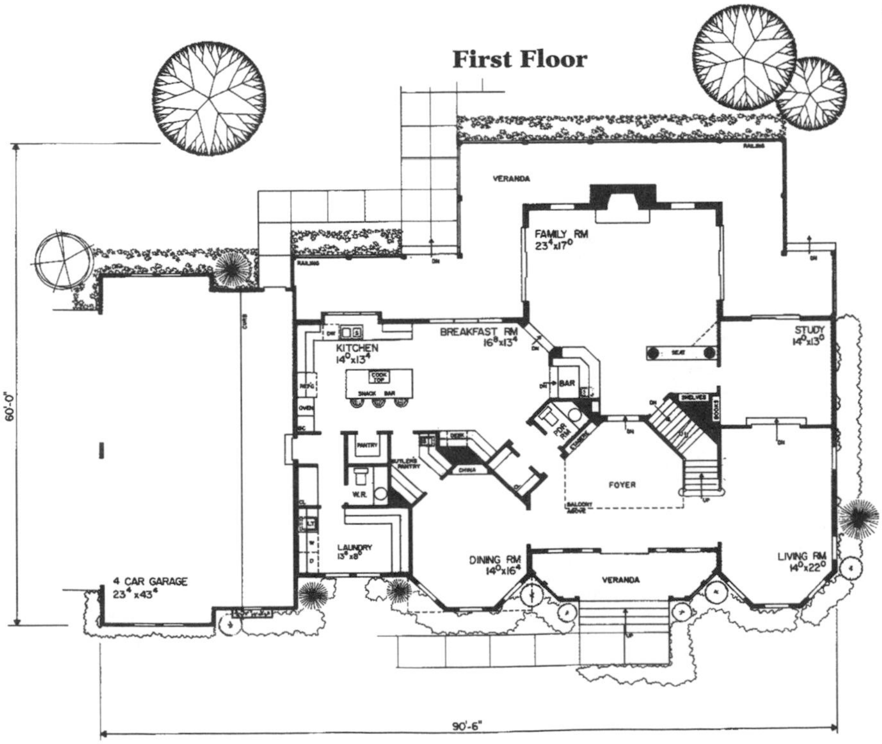

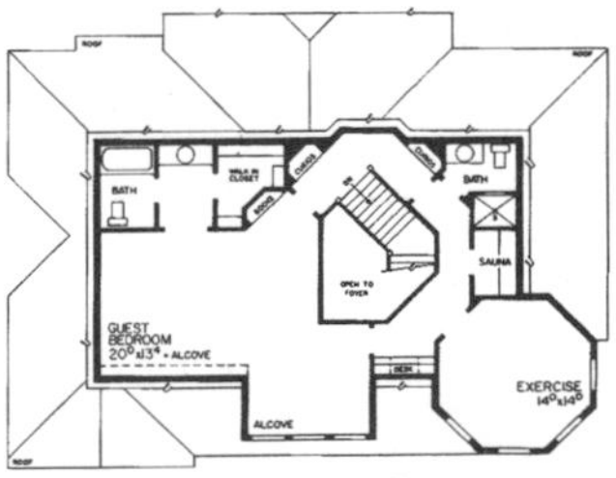

**Third Floor**

| | |
|---|---|
| *First Floor:* | *2,515 sq. ft.* |
| *Second Floor:* | *1,708 sq. ft.* |
| *Third Floor:* | *1,001 sq. ft.* |
| *Total:* | *5,224 sq. ft.* |

*(Foundation Type: Basement)*

# Design CP2562 Hudson

A circular drive and covered entrance with skylights are exterior focal points of this multi-level home. The foyer overlooks a planter on the lower level and a step-down gathering room with sloped ceiling and raised-hearth fireplace. Dramatic touches in the master suite include a sloped ceiling and a sunken tub. The upper level houses three bedrooms and a full bath. On the lower level, an activities room and two storage areas provide plenty of flexibility.

**Second Floor**

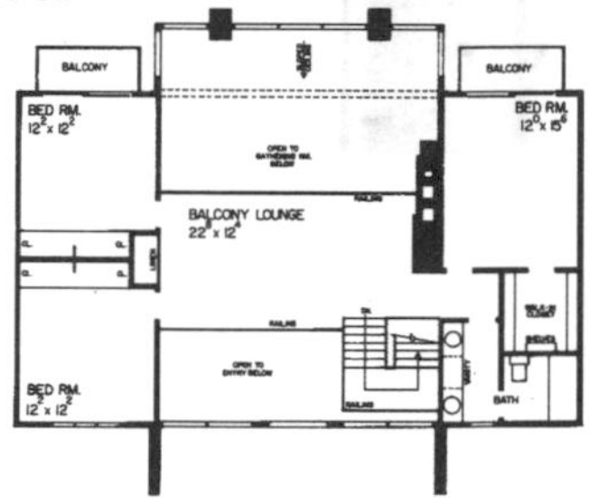

**First Floor**

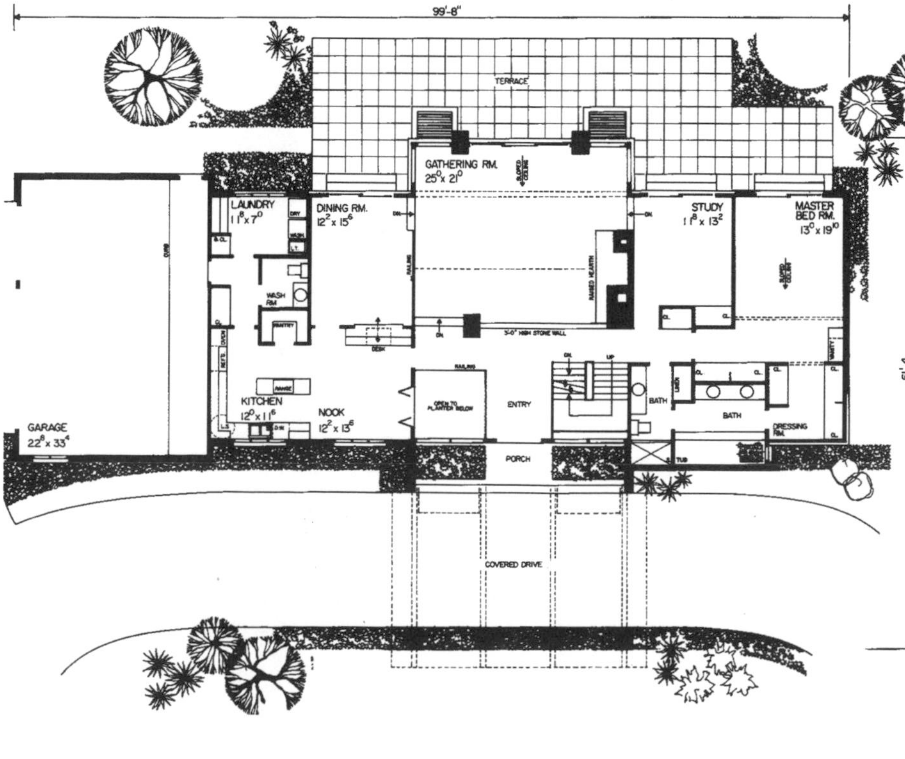

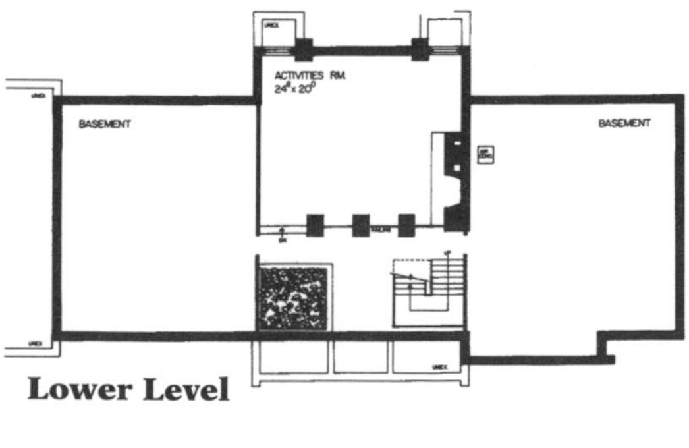

**Lower Level**

| | |
|---|---|
| *First Floor:* | *2,459 sq. ft.* |
| *Second Floor:* | *1,107 sq. ft.* |
| *Lower Level:* | *851 sq. ft.* |
| *Total:* | *4,417 sq. ft.* |

*(Foundation Type: Basement)*

# Springwater

**Design CP4127**

The wood and stone exterior of this home complements its contemporary style. This unusual floor plan provides a private master bedroom suite, with dressing room and walk-in closet, on the second floor. The main level includes three bedrooms, two baths, a family room with fireplace, a formal dining room and a kitchen with attached nook. The decks can be accessed through the breakfast and family rooms. The basement level has room for a recreation area or guest bedroom with outdoor patio access.

**First Floor**

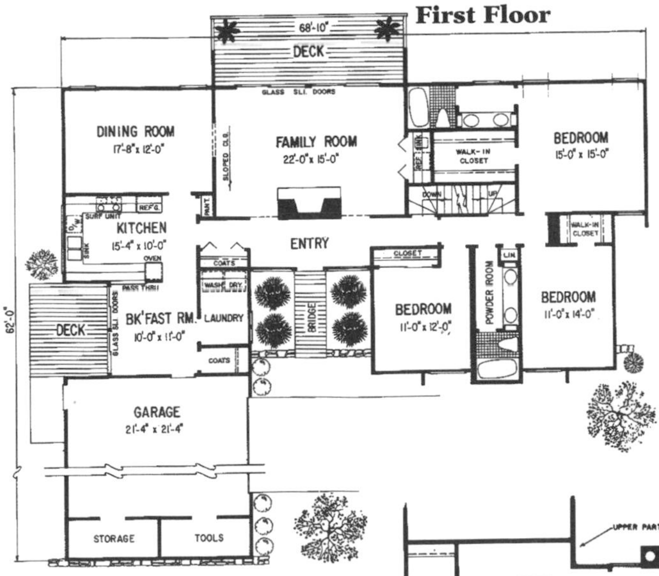

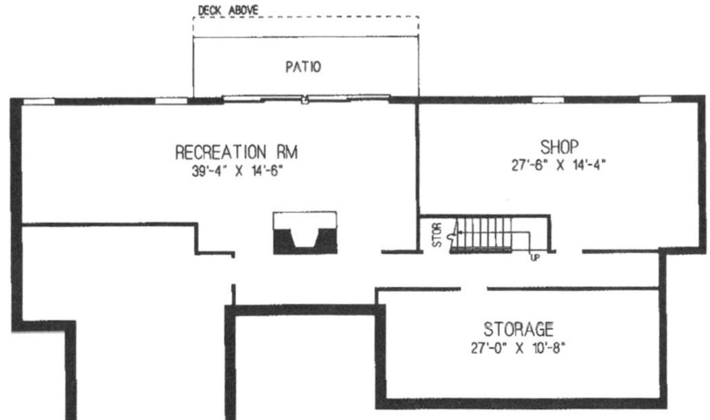

**Basement Level**

**Second Floor**

| | |
|---|---|
| *First Floor:* | *2,015 sq. ft.* |
| *Second Floor:* | *746 sq. ft.* |
| *Basement Level:* | *1,952 sq. ft.* |
| *Total:* | *4,713 sq. ft.* |

*(Foundation Type: Basement)*

## Design CP2392 **Flemington**

Two sets of front doors access this hillside contemporary. The lower entrance hall opens to the family room with fireplace. Each of the two bedrooms on this level has access to a balcony through sliding glass doors. The master suite and a third bedroom are located on the upper entrance level. The living room, adjoining dining room and kitchen with breakfast room, complete this floor. The lower level includes recreation room, hobby room and bathroom.

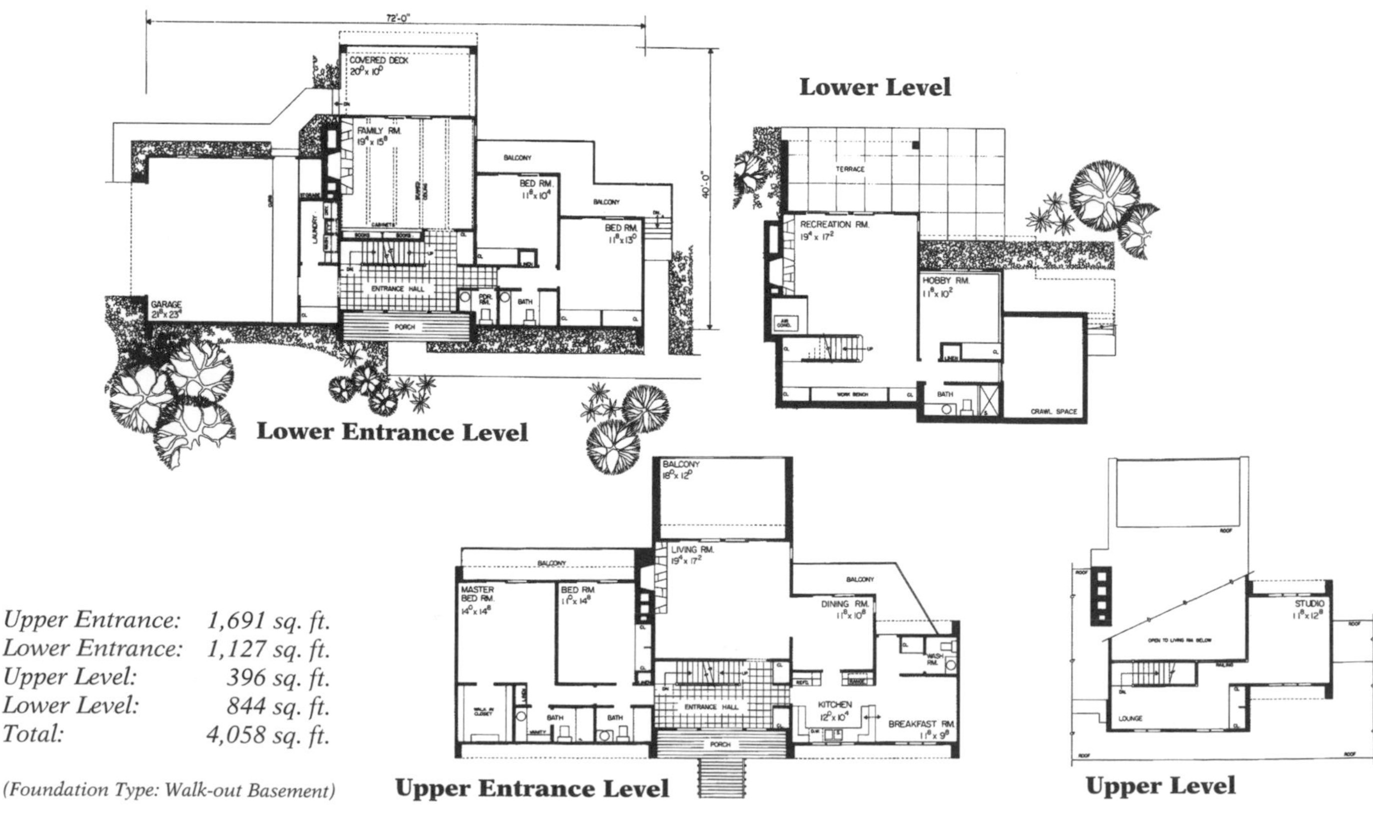


*Upper Entrance:* *1,691 sq. ft.*
*Lower Entrance:* *1,127 sq. ft.*
*Upper Level:* *396 sq. ft.*
*Lower Level:* *844 sq. ft.*
*Total:* *4,058 sq. ft.*

*(Foundation Type: Walk-out Basement)*

# Manchester

**Design CP4549**

Stone, glass and cedar-shingle siding create an interesting mix of textures on the exterior of this contemporary. An atrium foyer and planter are visible from the sunken living room. The oversized family room with huge stone fireplace has access to a spacious deck. The secluded master suite, with His and Her bathrooms, is tucked into a private corner. An island kitchen includes an adjoining breakfast nook. A playroom is found on the second floor.

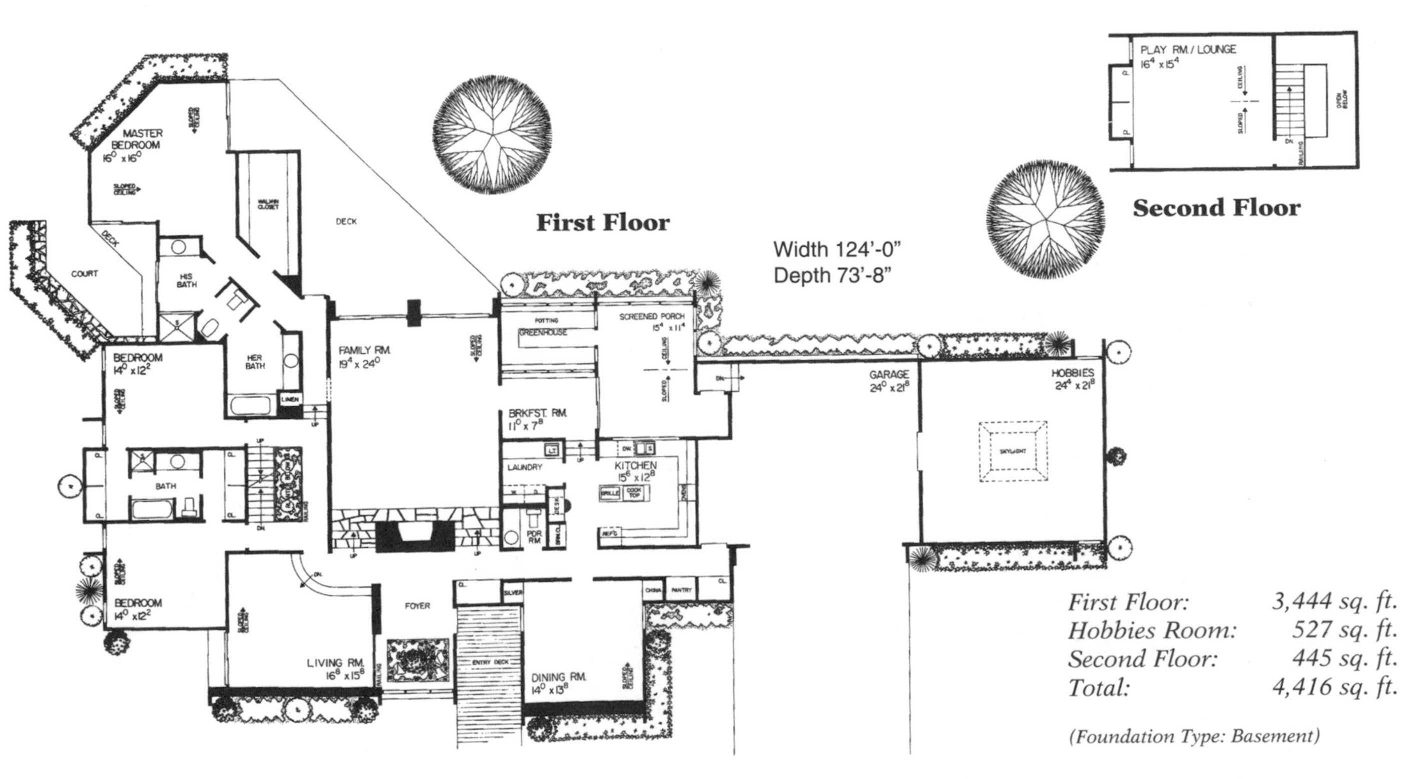


| | |
|---|---|
| *First Floor:* | *3,444 sq. ft.* |
| *Hobbies Room:* | *527 sq. ft.* |
| *Second Floor:* | *445 sq. ft.* |
| *Total:* | *4,416 sq. ft.* |

*(Foundation Type: Basement)*

## Design CP4547

# Ridgemont

The wood and stone exterior of this uniquely shaped home complements a contemporary style. Beyond the foyer is an enormous Great Room with conversation pit, fireplace and large windows for breathtaking views. The formal dining room, cozy library and kitchen with island and breakfast area are also found on this level. The master bedroom features a large bath and access to a private deck. The finished basement contains four bedrooms, three baths and a den with fireplace.

**First Floor**

Width 118'-0"
Depth 69'-0"

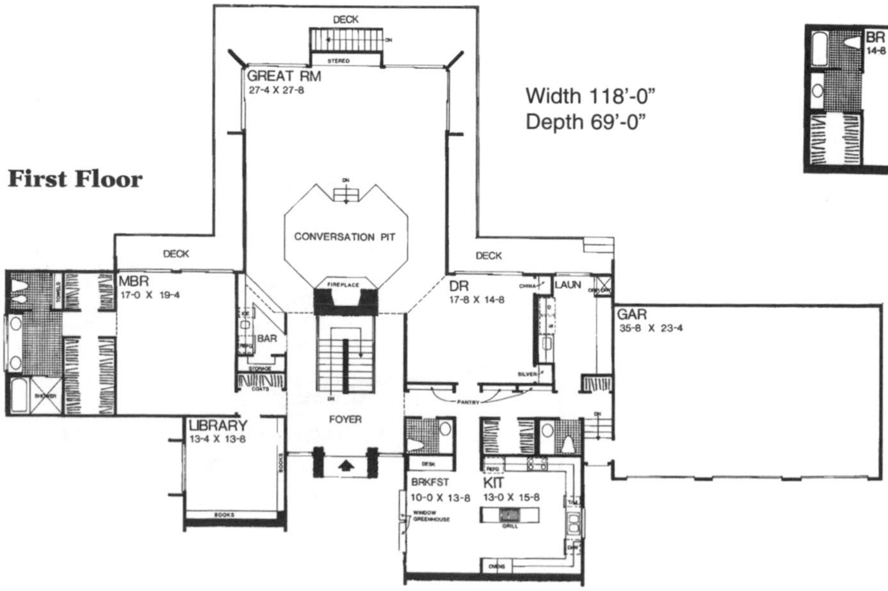

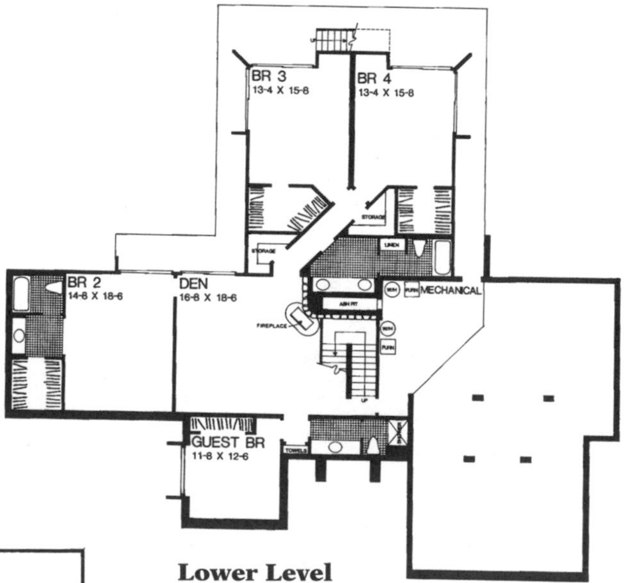

**Lower Level**

| | |
|---|---|
| *First Floor:* | *3,272 sq. ft.* |
| *Lower Level:* | *2,097 sq. ft.* |
| *Total:* | *5,369 sq. ft.* |

*(Foundation Type: Basement)*

# Flagstone

**Design CP4141**

A spacious, two-story living room is the centerpiece of this plan. With its massive fireplace and access to the rear deck, it is the perfect place for entertaining. The kitchen is flanked by a breakfast room and formal dining area. An enormous master suite with fireplace is also located on the main level. There are three bedrooms and a sewing room on the second floor. An apartment occupies the third level with recreation room, family room with fireplace, summer kitchen and laundry facilities.

Width 82'-8"
Depth 40'-0"

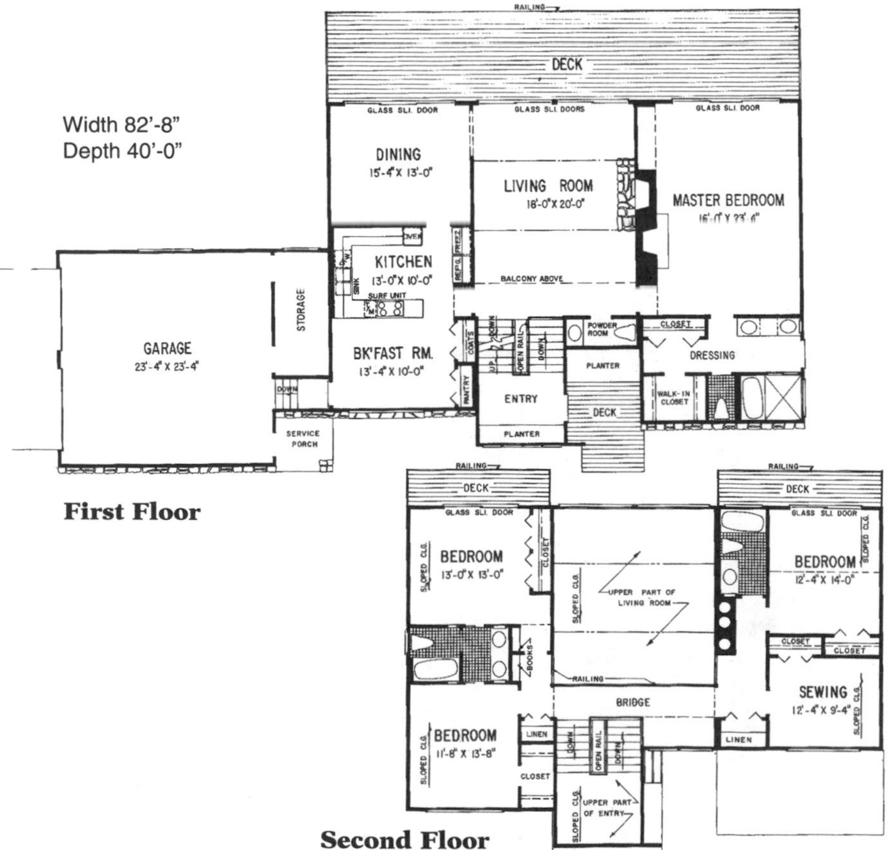


**First Floor**

**Second Floor**

**Third Floor**

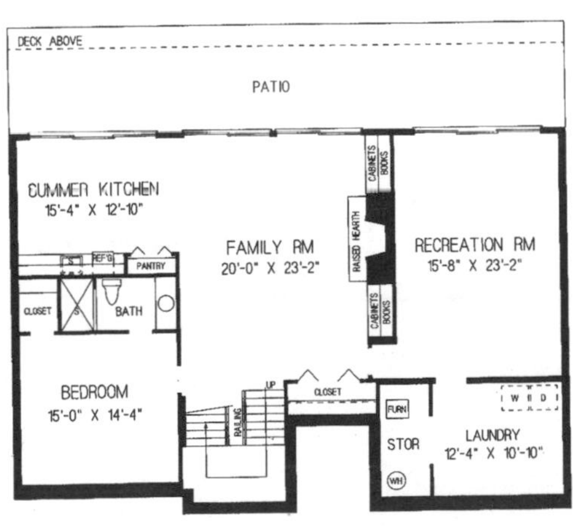


| | |
|---|---|
| *First Floor:* | *1,809 sq. ft.* |
| *Second Floor:* | *1,293 sq. ft.* |
| *Lower Level:* | *1,828 sq. ft.* |
| *Total:* | *4,930 sq. ft.* |

*(Foundation Type: Basement)*

Design CP4331

# Kingston

There's a lot to love about this wood-and-stone contemporary. The master bedroom, located on the first floor, includes private bath with dressing area and walk-in closet. A U-shaped kitchen serves both breakfast room and formal dining area. The two-story living room, with massive fireplace, has access to a spacious deck. The second floor is occupied by two bedrooms with an adjoined bath. A playroom, washroom and shop area are found on the lower level.

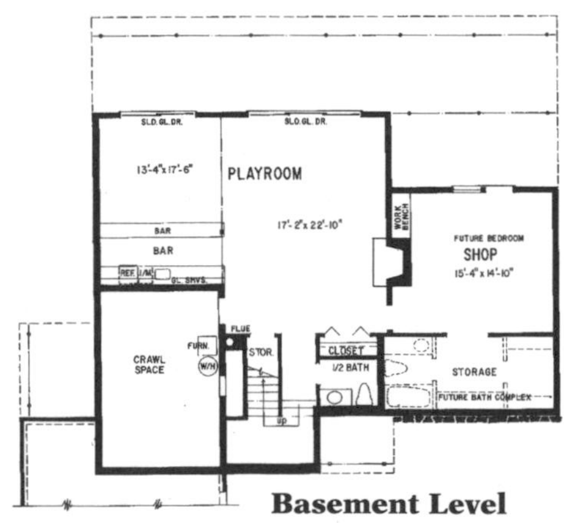


**Basement Level**

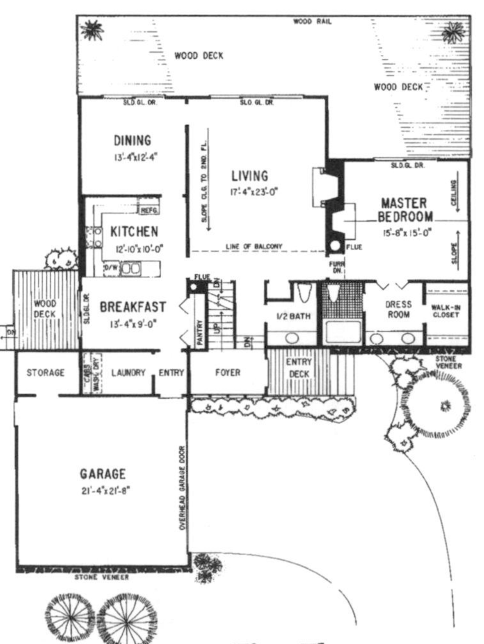


**First Floor**

Width 58'-0"
Depth 60'-0"

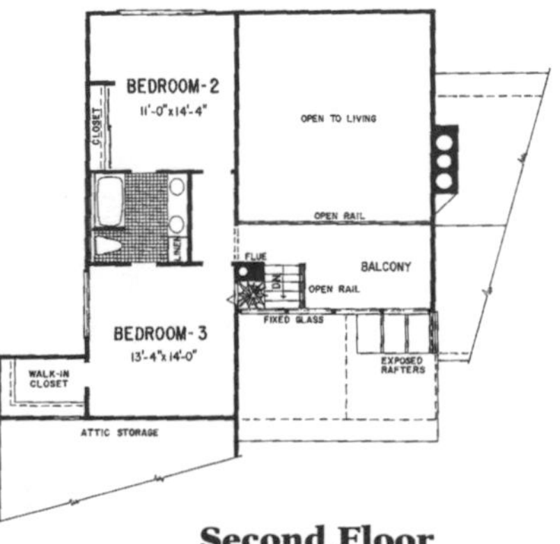


**Second Floor**

| | |
|---|---|
| *First Floor:* | *1,590 sq. ft.* |
| *Second Floor:* | *730 sq. ft.* |
| *Basement Level:* | *1,323 sq. ft.* |
| *Total:* | *3,643 sq. ft.* |

*(Foundation Type: Basement)*

# Sequoia

**Design CP4548**

Tall glass windows and a central chimney emphasize the height of this striking contemporary.The spacious living room opens to a curved deck. A U-shaped kitchen and adjoining breakfast room are found across the hall from the formal dining room. The spacious master bedroom opens to a private deck. Four bedrooms and two full baths are located on the second floor. The lower level features a separate storage room and a large recreation room.

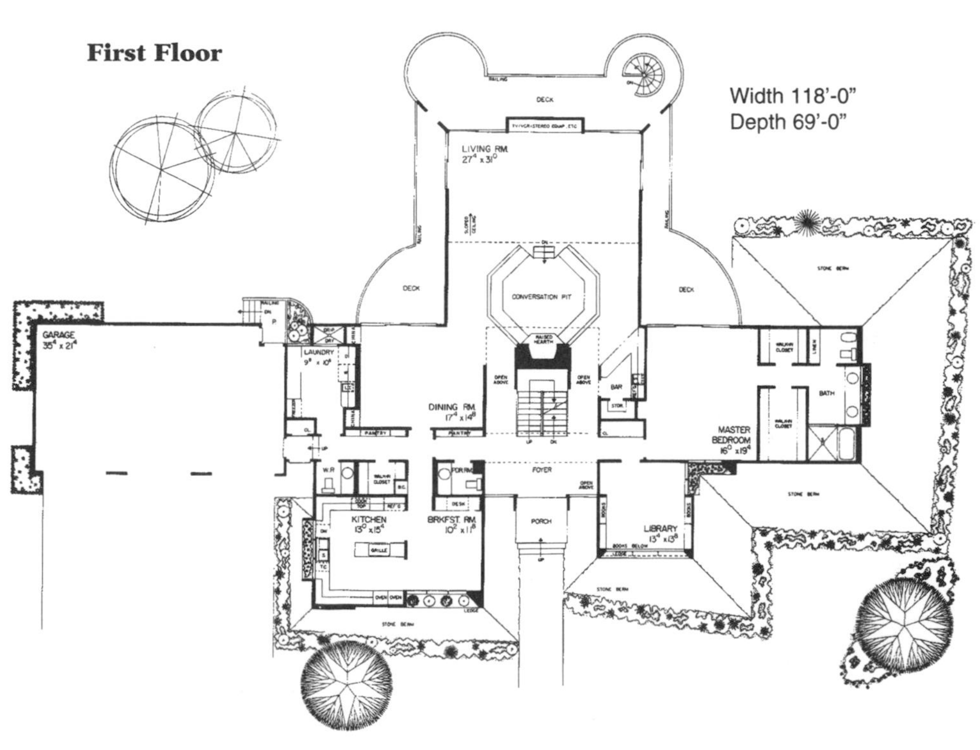


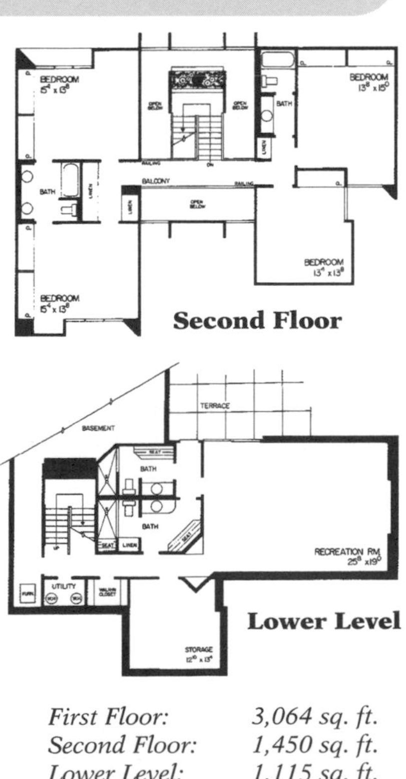


| | |
|---|---|
| *First Floor:* | *3,064 sq. ft.* |
| *Second Floor:* | *1,450 sq. ft.* |
| *Lower Level:* | *1,115 sq. ft.* |
| *Total:* | *5,629 sq. ft.* |

*(Foundation Type: Basement)*

## *Design CP3362* **Brenton**

This attractive multi-level home benefits from the comfort and ease of an open plan. The island kitchen is easily accessed by the dining room and spacious gathering room. The media room is separate for uninterrupted listening and viewing. Upstairs, the master suite with complete bathroom is joined by a bedroom with private bath and the balcony. The lower level is highlighted by an activities room with a raised hearth. A wet bar is perfect for entertaining.

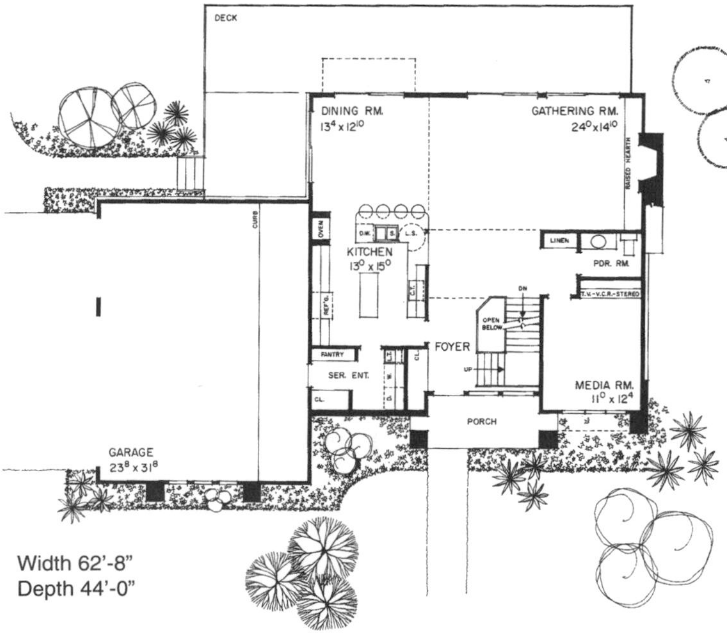

**Lower Level**

**First Floor**

Width 62'-8"
Depth 44'-0"

**Second Floor**

| | |
|---|---|
| *First Floor:* | *1,305 sq. ft.* |
| *Second Floor:* | *862 sq. ft.* |
| *Lower Level:* | *1,140 sq. ft.* |
| *Total:* | *3,307 sq. ft.* |

*(Foundation Type: Basement)*

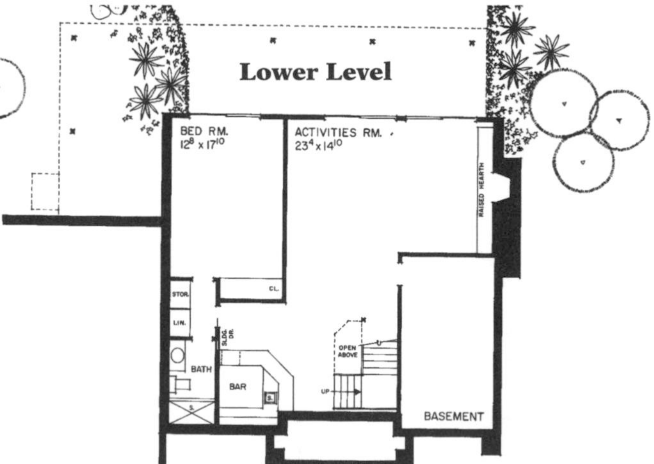

# Woodview

**Design CP3364**

A grand floor plan marks this impressive contemporary home. The rooms are set on different levels with the family room, living room, media room and atrium a few steps lower than the elegant foyer. The large L-shaped kitchen is highlighted by an island work center and a pass-through snack bar. The dining room accesses the kitchen through a butler's pantry. A double curved staircase leads to the second-floor bedrooms. The master suite sports a private deck, a whirlpool bath and a cozy fireplace.

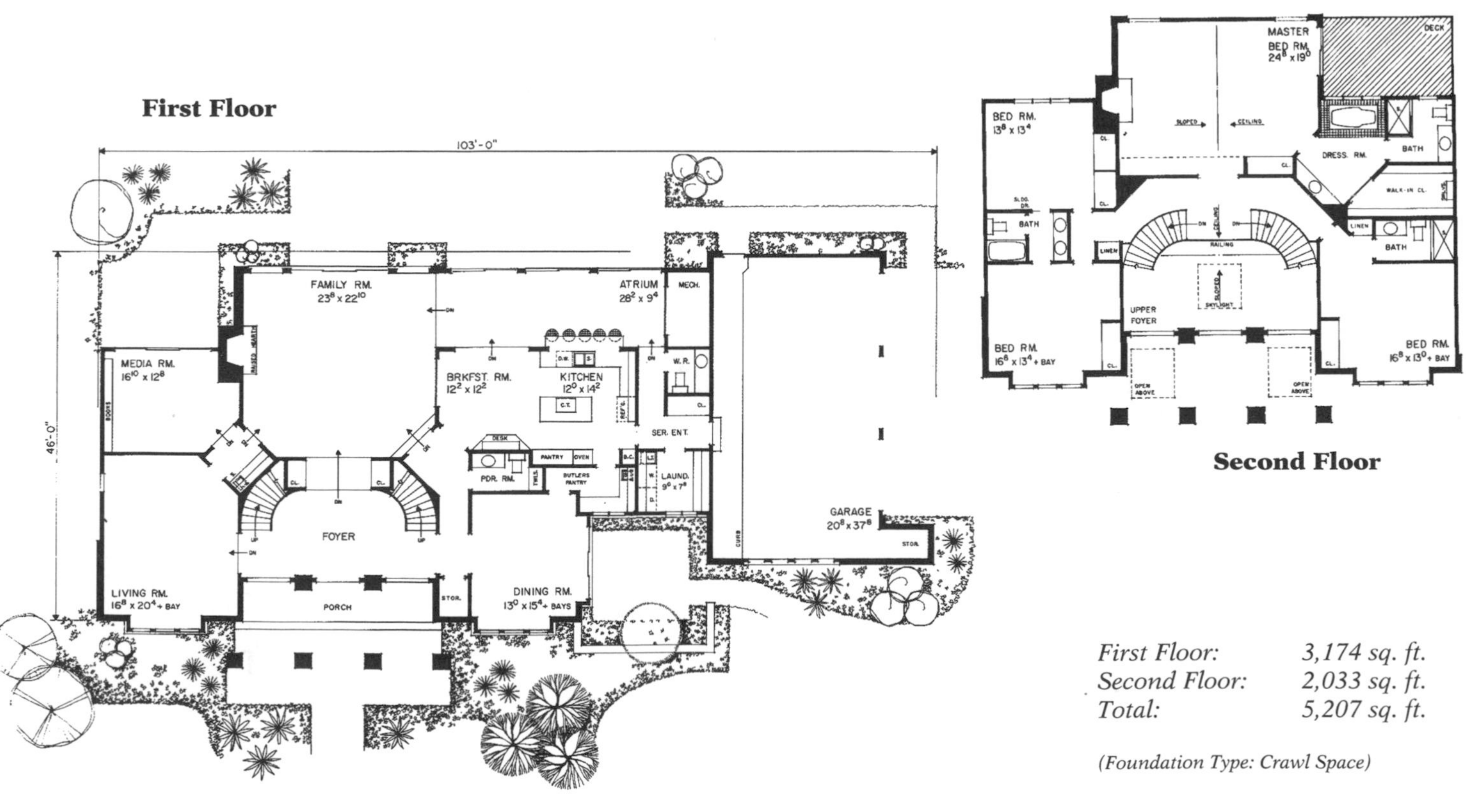


| | |
|---|---|
| *First Floor:* | *3,174 sq. ft.* |
| *Second Floor:* | *2,033 sq. ft.* |
| *Total:* | *5,207 sq. ft.* |

*(Foundation Type: Crawl Space)*

## Design CP2709

# Rudasill

An impressive two-story entry provides the convenience of a walk-in closet and a powder room. On the main level, expansive living areas, perfect for entertaining, surround an open railing above the lower-level conversation pit. The kitchen area is highlighted by a walk-in pantry and an attached breakfast nook with built-in desk. Four large bedrooms occupy the upper level. The lower level provides a family room with a planter and an activities room.

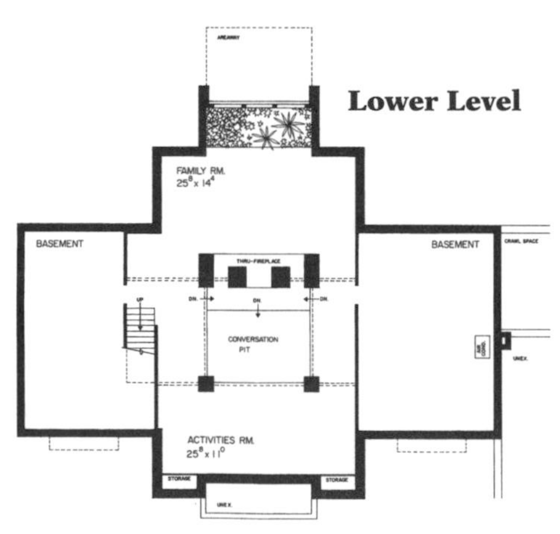


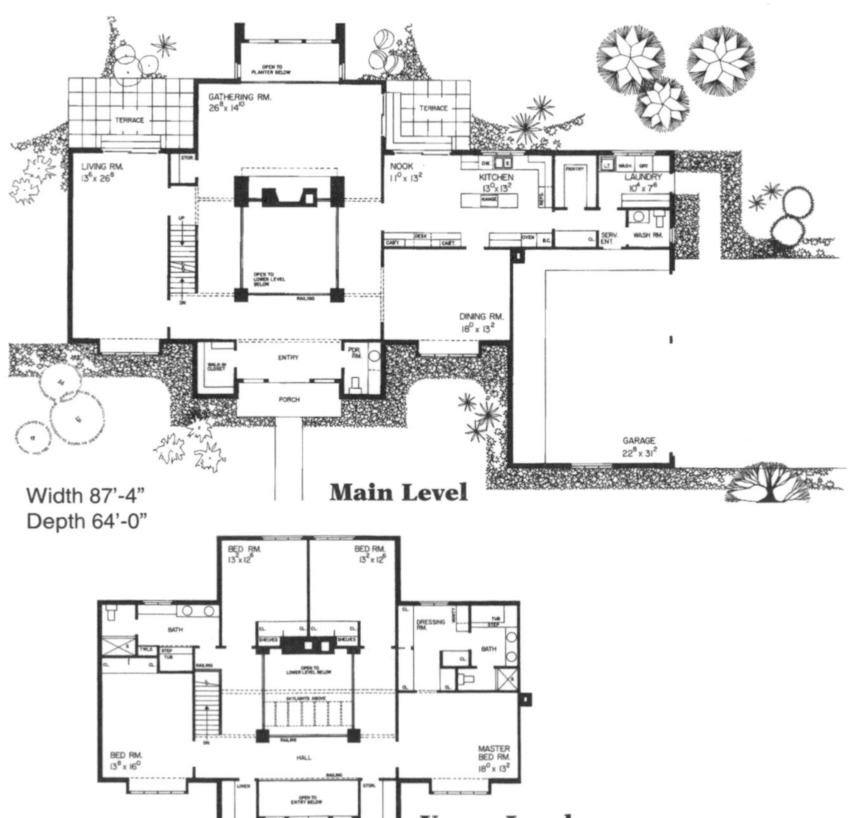


| | |
|---|---|
| *Main Level:* | *2,471 sq. ft.* |
| *Upper Level:* | *2,038 sq. ft.* |
| *Lower Level:* | *1,435 sq. ft.* |
| *Total:* | *5,944 sq. ft.* |

*(Foundation Type: Basement)*

# Copper Creek **Design CP2879**

This plush modern design seems to have it all, including an upper lounge and an atrium with a skylight above. A modern kitchen with snack bar service to a breakfast room enjoys a view of the atrium. A deluxe master bedroom includes its own whirlpool and a bay window. Three other bedrooms also are placed quietly at one end of the house. A spacious family room and living room each offer fireplaces. The three-car garage handles the family fleet easily.

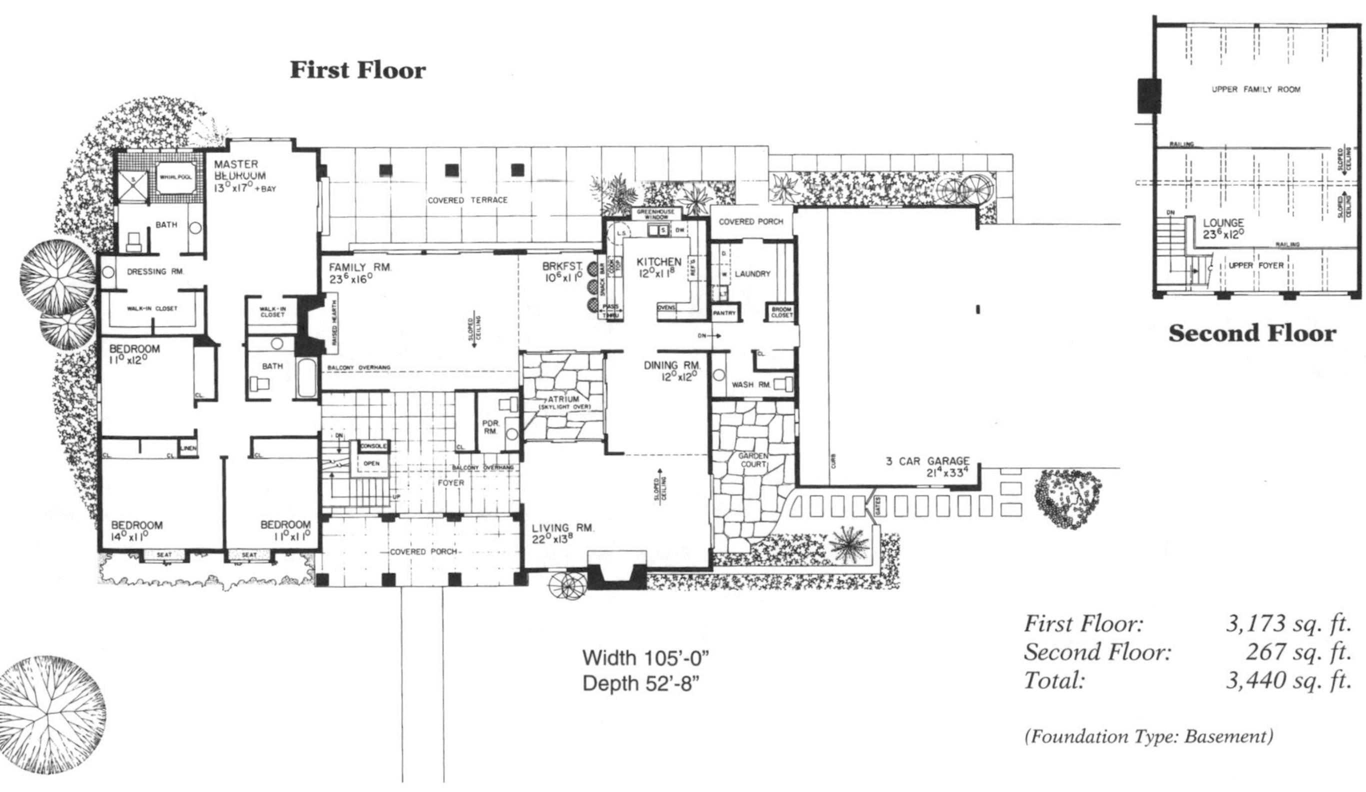


| | |
|---|---|
| *First Floor:* | *3,173 sq. ft.* |
| *Second Floor:* | *267 sq. ft.* |
| *Total:* | *3,440 sq. ft.* |

*(Foundation Type: Basement)*

## Design CP4540

# Alpine

Stone, bevel siding and a cedar-shake roof finish the exterior of this unique low-profile contemporary. Skylights sited over the rear porch and sliding glass doors allow light to enter the living room. A wet bar serves the family room, which opens to the terrace through sliding glass doors. The master bedroom occupies one end of the house. It includes an exercise/garden room, a whirlpool bath, dressing room and walk-in closets. The dining area is a step up from the U-shaped island kitchen.

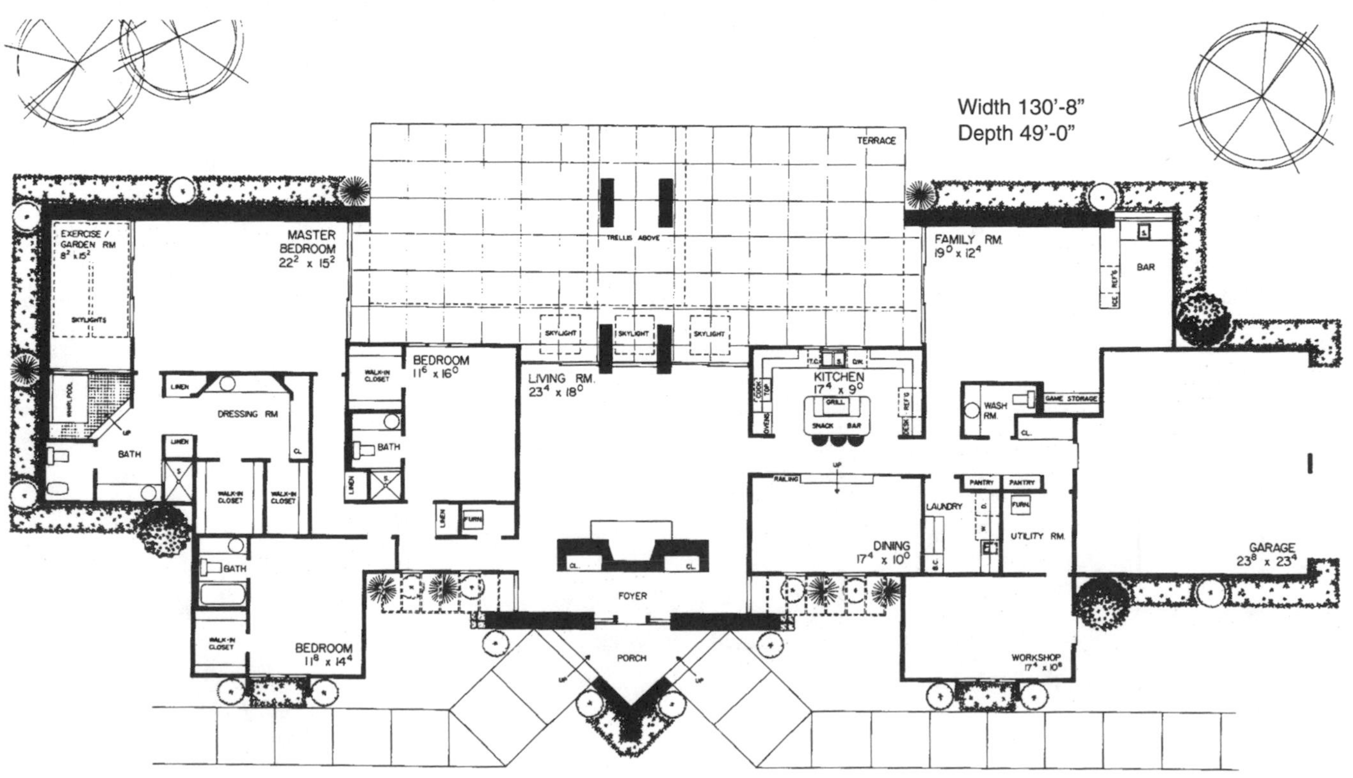


*Total:* *3,545 sq. ft.*

*(Foundation Type: Crawl Space)*

# Essex

## Design CP4546

The combination of stone and vertical wood siding graces the exterior of this contemporary home. The living room features an adjoining wet bar and deck that is ideal for entertaining. The library has access to the bar. The impressive family room opens to the front deck or screened porch. Upstairs, a corner fireplace is the focal point of a marvelous master bedroom with private deck, sauna and dressing room. Two additional bedrooms with private baths and a library complete the second floor.

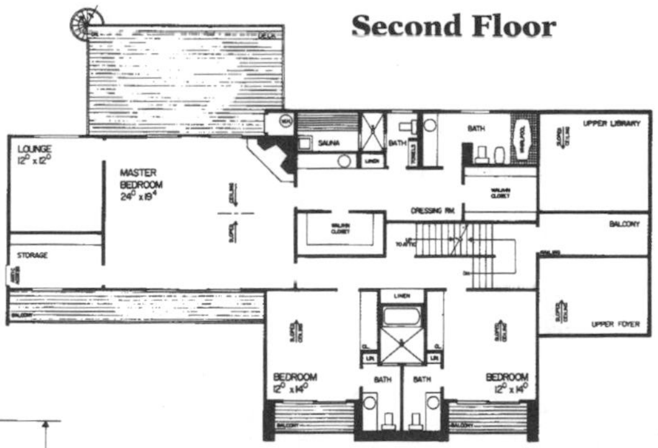

**Second Floor**

**First Floor**

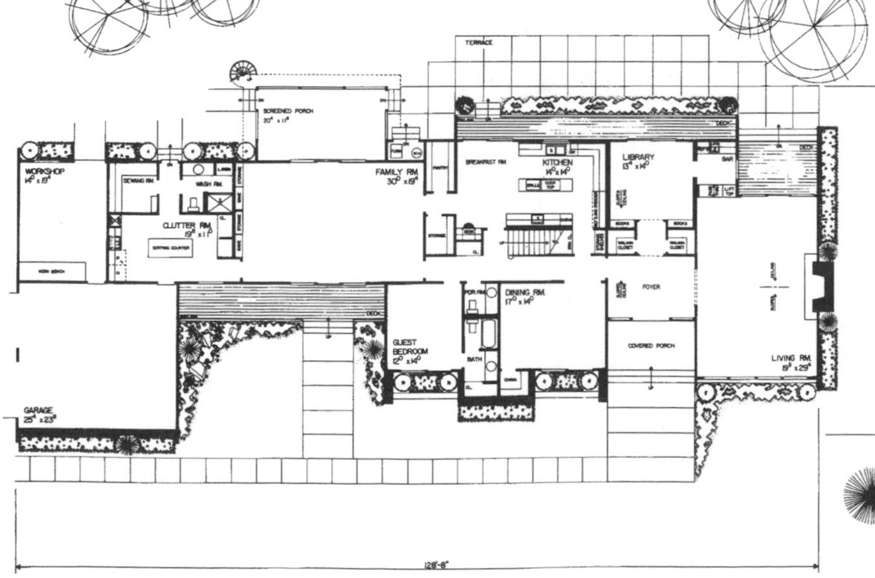

| | |
|---|---|
| *First Floor:* | *3,179 sq. ft.* |
| *Workshop:* | *353 sq. ft.* |
| *Second Floor:* | *2,474 sq. ft.* |
| *Total:* | *6,006 sq. ft.* |

*(Foundation Type: Crawl Space)*

## Design CP2951

# Jessica

A single prominent turret with two-story divided window draws attention to this stately Tudor home. The open foyer allows an uninterrupted view into the impressive, two-story Great Room with wet bar. The master suite features a sitting room, His and Her baths and closets, and a whirlpool. The formal dining area and casual family room flank an island kitchen and morning room. Upstairs, there is a guest suite, two bedrooms and a bathroom.

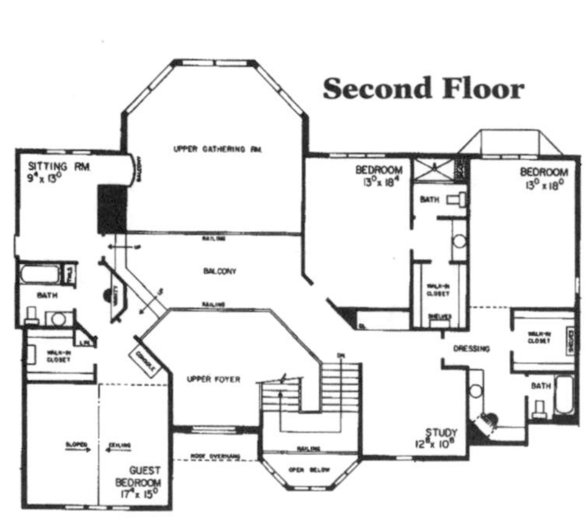


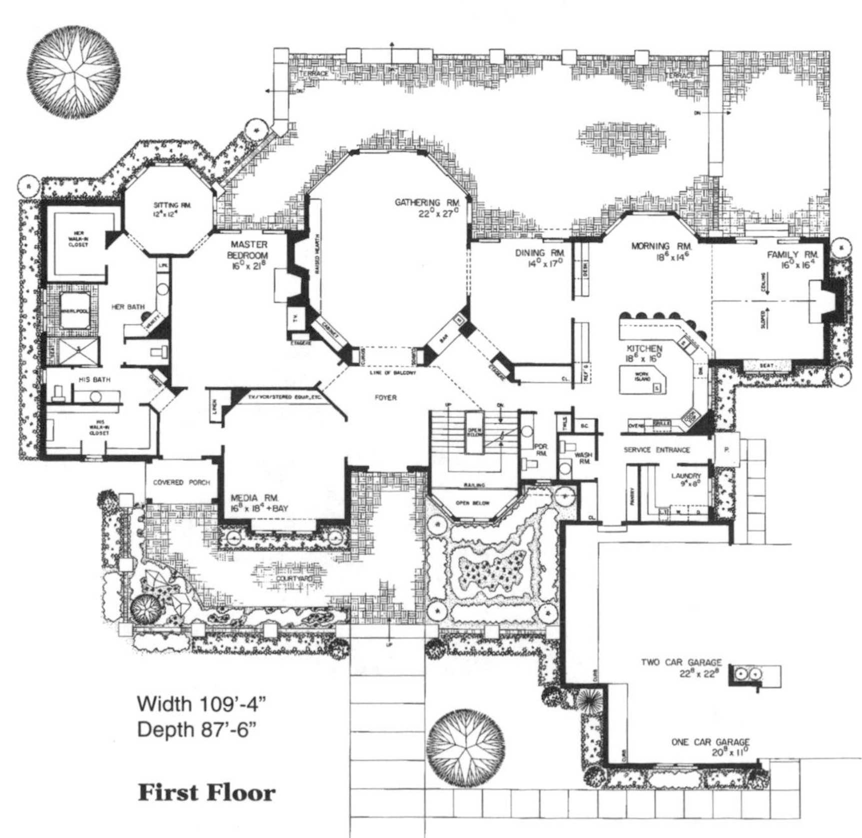


| | |
|---|---|
| *First Floor:* | *4,195 sq. ft.* |
| *Second Floor:* | *2,094 sq. ft.* |
| *Total:* | *6,289 sq. ft.* |

*(Foundation Type: Basement)*

# Dorchester

## Design CP2955

Cross-gables, half-timbers and three massive chimneys mark the exterior of this magnificent baronial Tudor. A circular staircase housed in the turret highlights the two-story foyer. Both, the living room and a sumptuous library with wet bar, feature massive fireplaces. An island kitchen serves the formal dining area, breakfast room and family room. The master bedroom includes sitting room and whirlpool. Four bedrooms with baths and a nursery or exercise area complete this floor.

**First Floor**

**Second Floor**

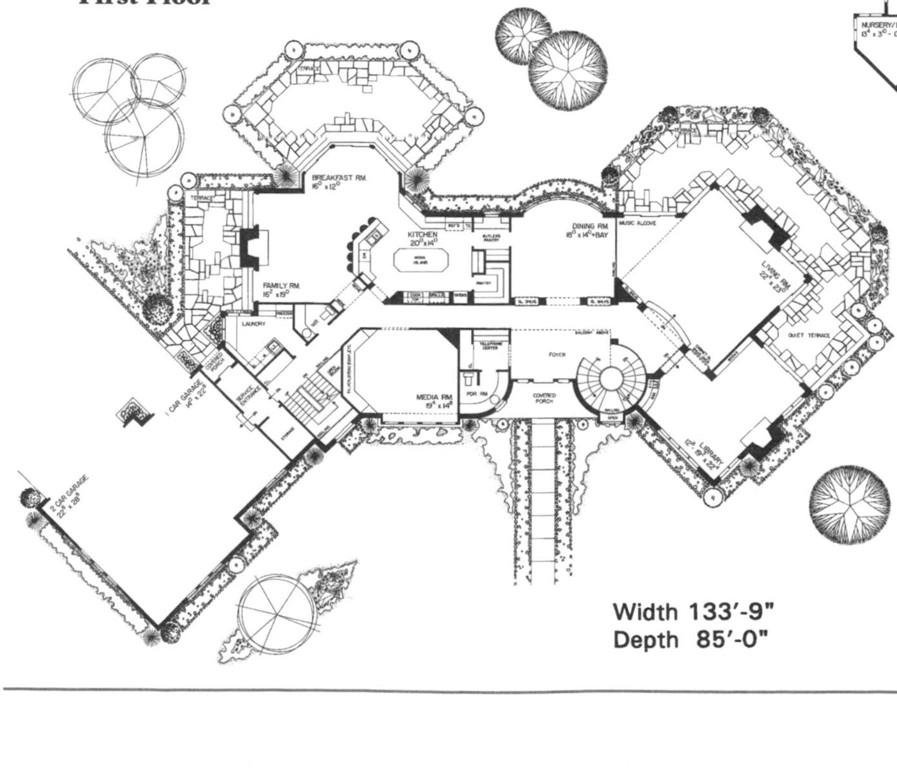

Width 133′-9″
Depth 85′-0″

| | |
|---|---|
| *First Floor:* | *3,840 sq. ft.* |
| *Second Floor:* | *3,435 sq. ft.* |
| *Total:* | *7,275 sq. ft.* |

*(Foundation Type: Basement)*

## Design CP3371

# Winchester

This fine home demonstrates the timelessness of the Tudor style. A two-story foyer leads to all living and working areas. The spacious living room is perfect for entertaining with its massive fireplace and complete bar. The library, family room and upstairs master suite are warmed by fireplaces. The island kitchen serves the dining room and breakfast area. Upstairs, there are three additional bedrooms, two baths and a balcony.

**Second Floor**

**First Floor**

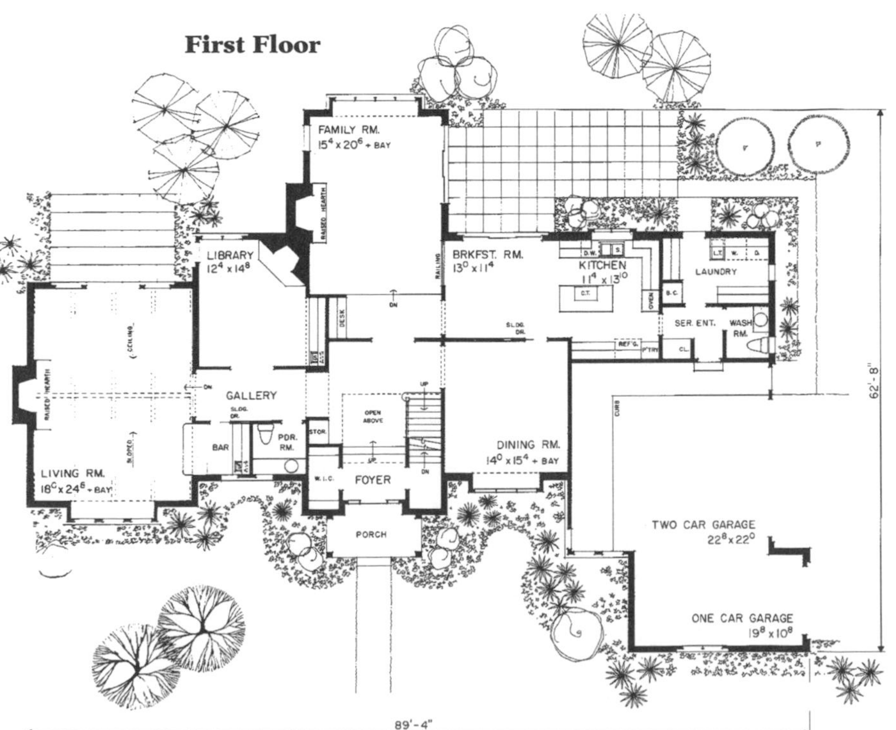


| | |
|---|---|
| *First Floor:* | *2,486 sq. ft.* |
| *Second Floor:* | *1,553 sq. ft.* |
| *Total:* | *4,039 sq. ft.* |

*(Foundation Type: Basement)*

# *Wrightstown*  **Design CP2966**

This Tudor adaptation is as dramatic inside as it is outside. The spacious foyer with its sloping ceiling looks up into the balcony-type lounge. It also looks down the open stairwell to the lower level. The focal point of the living zone is the delightful atrium. Both the formal living room and the informal family room feature a fireplace. Three bedrooms include a gorgeous master suite and two secondary bedrooms.

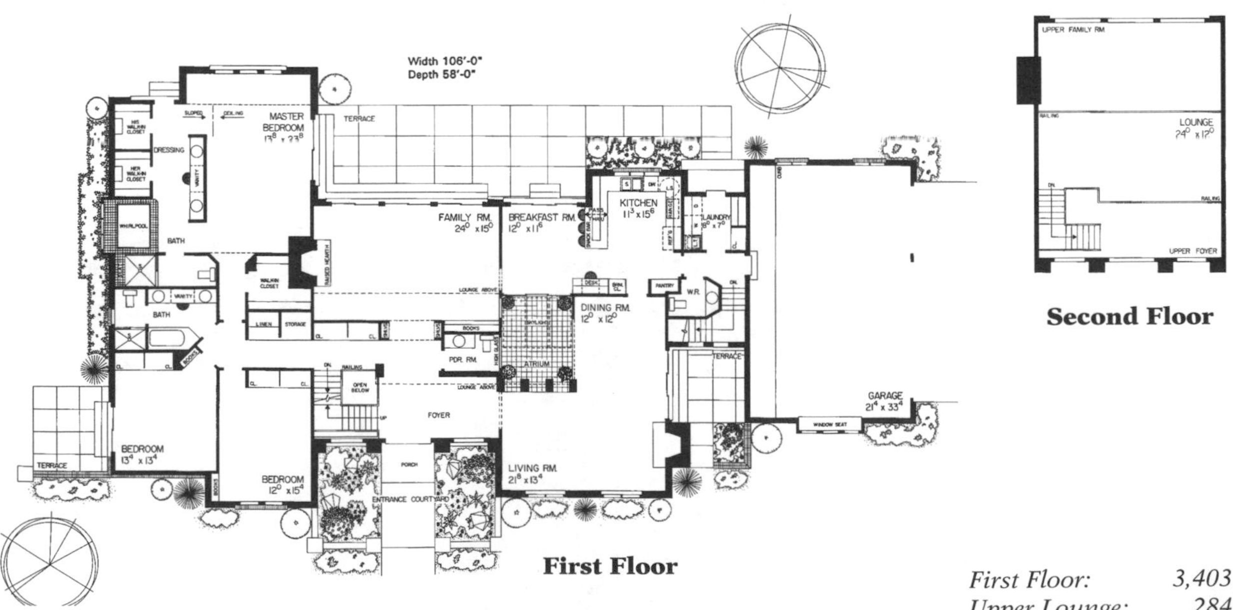


**First Floor**

**Second Floor**

| | |
|---|---|
| *First Floor:* | *3,403 sq. ft.* |
| *Upper Lounge:* | *284 sq. ft.* |
| *Total:* | *3,687 sq. ft.* |

*(Foundation Type: Basement)*

## Design CP3369

# Barrington

This graceful Tudor complements its surroundings in a grand manner. Living space abounds with a quiet library, a Great Hall with massive fireplace, a cozy family room with adjacent breakfast area and a laundry room that doubles as a hobbies center. An island kitchen provides easy access to the formal dining room. The second floor is occupied by three family bedrooms each with its own bath and a private master suite with garden whirlpool, His and Her closets and a double vanity.

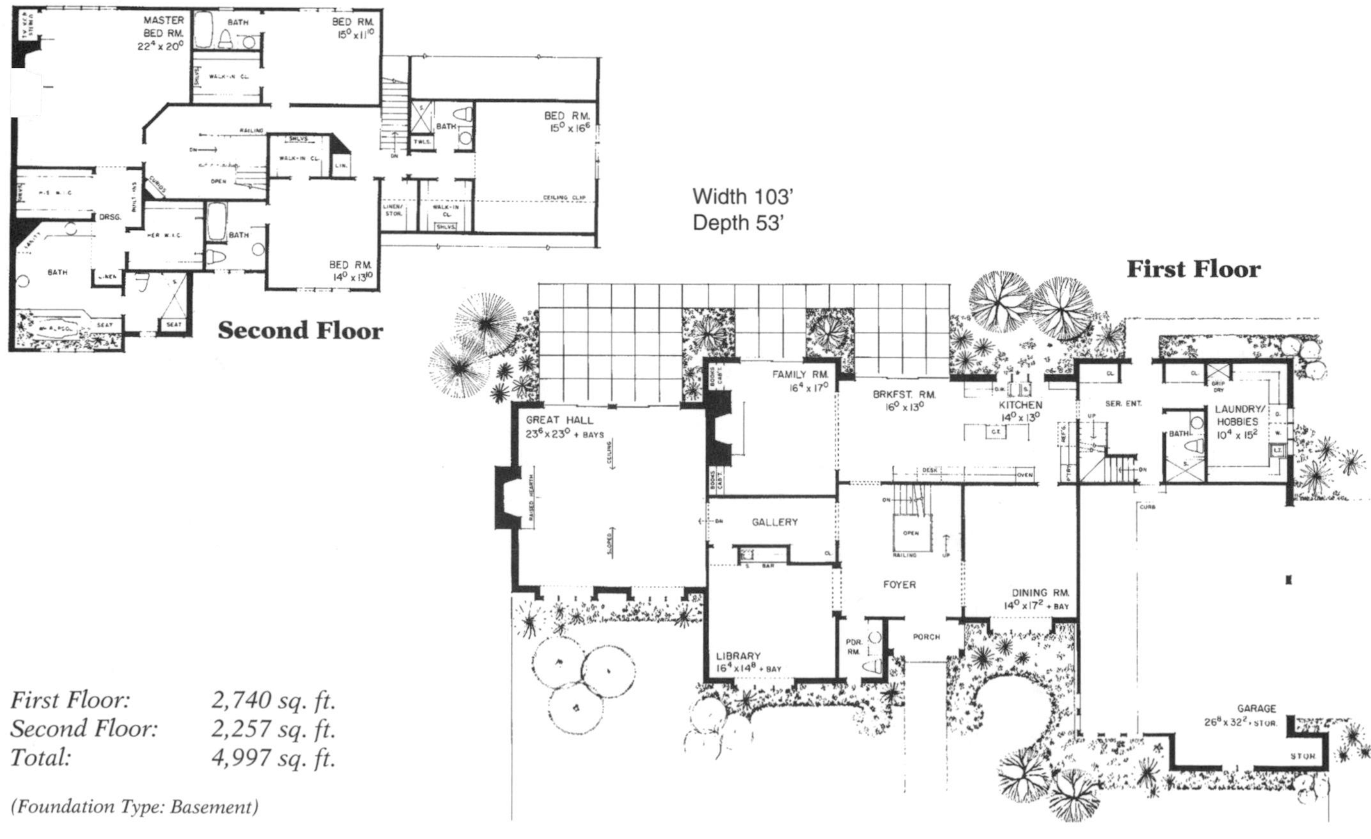


| | |
|---|---|
| *First Floor:* | *2,740 sq. ft.* |
| *Second Floor:* | *2,257 sq. ft.* |
| *Total:* | *4,997 sq. ft.* |

*(Foundation Type: Basement)*

# *Elizabeth* **Design CP3554**

A splendid garden entry greets visitors to this regal Tudor home. A quiet library is secluded directly off the foyer and has a box bay window, private powder room and sloped ceiling. Formal living takes place to the right of the foyer—an attached garden room shares a through fireplace with this area. Formal dining is accessed from the kitchen via a butler's pantry. The gathering room handles casual occasions. Upstairs is a grand master suite with lavish bath and sitting room and three secondary bedrooms.

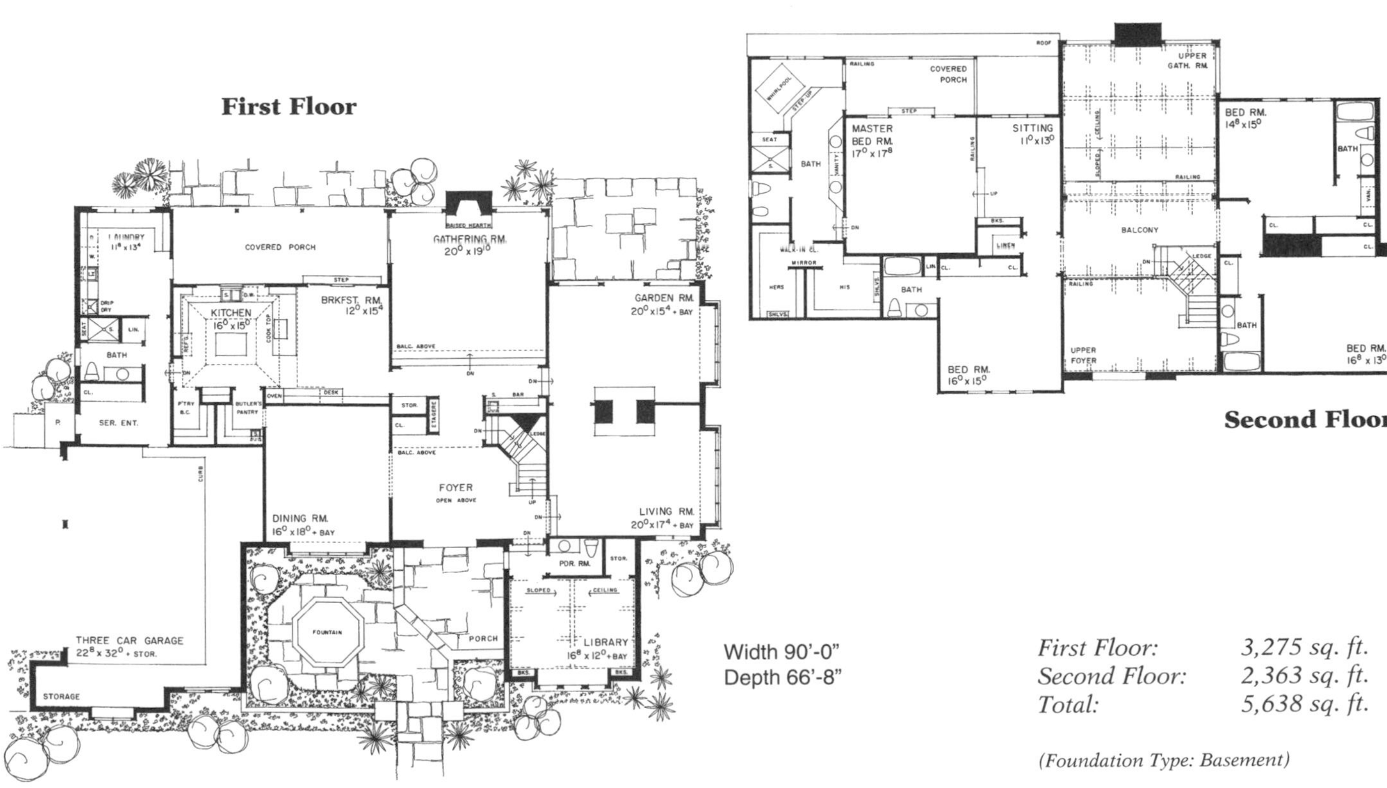


**First Floor**

**Second Floor**

Width 90'-0"
Depth 66'-8"

| | |
|---|---|
| *First Floor:* | *3,275 sq. ft.* |
| *Second Floor:* | *2,363 sq. ft.* |
| *Total:* | *5,638 sq. ft.* |

*(Foundation Type: Basement)*

## Design CP2965

# Belmont

An appealing mix of contrasting exterior materials distinguishes this expansive Tudor. Double front doors lead to a spacious foyer. The sunken living room, with balcony above, features a wet bar and fireplace. An island kitchen with breakfast room and pass-through dining area, is easily accessed by the family room. The master suite, with walk-in closet and whirlpool, is on the first floor. Upstairs, three bedrooms with private baths are joined by a lounge.

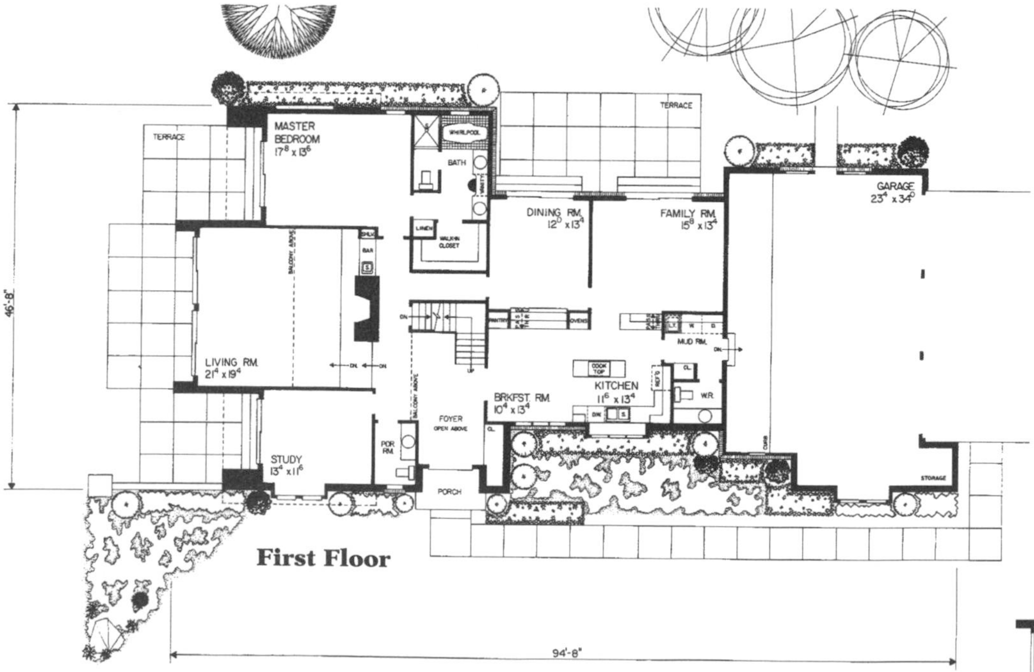

**First Floor**

**Second Floor**

| | |
|---|---|
| *First Floor:* | *2,313 sq. ft.* |
| *Second Floor:* | *1,314 sq. ft.* |
| *Total:* | *3,627 sq. ft.* |

*(Foundation Type: Basement)*

# Amanda

**Design CP2356**

Here is a truly exquisite Tudor adaptation. The exterior, with its interesting roof lines, window treatment and appealing use of brick and stucco, could hardly be more dramatic. The large receiving hall has a two-story ceiling and controls the flexible traffic patterns. The living and dining rooms, with the library nearby, will cater to the formal living pursuits. Four large bedrooms and a lounge occupy the second floor.

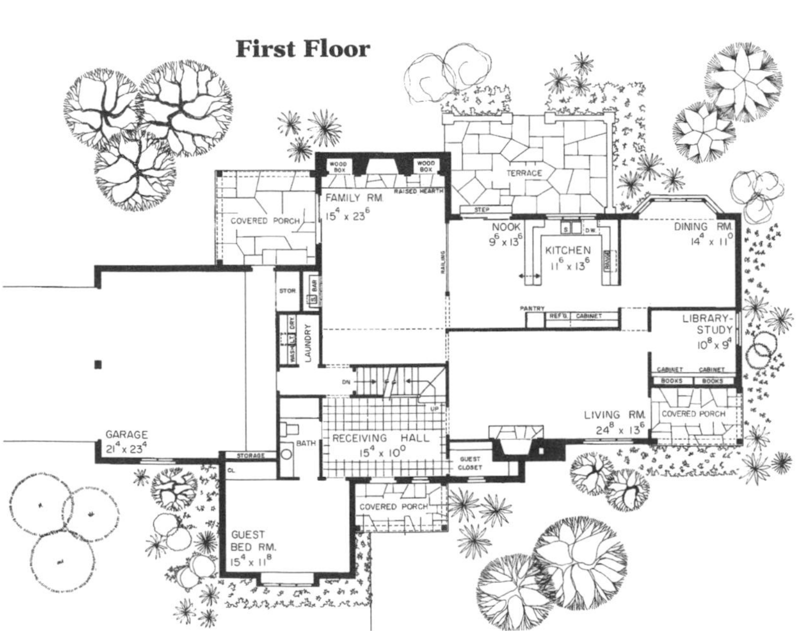

Width 79' 10"
Depth 53' 6"

| | |
|---|---|
| *First Floor:* | *1,969 sq. ft.* |
| *Second Floor:* | *1,702 sq. ft.* |
| *Total:* | *3,671 sq. ft.* |

*(Foundation Type: Basement)*

## Design CP9889 — Raintree

A blend of stucco and stone creates the charm in this country French home. The asymmetrical design and arched glass windows add to the European character. Inside, a living room and dining room flank the foyer, creating a functional formal area. The large den or family room is positioned at the rear of the home with convenient access to the kitchen, patio and covered arbor. Upstairs, the vaulted master suite and three large bedrooms provide private retreats.

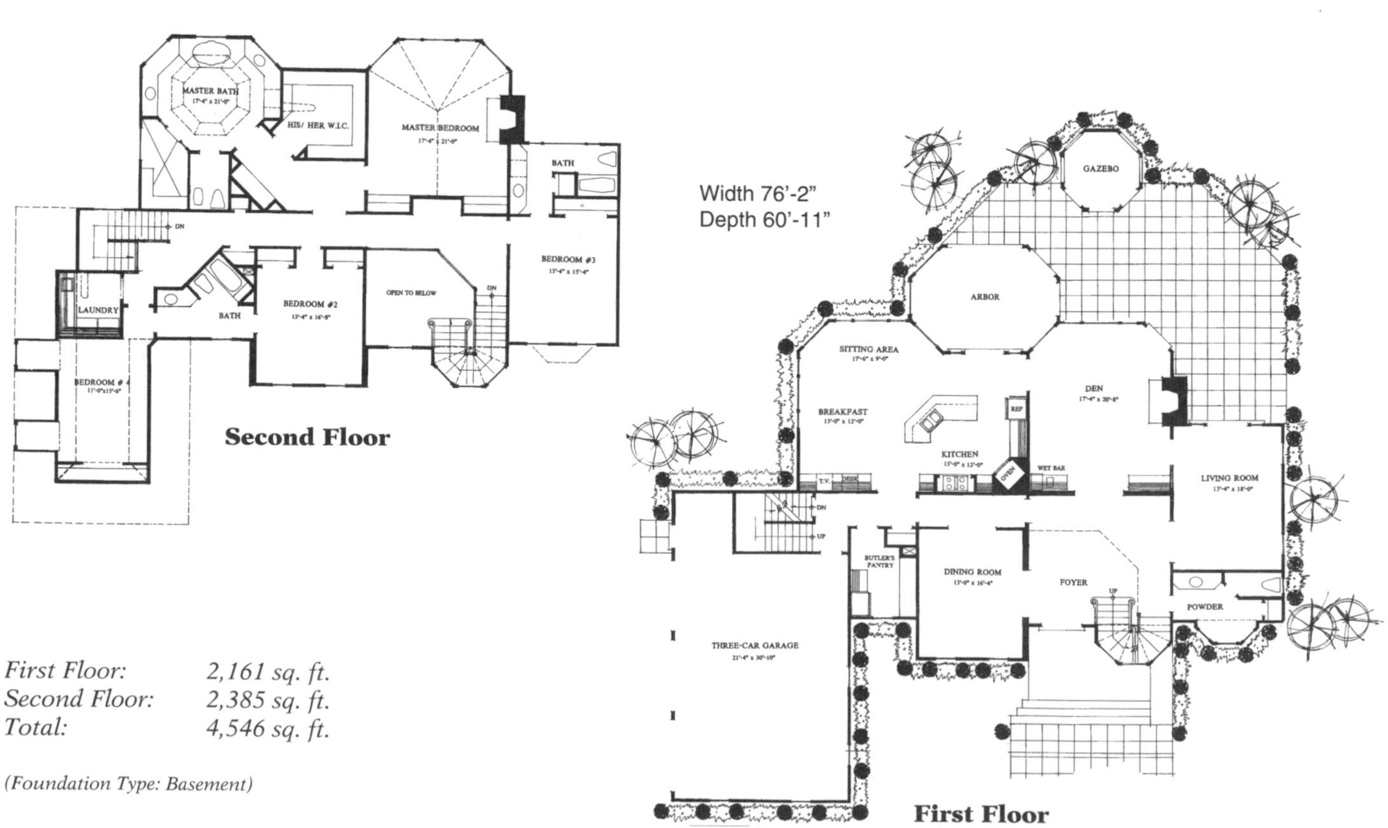


| | |
|---|---|
| *First Floor:* | *2,161 sq. ft.* |
| *Second Floor:* | *2,385 sq. ft.* |
| *Total:* | *4,546 sq. ft.* |

*(Foundation Type: Basement)*

# Patrick

**Design CP9887**

Multi-lite windows, double French doors and ornamental stucco detailing are complementary elements on the facade of this home. An impressive two-story foyer opens to the formal living and dining rooms. Natural light is available through the attractive windows in each room. The kitchen features a pass-through to the two-story family room and sky-lit breakfast room. The first-floor master suite offers an elegant vaulted ceiling, a bath with twin vanities, a separate shower and tub and two walk-in closets.

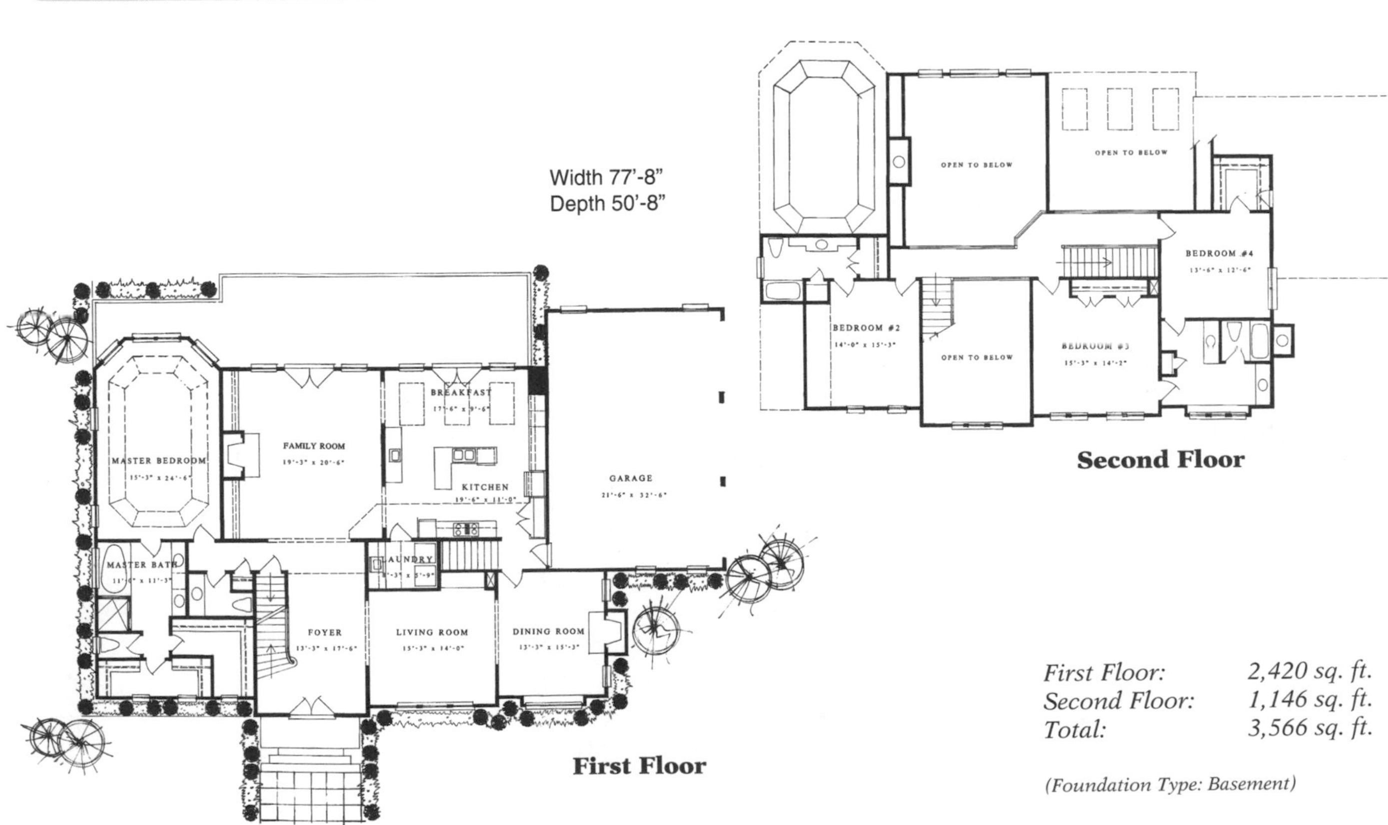


| | |
|---|---|
| *First Floor:* | *2,420 sq. ft.* |
| *Second Floor:* | *1,146 sq. ft.* |
| *Total:* | *3,566 sq. ft.* |

*(Foundation Type: Basement)*

## Design CP3568 **Carondolet**

Traditional styling takes on added dimension in this stately two-story home. An angled wing encloses the sunken living room and a roomy study. The resident gourmet will take great delight in the kitchen with its ample counter space and island cooktop. The breakfast room remains open to the kitchen and, through a pair of columns, the family room. The second floor offers excellent sleeping quarters with four bedrooms. The master suite spoils its occupants with a sloped ceiling, balcony and fireplace.

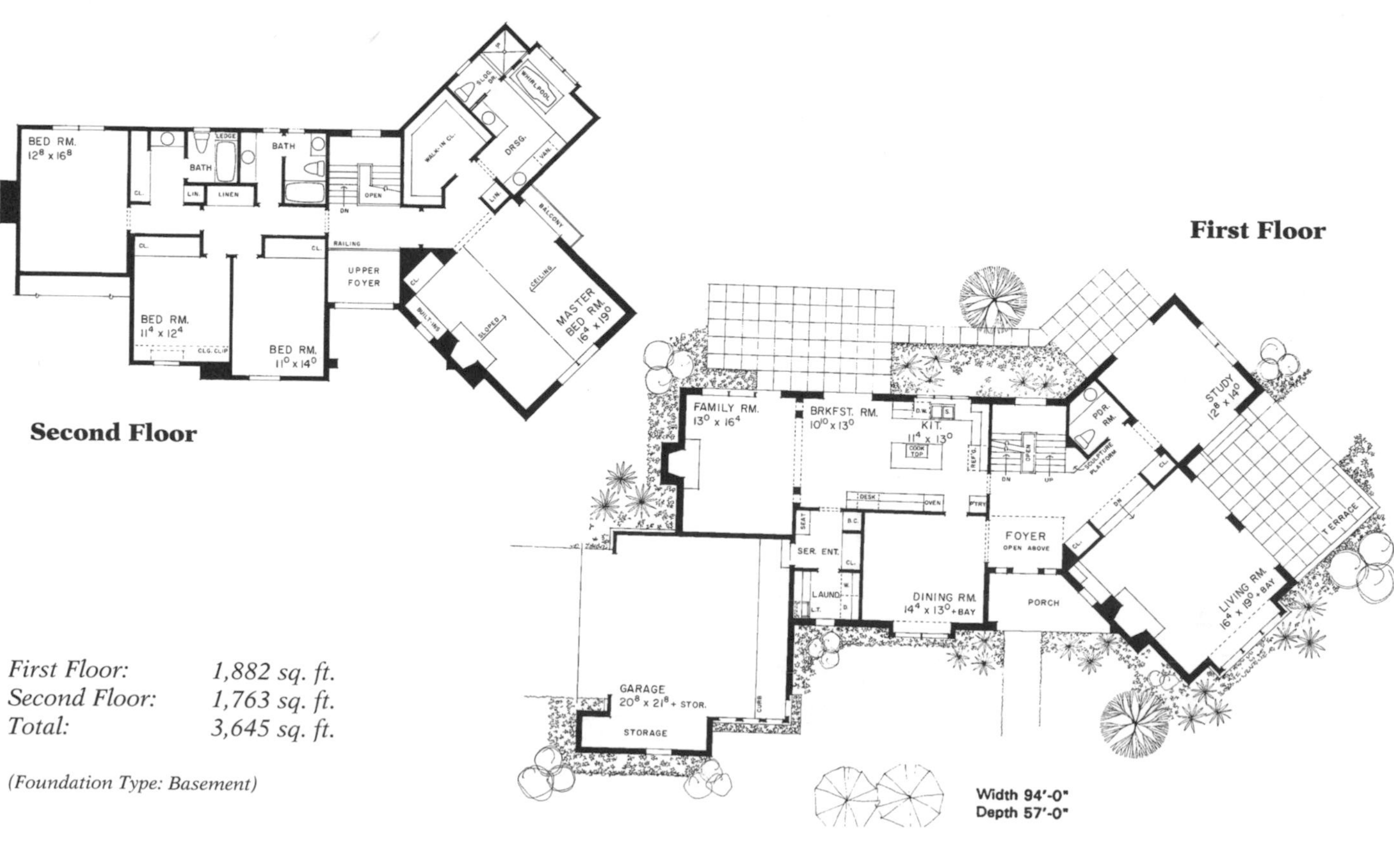


*First Floor:* *1,882 sq. ft.*
*Second Floor:* *1,763 sq. ft.*
*Total:* *3,645 sq. ft.*

*(Foundation Type: Basement)*

# Sterling Heights **Design CP3301**

With an abundance of shapes and angles, this Tudor is a true treasure. An angled kitchen features a cooktop, snack bar and breakfast nook with adjoined family room. The formal dining area is easily accessed through the kitchen and living room with wet bar and raised hearth. A media room is an added highlight. The master suite includes a whirlpool and dressing areas. A private guest suite with lounge and sitting room, and three bedrooms with private baths occupy the second floor.

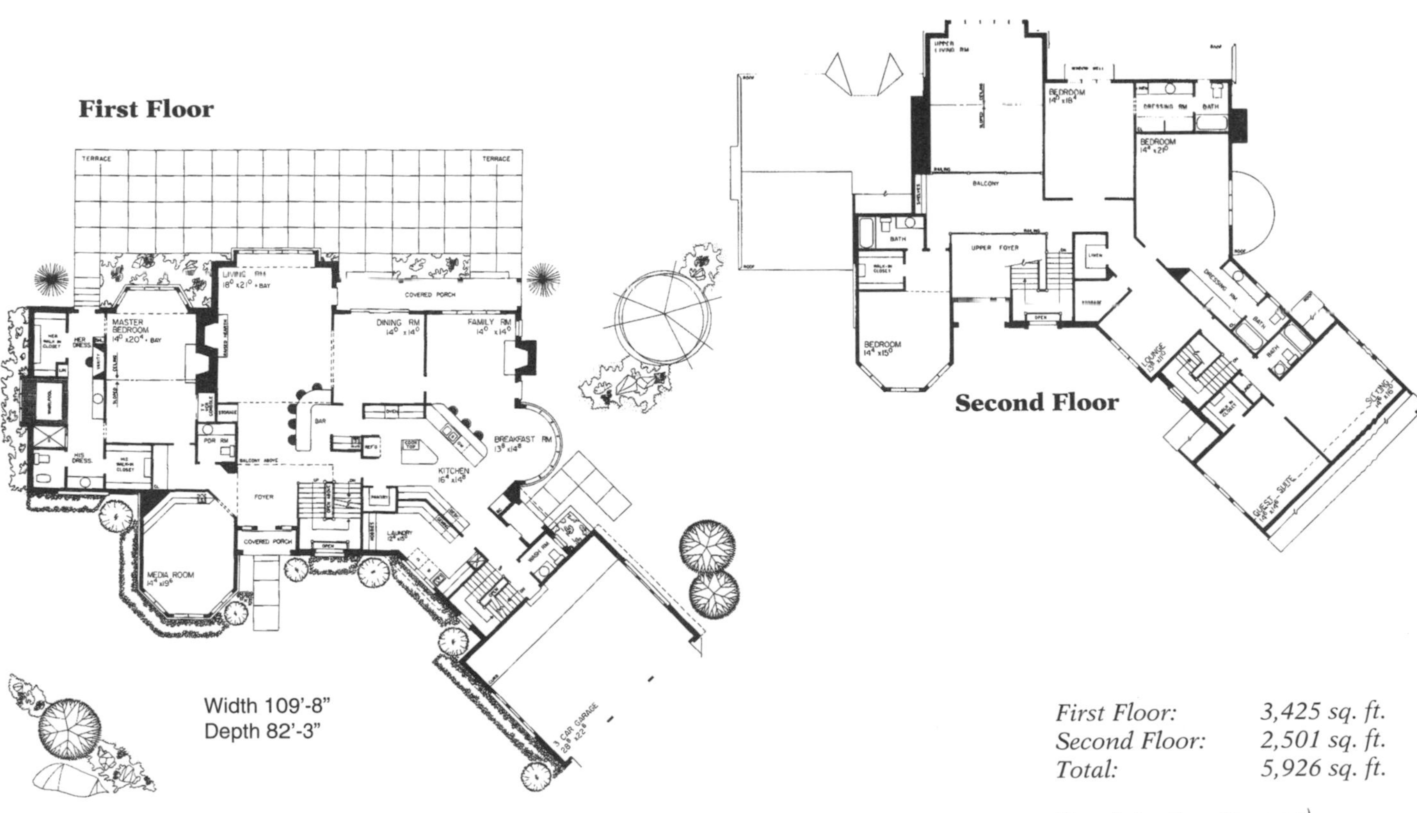


Width 109'-8"
Depth 82'-3"

| | |
|---|---|
| *First Floor:* | *3,425 sq. ft.* |
| *Second Floor:* | *2,501 sq. ft.* |
| *Total:* | *5,926 sq. ft.* |

*(Foundation Type: Basement)*

**Design CP2791**

# Sante Fe

The exterior of this unique contemporary home is accented by vertical paned windows and a wide, overhanging roof. A sunlit, sunken atrium is the center of an open plan, surrounded by the dining room, spacious living room, lounge and foyer. There is a massive fireplace in the living room. A U-shaped kitchen is conveniently adjoined by the family room. The master suite, with two separate entrance doors, is highlighted by a large bay window.

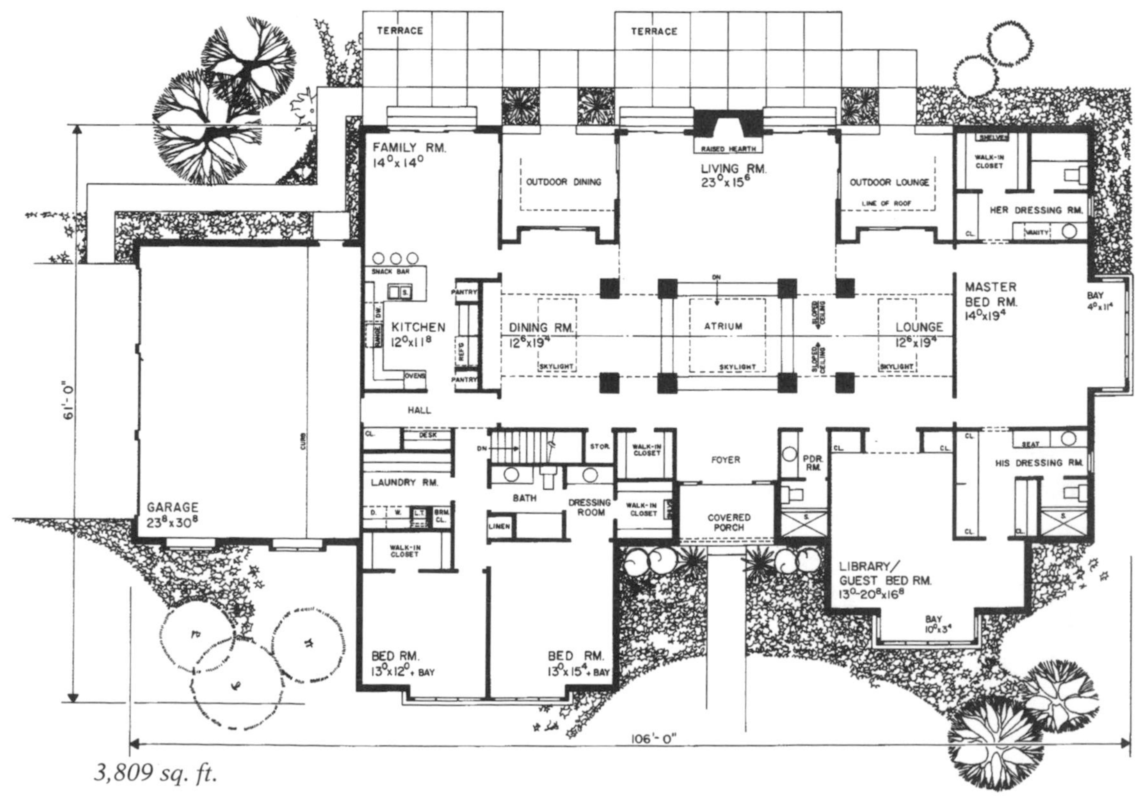


*Total:* *3,809 sq. ft.*

*(Foundation Type: Basement)*

# San Angelo

**Design CP2938**

A semi-circular fanlight and sidelights grace the entrance of this striking contemporary. The lofty foyer leads to an elegant, two-story living room with a fireplace. The family room leads to a glorious sun room with dramatic, sloped ceilings. An executive-sized, first-floor master suite offers privacy and relaxation. Two second-floor bedrooms with private baths round out the livability in this home.

**First Floor**

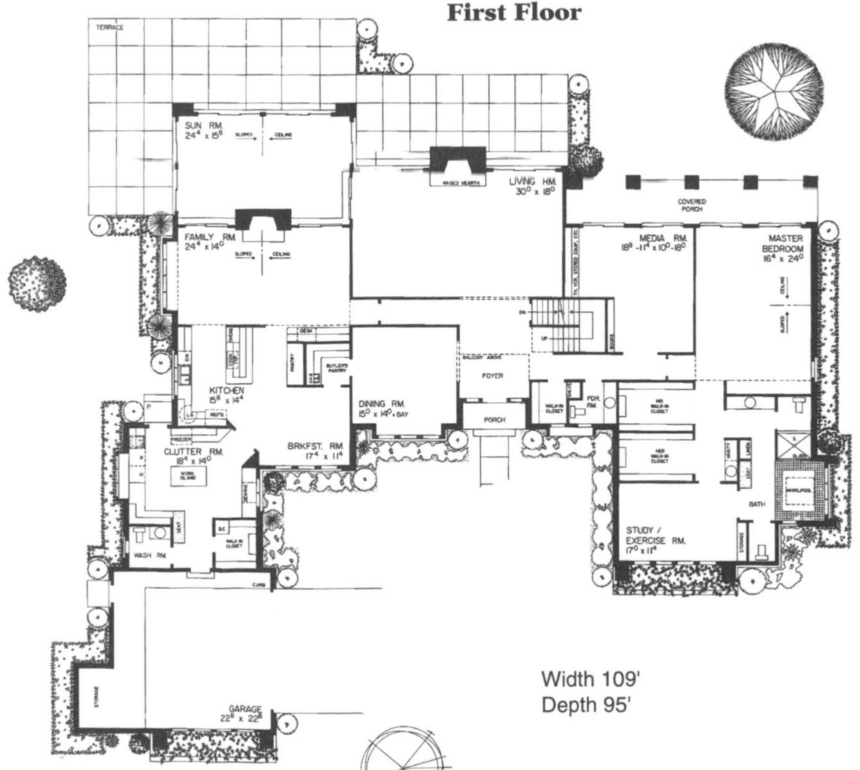


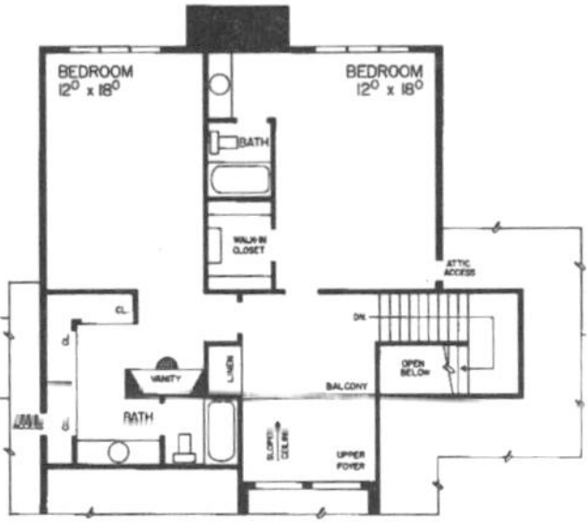


**Second Floor**

| | |
|---|---|
| *First Floor:* | *4,518 sq. ft.* |
| *Second Floor:* | *882 sq. ft.* |
| *Total:* | *5,400 sq. ft.* |

*(Foundation Type: Basement)*

## Design CP3361 — Rolling Hills

This hillside home is perfect for both formal and informal entertaining. The foyer leads to a gathering room/dining room combination. Both are warmed by a massive fireplace and have a view of the spacious deck. A U-shaped kitchen adjoins the breakfast room and is connected to the dining area through a butler's pantry. The master suite features a step-up tub and His and Her walk-in closets. Downstairs, the activities room is enhanced with a fireplace and summer kitchen.

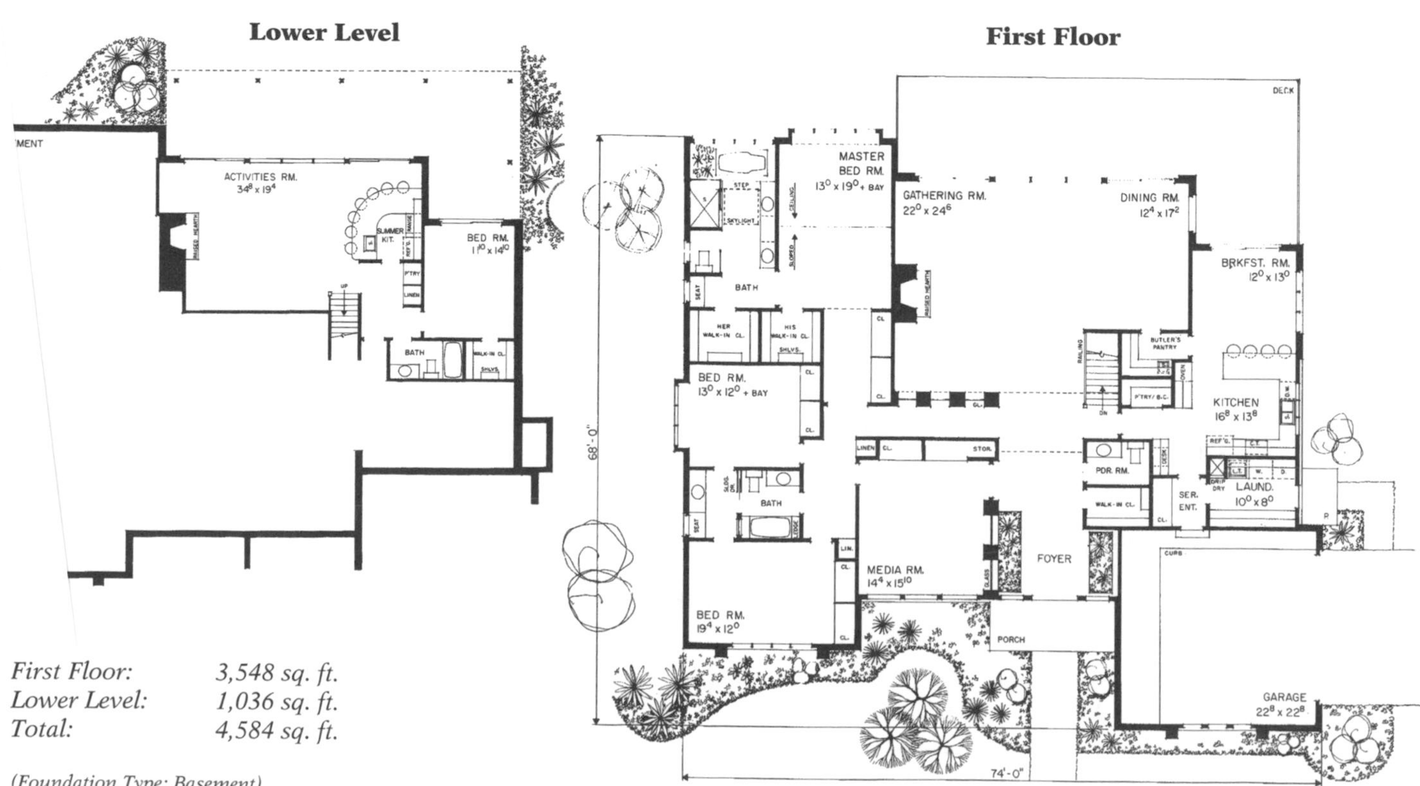


| | |
|---|---|
| *First Floor:* | *3,548 sq. ft.* |
| *Lower Level:* | *1,036 sq. ft.* |
| *Total:* | *4,584 sq. ft.* |

*(Foundation Type: Basement)*

# Woodspring

**Design CP3354**

This home is distinguished by its unique amenities. The country kitchen, with large bay window, includes a cooktop island and snack bar. The adjoining sun room has a sloped ceiling and is perfect for informal gatherings. Formal spaces include living and dining rooms, and a media room. A clutter room includes a work island, work bench and a porch. The master suite is complete with an exercise room, whirlpool bath and room-sized walk-in closet. Upstairs, there are two bedrooms and a shared bathroom.

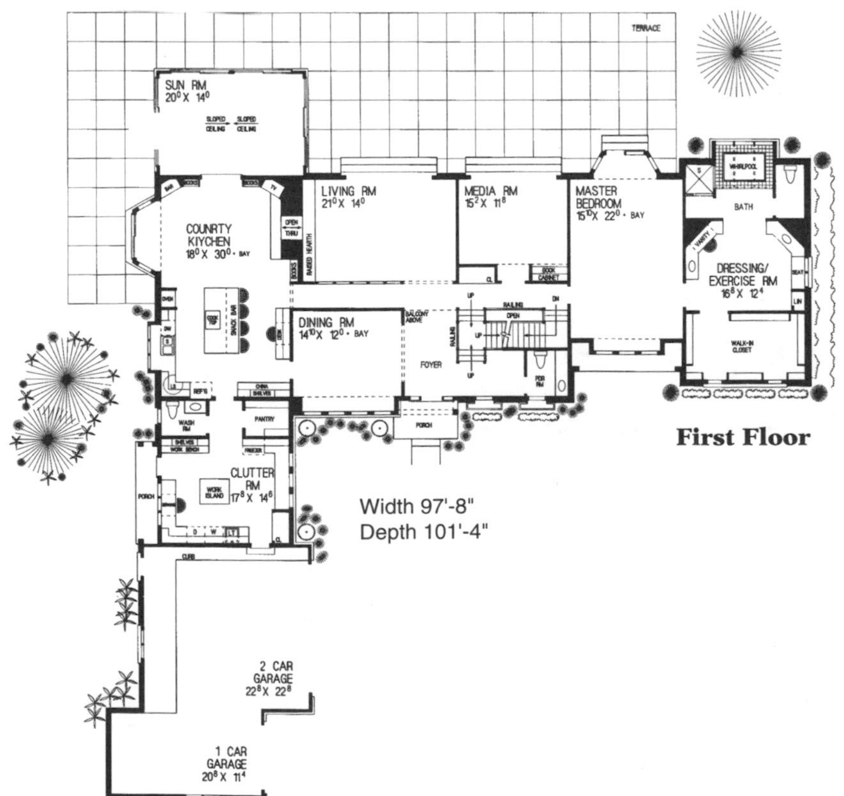


**First Floor**

**Second Floor**

| | |
|---|---|
| *First Floor:* | *3,260 sq. ft.* |
| *Second Floor:* | *684 sq. ft.* |
| *Sun Room:* | *296 sq. ft.* |
| *Total:* | *4,240 sq. ft.* |

*(Foundation Type: Basement)*

## Design CP3404

# Oakcreek

This farmhouse design is distinguished by its unusual elegance. Most of the living space is found on the first floor. A massive fireplace is the focal point in a gigantic family room. The master bedroom adjoins a private bathroom with whirlpool tub and walk-in closet. The living and dining areas access a covered porch. Upstairs, two bedrooms adjoin a large balcony.

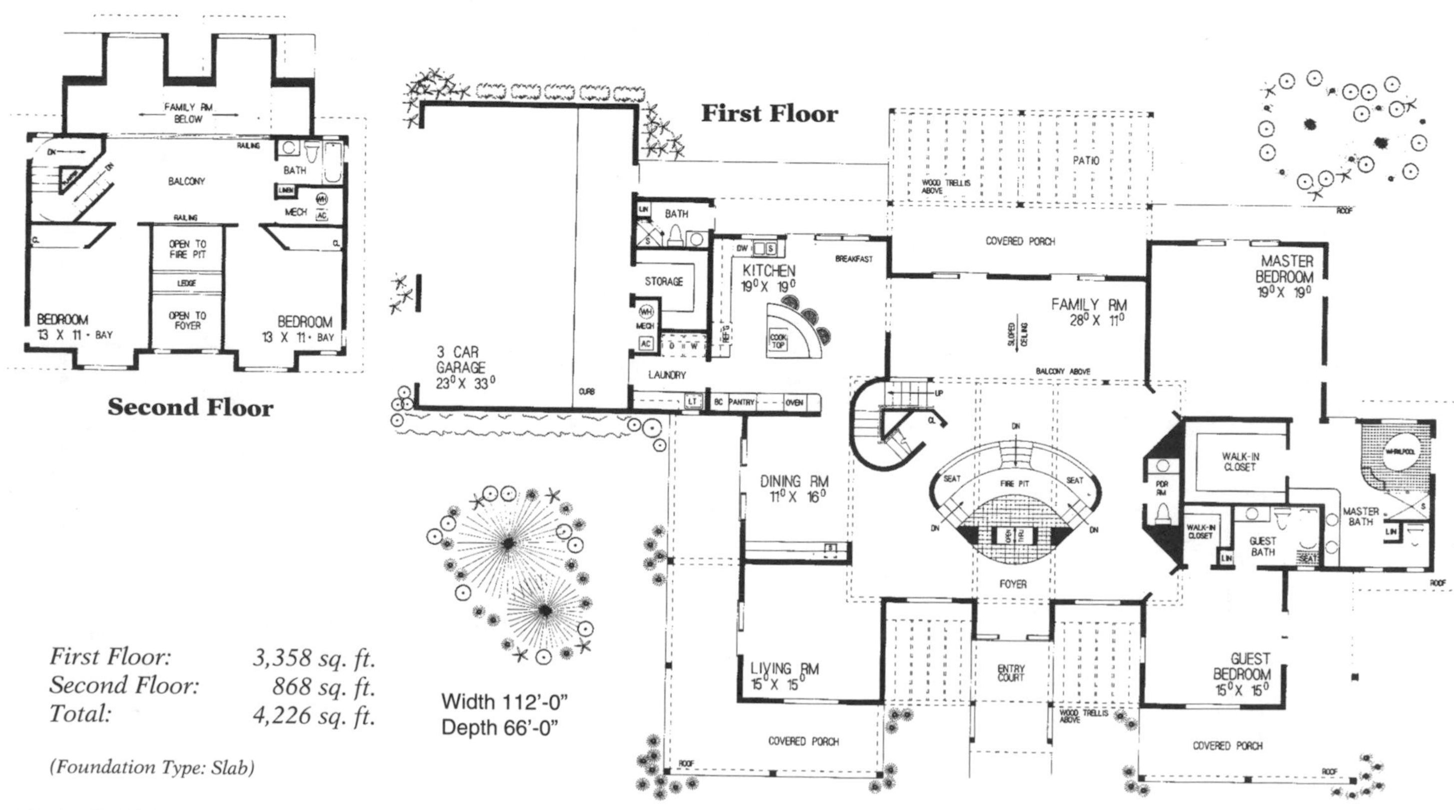


*First Floor:* *3,358 sq. ft.*
*Second Floor:* *868 sq. ft.*
*Total:* *4,226 sq. ft.*

*(Foundation Type: Slab)*

Width 112'-0"
Depth 66'-0"

# Westhaven

**Design CP3311**

This hillside haven offers an abundence of space. A columned portico ushers guests through a large entry hall. The gathering room, warmed by a massive fireplace, adjoins a formal dining area. The kitchen has a snack bar and serves a sitting area and breakfast room. The master suite boasts a private bathroom with His and Her closets and a whirlpool bath. Downstairs, two bedrooms and a full bath are joined by a large activities room with a fireplace and a summer kitchen.

**First Floor**

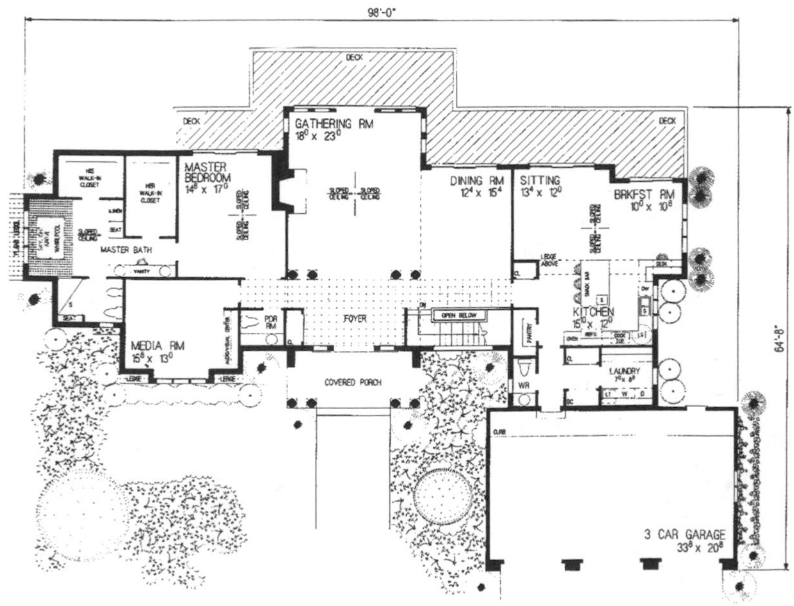


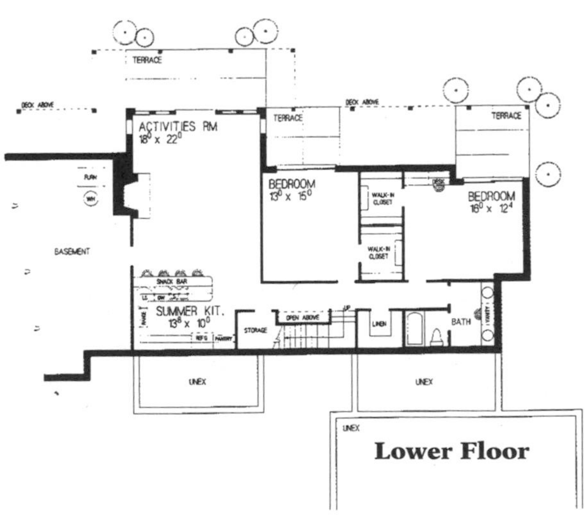


**Lower Floor**

| | |
|---|---|
| *First Floor:* | *2,662 sq. ft.* |
| *Lower Level:* | *1,548 sq. ft.* |
| *Total:* | *4,210 sq. ft.* |

*(Foundation Type: Basement)*

**Design CP4530**

# Ionna

The exterior of this large, country-style home is decorated with board-and-batten siding combined with stone. A formal entry leads to a gallery and the living room with fireplace and beamed ceiling. The family room offers a built-in bookcase, a fireplace and a sloping, beamed ceiling. The master suite features His and Her closets and dressing areas. Two bedrooms with full baths occupy the second floor. The lower level includes a game room with fireplace, and two bedrooms with a shared bath.

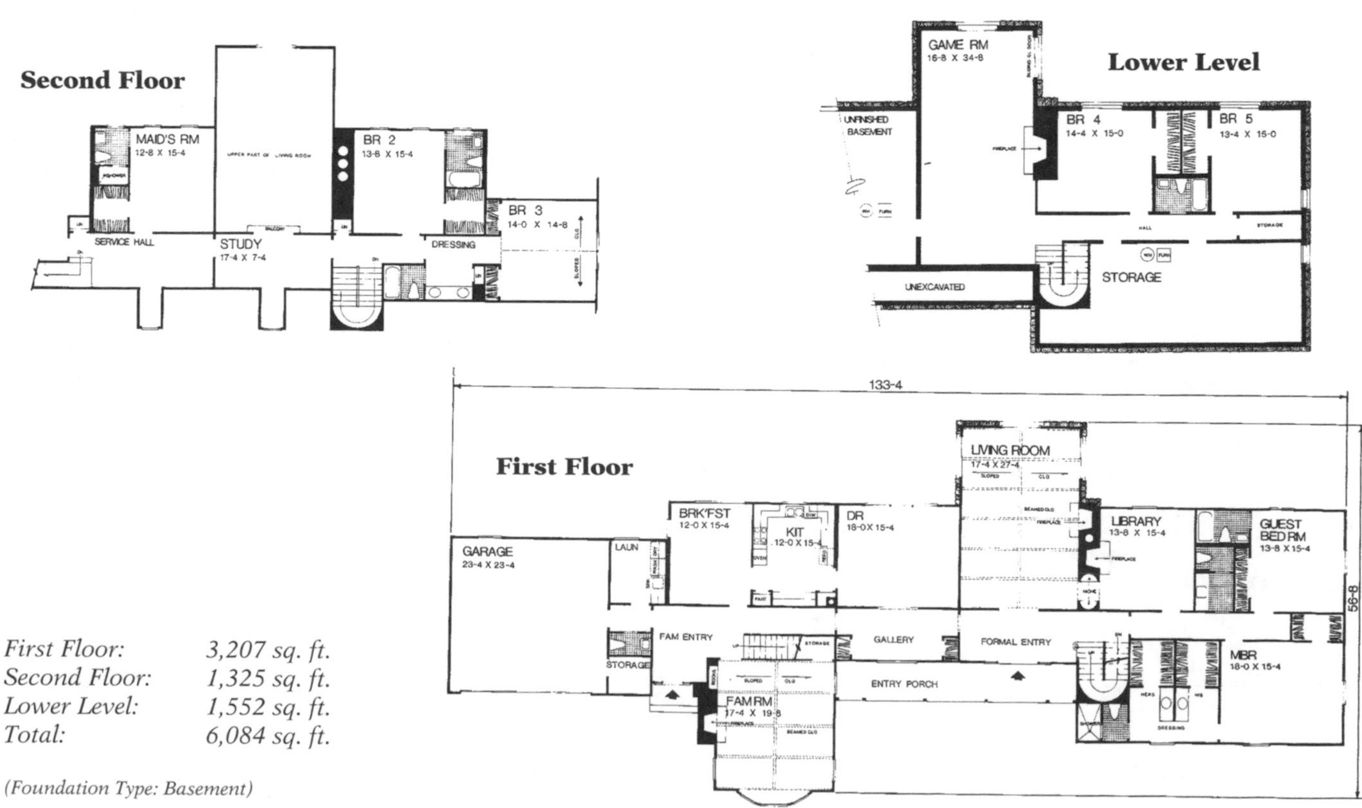


| | |
|---|---|
| *First Floor:* | *3,207 sq. ft.* |
| *Second Floor:* | *1,325 sq. ft.* |
| *Lower Level:* | *1,552 sq. ft.* |
| *Total:* | *6,084 sq. ft.* |

*(Foundation Type: Basement)*

# Cape Cod

**Design CP2921**

This sprawling Cape Cod has been carefully designed to offer the most useful amenities. An impressive raised hearth occupies one wall in the living room. The country kitchen with work island is the center of daily life and entertaining. It is brightened and warmed by an attached sun room featuring dramatic window walls and a glass gable. The master bedroom is balanced by elegant bay windows. Two bedrooms, a lounge and a convenient central bath are found on the second floor.

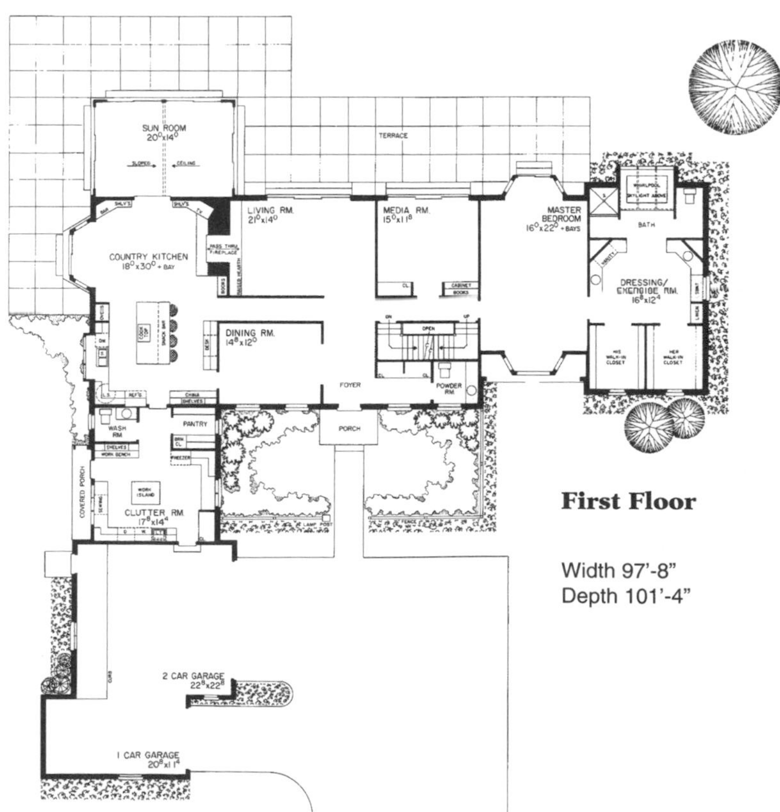


**First Floor**

Width 97'-8"
Depth 101'-4"

**Second Floor**

| | |
|---|---|
| *First Floor:* | *3,215 sq. ft.* |
| *Second Floor:* | *711 sq. ft.* |
| *Total:* | *3,926 sq. ft.* |

*(Foundation Type: Basement)*

## Design CP4555

# Omaha

The exterior of this long, low country farmhouse is beautified with vertical boards and battens, and a cedar-shake roof. The expansive Great Room, with its dramatic proportions and sloped ceiling, is the focal point of this home. There are three family bedrooms, each with its own bath and spacious closet. A playroom, which could double as a guest room, completes the wing. The master suite includes an adjoined study and a complete private bathroom.

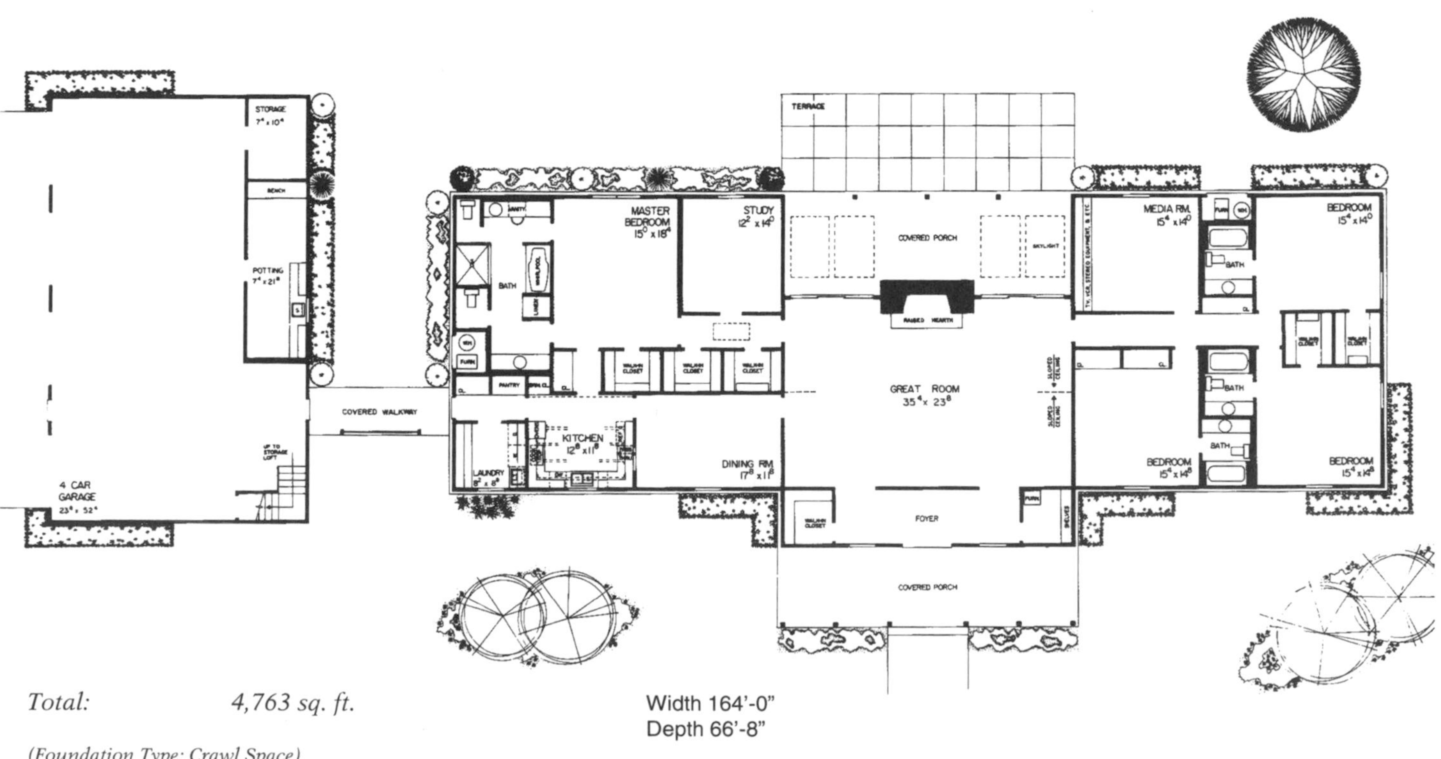


*Total:* *4,763 sq. ft.*

*(Foundation Type: Crawl Space)*

Width 164'-0"
Depth 66'-8"

# Laredo

## Design CP2920

A private courtyard creates a welcoming entrance to this home. An island work center with cooktop and snack bar serves as the informal gathering point for family or guests, while the adjoining sun room supplies light and warmth to the room. The impressive master suite includes exercise room, whirlpool bath and two vanities. The media room has extra closet space and opens to the terrace, as do the living room, sun room and master bedroom.

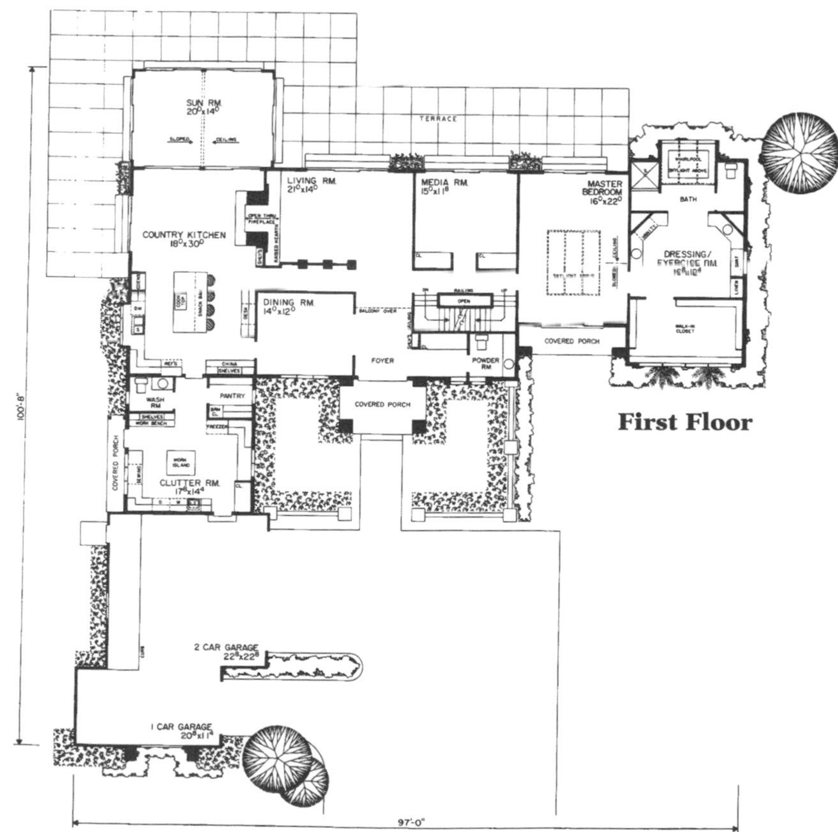

**First Floor**

**Second Floor**

| | |
|---|---|
| *First Floor:* | *3,067 sq. ft.* |
| *Second Floor:* | *648 sq. ft.* |
| *Total:* | *3,715 sq. ft.* |

*(Foundation Type: Basement)*

## Design CP2214

# Madrid

This Spanish hacienda has a distinguished exterior and many unique amenities. A square foyer opens to a massive living room that sports a fireplace, built-in storage units and a special plant area with work bench. The dining room and family room flank the kitchen and adjoined breakfast nook. The master bedroom, with private bathroom and dressing area, shares the second floor with four family bedrooms and a sleeping porch.

**Second Floor**

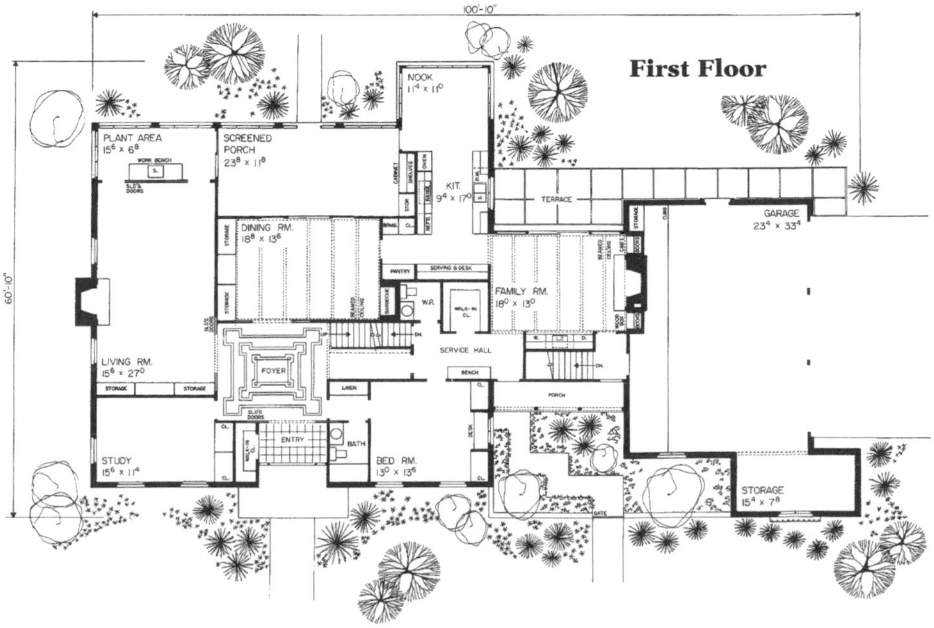

**First Floor**

| | |
|---|---|
| *First Floor:* | *3,011 sq. ft.* |
| *Second Floor:* | *2,297 sq. ft.* |
| *Total:* | *5,308 sq. ft.* |

*(Foundation Type: Basement)*

# Barcelona

**Design CP4551**

The front garden court, with its wrought-iron gate, helps create a distinctive exterior for this home. An equally distinguished interior features formal dining and living rooms flanking the entry, a large family room to the rear and a spacious kitchen with snack bar and breakfast area. Seven bedrooms and five baths will accommodate even the largest of families. A covered porch at the rear of the house is perfect for entertaining.

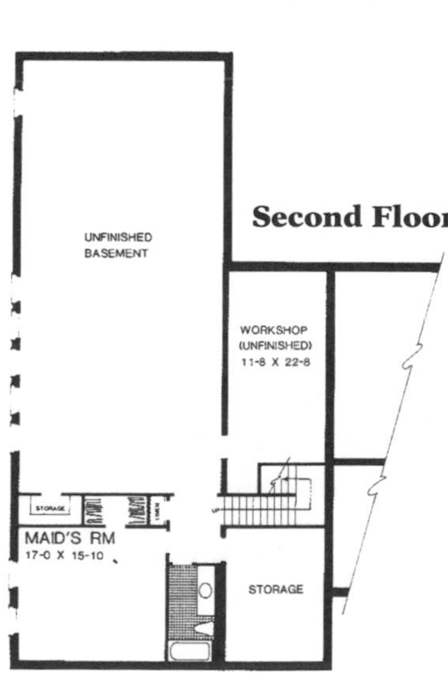


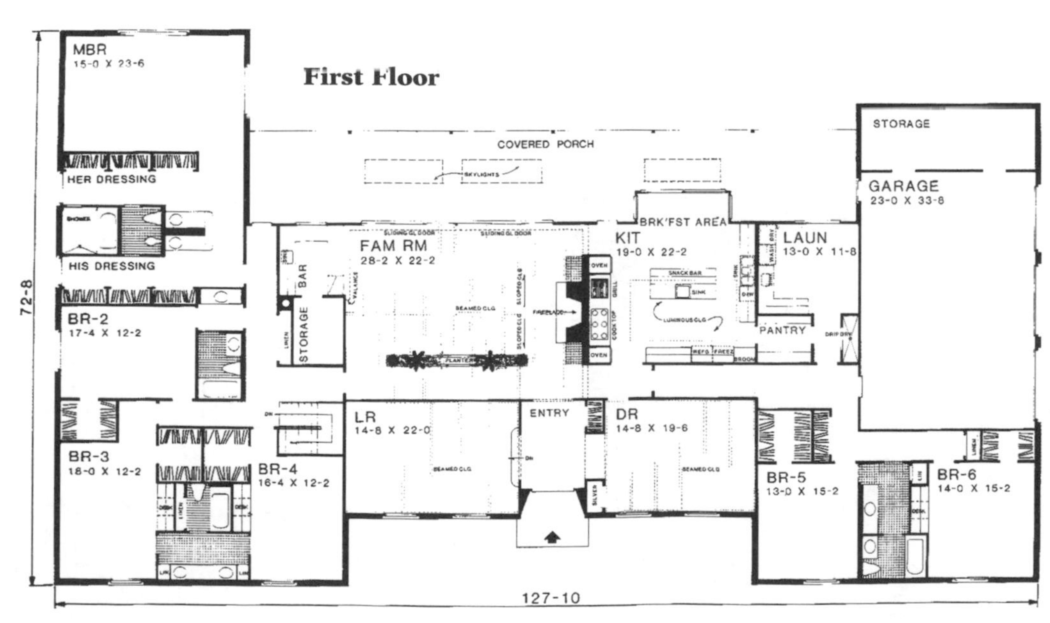


| | |
|---|---|
| *First Floor:* | *5,632 sq. ft.* |
| *Second Floor:* | *525 sq. ft.* |
| *Total:* | *6,157 sq. ft.* |

*(Foundation Type: Basement)*

## Design CP4553

# Fieldcrest

This home, planned as three separate pavilions joined by glazed passages, will fit a lot that slopes to the right. The left pavilion contains a study, a guest room and bath, and a master suite with two large walk-in closets and a compartmented bath. The center pavilion contains the living areas and is highlighted by a spacious family room with massive fireplace. Three children's rooms are found in the right pavilion. An open staircase leads to the basement.

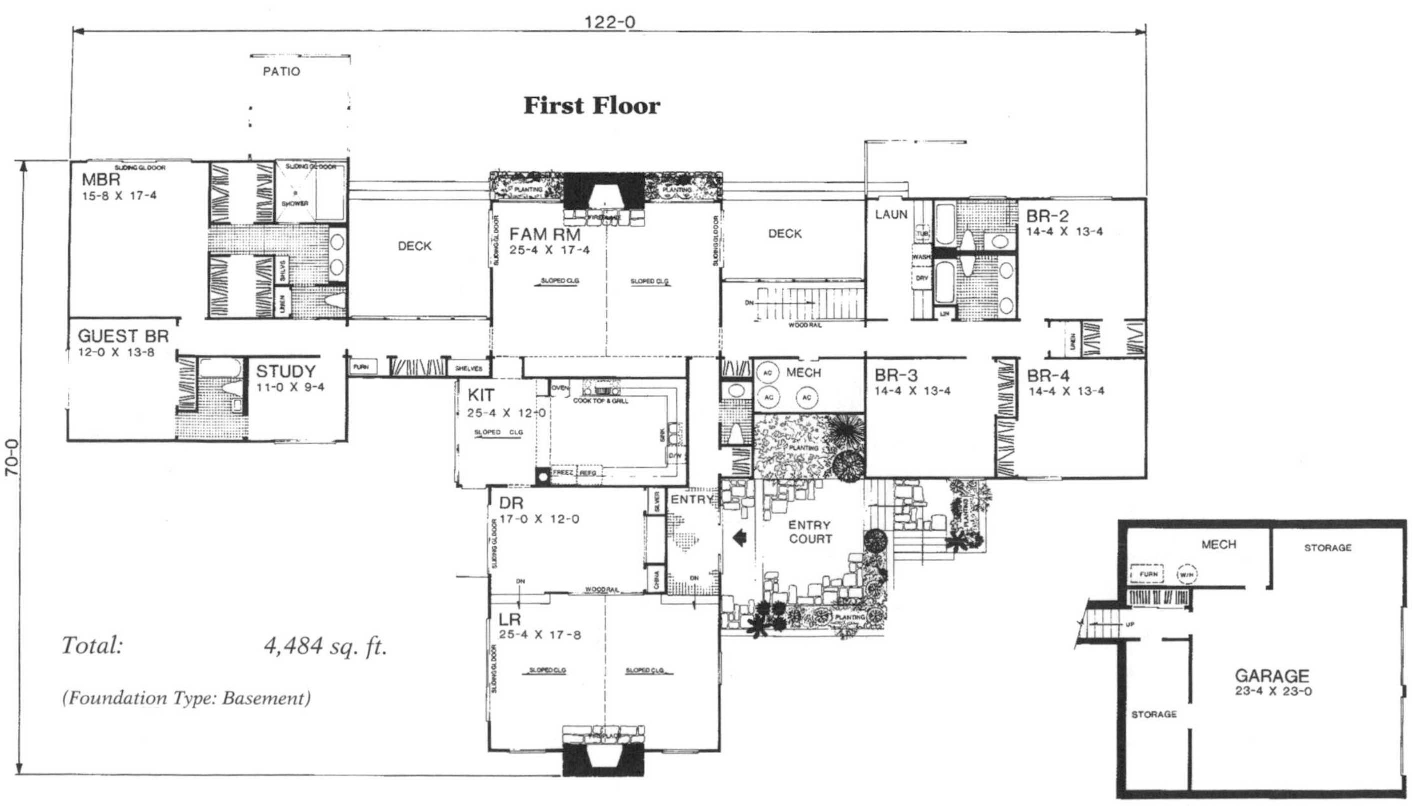


*Total:* *4,484 sq. ft.*

*(Foundation Type: Basement)*

# Pantano

## Design CP4261

This house includes special features including five bedrooms, 3 1/2 baths, a large family room, a spacious foyer separating living space on the first floor, a long kitchen with snack bar, a light-filled studio on the second floor, window greenhouse, deck, lots of storage and closet space, and a large fireplace in the beam-ceilinged living room. Without a doubt, this is a plan that could well become the talk of the town.

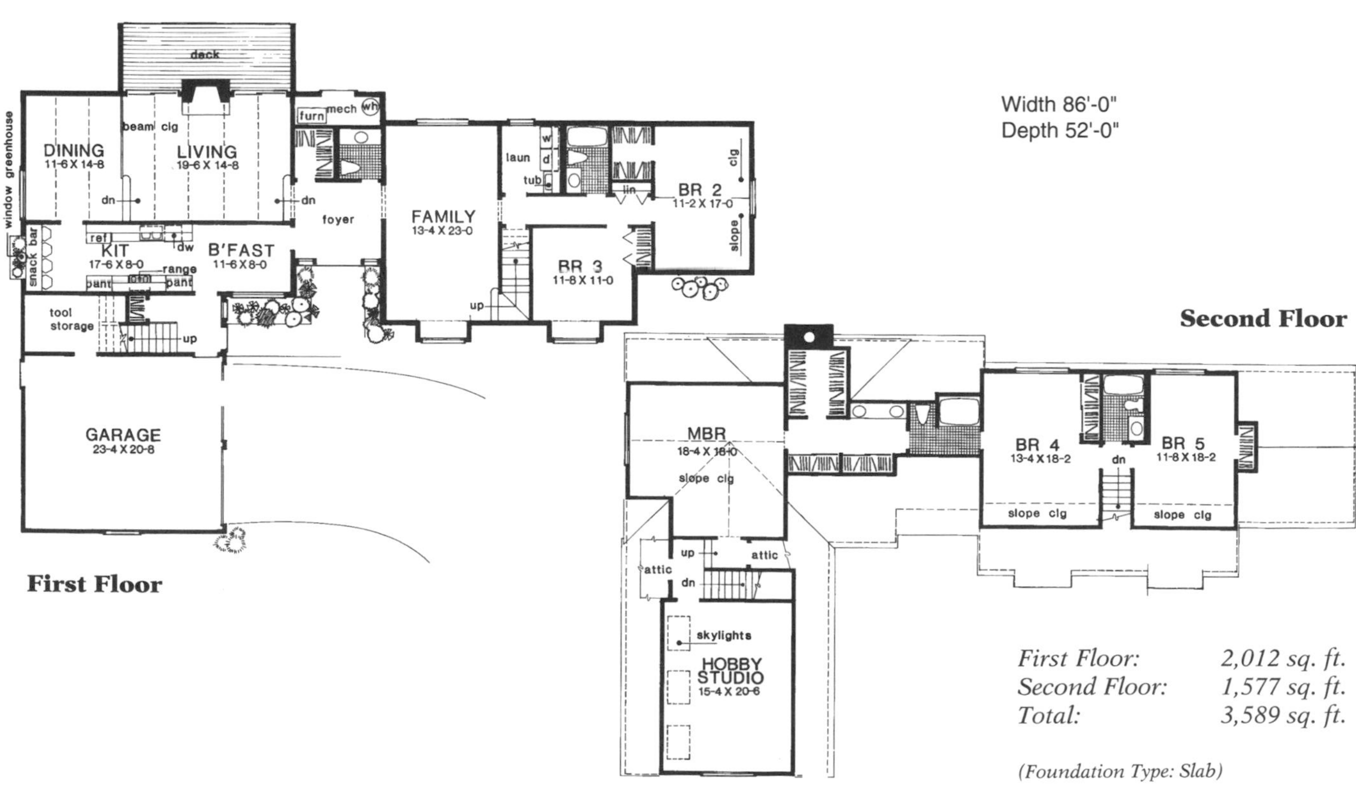


Width 86'-0"
Depth 52'-0"

**First Floor**

**Second Floor**

| | |
|---|---|
| *First Floor:* | *2,012 sq. ft.* |
| *Second Floor:* | *1,577 sq. ft.* |
| *Total:* | *3,589 sq. ft.* |

*(Foundation Type: Slab)*

# Design CP2835 Alderwood

Passive solar techniques and an active solar component heat and cool this striking contemporary design. The lower level solarium admits sunlight during the day. The earth berms on the three sides of the lower level help keep out the winter cold and summer heat. The active system uses collector panels to gather the sun's heat, which is circulated throughout the house by a heat exchanger. Note that where active solar collectors are a design OPTION, they must be contracted locally.

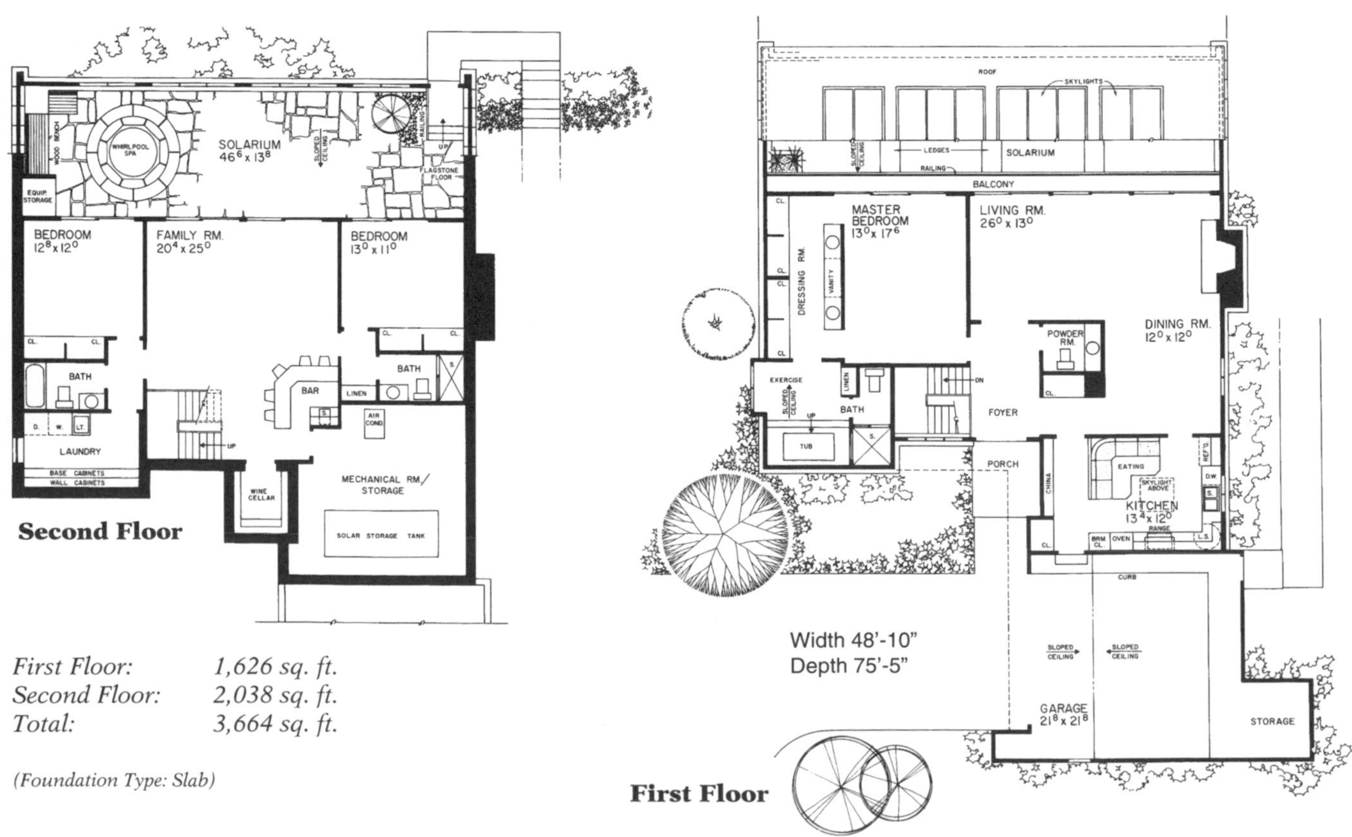


| | |
|---|---|
| *First Floor:* | *1,626 sq. ft.* |
| *Second Floor:* | *2,038 sq. ft.* |
| *Total:* | *3,664 sq. ft.* |

*(Foundation Type: Slab)*

# Catalina

**Design CP2834**

This passive solar design offers 3,900 square feet of livability situated on three levels. The primary passive element will be the lower-level sun room which admits sunlight for direct-gain heating. The solar warmth collected here will radiate into the rest of the house. During the summer months, shades are put over the skylight. Solar heating panels may be installed on the south-facing portion of the roof. An attic fan exhausts any hot air out of the house in the summer and circulates air in the winter.

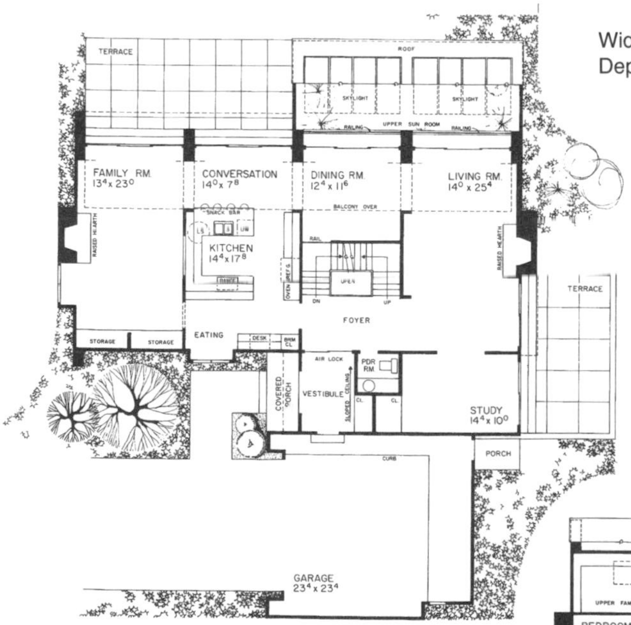

Width 60'-0"
Depth 73'-4"

**First Floor**

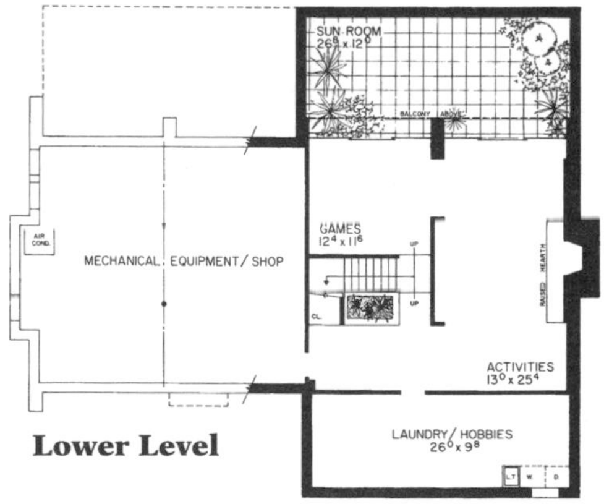

**Lower Level**

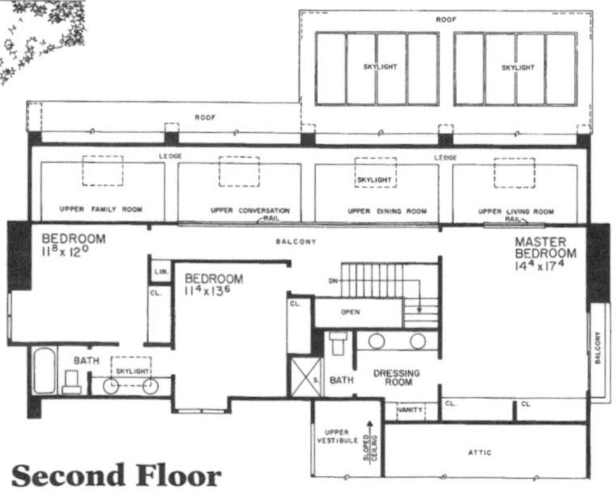

**Second Floor**

| | |
|---|---|
| *First Floor:* | *1,775 sq. ft.* |
| *Second Floor:* | *1,041 sq. ft.* |
| *Lower Level:* | *1,128 sq. ft.* |
| *Total:* | *3,944 sq. ft.* |

*(Foundation Type: Slab)*

## Design CP2169

# Cinnabar

Orienting the living areas to the rear of the plan allows you to enjoy nature's scenery. In addition to greater enjoyment of the landscape, such floor planning will provide extra privacy from the street. The angular configuration adds appeal to the exterior of the design. The upper level rooms have direct access to the decks and balcony. With five bedrooms, plus a library and a game and hobby room, the active family will have an abundance of space for individual pursuits.

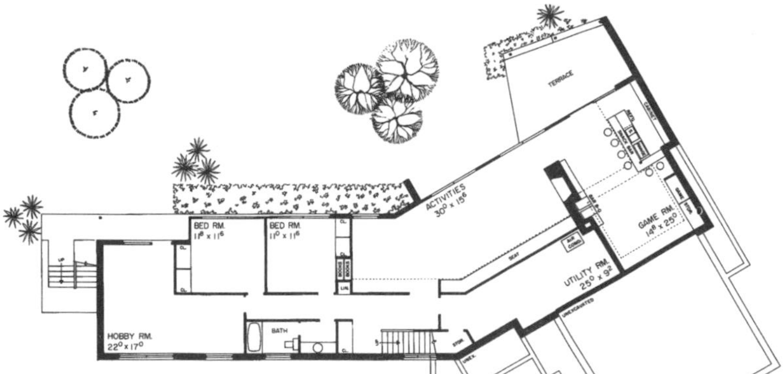

**Second Floor**

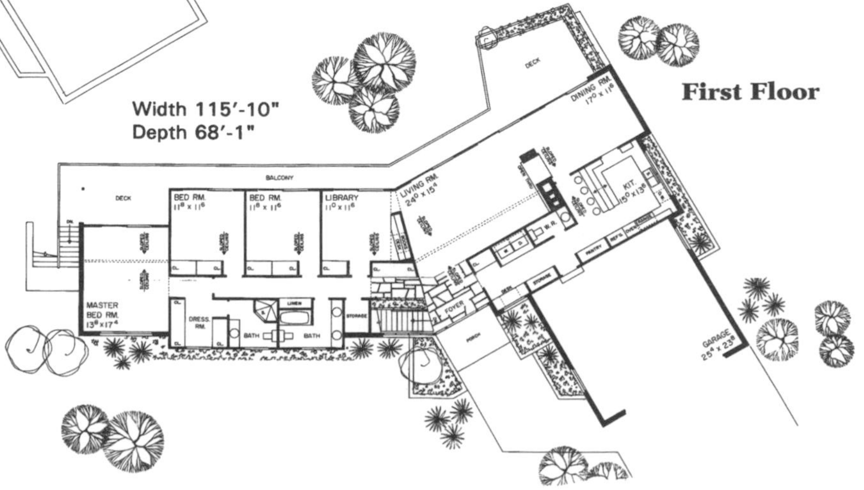

**First Floor**

Width 115'-10"
Depth 68'-1"

| | |
|---|---|
| *First Floor:* | *2,381 sq. ft.* |
| *Second Floor:* | *2,010 sq. ft.* |
| *Total:* | *4,391 sq. ft.* |

*(Foundation Type: Basement)*

# Highland

**Design CP2579**

A huge gathering room, 27 feet long, has a raised-hearth fireplace in the center, sloped ceilings, two balconies, a deck and separate areas for dining and games. A family room on the lower level is of equal size and features its own central fireplace and terrace access. An activities room provides even more living space. An efficient kitchen is accompanied by a breakfast nook with a built-in desk. Four bedrooms include a master suite with private bath, walk-in closets and a private balcony.

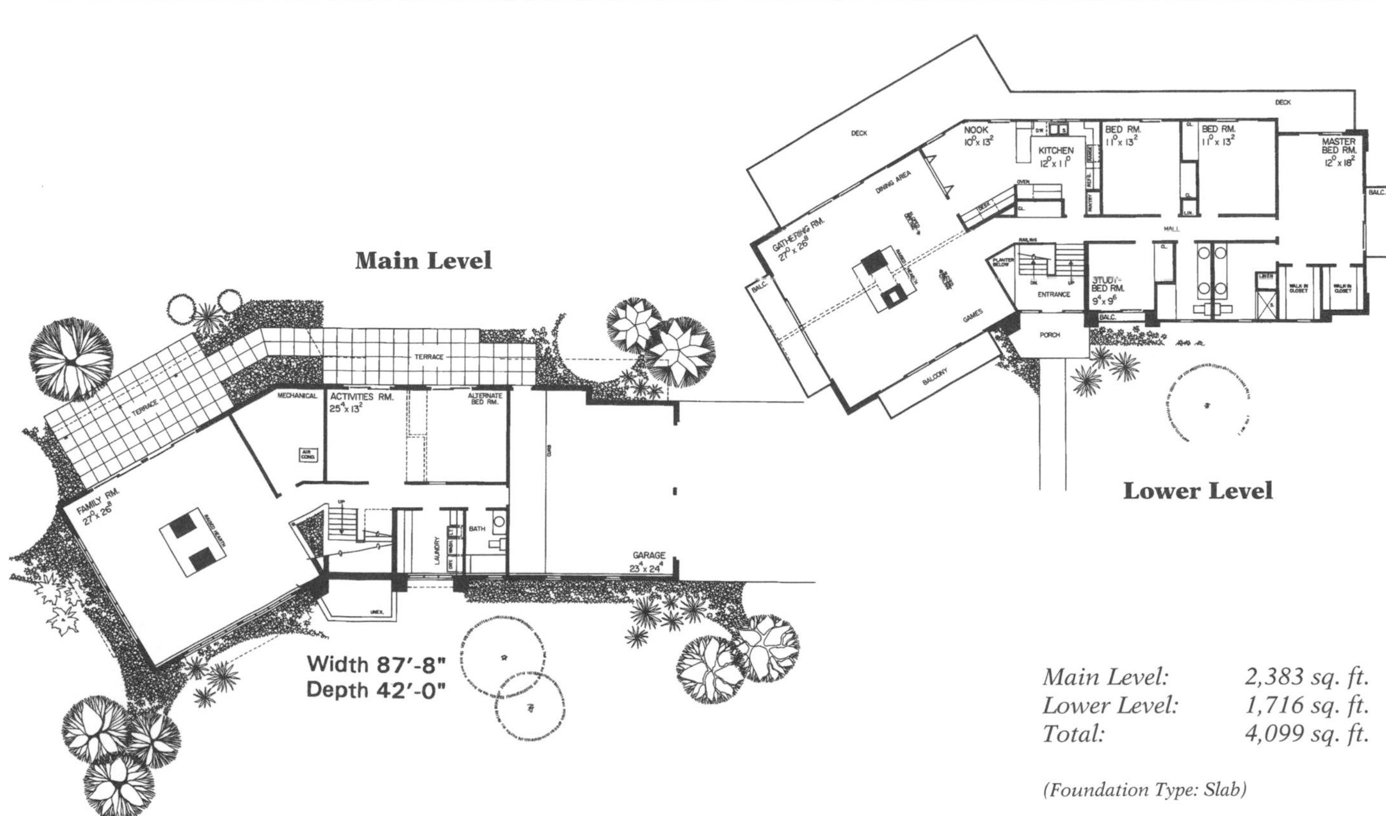


*Main Level:* *2,383 sq. ft.*
*Lower Level:* *1,716 sq. ft.*
*Total:* *4,099 sq. ft.*

*(Foundation Type: Slab)*

## Design CP2719

# Quentin

This design offers three large living areas: gathering room, family room and all-purpose activity room. Note the features in each of the three: balcony, sloping ceiling and through-fireplace in the gathering room; deck and eating area in the family room, and terrace and raised-hearth fireplace in the activity room. The staircase to the lower level is open, which adds to the spacious appeal of the entry hall. There are three bedrooms, with the master suite on the main level and two bedrooms on the lower level.

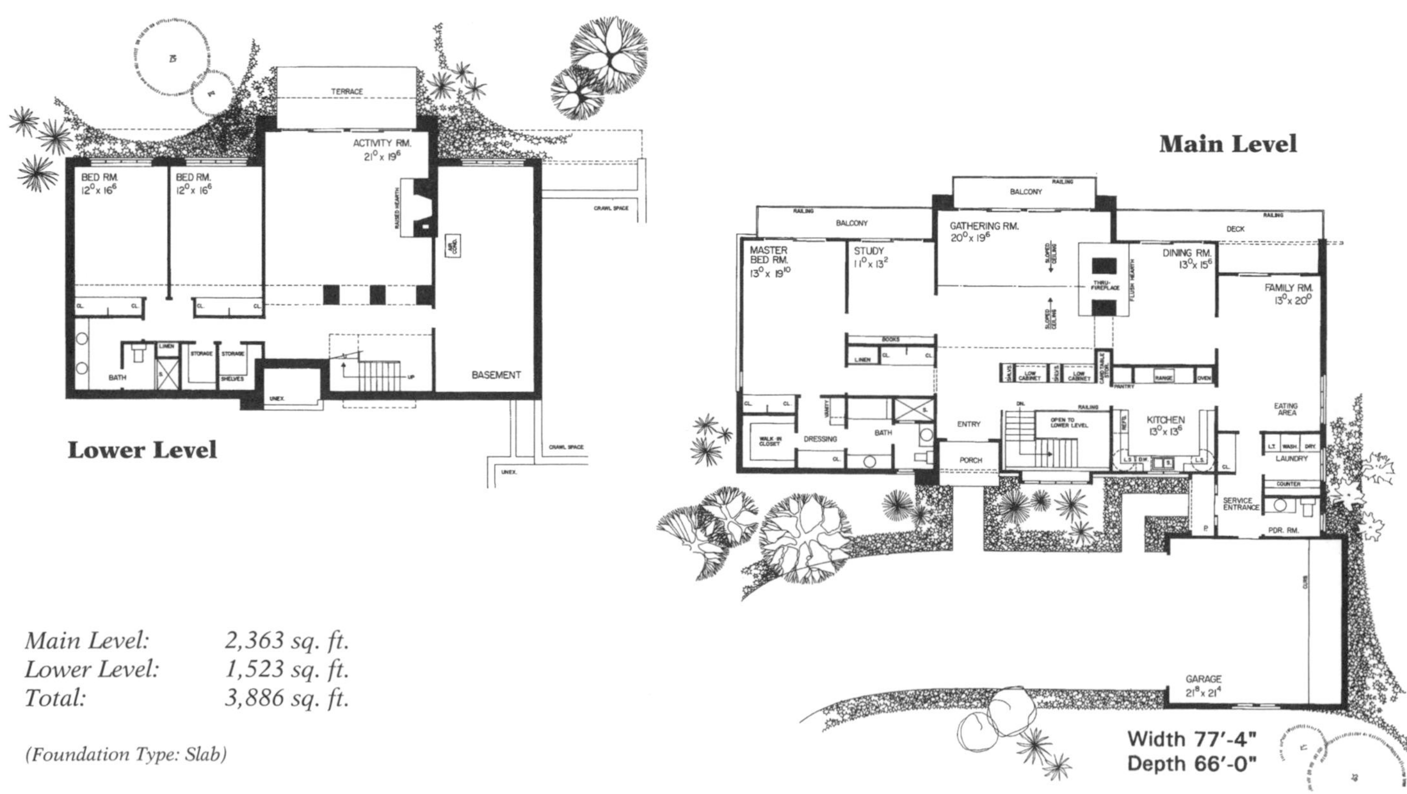


*Main Level:* *2,363 sq. ft.*
*Lower Level:* *1,523 sq. ft.*
*Total:* *3,886 sq. ft.*

*(Foundation Type: Slab)*

# Skyline

**Design CP2504**

A front court area welcomes guests on their way to the double front doors. These doors, flanked by floor-to-ceiling glass panels, are sheltered by the porch. Adjacent to this area are the sliding glass doors off the breakfast nook, which display the beauty of the front yard. This design takes advantage of a sloping site to open up the lower level. In this case, the lower level has virtually the same glass treatment as its corresponding room above.

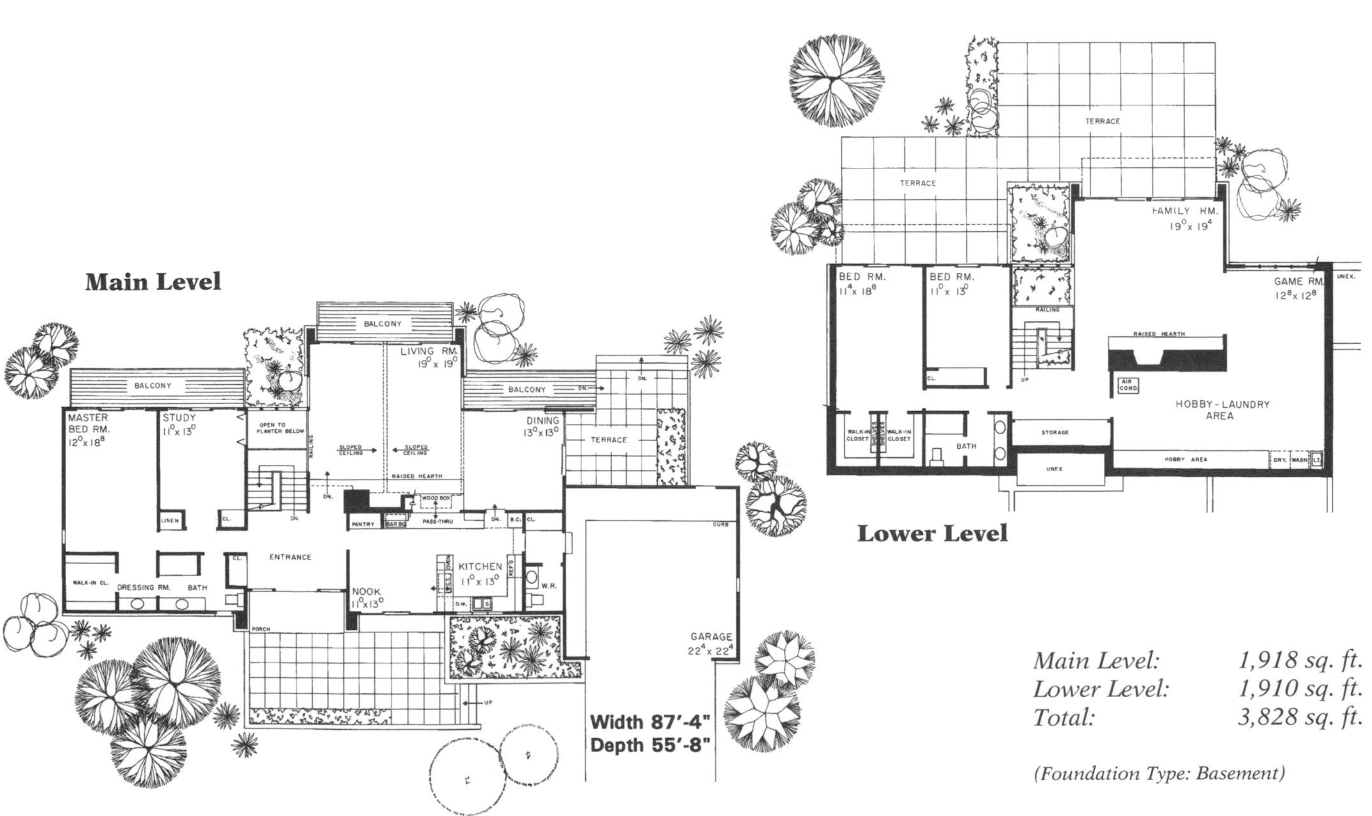


| | |
|---|---|
| *Main Level:* | *1,918 sq. ft.* |
| *Lower Level:* | *1,910 sq. ft.* |
| *Total:* | *3,828 sq. ft.* |

*(Foundation Type: Basement)*

## Design CP2549

# Garrick

This hillside home gives all the appearances of a one-story ranch home; and what a delightful one at that! Should the contours of your property slope to the rear, this plan permits the exposing of the lower level. This results in the activities room and bedroom/study gaining direct access to outdoor living. The large and growing family will be admirably served with five bedrooms and three baths. An extra washroom and separate laundry add to the living potential.

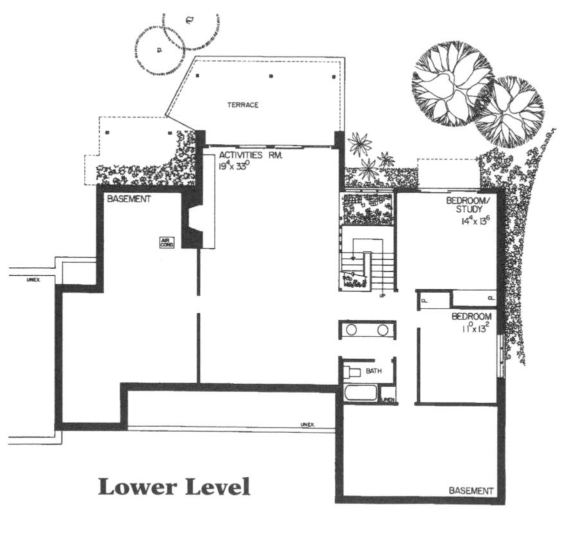


**Lower Level**

**Main Level**

Width 86'-0"
Depth 52'-0"

| | |
|---|---|
| *Main Level:* | *2,260 sq. ft.* |
| *Lower Level:* | *1,406 sq. ft.* |
| *Total:* | *3,666 sq. ft.* |

*(Foundation Type: Basement)*

# Mikado

## Design CP2502

This design appears to be a one-story, L-shaped home from the street. However, a sloping terrain reveals a lower level with terrace access. The main level features several terraces in addition to a large balcony and an entrance court. The formal living room is sunken and includes a raised-hearth fireplace. A second fireplace is found in the family room. The sleeping areas are placed at opposite ends of the home for quiet and privacy. The lower level provides a huge activities room, a game room and a summer kitchen.

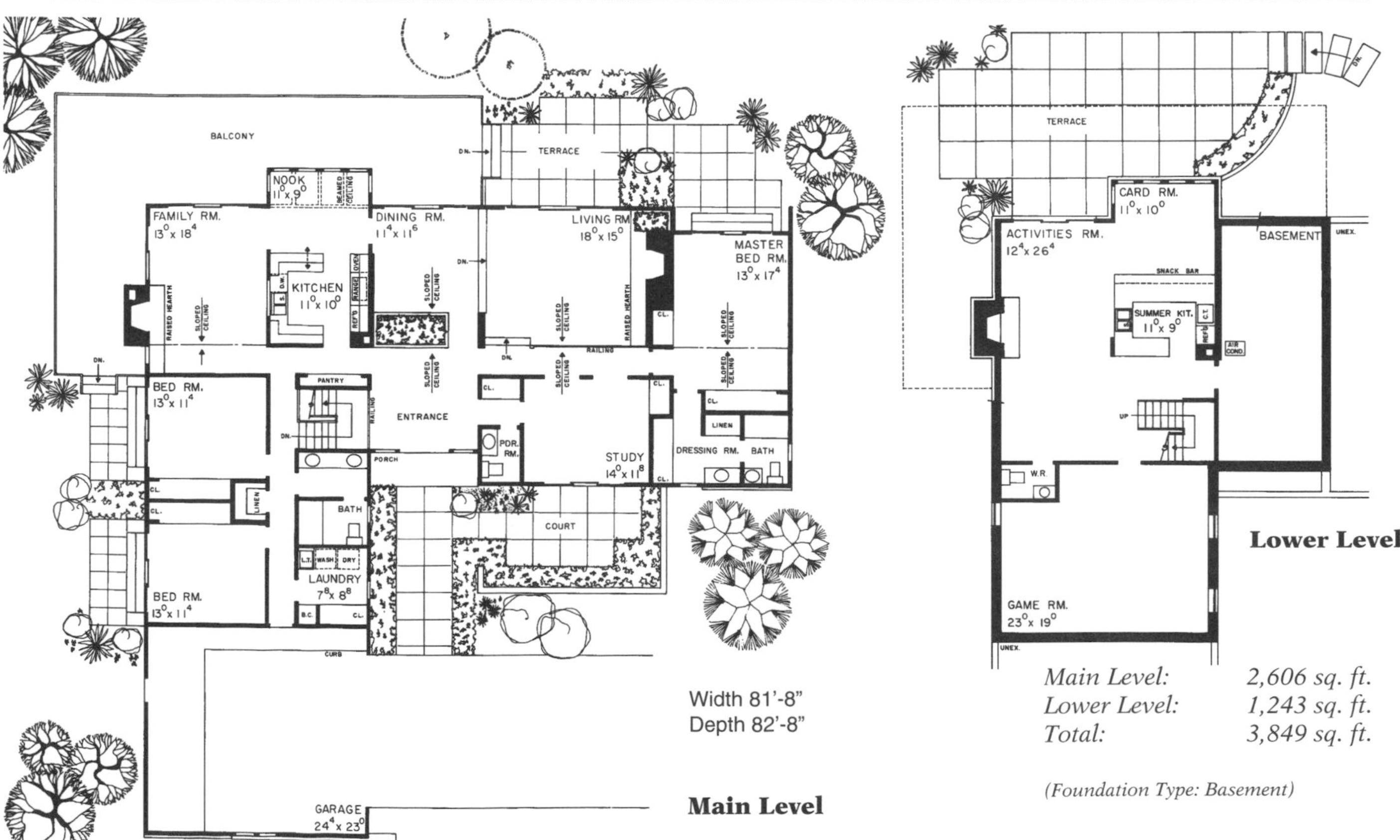


| | |
|---|---|
| *Main Level:* | *2,606 sq. ft.* |
| *Lower Level:* | *1,243 sq. ft.* |
| *Total:* | *3,849 sq. ft.* |

*(Foundation Type: Basement)*

## Design CP2856

# Sceptre

This attractive, contemporary bi-level will overwhelm you with its features: two balconies, an open staircase with planter below, two lower-level bedrooms, six sets of sliding glass doors and an outstanding master suite loaded with features. The gathering room and family room provide plenty of space for entertaining. The occupants of this house will love the large exercise room. After a tough workout, you can relax in the whirlpool or the sauna.

**Upper Level**

**Lower Level**

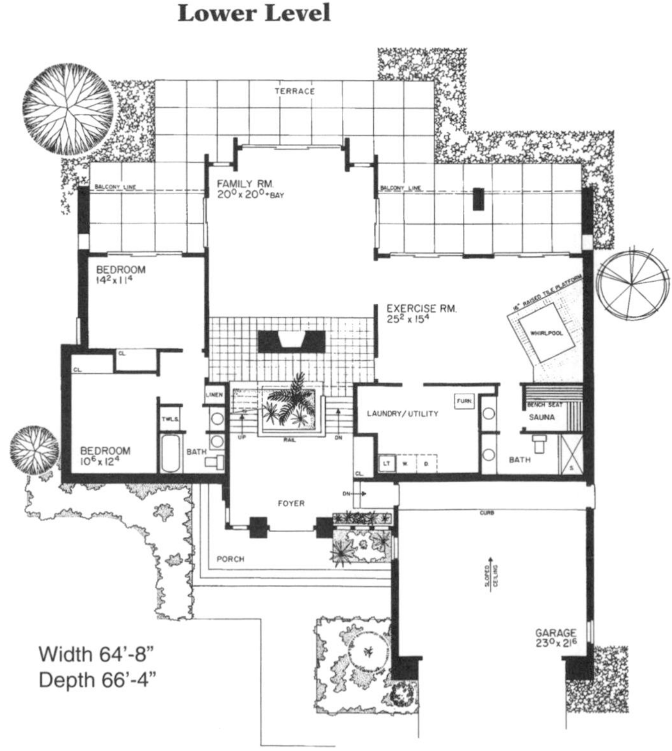


Width 64'-8"
Depth 66'-4"

*Upper Level:* *1,801 sq. ft.*
*Lower Level:* *2,170 sq. ft.*
*Total:* *3,971 sq. ft.*

*(Foundation Type: Basement)*

# Raven

## Design CP2934

This contemporary provides split-bedroom planning. The main-level master bedroom is a delightful retreat, with a balcony, a massive bath including a whirlpool tub and a dressing area with His and Hers walk-in closets. Three bedrooms and two full baths are on the lower level. Living areas include a living room with fireplace, a media room, a family room with snack bar, a formal dining room and a lower-level activities room with a game room and a bar nearby.

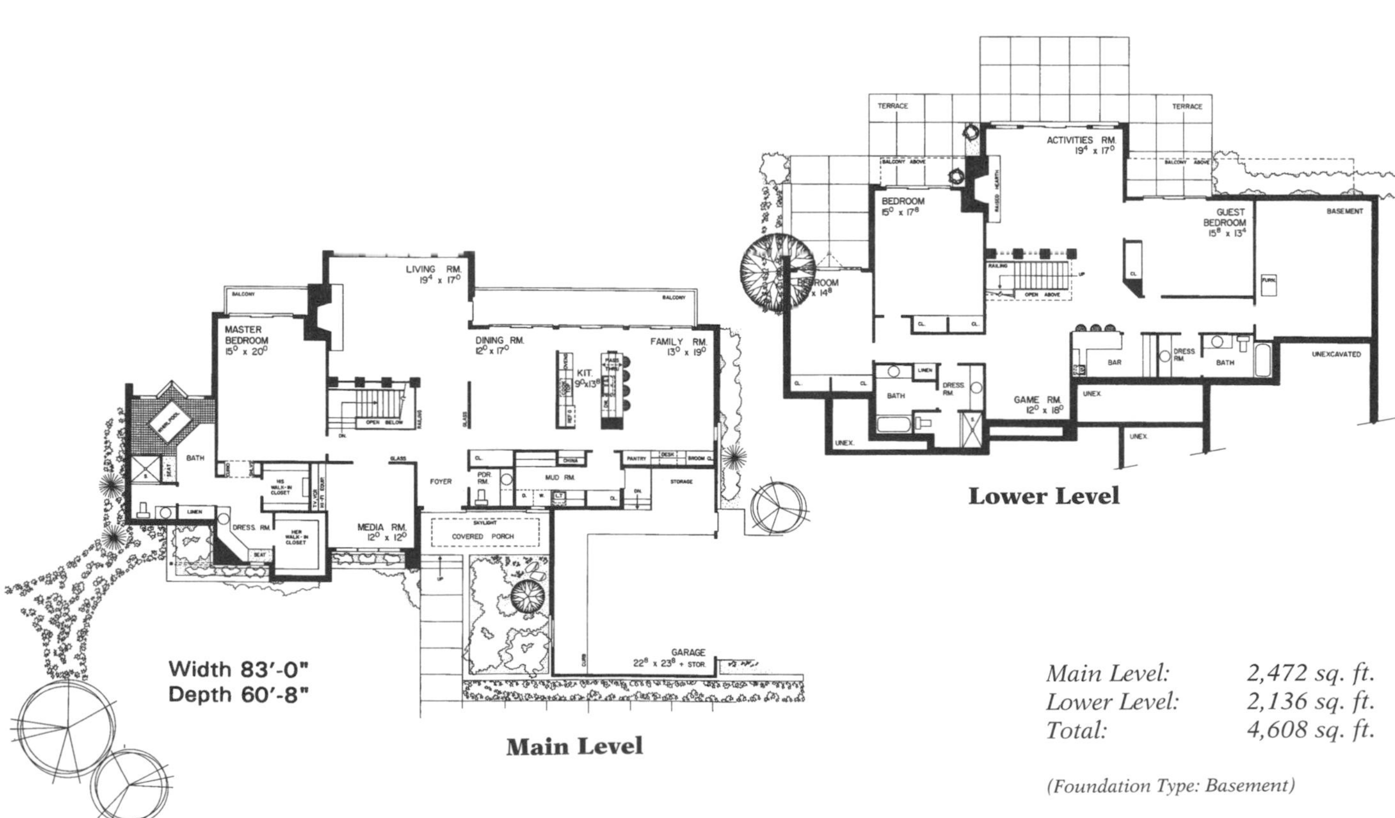


Width 83'-0"
Depth 60'-8"

**Main Level**

**Lower Level**

| | |
|---|---|
| *Main Level:* | *2,472 sq. ft.* |
| *Lower Level:* | *2,136 sq. ft.* |
| *Total:* | *4,608 sq. ft.* |

*(Foundation Type: Basement)*

## Design CP2730 — Oakwood

Here is a basic one-story home loaded with livability on the first floor and a bonus of 1,086 square feet on a lower level. Just beyond the entry, a balcony looks down to a dramatic planting area. The main-level traffic patterns flow around this impressive and distinctive feature. In addition to the gathering room, study and family room, there is a lounge plus an activity room. The master bedroom is outstanding with a large bath and two walk-in closets.

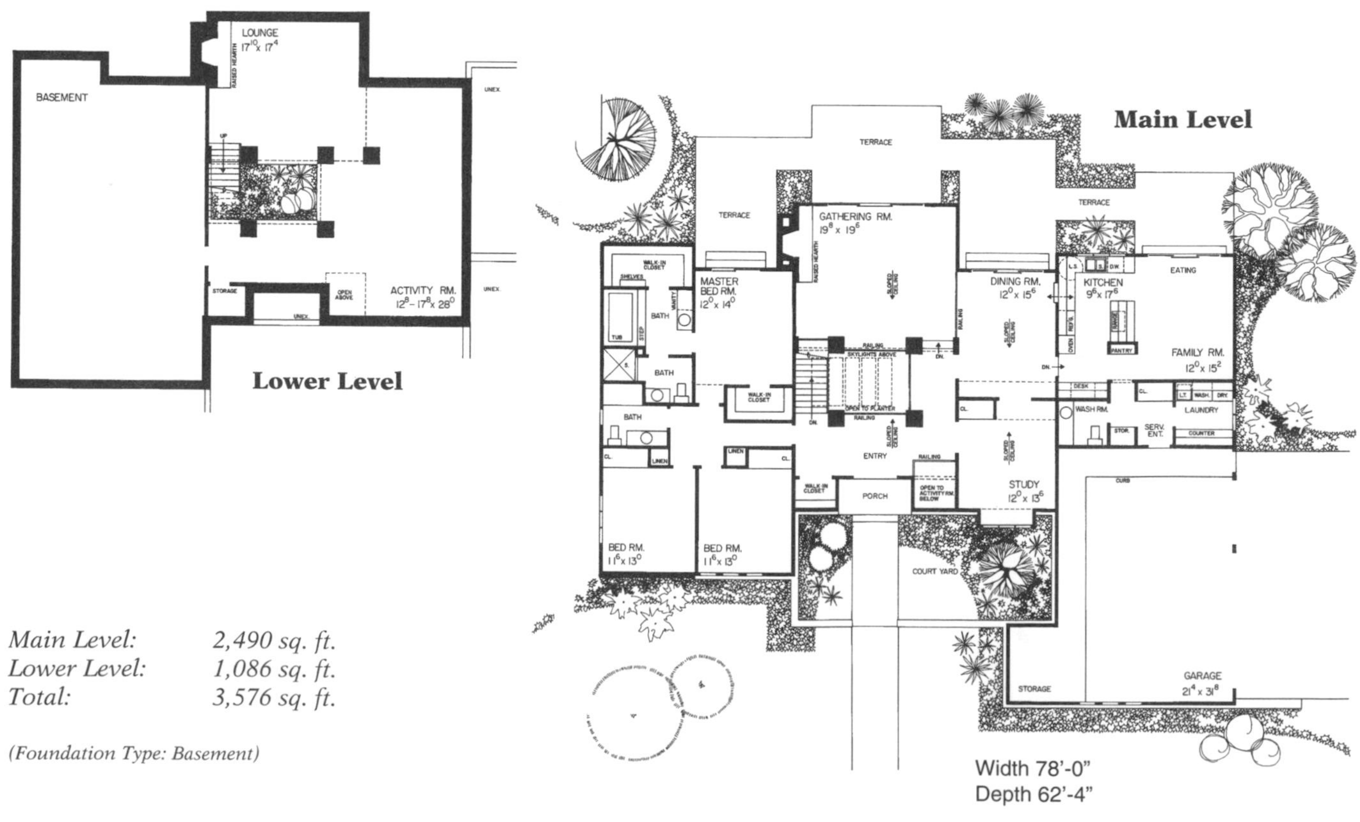


*Main Level:* *2,490 sq. ft.*
*Lower Level:* *1,086 sq. ft.*
*Total:* *3,576 sq. ft.*

*(Foundation Type: Basement)*

# Sherwood

**Design CP2895**

This contemporary hillside is ideal for those with a flair for something different. A large kitchen with adjacent breakfast room offers easy access to the terraces as does the dining room. Other main-floor areas include: a master bedroom suite with private terrace and access to the rear balcony, a family room and a sunken living room. The lower level has two more bedrooms, an activity room and a lounge with built-in bar.

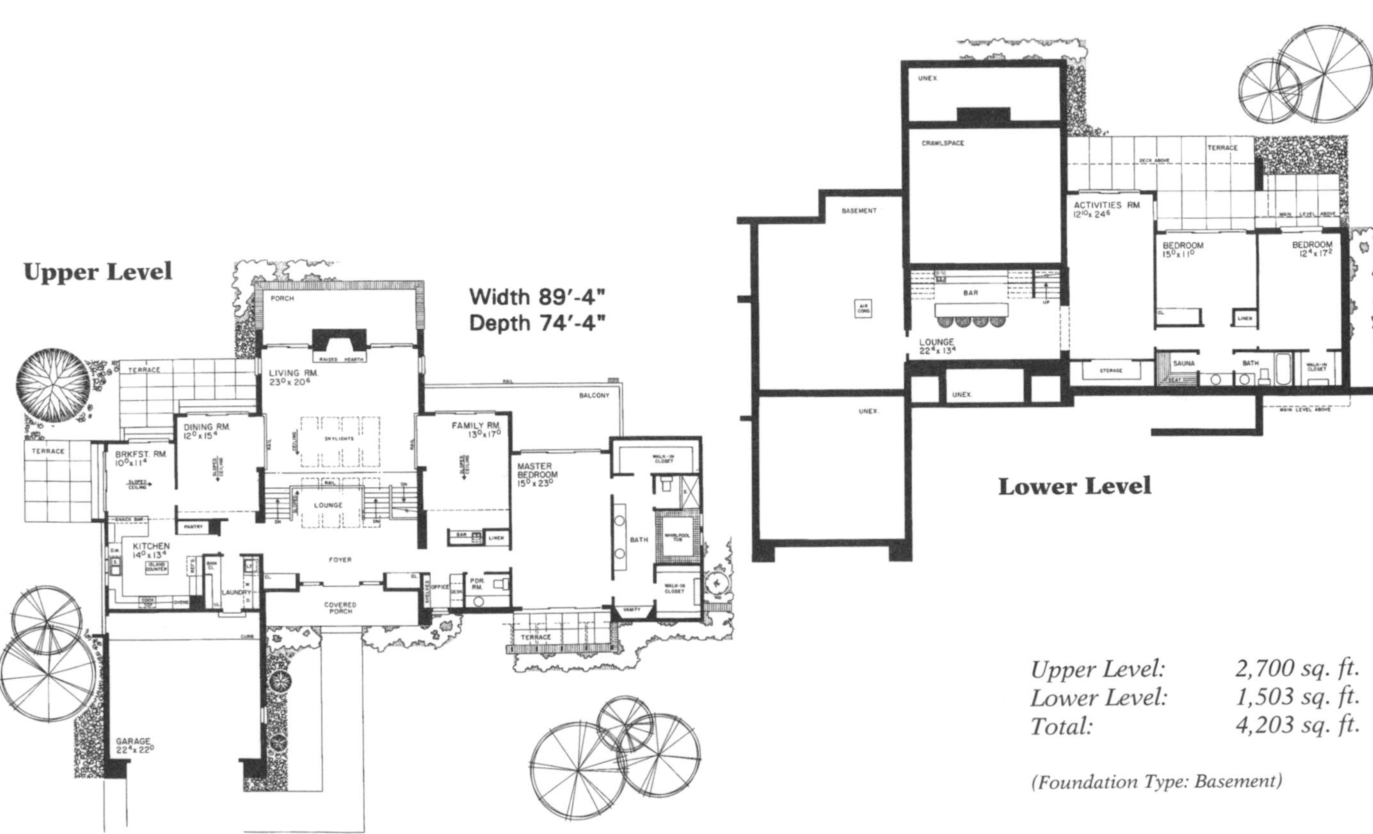

## Design CP2904

# Campbell

This four-bedroom contemporary trend home is loaded with extras that include a spacious garden room with its own whirlpool, snack bar off the kitchen and a deluxe master suite. The master bedroom has access to an exercise room with its own bath and a view of the back-yard terrace. Adjacent to the master bedroom is a spacious living room with sloped ceiling. Three other bedrooms, two with private balconies, are on the second floor.

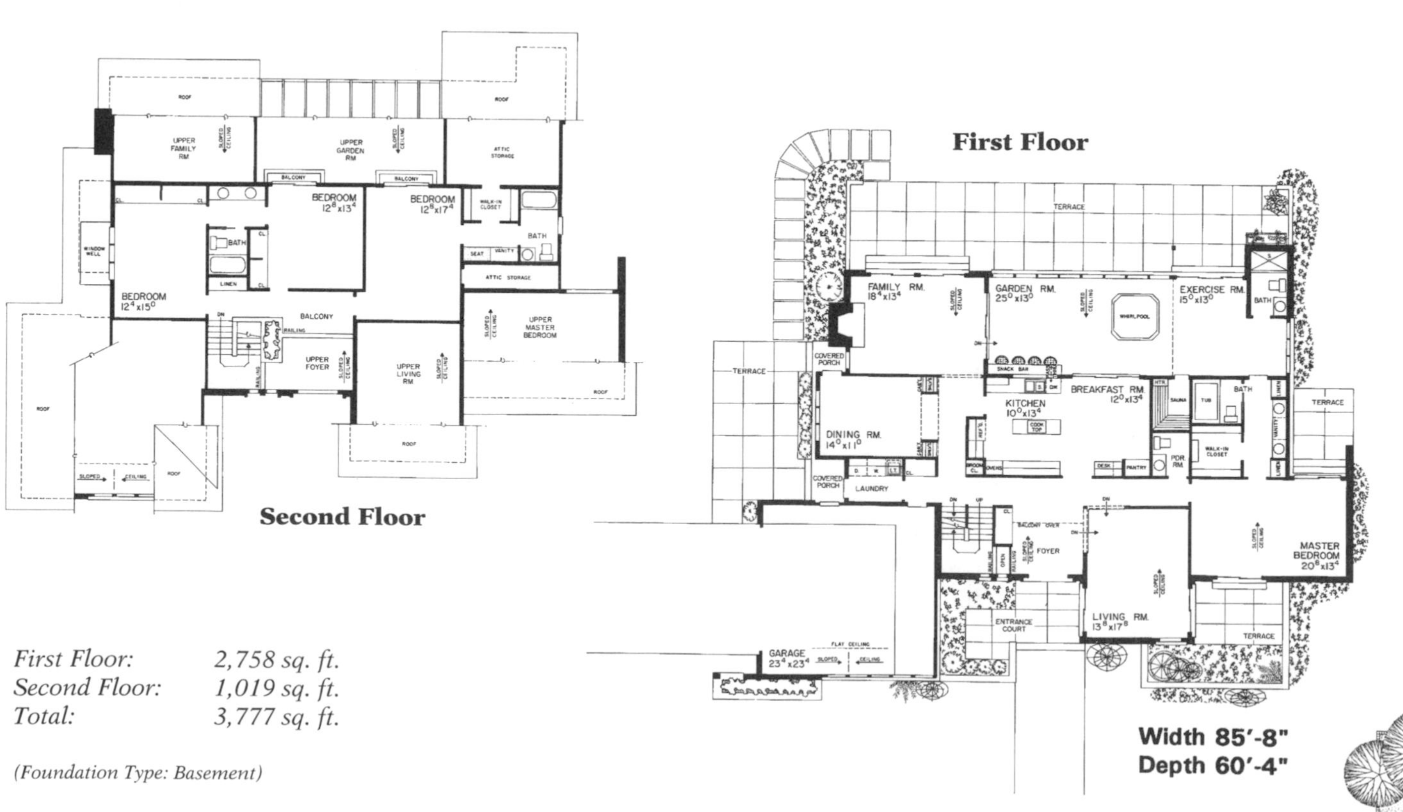


| | |
|---|---|
| *First Floor:* | *2,758 sq. ft.* |
| *Second Floor:* | *1,019 sq. ft.* |
| *Total:* | *3,777 sq. ft.* |

*(Foundation Type: Basement)*

# Wilmot

## Design CP3557

The owners of this home will be giving themselves a real treat. A large master bedroom is accompanied by a pampering master bath and dressing area with walk-in closet. The master suite also provides access to the media room with bay window and fireplace. A sunken gathering room suits formal or informal occasions. The kitchen contains a snack bar and is convenient to the breakfast and dining rooms. Two large bedrooms upstairs are accompanied by two full baths.

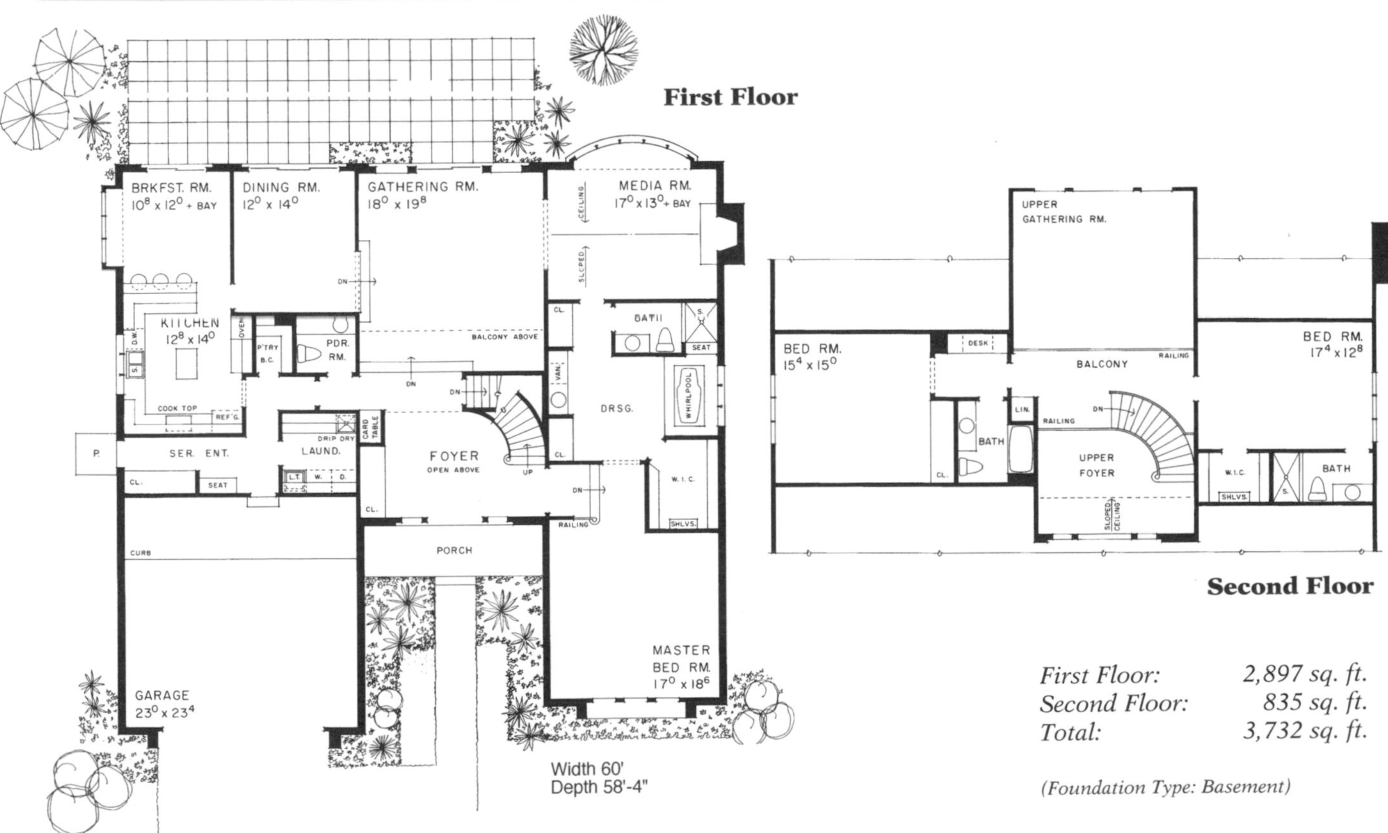


*First Floor:* *2,897 sq. ft.*
*Second Floor:* *835 sq. ft.*
*Total:* *3,732 sq. ft.*

*(Foundation Type: Basement)*

## Design CP4511

# Bordeaux

A stucco exterior and decorative corner quoins add flair to this French chateau. A fireplace, cathedral ceiling and tall windows are dramatic accents in the oversized living room. A playroom with fireplace, pool room and storage space is positioned behind the breakfast room. The master suite includes a fireplace, oversized bath and three walk-in closets in the dressing room. The second floor features six bedrooms and three full baths.

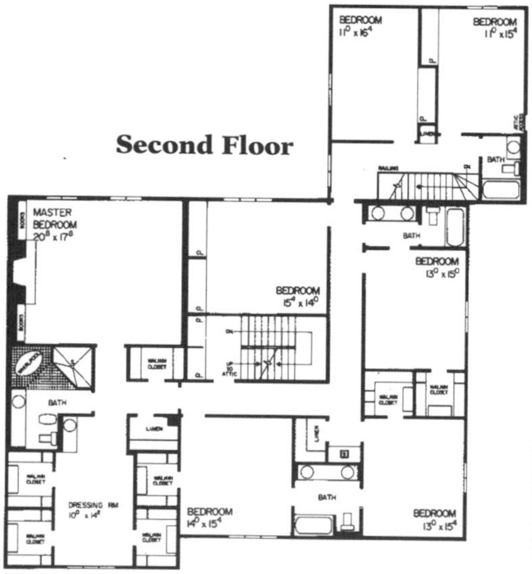

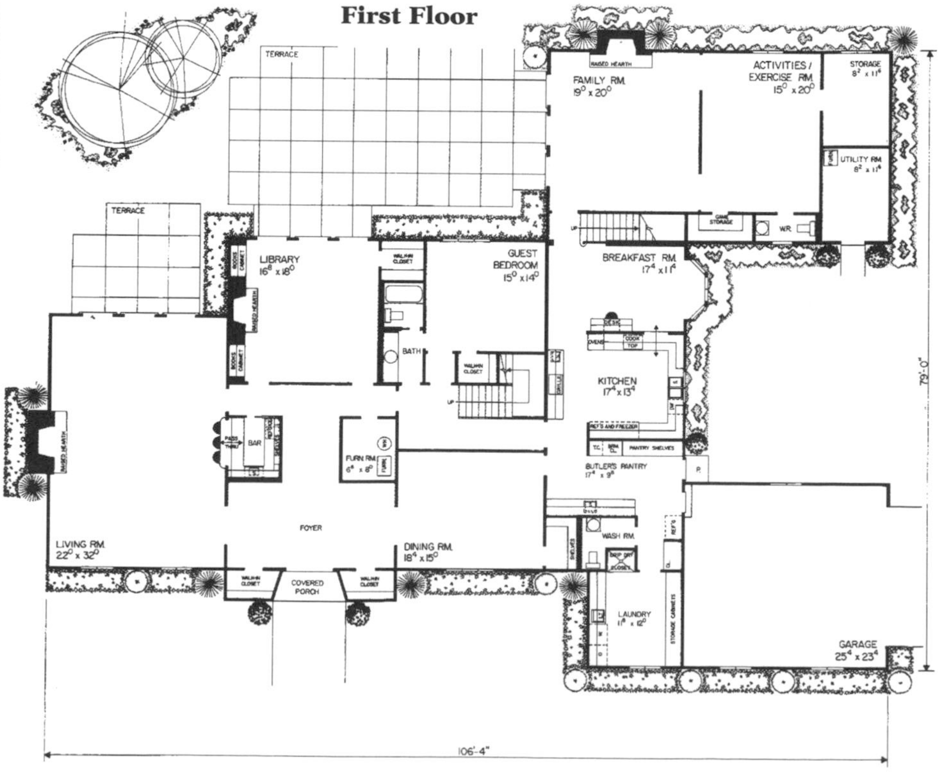

**Second Floor**

**First Floor**

| | |
|---|---|
| *First Floor:* | *4,480 sq. ft.* |
| *Second Floor:* | *3,178 sq. ft.* |
| *Total:* | *7,658 sq. ft.* |

*(Foundation Type: Slab)*

# Gainsborough

**Design CP4391**

Hillside living takes on elegant proportions in this thoughtful plan. The living and dining rooms flank a formal entry. The family room includes a massive fireplace and large bay window. A U-shaped kitchen adjoins the breakfast room, which looks out onto a large deck. Upstairs, a master suite features a whirlpool tub and walk-in closets. Two bedrooms share a bath. A bonus space to the front makes a perfect office or computer room.

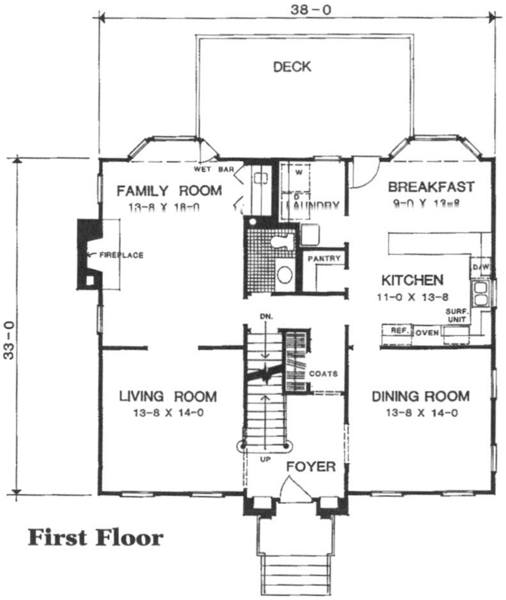

38-0
DECK
FAMILY ROOM 13-8 X 18-0
WET BAR
LAUNDRY
BREAKFAST 9-0 X 13-8
FIREPLACE
PANTRY
KITCHEN 11-0 X 13-8
D/W
SURF. UNIT
REF.
OVEN
DN.
COATS
33-0
LIVING ROOM 13-8 X 14-0
DINING ROOM 13-8 X 14-0
UP
FOYER

**First Floor**

**Second Floor**

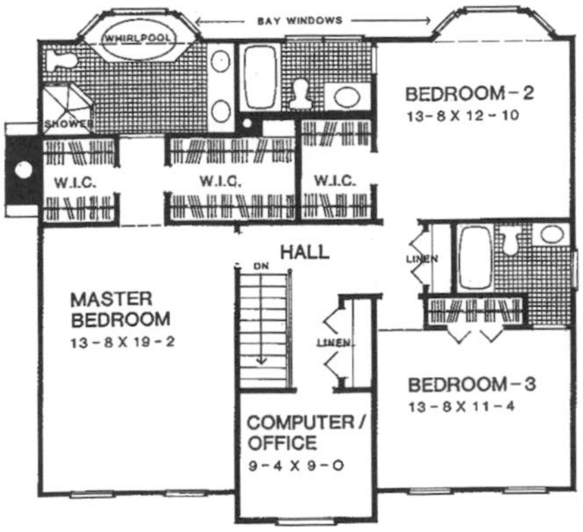

BAY WINDOWS
WHIRLPOOL
SHOWER
BEDROOM-2 13-8 X 12-10
W.I.C.
W.I.C.
W.I.C.
HALL
LINEN
DN
MASTER BEDROOM 13-8 X 19-2
LINEN
BEDROOM-3 13-8 X 11-4
COMPUTER / OFFICE 9-4 X 9-0

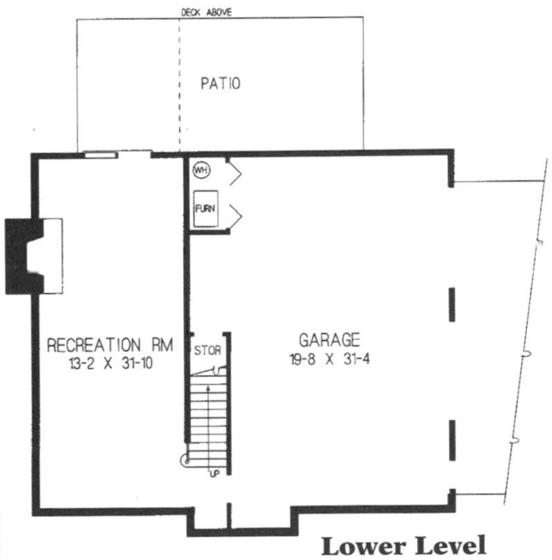

DECK ABOVE
PATIO
WH
FURN
RECREATION RM 13-2 X 31-10
STOR
GARAGE 19-8 X 31-4
UP

**Lower Level**

| | |
|---|---|
| *First Floor:* | *1,315 sq. ft.* |
| *Second Floor:* | *1,312 sq. ft.* |
| *Lower Level:* | *1,273 sq. ft.* |
| *Total:* | *3,900 sq. ft.* |

*(Foundation Type: Basement)*

## Design CP3503

# Hearthstone

A brick exterior serves as a nice introduction to a charming home perfect for narrow lots. Enter the eleven-foot-high foyer and take a seat in the living room with a focal-point fireplace. The kitchen with island and snack bar opens up into a conversation room with bay and fireplace. This house features four bedrooms: the master with fireplace, walk-in closet and whirlpool; two family bedrooms that share a full bath with double-bowl vanity; and a guest bedroom that shares the third floor with the library.

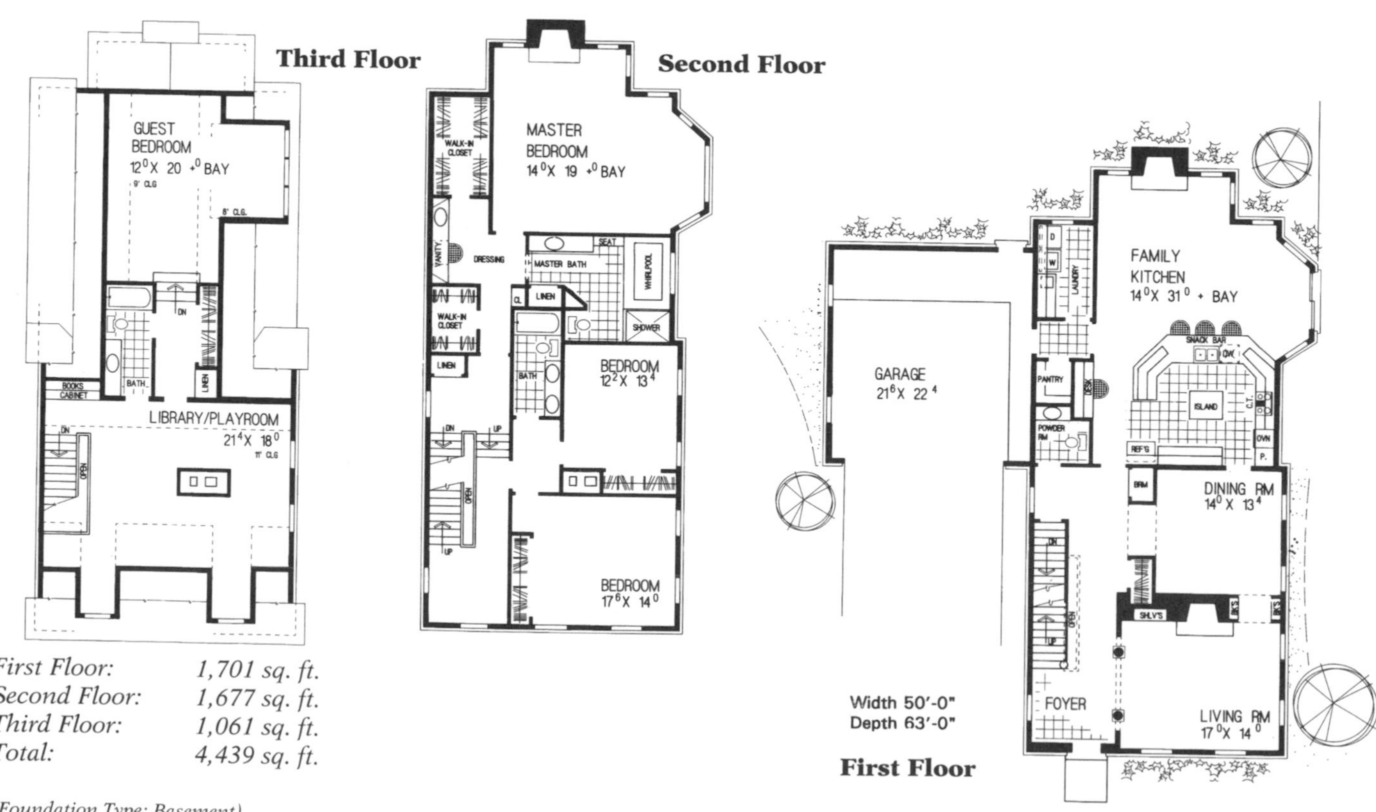


*First Floor:* *1,701 sq. ft.*
*Second Floor:* *1,677 sq. ft.*
*Third Floor:* *1,061 sq. ft.*
*Total:* *4,439 sq. ft.*

*(Foundation Type: Basement)*

# Magnolia

**Design CP3570**

The unique design of this Colonial will satisfy the most refined tastes. The family room and its fireplace create a warm atmosphere for playing a board game with the kids or just relaxing. The kitchen features an island cooktop and view onto the back porch. Take in the good weather from the second-floor balcony or slip into the master bath's whirlpool. With an additional three bedrooms and two bathrooms, as well as a large bonus room above the garage, your family will have plenty of room to grow.

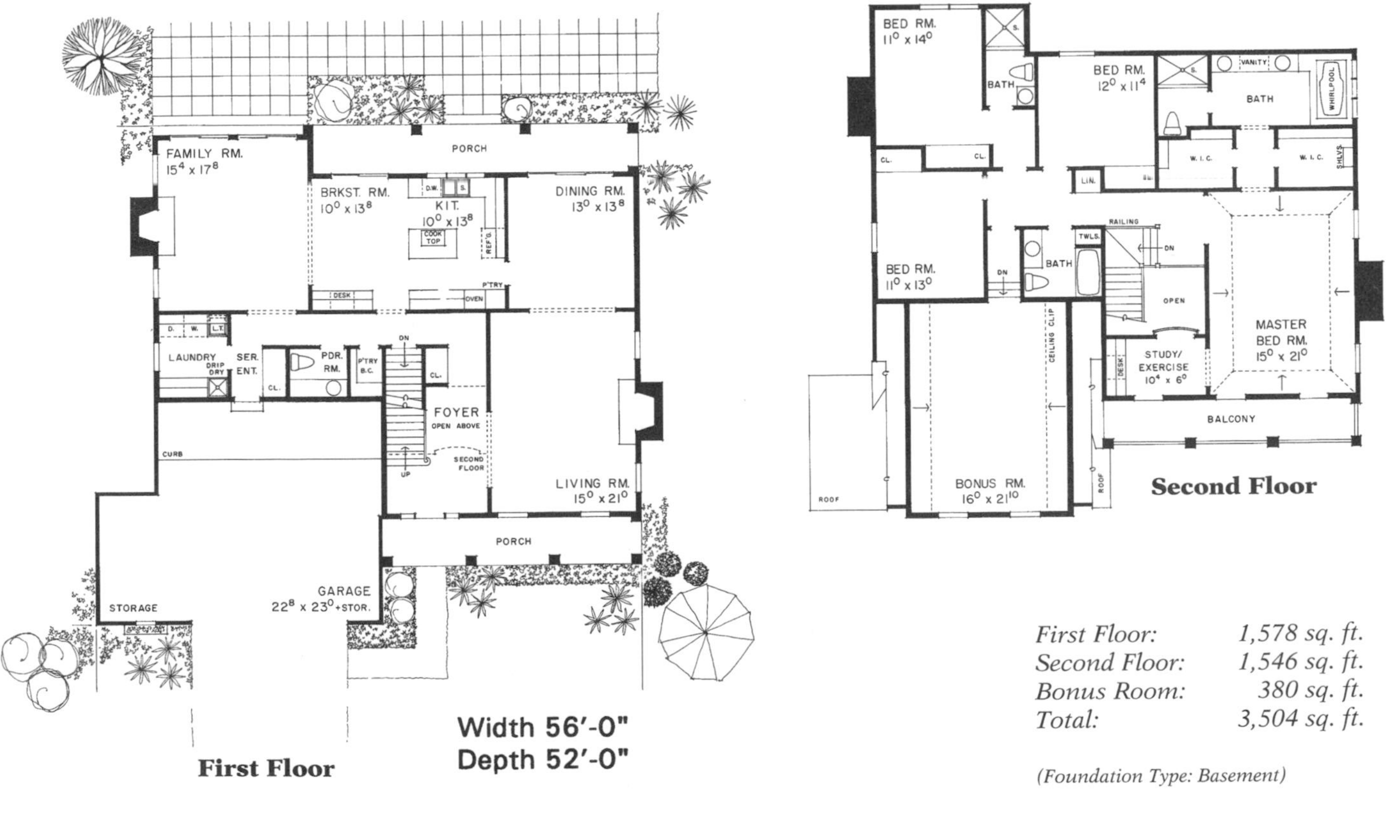


**First Floor**

**Second Floor**

| | |
|---|---|
| *First Floor:* | *1,578 sq. ft.* |
| *Second Floor:* | *1,546 sq. ft.* |
| *Bonus Room:* | *380 sq. ft.* |
| *Total:* | *3,504 sq. ft.* |

*(Foundation Type: Basement)*

## Design CP9514 **Kevin**

A striking facade opens to an impressive two-story foyer with a plant shelf. The formal living room and the dining room are open to each other. The kitchen features an island cooktop, a pantry and a planning desk. It is convenient to the breakfast room with bay and the family room with fireplace. Double doors open to the master suite with walk-in closet and bath with spa tub. Three family bedrooms share a compartmented bath. A 30-foot bonus room over the three-car garage is near a second stairway.

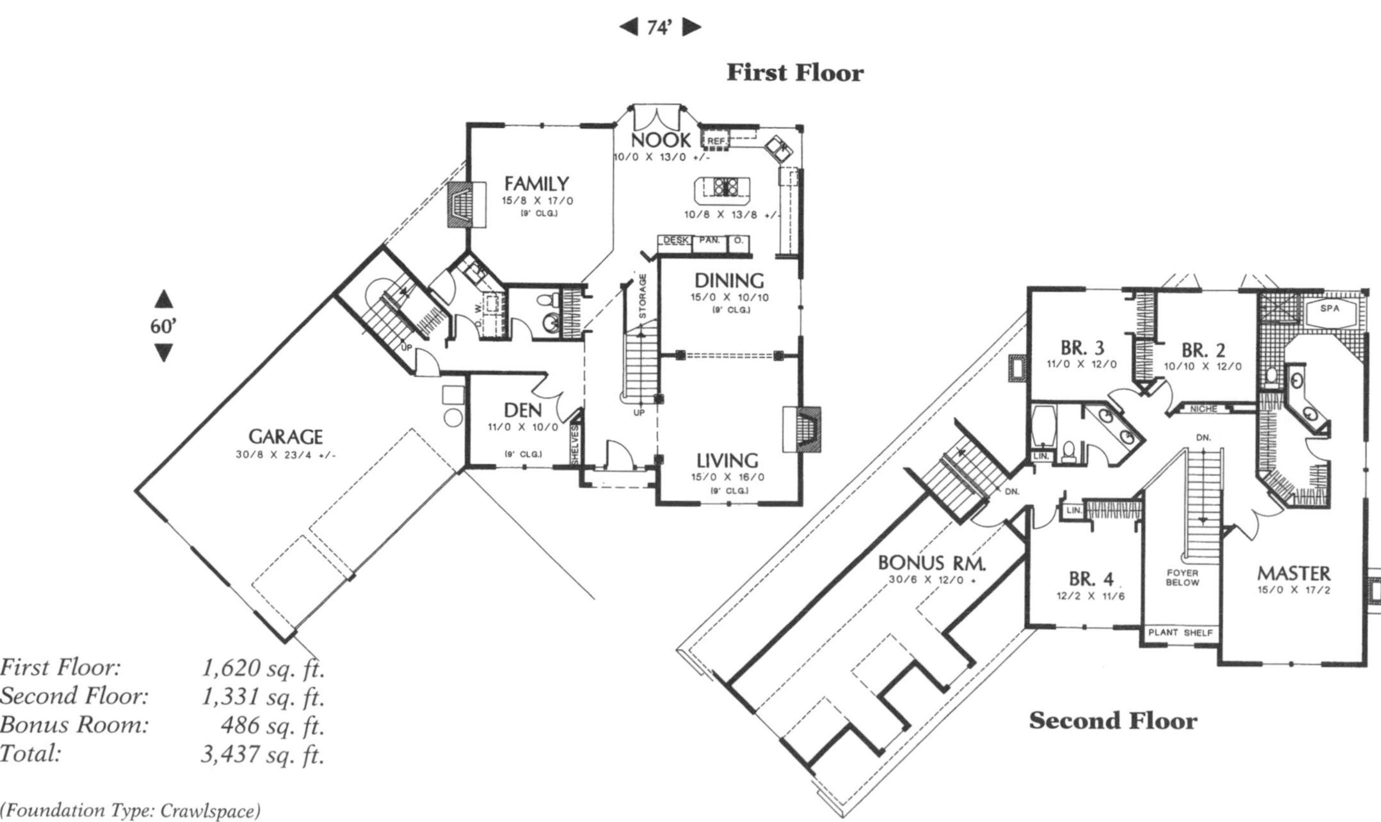


*First Floor:* *1,620 sq. ft.*
*Second Floor:* *1,331 sq. ft.*
*Bonus Room:* *486 sq. ft.*
*Total:* *3,437 sq. ft.*

*(Foundation Type: Crawlspace)*

# Frankfort

**Design CP4278**

A covered porch is a welcoming sight and leads guests to the formal entry of this two-story home. The focal point of the first floor is the adjoined family room, breakfast area and U-shaped kitchen. A fireplace with a raised hearth and bay windows are added amenities. The master bedroom has a private bath and joins three family bedrooms on the second floor. A large, open recreation room occupies the basement space.

**First Floor**

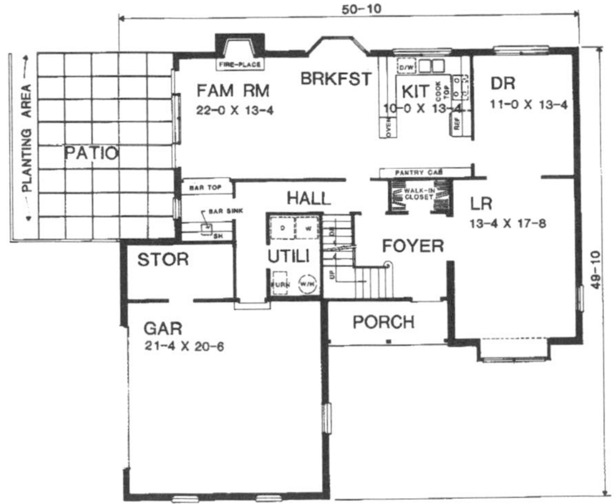


**Second Floor**

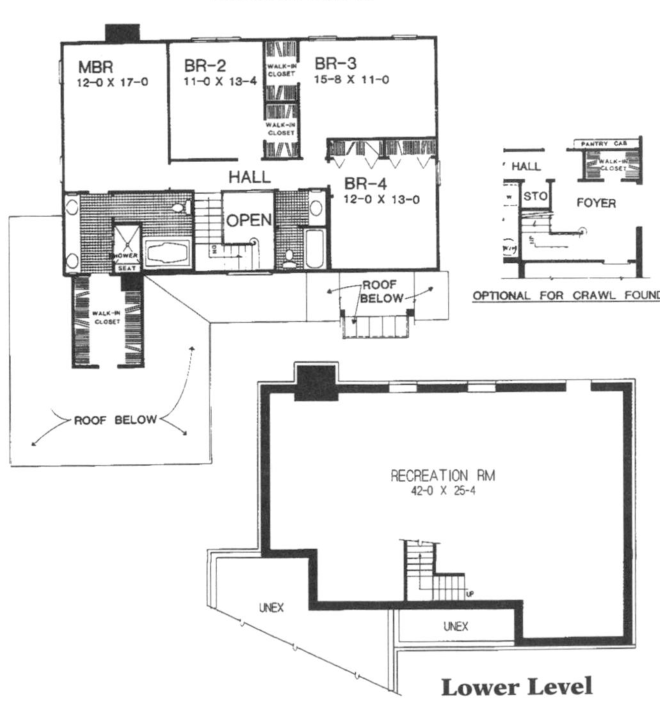


**Lower Level**

| | |
|---|---|
| *First Floor:* | *1,269 sq. ft.* |
| *Second Floor:* | *1,203 sq. ft.* |
| *Lower Level:* | *1,232 sq. ft.* |
| *Total:* | *3,704 sq. ft.* |

*(Foundation Type: Basement)*

## Design CP9803

# Old Roswell

This American Country-styled home, with wood siding and shuttered windows, echoes images of the warmth and strength of traditional Southern living. The two-story foyer opens to a dining room and formal parlor. Then pass the open rail stairs to the large family room with its fireplace, flanking book-cases and squared column supports. The kitchen has a breakfast area which opens to the outside. Upstairs, the master suite has its own sitting area and a vaulted ceiling.

*First Floor:* *1,850 sq. ft.*
*Second Floor:* *1,760 sq. ft.*
*Total:* *3,610 sq. ft.*

*(Foundation Type: Basement)*

# Scarlett

**Design CP9458**

Though its facade says country casual, this home has a floor plan that is as elegant and modern as any. The large family room features a vaulted ceiling and fireplace. It blends into the bay-windowed nook adjacent to the L-shaped island kitchen. A powder room separates the space between the kitchen and formal dining room with boxed window. Up an open staircase is the four-bedroom second floor. The master suite has a vaulted ceiling, large walk-in closet and bath with spa.

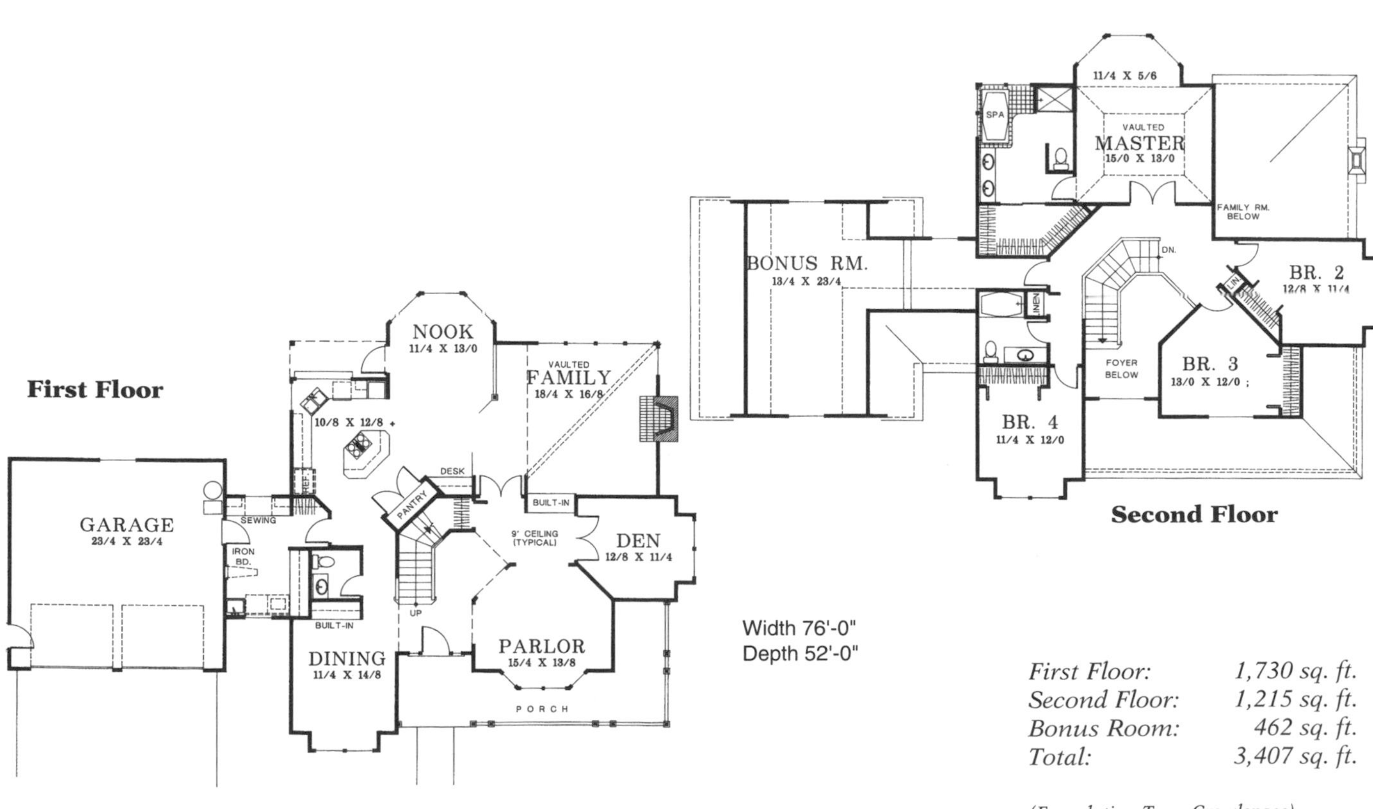


| | |
|---|---|
| *First Floor:* | *1,730 sq. ft.* |
| *Second Floor:* | *1,215 sq. ft.* |
| *Bonus Room:* | *462 sq. ft.* |
| *Total:* | *3,407 sq. ft.* |

*(Foundation Type: Crawlspace)*

# Design CP3567 Alvernon

Spring breezes and summer nights will be a joy to take in on the verandas and balcony of this Southern Colonial. If you prefer, sit back and enjoy a good book in the library, or invite an old friend over for a chat in the conversation room. The first floor also includes formal dining and living rooms, a service entry with laundry and a three-car garage. The master bedroom sports a fireplace, two walk-in closets, a double-bowl vanity, a shower and a whirlpool tub. Three other bedrooms occupy the second floor.

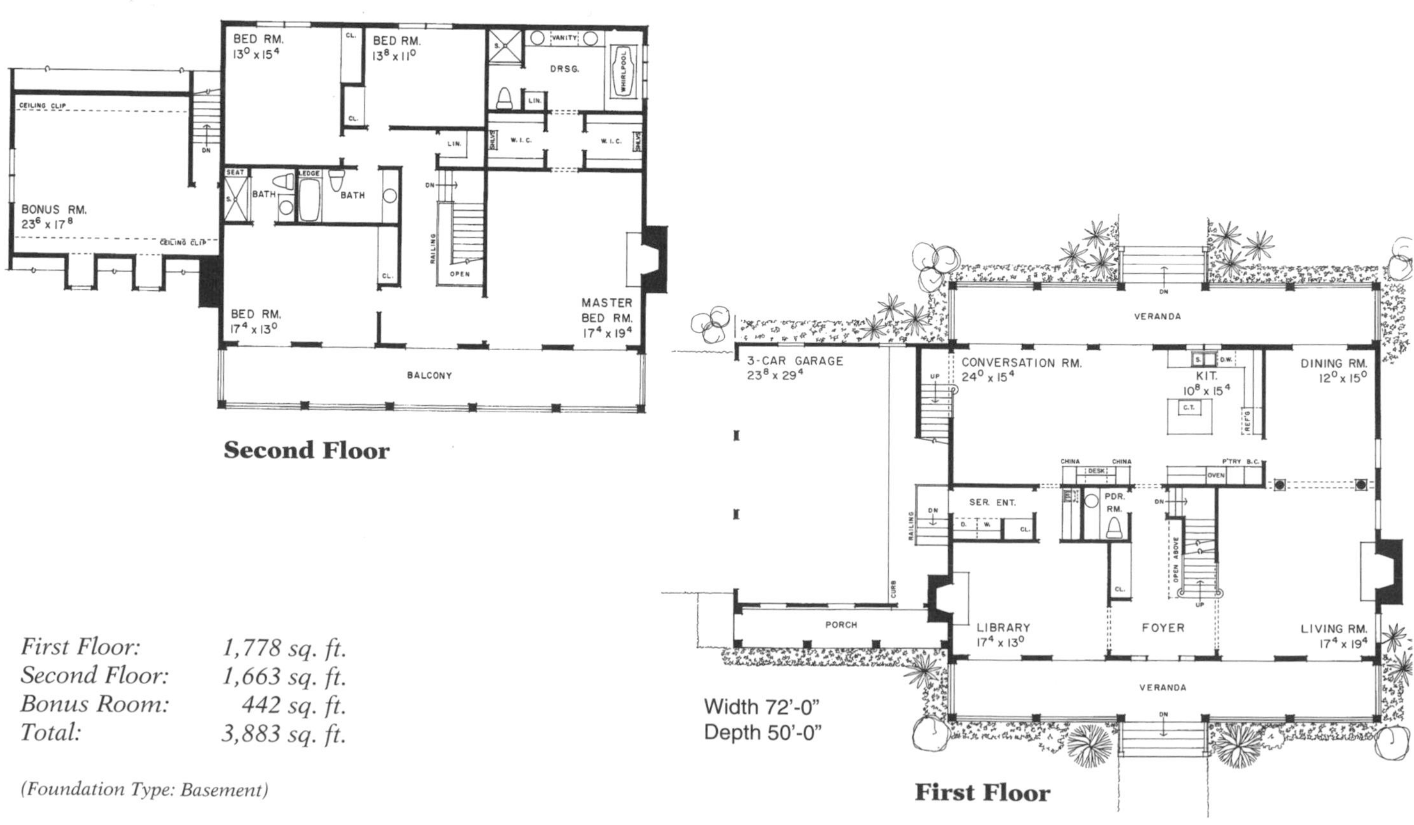


**Second Floor**

**First Floor**

Width 72'-0"
Depth 50'-0"

| | |
|---|---|
| *First Floor:* | *1,778 sq. ft.* |
| *Second Floor:* | *1,663 sq. ft.* |
| *Bonus Room:* | *442 sq. ft.* |
| *Total:* | *3,883 sq. ft.* |

*(Foundation Type: Basement)*

# Prospect Place

## Design CP2694

This two-story design faithfully recalls the 18th-Century homestead of Secretary of Foreign Affairs John Jay. First-floor livability includes a grand living room with fireplace and music alcove; a library with another fireplace and built-in bookshelves; a light-filled dining room; a large country kitchen with still another fireplace and snack bar; and a handy clutter room adjacent to the mud room. Three upstairs bedrooms include a large master suite with walk-in closet, vanity seating, and double sinks.

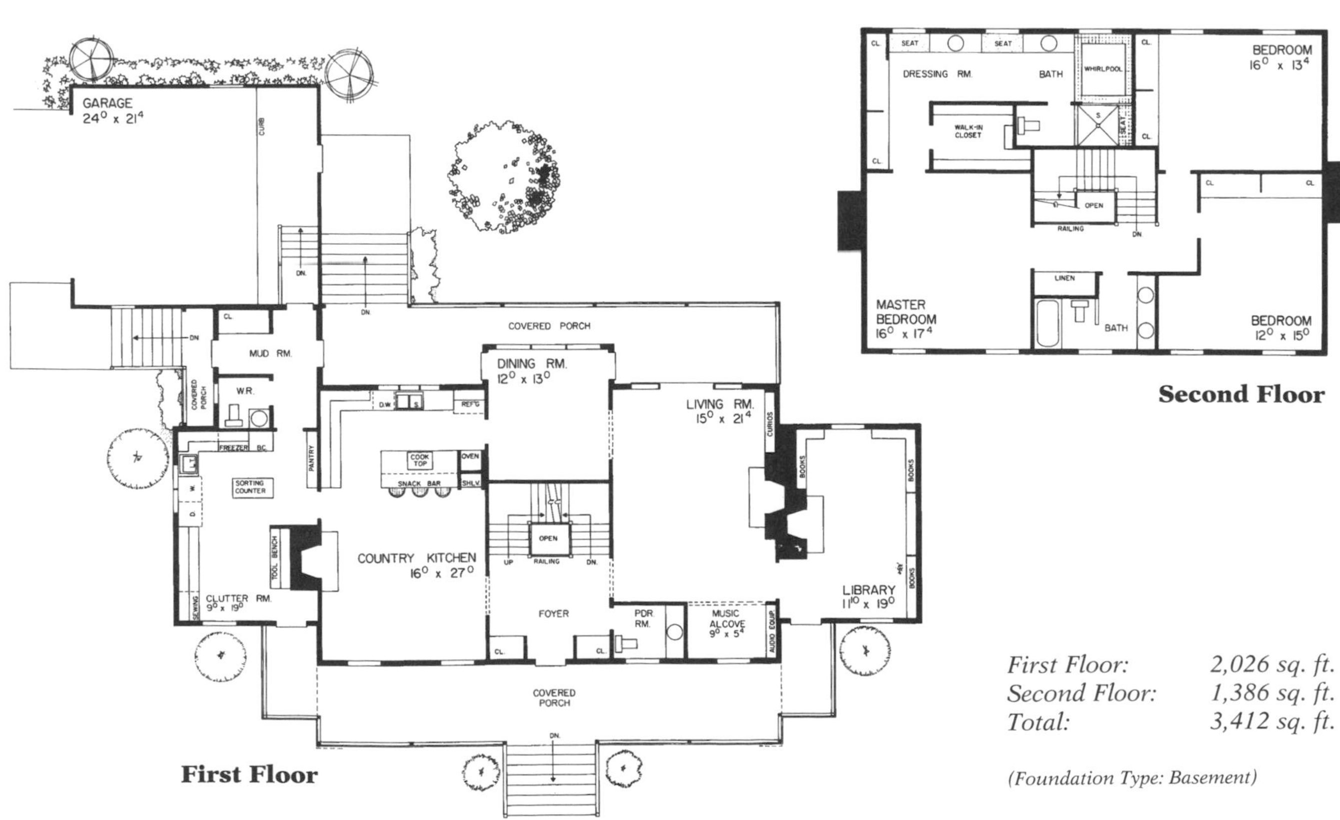


**First Floor**

**Second Floor**

| | |
|---|---|
| *First Floor:* | *2,026 sq. ft.* |
| *Second Floor:* | *1,386 sq. ft.* |
| *Total:* | *3,412 sq. ft.* |

*(Foundation Type: Basement)*

**Design CP2542**

# Rincon

Here is a fieldstone farmhouse that has its roots in the rolling countryside of Pennsylvania. In addition to its stone exterior, the charm of such a house is characterized by various appendages. These additions came into being as the size of the family increased. This updated version includes a very livable floor plan with four bedrooms and five fireplaces.

Width 76'-8"
Depth 76'-4"

**Second Floor**

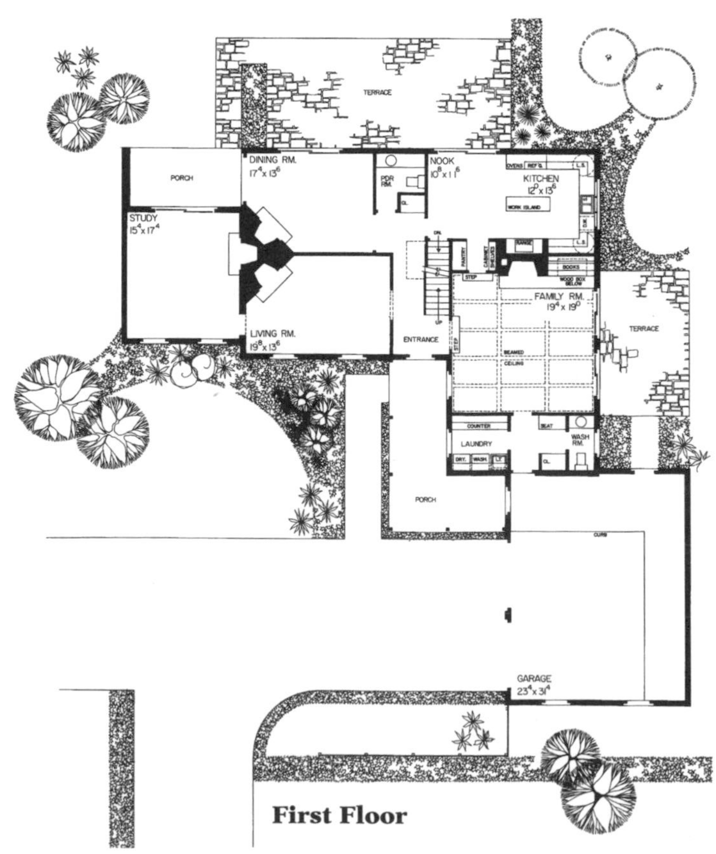


**First Floor**

| | |
|---|---|
| *First Floor:* | *2,025 sq. ft.* |
| *Second Floor:* | *1,726 sq. ft.* |
| *Total:* | *3,751 sq. ft.* |

*(Foundation Type: Basement)*

# *Harrison* Design CP3502

The columned front porch of this stone farmhouse leads to a formal foyer with living room on the left and library on the right. The formal dining room connects directly to the living room and to the island kitchen through a butler's pantry. The family room and breakfast room have beamed ceilings. A covered veranda is accessed from the breakfast room and leads to a side yard. On the second floor are three bedrooms and a guest room with private bath. The master bedroom has a fireplace and a fine bath.

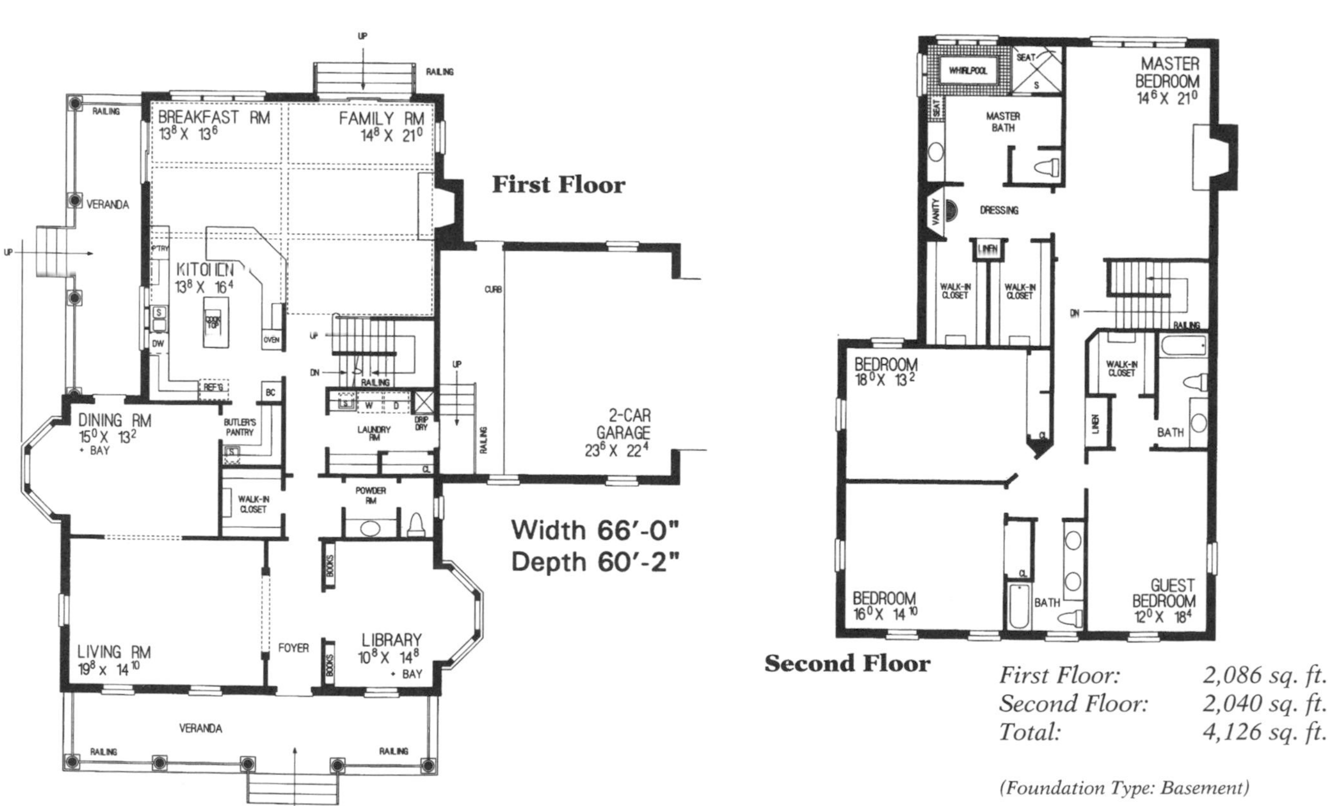


| | |
|---|---|
| *First Floor:* | *2,086 sq. ft.* |
| *Second Floor:* | *2,040 sq. ft.* |
| *Total:* | *4,126 sq. ft.* |

*(Foundation Type: Basement)*

## Design CP3381 — Silverbell

A central foyer allows access to every part of the home. To the left sits the spacious gathering room with fireplace and music alcove. Straight ahead, the open living and dining rooms offer sweeping views of the back yard. The modern kitchen and conversation area are situated to the right of the home. Near the entrance, a library with bay window and built-in bookcase is found. Extra amenities throughout the home include: curio cabinets; built-in desk; walk-in closet, and a second fireplace.

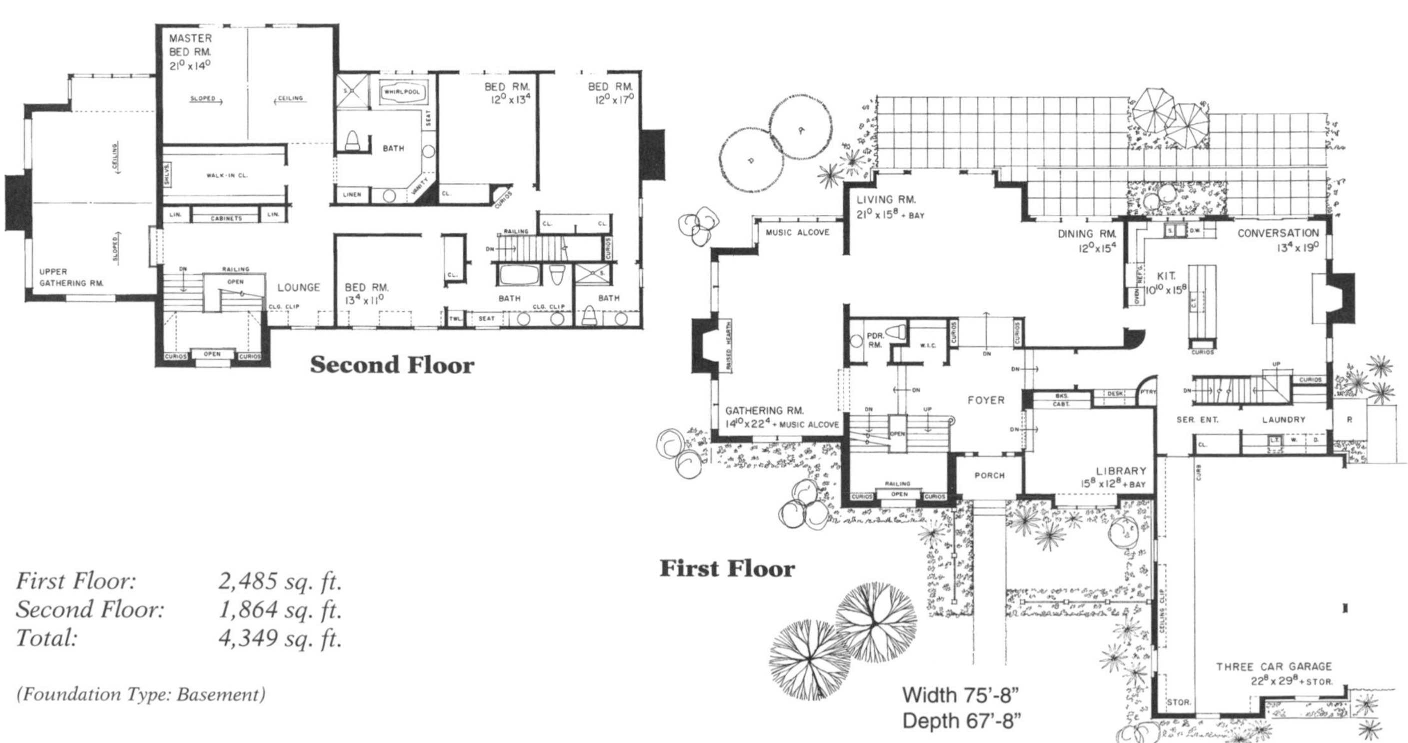


*First Floor:* *2,485 sq. ft.*
*Second Floor:* *1,864 sq. ft.*
*Total:* *4,349 sq. ft.*

*(Foundation Type: Basement)*

# Toronto

## Design CP3378

This large traditional home fits right in whether built in the busy city or a secluded rural area. Living areas on the first floor include a media room with bay window, gathering room with raised-hearth fireplace and a formal dining room. The kitchen area supplies room enough for a crowd with a snack bar and a 17-foot breakfast room with terrace access. A convenient first-floor master suite also includes terrace access, along with a sitting room and a dressing and bath area fit for a king.

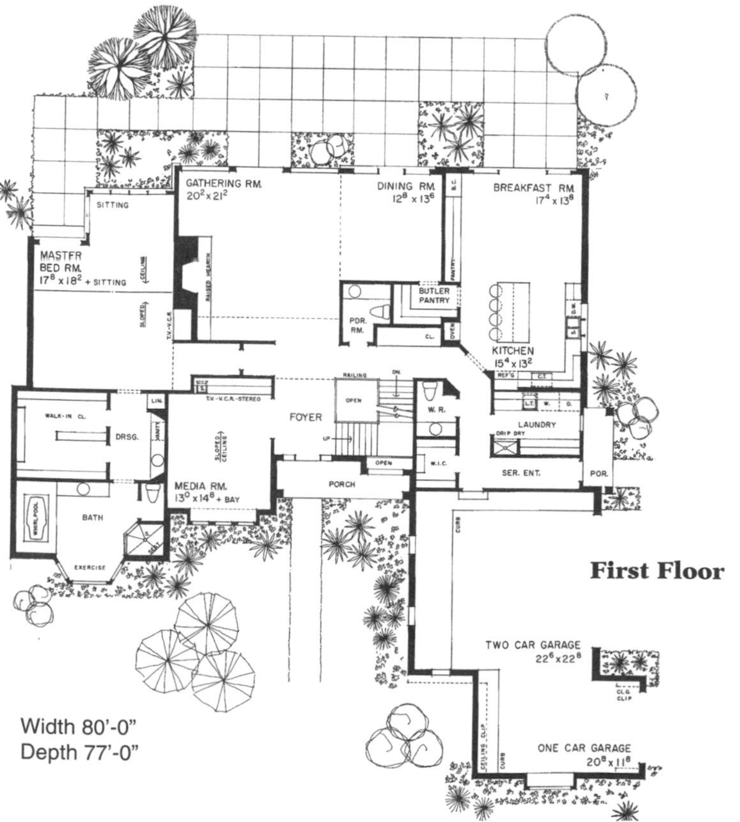


**First Floor**

Width 80'-0"
Depth 77'-0"

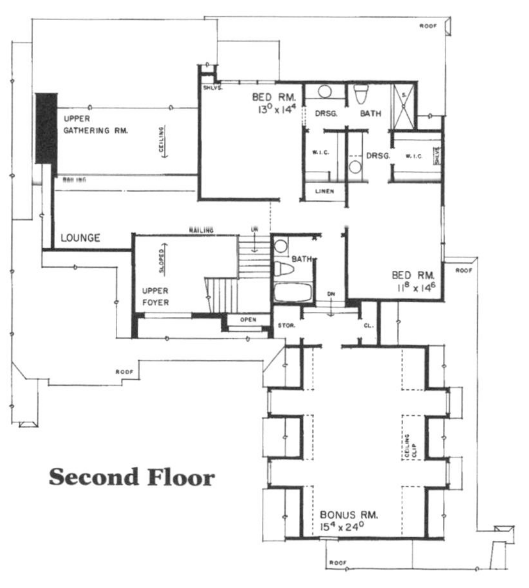


**Second Floor**

| | |
|---|---|
| *First Floor:* | *2,959 sq. ft.* |
| *Second Floor:* | *1,440 sq. ft.* |
| *Total:* | *4,399 sq. ft.* |

*(Foundation Type: Basement)*

## Design CP2599 — Adelaide

This traditional two-story with its projecting one-story wings is delightfully proportioned. The massive field stone arch projects from the front line of the house, providing a sheltered entrance. Inside, there is a large foyer with a curving, open staircase to the second floor. Along with the formal living and informal family rooms, there is the quiet study. A sizeable breakfast nook and separate dining room provide mealtime options. The second floor may function as a three- or four-bedroom sleeping zone.

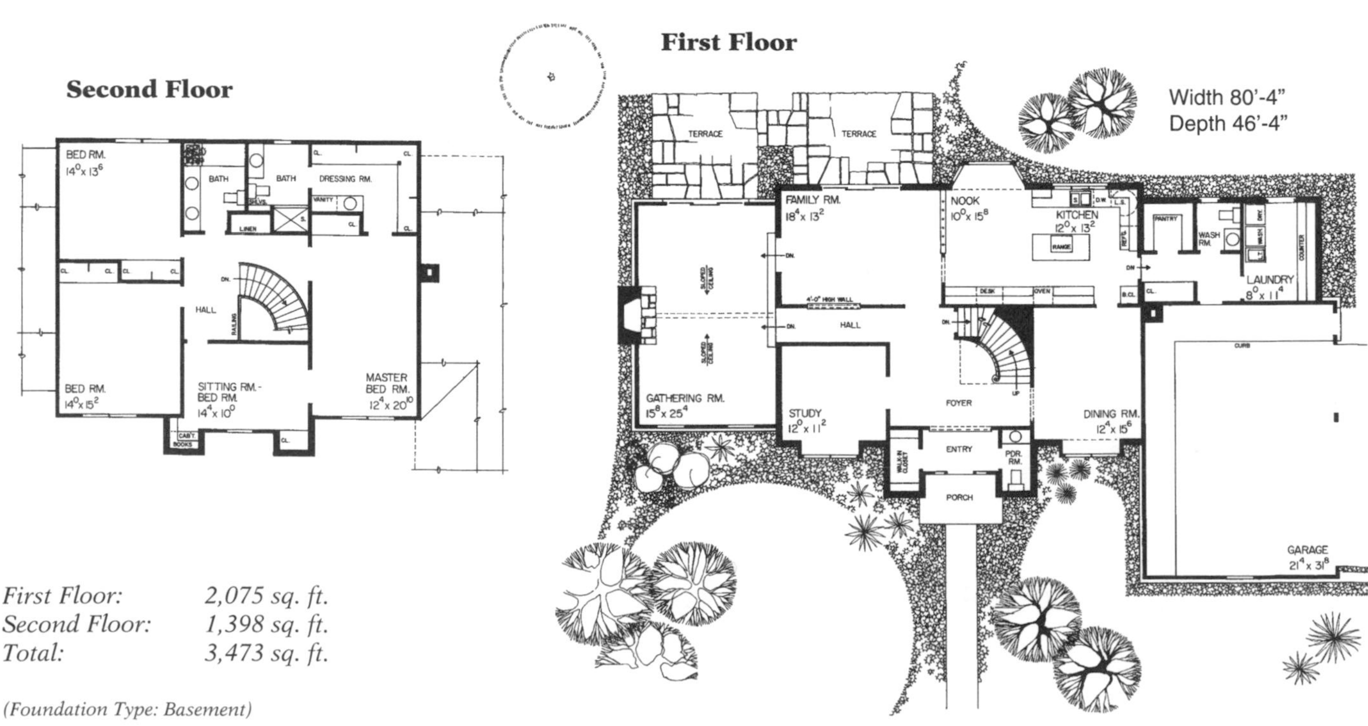


| | |
|---|---|
| *First Floor:* | *2,075 sq. ft.* |
| *Second Floor:* | *1,398 sq. ft.* |
| *Total:* | *3,473 sq. ft.* |

*(Foundation Type: Basement)*

# Dakota

## Design CP3555

Round-top windows add elegance to the interior and exterior of this traditional home. Large gathering areas on the first floor flow together for ease in entertaining. The sunken gathering room stretches from the front of the house to the back, with a terrace at each end and a fireplace in the middle. Another fireplace is found in the conversation area adjoining the kitchen. The formal dining room features a bay window. Sleeping areas upstairs include a master bedroom, three family bedrooms and two full baths.

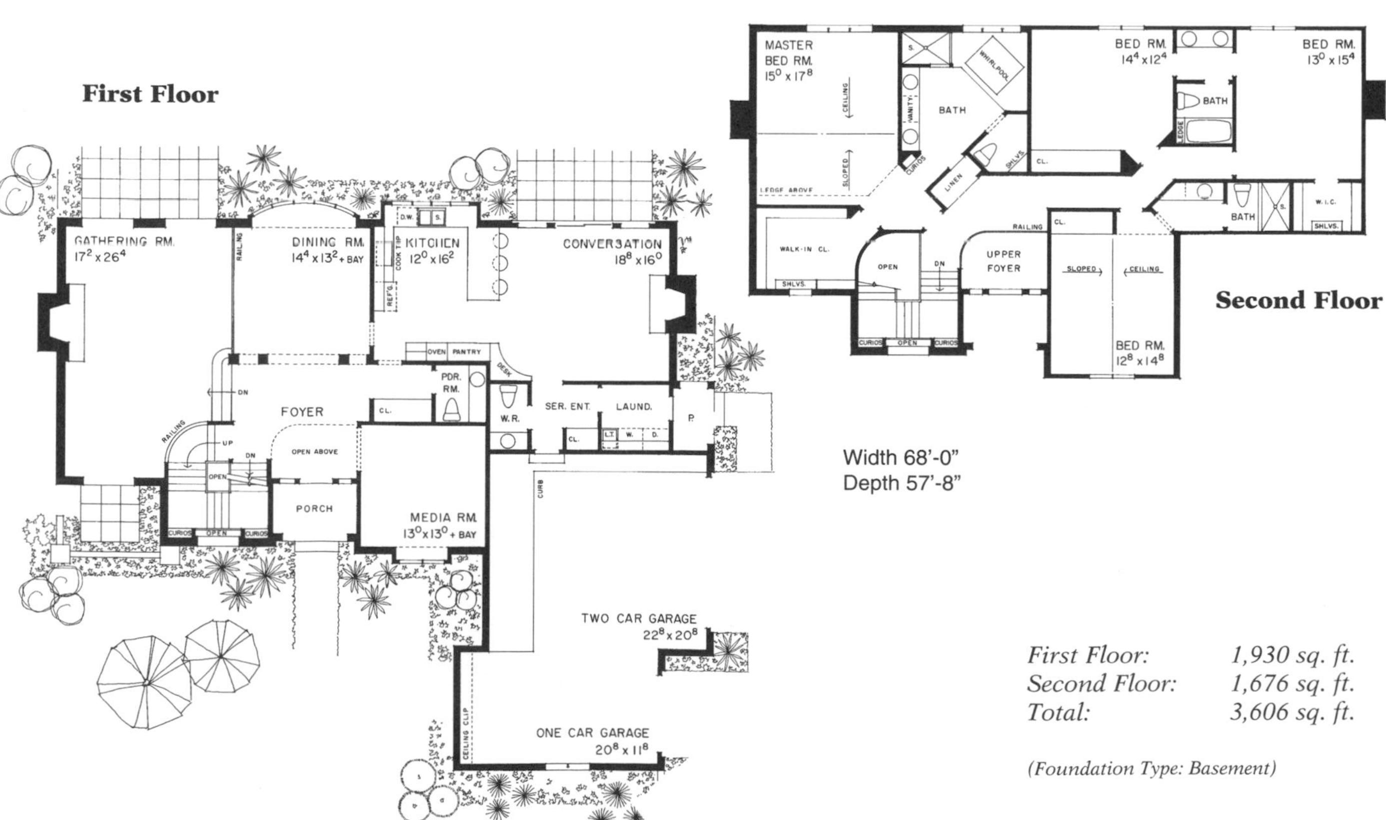


| | |
|---|---|
| *First Floor:* | *1,930 sq. ft.* |
| *Second Floor:* | *1,676 sq. ft.* |
| *Total:* | *3,606 sq. ft.* |

*(Foundation Type: Basement)*

## Design CP4554

# Greendale

The center section of this T-shaped house is made of stone veneer with vertical boards and battens. The entry leads to a living room with a large fireplace. The island kitchen has a barbecue grill built into the back of the family-room fireplace. A recessed buffet is an added convenience in the dining room. The master bedroom has a two-door walk-in closet with separate spaces for His and Hers. Two baths serve the three bedrooms on the second floor.

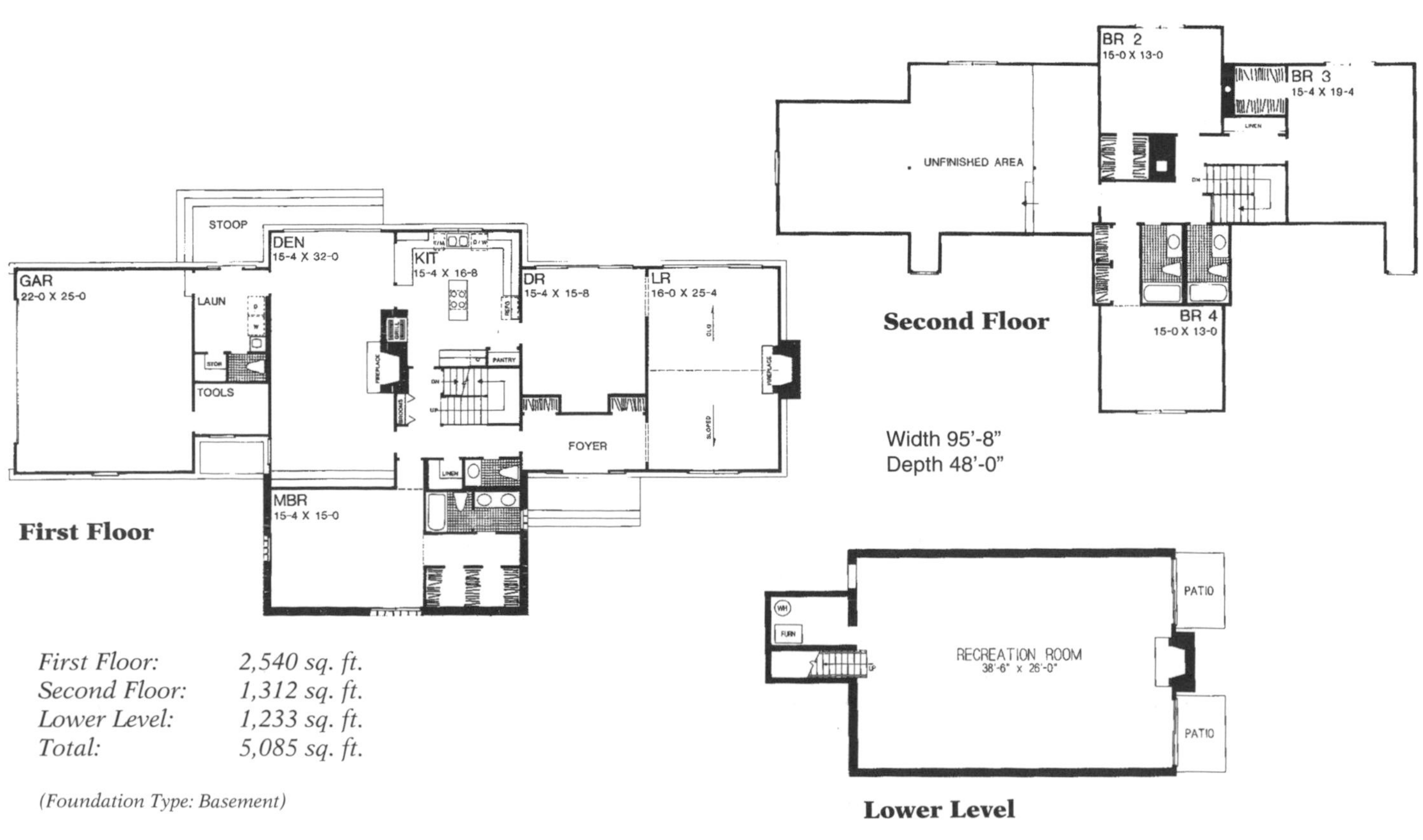


*First Floor:* *2,540 sq. ft.*
*Second Floor:* *1,312 sq. ft.*
*Lower Level:* *1,233 sq. ft.*
*Total:* *5,085 sq. ft.*

*(Foundation Type: Basement)*

## *Executive* **Design CP4403**

The exterior of this multi-level home is distinguished by a combination of stone and vertical board. A sunken Great Room is the highlight of the first floor with its massive fireplace and access to an expansive deck. The kitchen and breakfast room has a work island and large pantry. Nearby, there is a formal dining room with a built-in china cabinet. The master bedroom has a complete bath with walk-in closets. Upstairs, there are two bedrooms and a shared bathroom. The lower level offers a recreation room and a shop area.

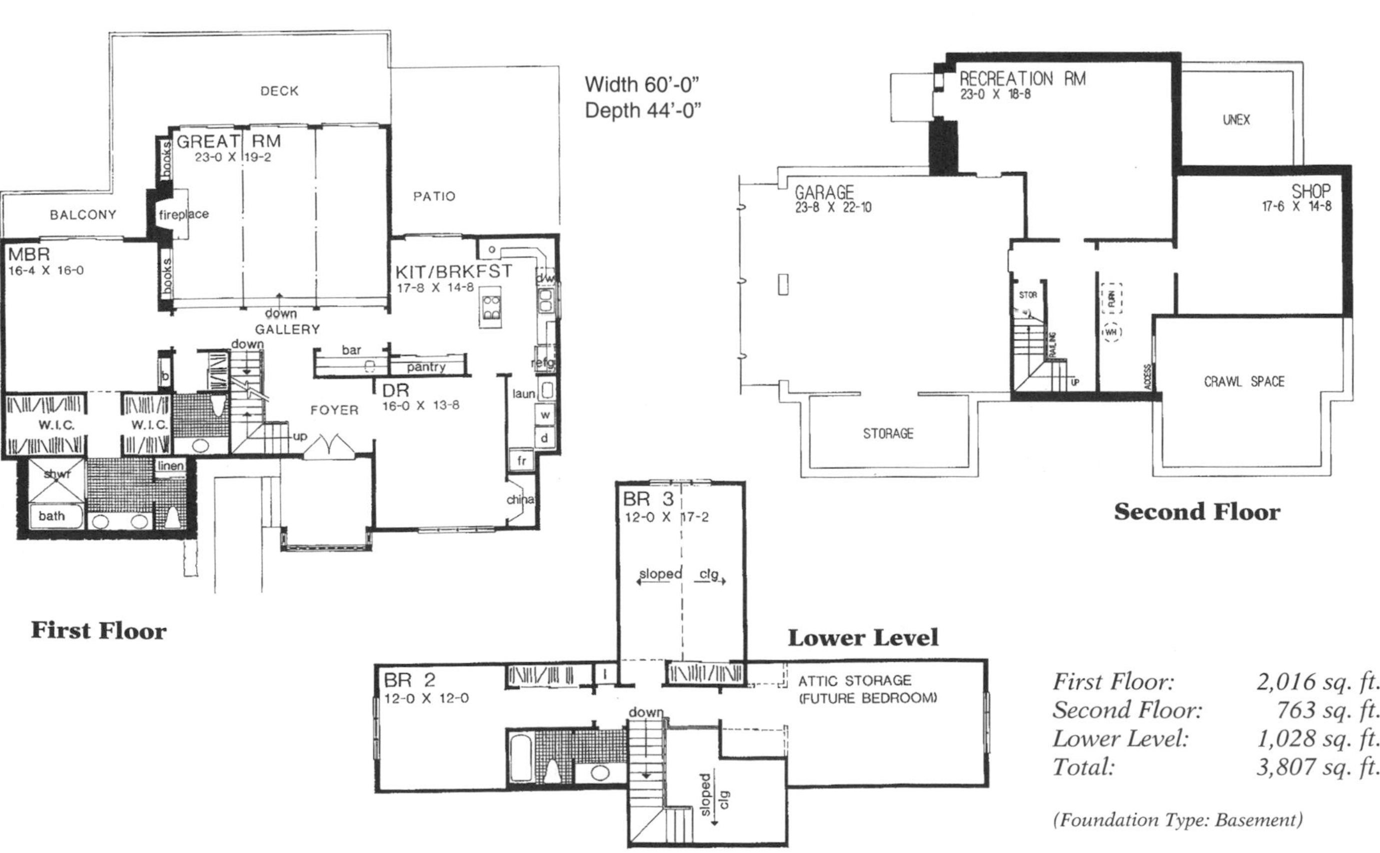


| | |
|---|---|
| *First Floor:* | *2,016 sq. ft.* |
| *Second Floor:* | *763 sq. ft.* |
| *Lower Level:* | *1,028 sq. ft.* |
| *Total:* | *3,807 sq. ft.* |

*(Foundation Type: Basement)*

## Design CP3360 — Crestview

This plan has the best of both worlds—a traditional exterior and a modern multi-level floor plan. The central foyer routes traffic effectively to all areas: the kitchen, gathering room, bedrooms, media room and the stairs leading to the lower level. A complete kitchen includes a breakfast area that adjoins the dining room. The master bedroom suite includes a luxurious bath. On the lower level, there is an activities room with fireplace and convenient kitchen.

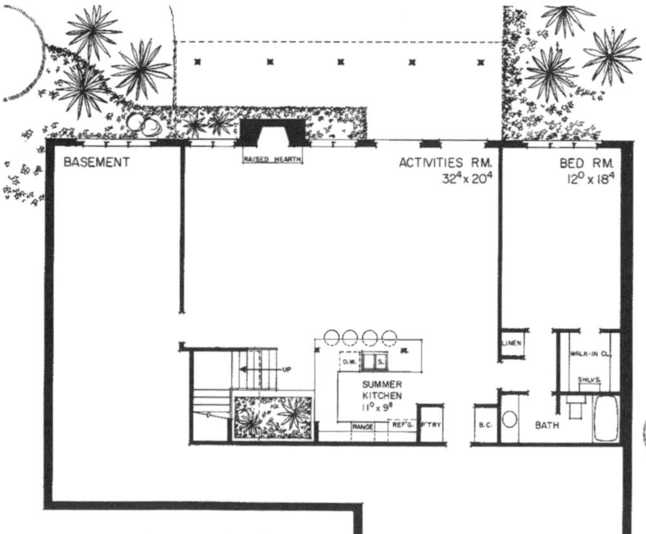

**Second Floor**

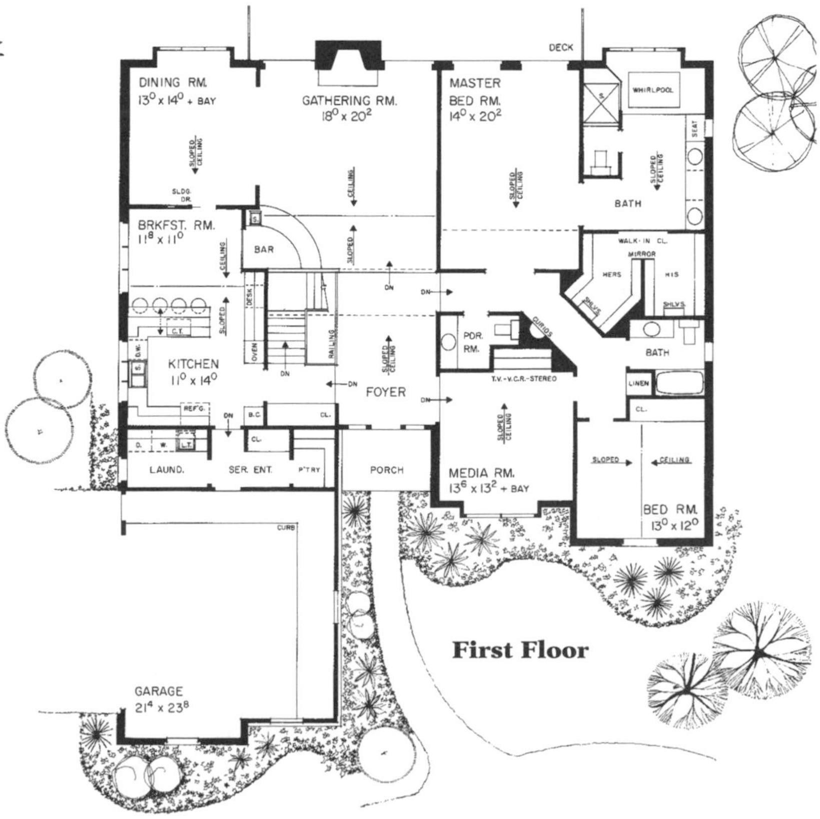

**First Floor**

| | |
|---|---|
| *First Floor:* | *2,673 sq. ft.* |
| *Second Floor:* | *1,389 sq. ft.* |
| *Total:* | *4,062 sq. ft.* |

Width 60'-0"
Depth 70'-0"

*(Foundation Type: Basement)*

# Simpson

## Design CP3370

The combination of stone and brick creates an impressive facade on this traditional two-story. The symmetrically designed interior will provide efficient traffic patterns. Note the formal living and dining areas to the right and huge family room to the rear. The U-shaped kitchen has an attached breakfast room and built-ins. There are four bedrooms on the second floor. The master features a walk-in closet, double vanity and whirlpool tub.

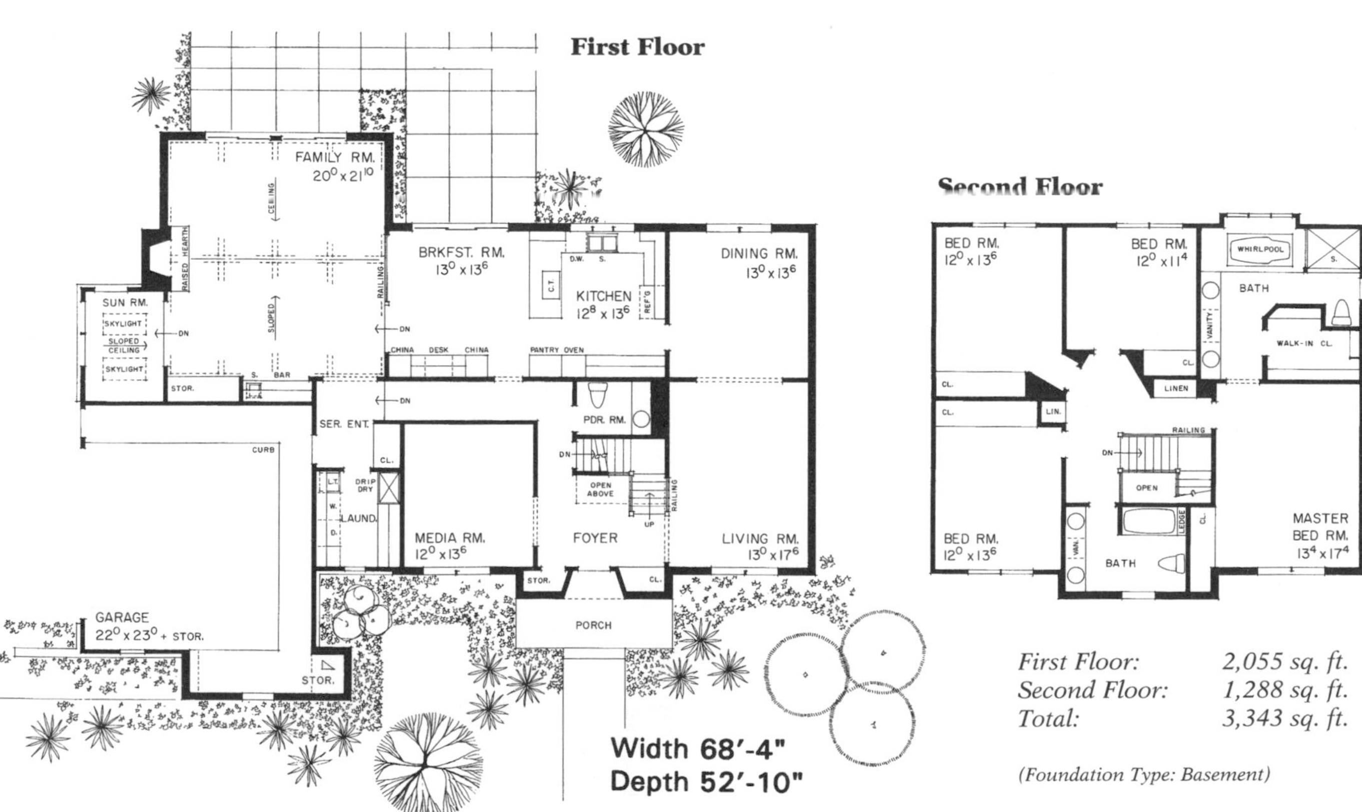


| | |
|---|---|
| *First Floor:* | *2,055 sq. ft.* |
| *Second Floor:* | *1,288 sq. ft.* |
| *Total:* | *3,343 sq. ft.* |

*(Foundation Type: Basement)*

## *Design CP4503*

# *Marietta*

This home was designed for the family that entertains. Both the dining and living rooms, which flank the entry, can handle large groups of people. The living room can be further expanded by opening the double doors to the den. The kitchen includes a breakfast room that acesses the patio. The master bath has both a stall shower and a separate tub. Two bedrooms on the second floor are joined by private baths. An optional recreation room in the basement serves informal entertaining.

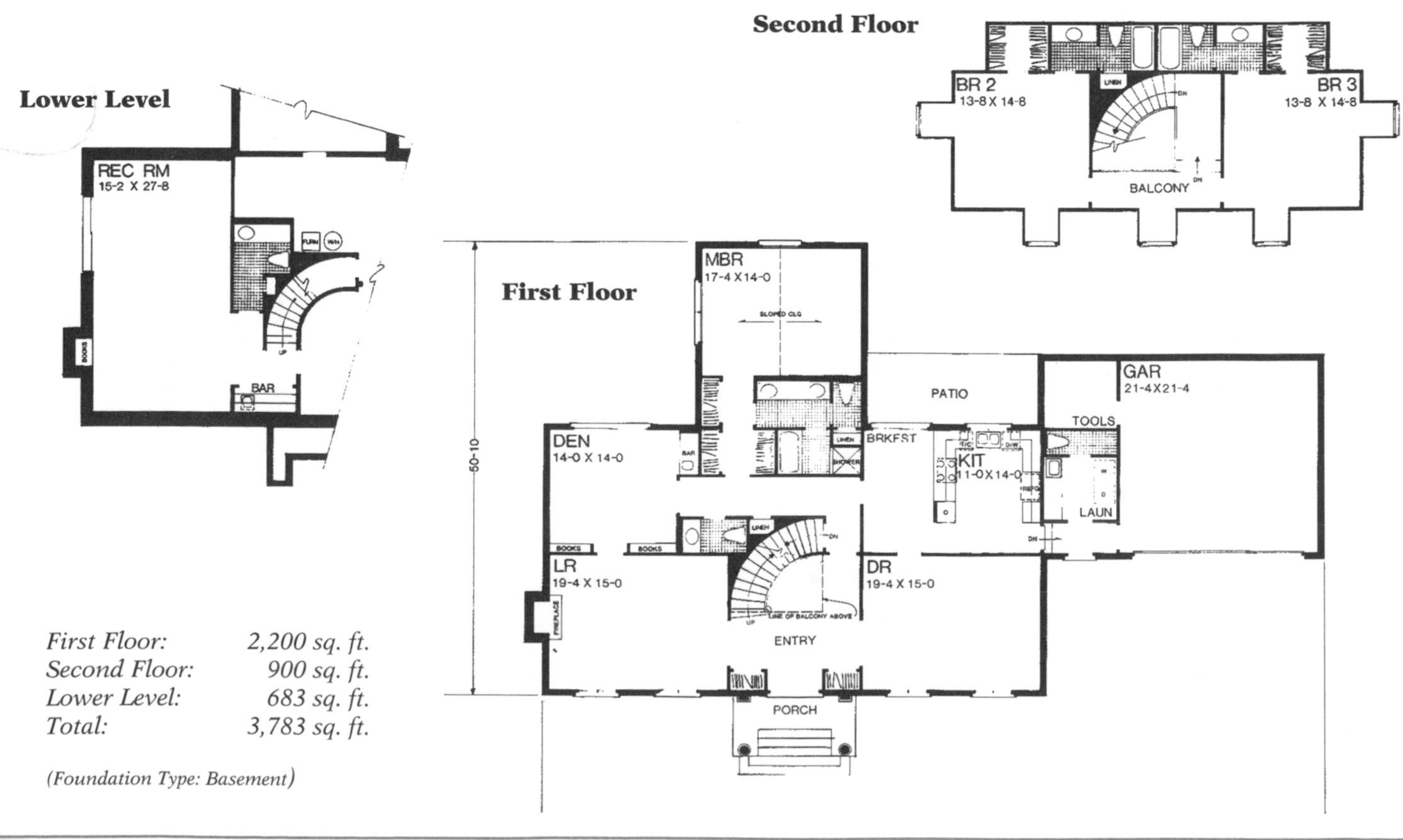


| | |
|---|---|
| *First Floor:* | *2,200 sq. ft.* |
| *Second Floor:* | *900 sq. ft.* |
| *Lower Level:* | *683 sq. ft.* |
| *Total:* | *3,783 sq. ft.* |

*(Foundation Type: Basement)*

# Southerland

## Design CP4405

A complicated roofline marks the exterior of this distinguished two-story home. The entrance ushers guests to the immediate living room area with massive fireplace. The island kitchen features a greenhouse and adjoins the dining room. Both the dining area and the master bedroom have access to private decks. The master bath includes a whirlpool bath and spacious walk-in closet. Upstairs, there are two bedrooms with private baths. A recreation room and a shop are found on the lower level.

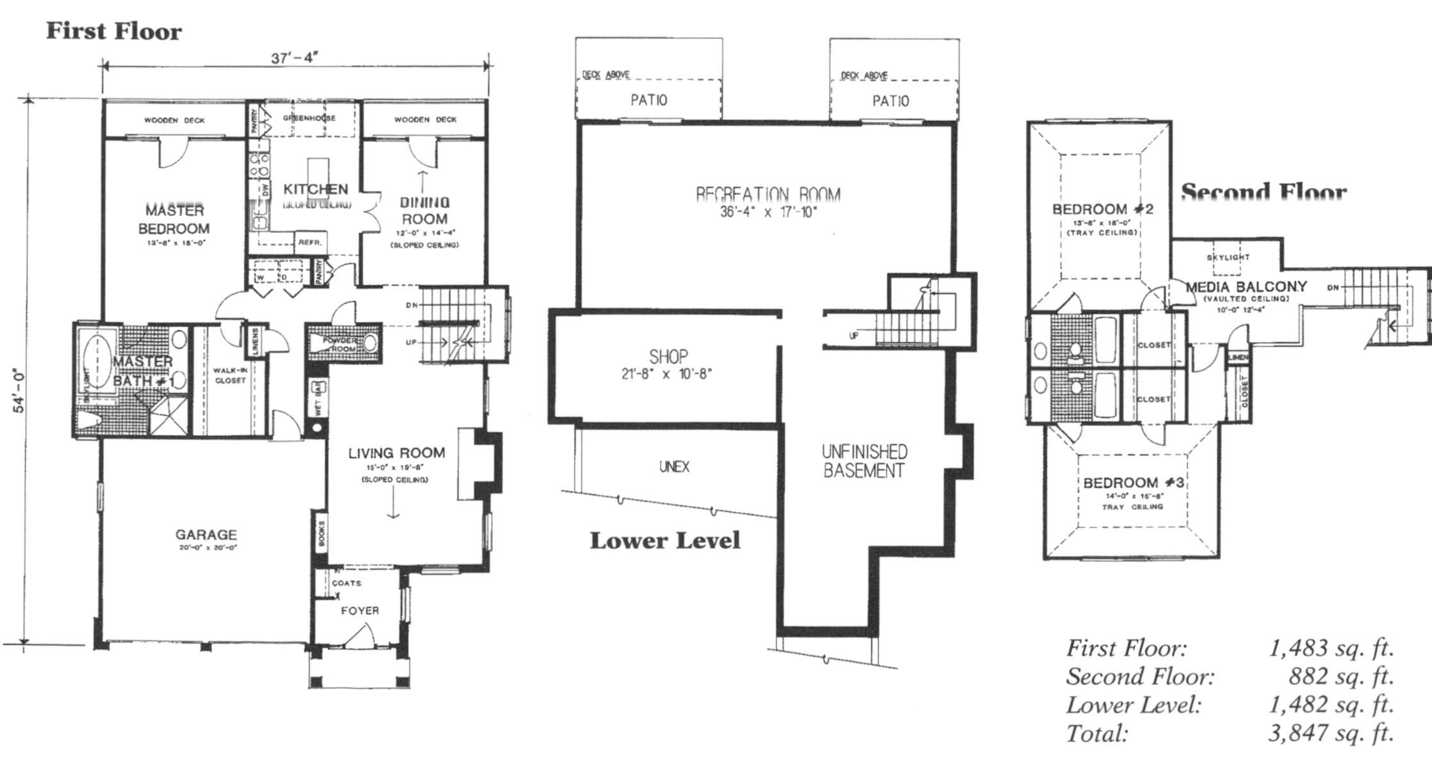


| | |
|---|---|
| *First Floor:* | *1,483 sq. ft.* |
| *Second Floor:* | *882 sq. ft.* |
| *Lower Level:* | *1,482 sq. ft.* |
| *Total:* | *3,847 sq. ft.* |

*(Foundation Type: Basement)*

## Design CP4404

# Sussex

This home is enhanced by an expansive rear and side deck. The large central dining room has access to the deck and leads to the sunken living room with sloped ceiling, bay window and fireplace. The island kitchen includes a breakfast nook. Upstairs, the master bedroom sports a complete bath. Two family bedrooms and a bathroom complete the second floor. The family and recreation rooms are found on the lower level.

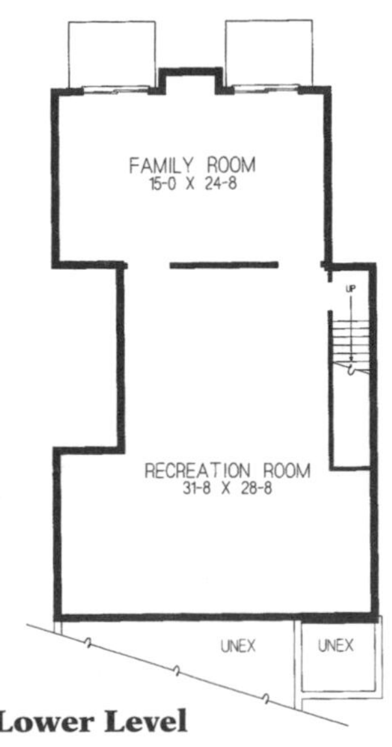


**Lower Level**

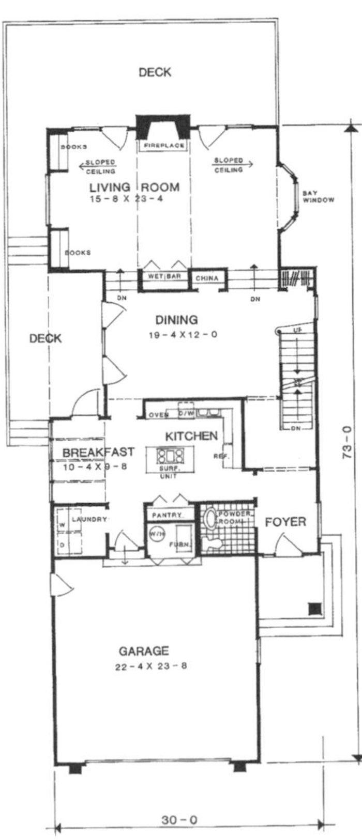


**First Floor**

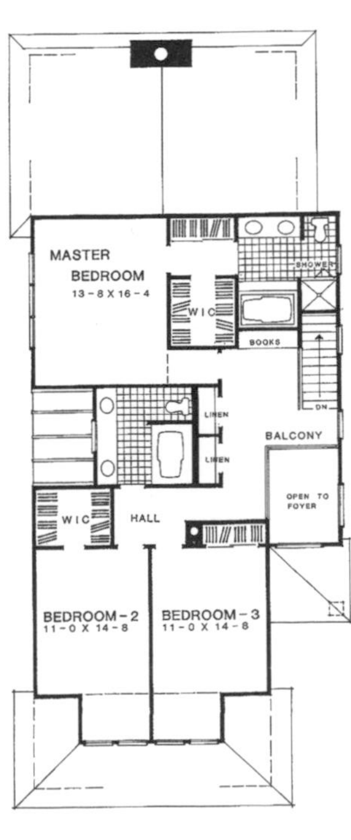


**Second Floor**

| | |
|---|---|
| *First Floor:* | *1,336 sq. ft.* |
| *Second Floor:* | *1,210 sq. ft.* |
| *Lower Level:* | *1,321 sq. ft.* |
| *Total:* | *3,867 sq. ft.* |

*(Foundation Type: Basement)*

# Chantilly

**Design CP4513**

Arched window heads and dormers, a steeply pitched roof and a stucco exterior give this design a French country flavor. Identically sized formal living room and dining rooms flank the center entry. The den includes a wet bar and opens to the living room. The kitchen is adjoined by a breakfast room. The master suite has a sloping ceiling, a separate shower and tub, and a double vanity. Each of two large second-floor bedrooms has a private bath and a large walk-in closet.

**Second Floor**

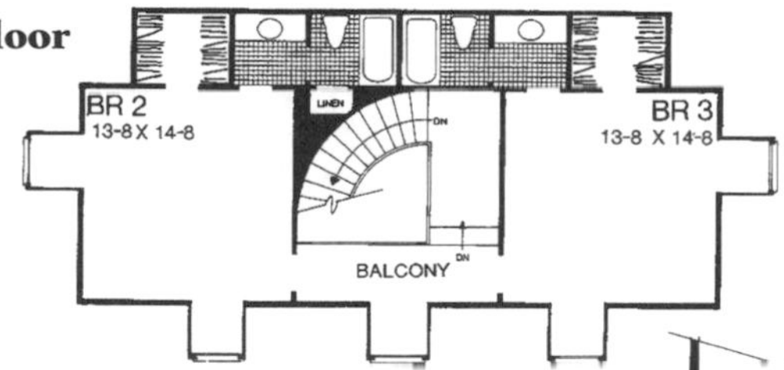

**First Floor**

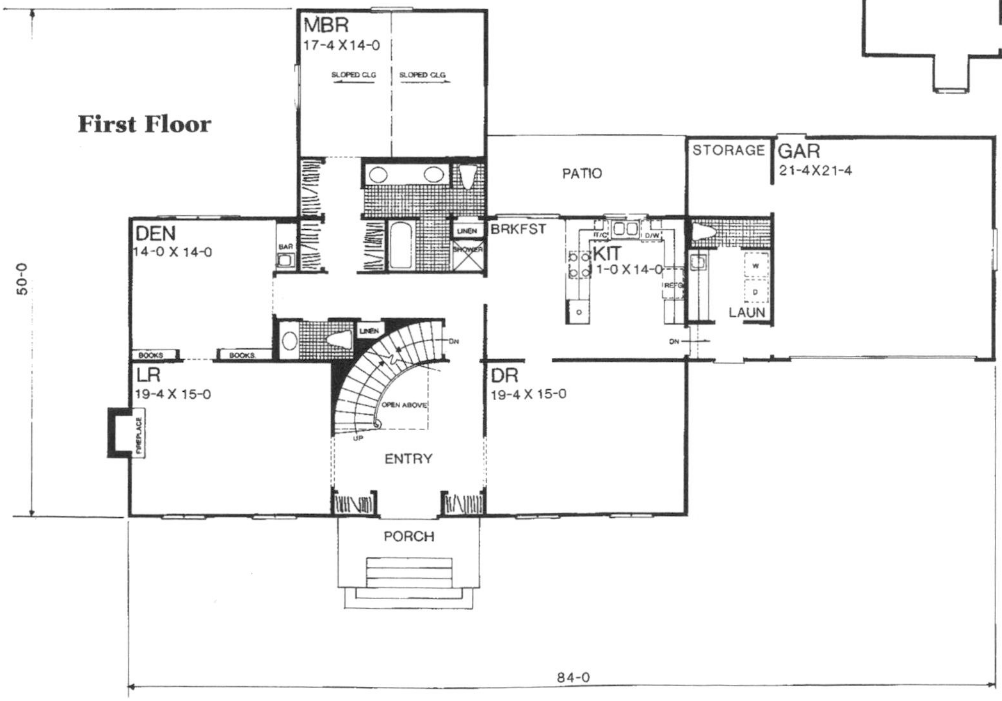

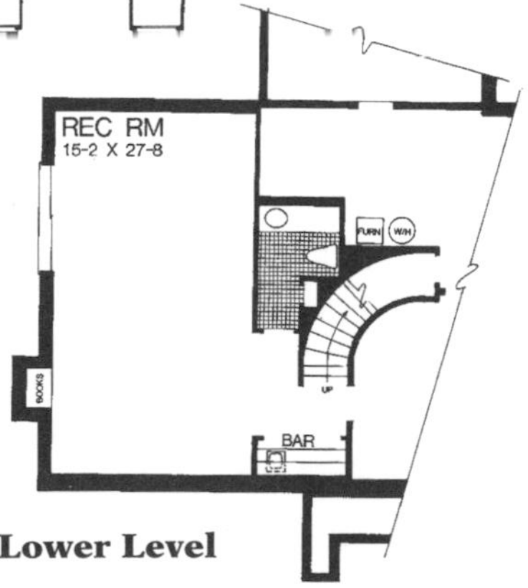

**Lower Level**

| | |
|---|---|
| *First Floor:* | *2,112 sq. ft.* |
| *Second Floor:* | *932 sq. ft.* |
| *Lower Level:* | *658 sq. ft.* |
| *Total:* | *3,702 sq. ft.* |

*(Foundation Type: Basement)*

**Design CP1993**

# Oracle

The elegance of pleasing proportion and detailing has seldom been better exemplified than by this classic French country manor adaptation. Approaching the house across the drive court, the majesty of this multi-roofed structure is breathtaking. The maid's suite is an outstanding feature. It is located above the garage and is easily reached by use of the covered porch connecting the laundry room to the garage. The large master suite with window seats occupies its own level.

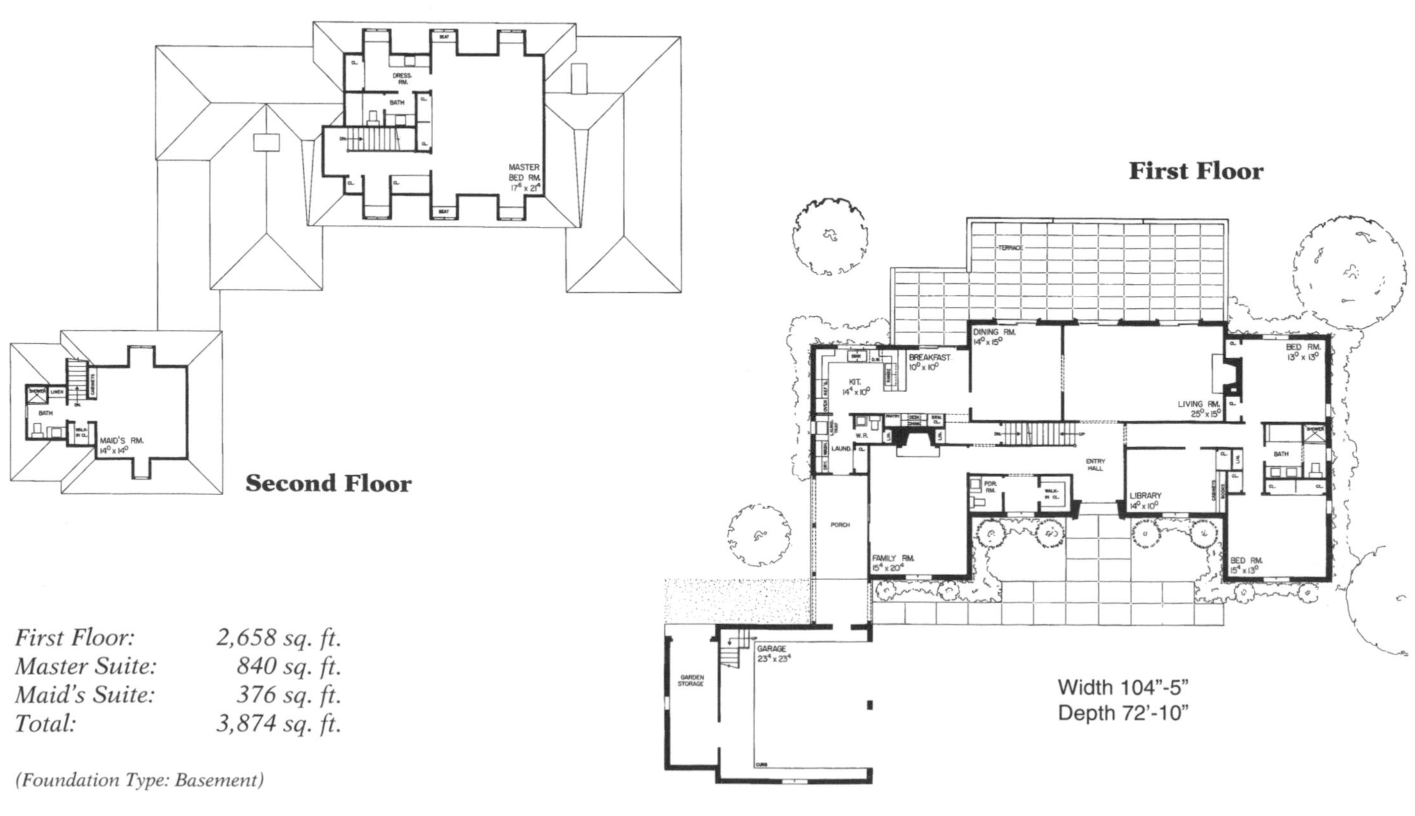


| | |
|---|---|
| *First Floor:* | *2,658 sq. ft.* |
| *Master Suite:* | *840 sq. ft.* |
| *Maid's Suite:* | *376 sq. ft.* |
| *Total:* | *3,874 sq. ft.* |

*(Foundation Type: Basement)*

# *Wilcox*

**Design CP2543**

This best-selling French adaptation is highlighted by effective window treatment, delicate cornice detailing, appealing brick quoins and excellent proportion. Inside are an expansive gathering room, formal living and dining rooms, a quiet study, gourmet kitchen with breakfast room and four upstairs bedrooms, including a master suite with a fireplace and plenty of closet space. A rear terrace allows for outdoor entertaining.

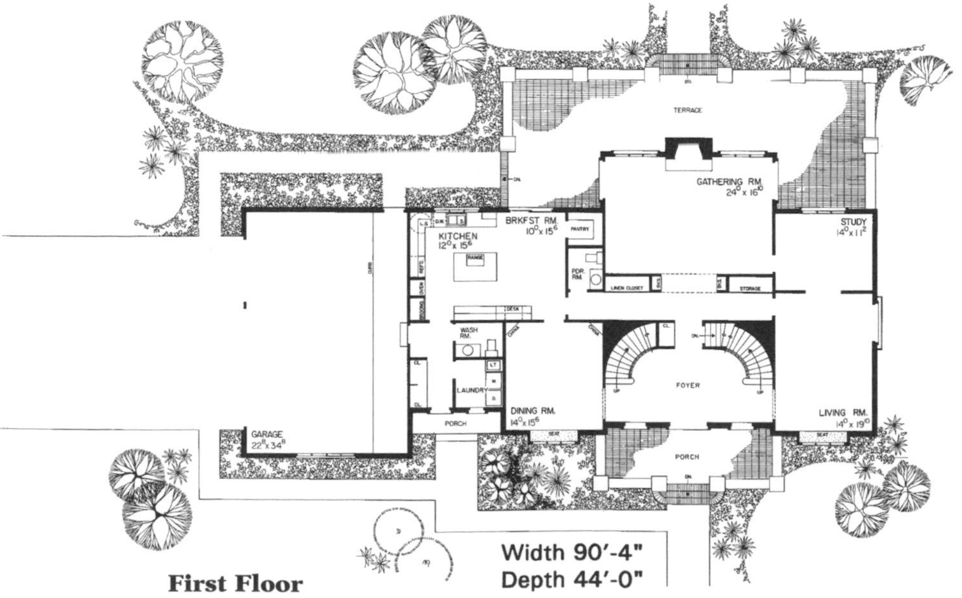


**First Floor**

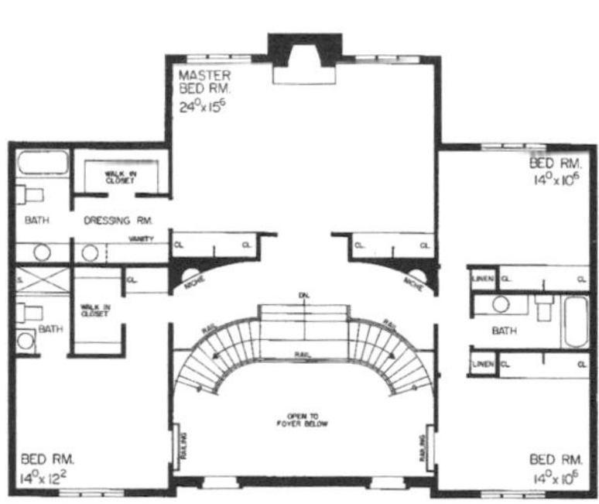


**Second Floor**

*First Floor:* *2,345 sq. ft.*
*Second Floor:* *1,687 sq. ft.*
*Total:* *4,032 sq. ft.*

*(Foundation Type: Basement)*

## Design CP9163

# Spruce

The steeply pitched roof, massive brick chimney and copper-roofed bay window are features often associated with traditional homes of the 1920s. The front door opens into an impressive area combining dining and living rooms along with gallery and grand curved staircase. The kitchen with island cooktop overlooks the breakfast area and family room. The master bedroom boasts His and Hers closet space as well as an elegant tub. Upstairs are Bedrooms 2, 3 and 4 and a library loft with built-in bookcase.

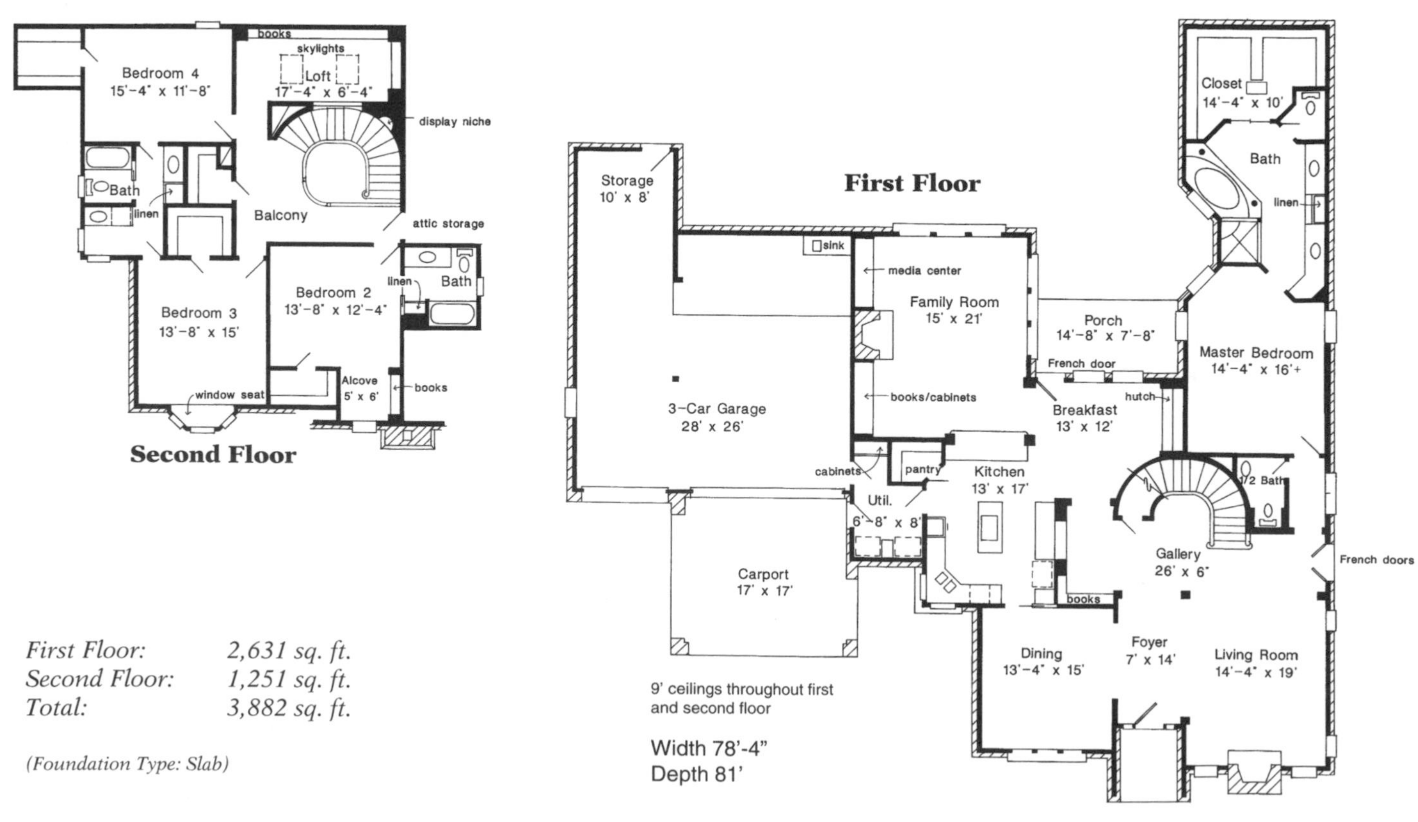


*First Floor:* *2,631 sq. ft.*
*Second Floor:* *1,251 sq. ft.*
*Total:* *3,882 sq. ft.*

*(Foundation Type: Slab)*

# Rancho Vista **Design CP3380**

Reminiscent of a Mediterranean villa, this grand manor is a showstopper on the outside and a comfortable residence on the inside. An elegant receiving hall boasts a double staircase and is flanked by the formal dining room and the library. A huge gathering room is found to the back. The master bedroom is found on the first floor for privacy. Upstairs are four additional bedrooms and two full baths.

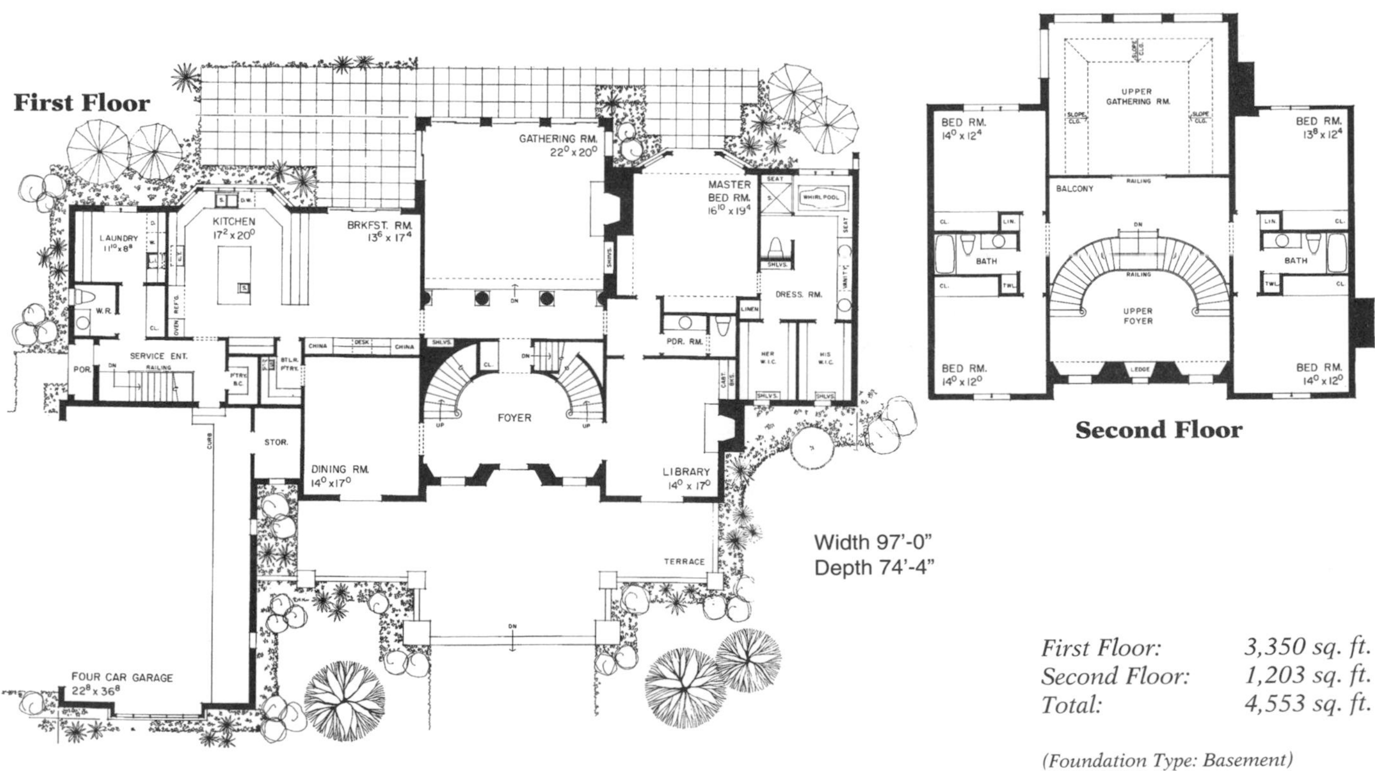


| | |
|---|---|
| *First Floor:* | *3,350 sq. ft.* |
| *Second Floor:* | *1,203 sq. ft.* |
| *Total:* | *4,553 sq. ft.* |

*(Foundation Type: Basement)*

## Design CP2922

# Hermosilla

Loaded with custom features, this plan seems to have everything imaginable. There's an enormous sunken gathering room and cozy study with a fireplace. The country-style kitchen contains an efficient work area, as well as space for relaxing in the morning and sitting rooms. The master bedroom features an alcove with a raised-hearth fireplace and built-in seats. The master bath includes His and Hers closets and a grand whirlpool bath.

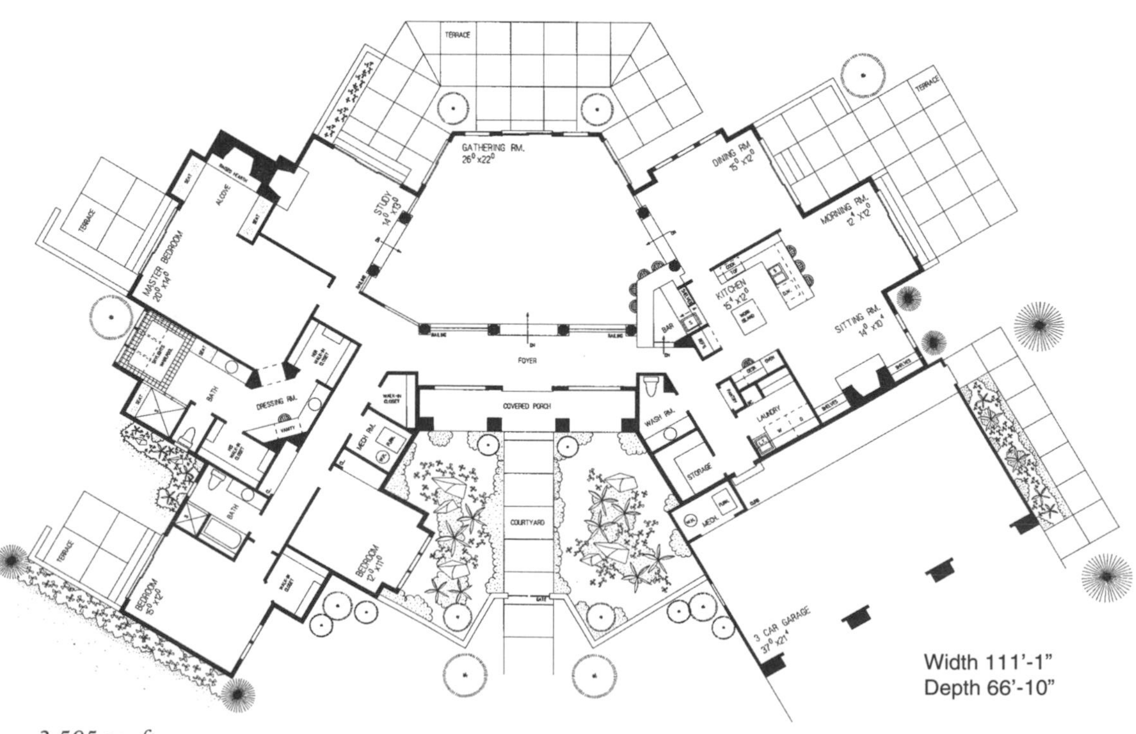


*Total:* *3,505 sq. ft.*

*(Foundation Type: Slab)*

# Almond

**Design CP3448**

Spacious rooms are the rule in this home. A sunken living room stretches for a full 25 feet. The family room with fireplace is impressive in size, and even the kitchen abounds in space, with a separate eating area (with coffered ceiling), a snack bar, an island cooktop and a walk-in pantry. The first-floor master suite contains His and Hers walk-in closets, a three-way fireplace, whirlpool and double-bowl vanity. Three bedrooms upstairs share a compartmented bath.

**First Floor**

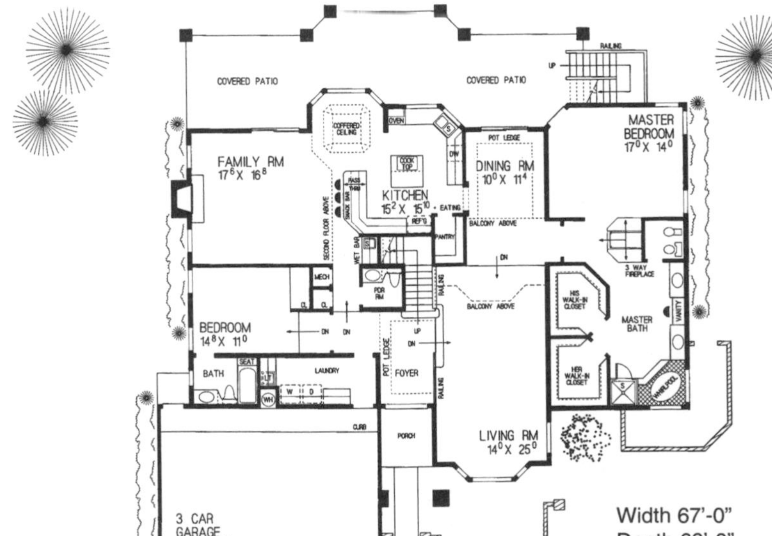


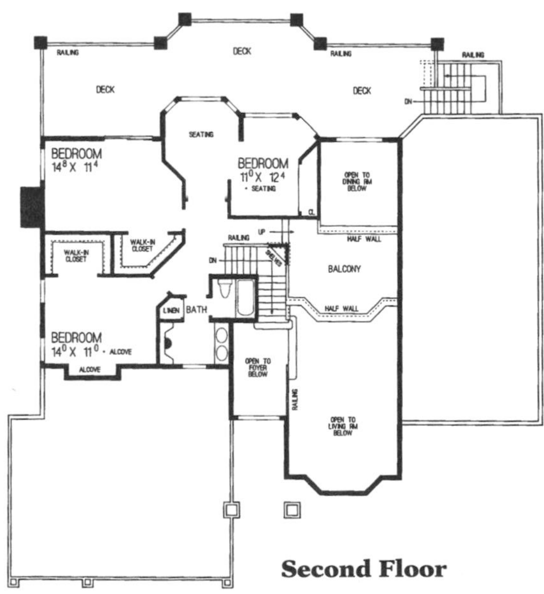


**Second Floor**

| | |
|---|---|
| *First Floor:* | *2,495 sq. ft.* |
| *Second Floor:* | *1,080 sq. ft.* |
| *Total:* | *3,575 sq. ft.* |

*(Foundation Type: Slab)*

## Design CP2850

# Felicidad

You'd be hard pressed to find a better looking and better planned Spanish-style design. The main level offers a family room with raised-hearth fireplace and sloped ceiling, rear terrace, and a small porch. Down below is just the right spot for kids and teens: a 300-square-foot activity room, with a fireplace and access to a covered terrace out back. Here are a study and an extra bedroom. The upper level features three bedrooms, including a master suite with a dressing room, walk-in closet, and private balcony.

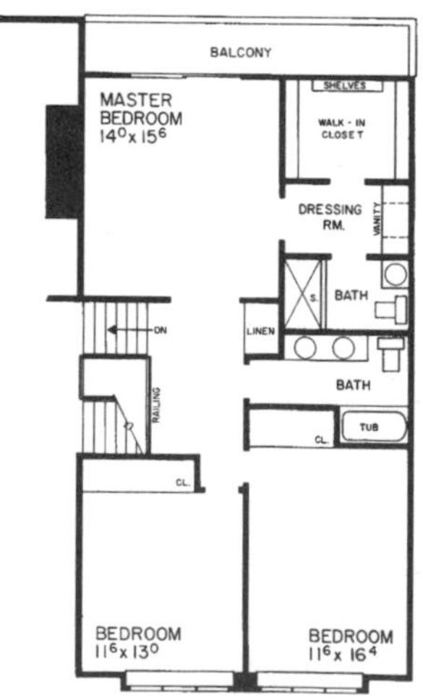


**Upper Level**

| | |
|---|---|
| *Main Level:* | *1,530 sq. ft.* |
| *Upper Level:* | *984 sq. ft.* |
| *Lower Level:* | *951 sq. ft.* |
| *Total:* | *3,465 sq. ft.* |

*(Foundation Type: Basement)*

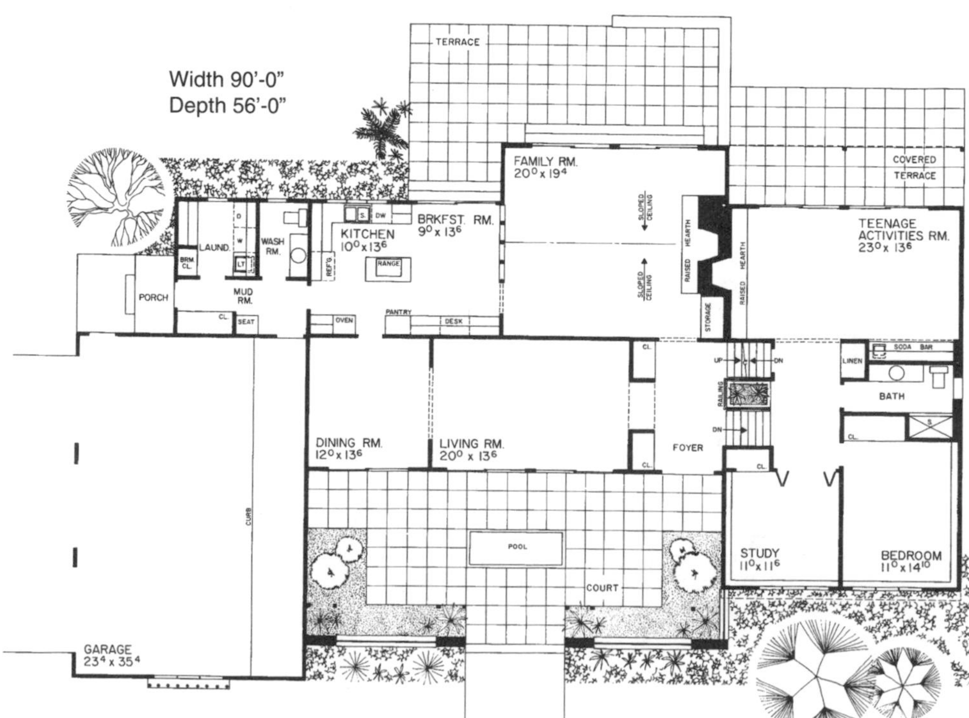


**Main Level**

# Rancho Benito

The street view of this Spanish design shows a beautifully fashioned one-story home, but this home has been designed to be built into a hill so the lower level can be opened to the sun. By so doing, the total livability is almost doubled. Three fireplaces add charm to the living areas on both levels. The lower level offers a helpful summer kitchen, a games room, a lounge with raised-hearth fireplace and a guest room with a full bath.

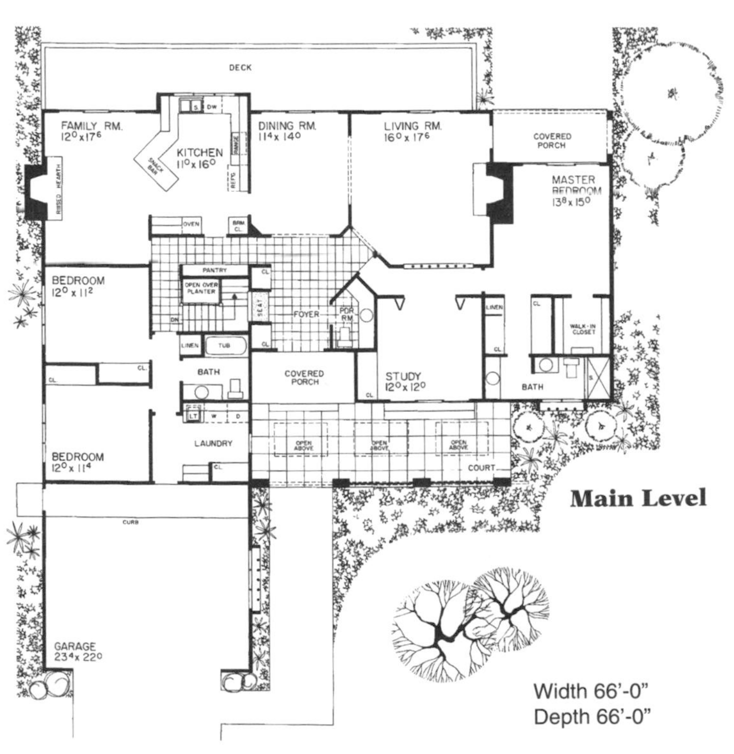


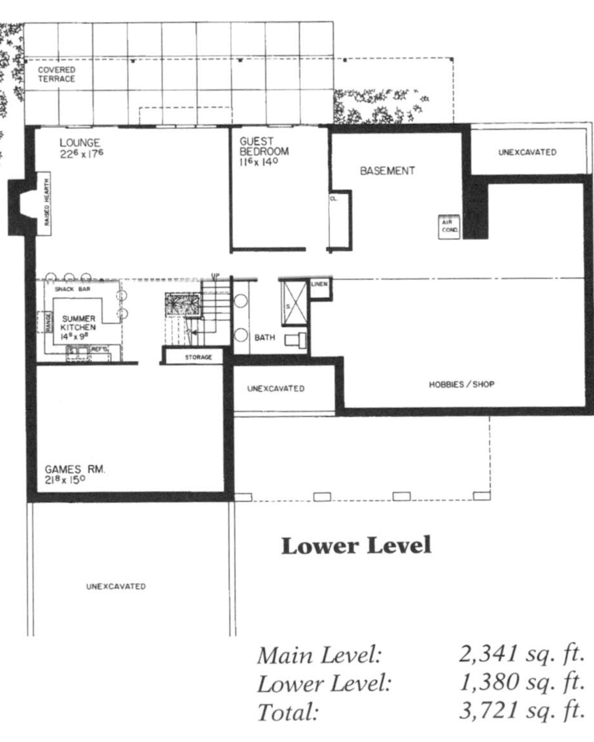


*(Foundation Type: Slab)*

## Design CP9455

# Conner

Besides all the great living on the main level of this house, there is additional space under the right side, available for later development. It will complement first-floor living areas: formal living and dining rooms, private den, family room and breakfast nook. The kitchen has an island work area and overlooks the wooden deck reached from the nook. Fireplaces warm both the family room and the living room. A handy three-car garage allows space for all family vehicles.

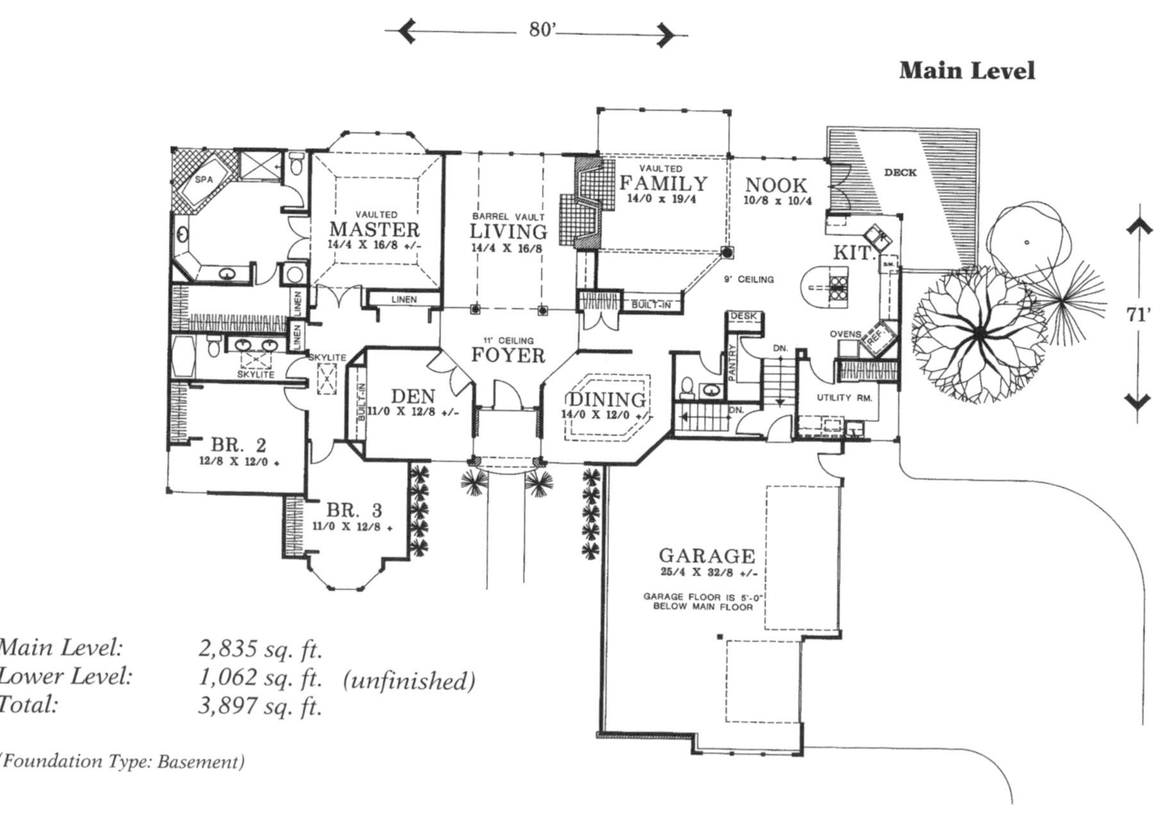


| | | |
|---|---|---|
| *Main Level:* | *2,835 sq. ft.* | |
| *Lower Level:* | *1,062 sq. ft.* | *(unfinished)* |
| *Total:* | *3,897 sq. ft.* | |

*(Foundation Type: Basement)*

# Emerald

**Design CP9179**

This grand brick home offers a lovely European facade for outside appeal with a luxurious floor plan inside to meet every lifestyle need. To the right of the entry foyer is a formal dining room connecting to the kitchen. To the left is the living room with fireplace and built-ins and a columned gallery leading to the study, library and master suite. A glass-enclosed breakfast room complements the island kitchen. The master suite features a bright sitting room, huge walk-in closet and well-appointed bath.

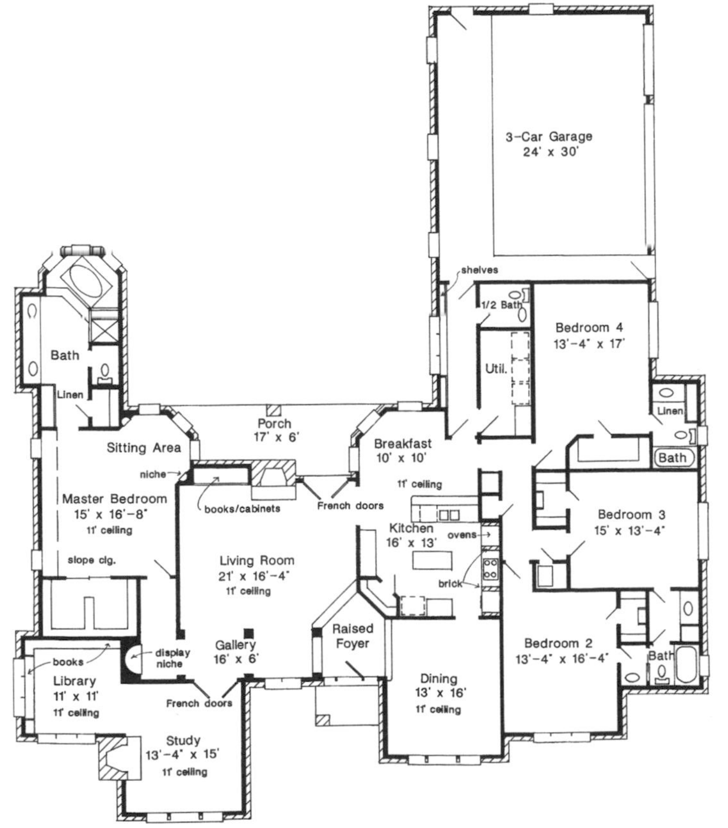


Width 79'-0"
Depth 66'-4"

*Total:* *3,538 sq. ft.*

*(Foundation Type: Slab)*

## Design CP3471 **Rancho Encanto**

Western farmhouse living is captured in this handsome design. The entrance leads into a cozy parlor where half walls provide a view of the dining room with a built-in china alcove, service counter and fireplace. The country kitchen overlooks the gathering room with its full wall of glass. One of the first-floor bedrooms may be used as a study, the other as a guest room. Two bedrooms and attic storage make up the second floor. Note the separate garage and guest house which make this such a winning design.

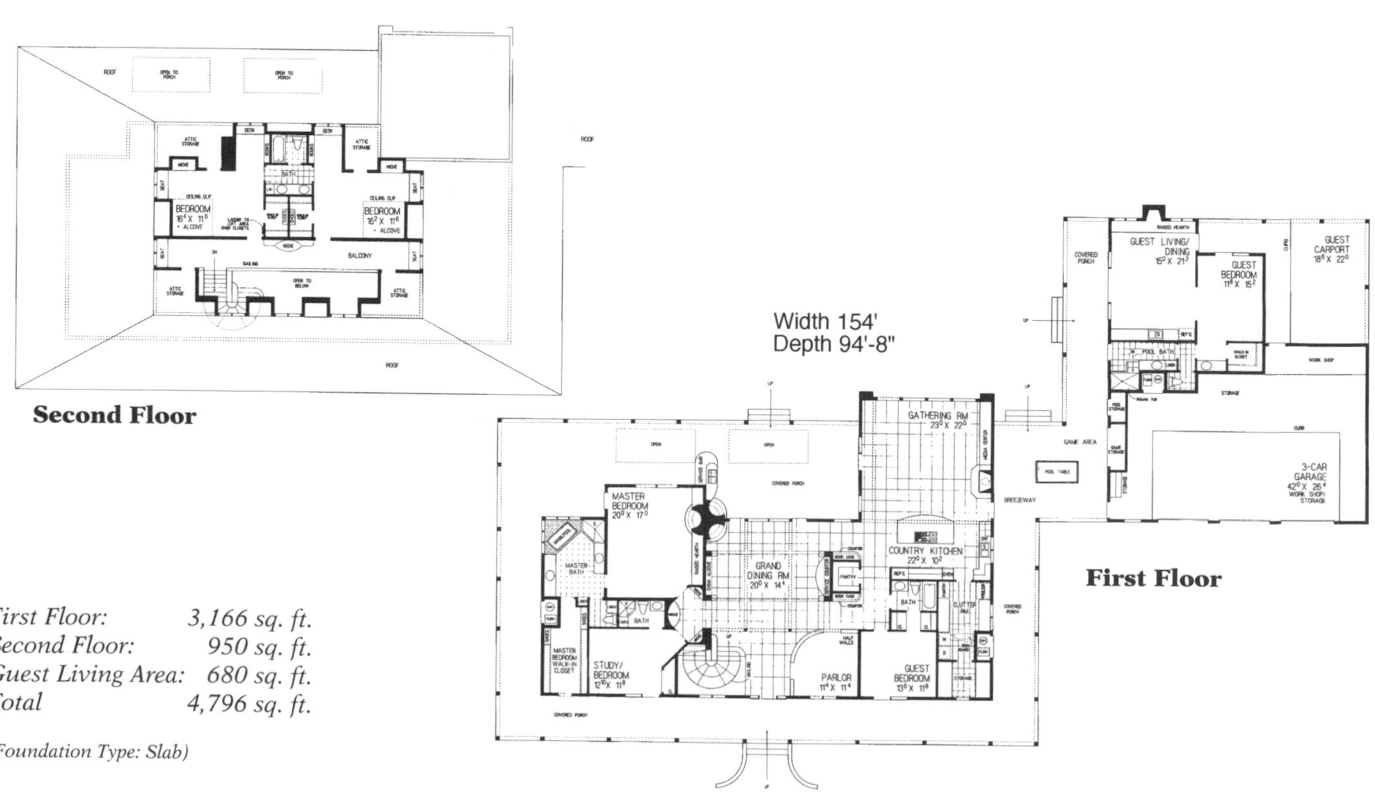


**Second Floor**

**First Floor**

| | |
|---|---|
| *First Floor:* | *3,166 sq. ft.* |
| *Second Floor:* | *950 sq. ft.* |
| *Guest Living Area:* | *680 sq. ft.* |
| *Total* | *4,796 sq. ft.* |

*(Foundation Type: Slab)*

# Buena Vista

## Design CP8932

This design showcases a front porch and a dual-pitched hipped roof—both of which are typical features of the French Colonial style. A central foyer leads to a dining room and a living room with a two-way fireplace. The kitchen provides easy access to the dining room, family room and breakfast area. The sunroom encompasses French doors and a spiral staircase leading up to the loft. Three bedrooms define the upstairs. The master bedroom, with a sitting area, remains on the first floor for privacy.

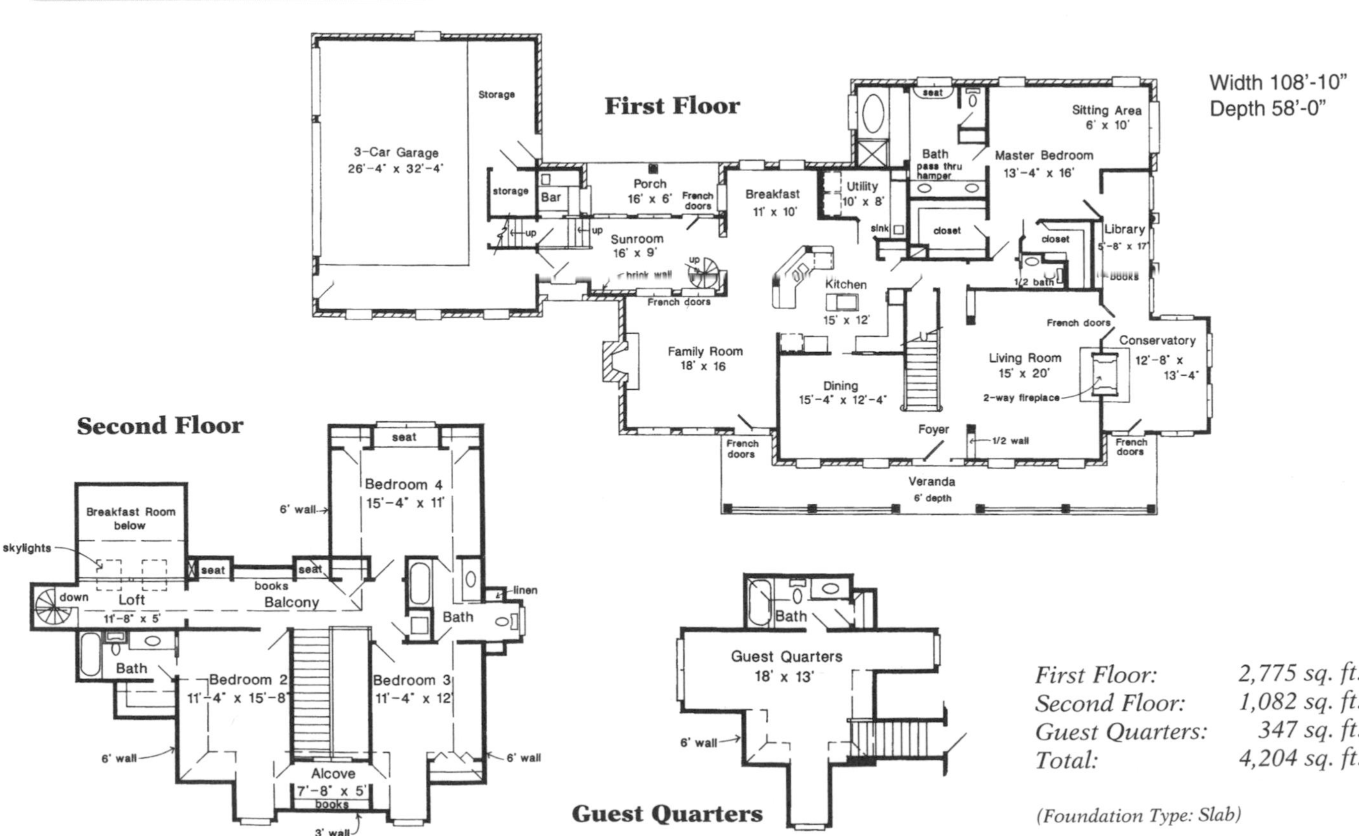


| | |
|---|---|
| *First Floor:* | *2,775 sq. ft.* |
| *Second Floor:* | *1,082 sq. ft.* |
| *Guest Quarters:* | *347 sq. ft.* |
| *Total:* | *4,204 sq. ft.* |

*(Foundation Type: Slab)*

## Design CP9463

# Shadetree

Luxury abounds in this wonderfully appointed design. From the double entry doors to the three-car garage, this plan holds a wealth of amenities. A formal living room with coffered ceiling and fireplace is complemented by a formal dining room with bay window. Just beyond is the island kitchen with bay-windowed nook. A family room with another fireplace opens off the kitchen. An angled staircase leads to the four-bedroom second floor. The master suite occupies the entire left side of this floor.

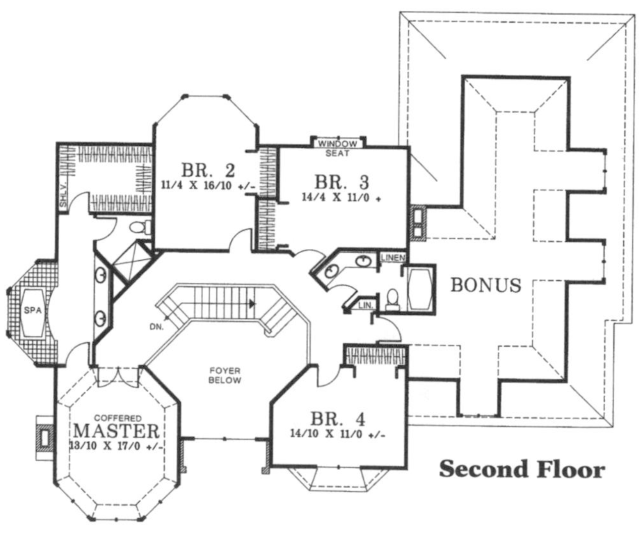


**Second Floor**

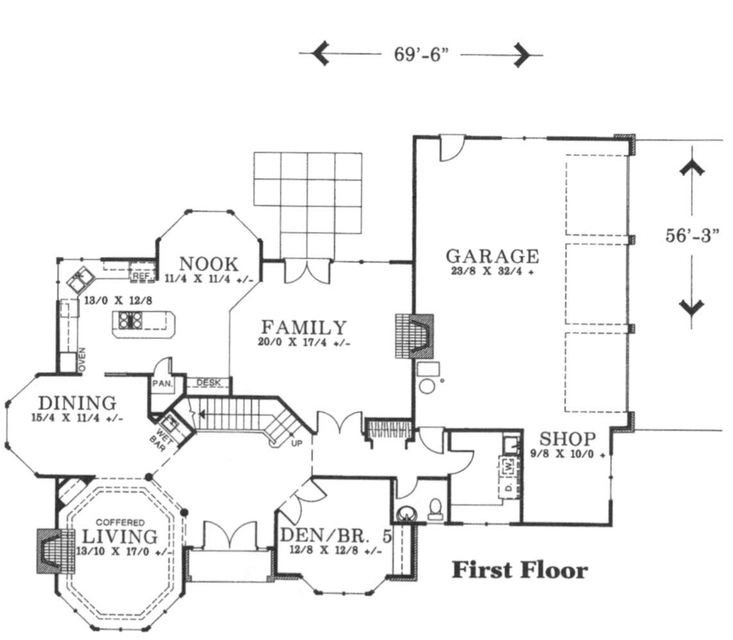


**First Floor**

| | |
|---|---|
| *First Floor:* | *1,738 sq. ft.* |
| *Second Floor:* | *1,362 sq. ft.* |
| *Bonus Room:* | *550 sq. ft.* |
| *Total:* | *3,650 sq. ft.* |

*(Foundation Type: Crawlspace)*

# Havana

**Design CP9485**

Luxury abounds in this magnificent contemporary plan. The entry foyer gives way to a den on the left and formal living and dining rooms on the right. A curving staircase leads upstairs to the master suite, and two family bedrooms sharing a full bath. The rear of the plan holds a family room separated from the kitchen/nook area by built-in shelves. A back staircase here makes the upstairs even more accessible. Note special features such as the three-car garage, island prep in the kitchen and bonus room.

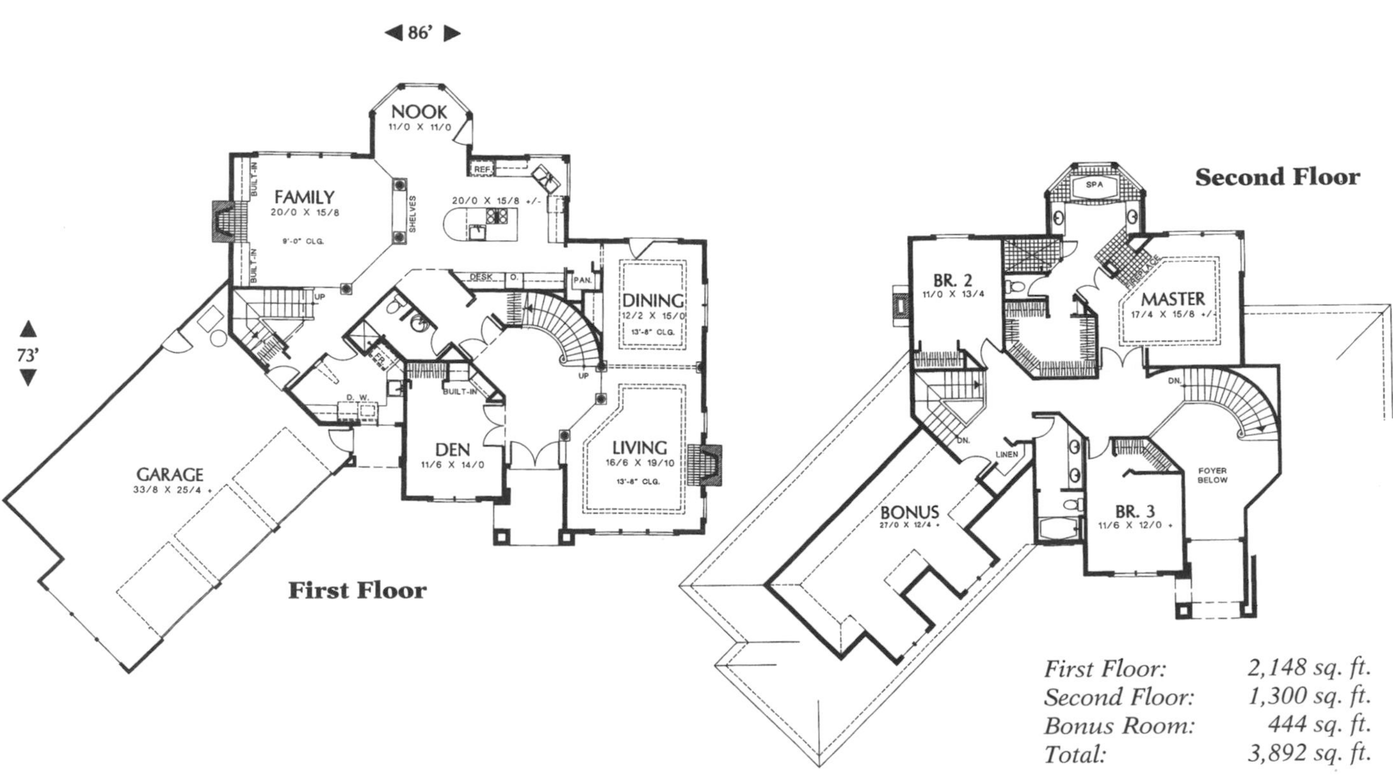


| | |
|---|---|
| *First Floor:* | *2,148 sq. ft.* |
| *Second Floor:* | *1,300 sq. ft.* |
| *Bonus Room:* | *444 sq. ft.* |
| *Total:* | *3,892 sq. ft.* |

*(Foundation Type: Crawlspace)*

## Design CP9405

# Kannada

This impressive contemporary has a plan that works well for steep, sloping lots. A two-story, covered entry has a curved balcony overlooking the front yard. The grand master suite is conveniently located on the entry level and includes a private sun deck. The 14-foot-high living room has a stair up to the dining room. Note the bridge on the upper level with a view of the two-story nook on one side and the foyer on the other. Each of the four bedrooms and the den have direct access to a bathroom.

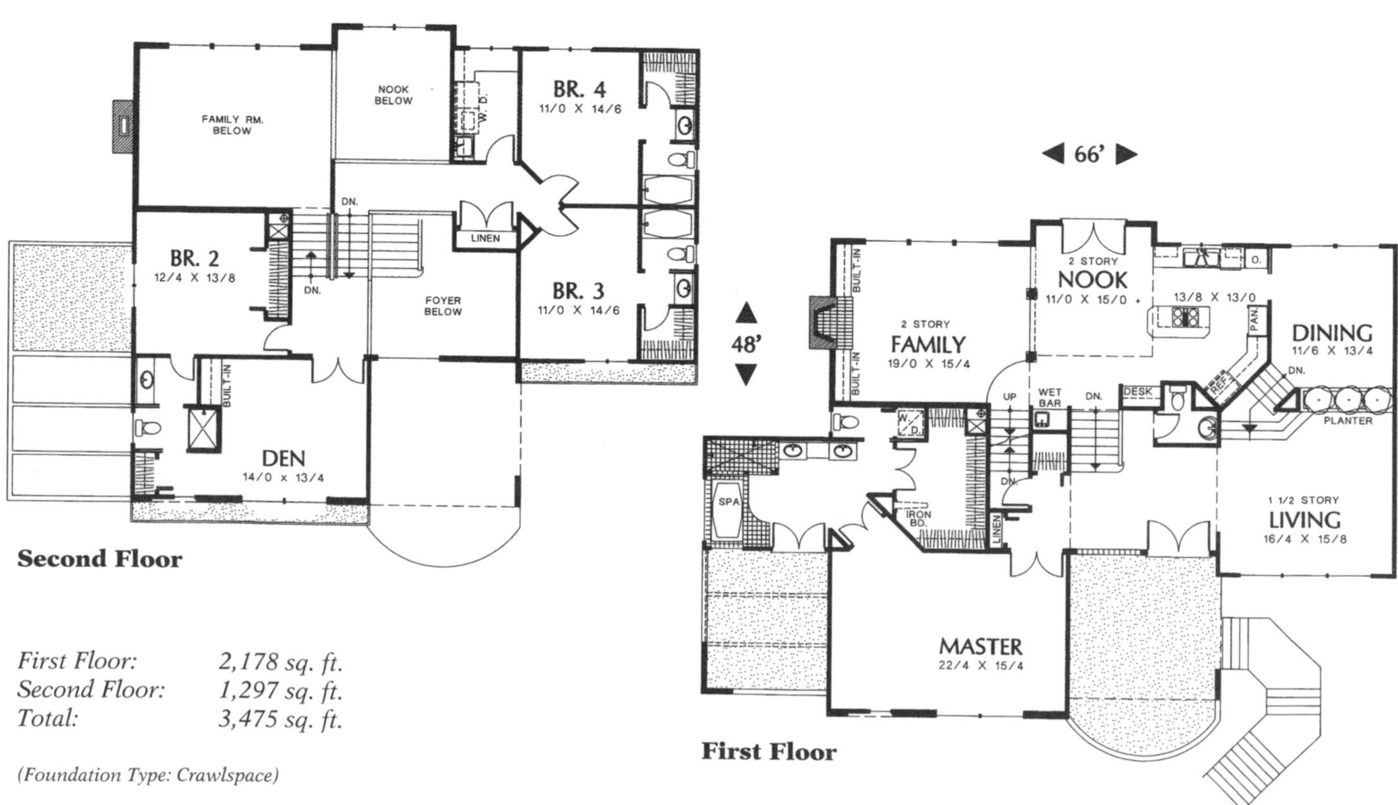


**Second Floor**

**First Floor**

| | |
|---|---|
| *First Floor:* | *2,178 sq. ft.* |
| *Second Floor:* | *1,297 sq. ft.* |
| *Total:* | *3,475 sq. ft.* |

*(Foundation Type: Crawlspace)*

# Seville

## Design CP9417

This refined Georgian home is designed for lots that fall off toward the rear and works especially well with a view out the back. The kitchen and eating nook wrap around the vaulted family room with its arched transom windows flanking the fireplace. Directly off the nook is a covered deck. The open living and dining rooms are distinguished by ceiling treatment. A den to the front of the home may serve as a media room. Don't miss the huge game room on the lower level.

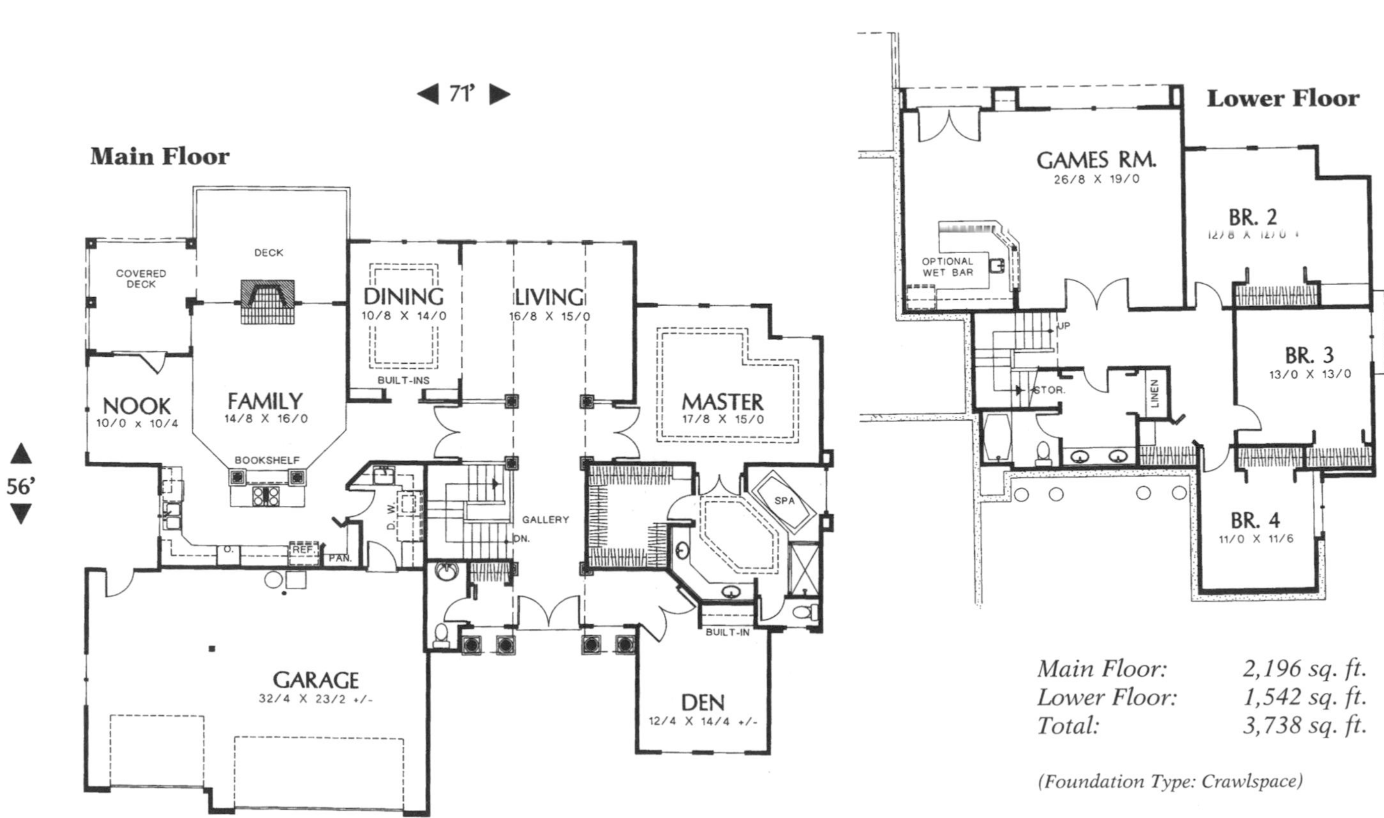


| | |
|---|---|
| *Main Floor:* | *2,196 sq. ft.* |
| *Lower Floor:* | *1,542 sq. ft.* |
| *Total:* | *3,738 sq. ft.* |

*(Foundation Type: Crawlspace)*

## Design CP9433 **Halcyon**

European styling is evident in this spectacular home. Note the dramatic split stair in the foyer. A second stairway leads up to a huge bonus room over the four-car garage. A large den on the main floor, with an adjacent full bath, makes a perfect guest suite. A large living room with fireplace overlooks the foyer. The two-story family room also features a fireplace and has access to the rear yard. A covered patio adds outdoor dining space to the breakfast nook. Upstairs are four bedrooms, including the master suite.

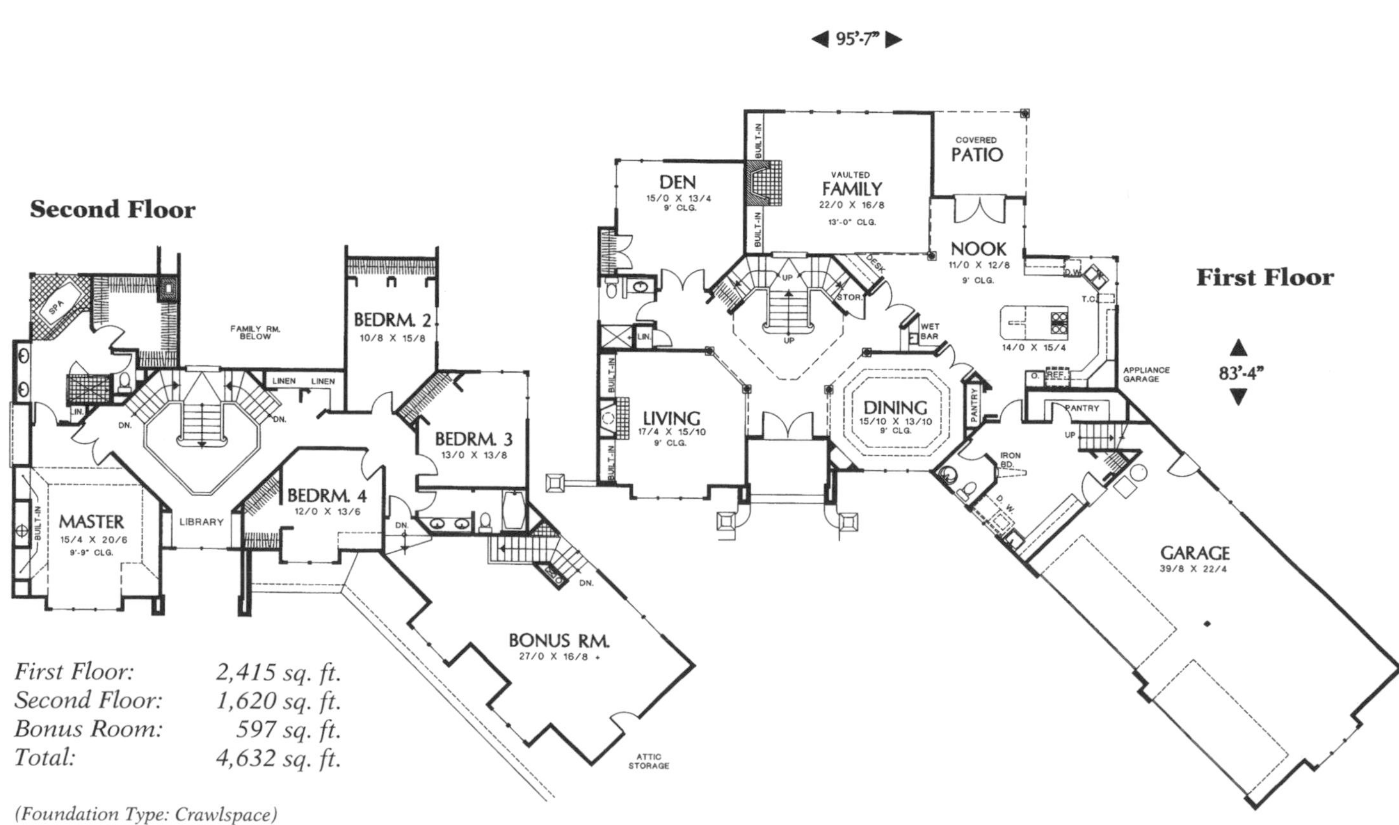


*First Floor:* *2,415 sq. ft.*
*Second Floor:* *1,620 sq. ft.*
*Bonus Room:* *597 sq. ft.*
*Total:* *4,632 sq. ft.*

*(Foundation Type: Crawlspace)*

# Ricardo

**Design CP9445**

Beyond a spacious foyer, double doors lead to a den on the left, while a living room with fireplace and vaulted ceiling awaits on the right. The island kitchen features a planning desk and a bayed breakfast nook. It is placed between the formal dining room and the family room with fireplace and built-in bookshelves. The master bedroom lies behind double doors. Special amenities in this room include a vaulted ceiling, private deck, and a bath with a walk-in closet, dual vanities and a spa in a bay window.

70'

54'

**Main Floor**

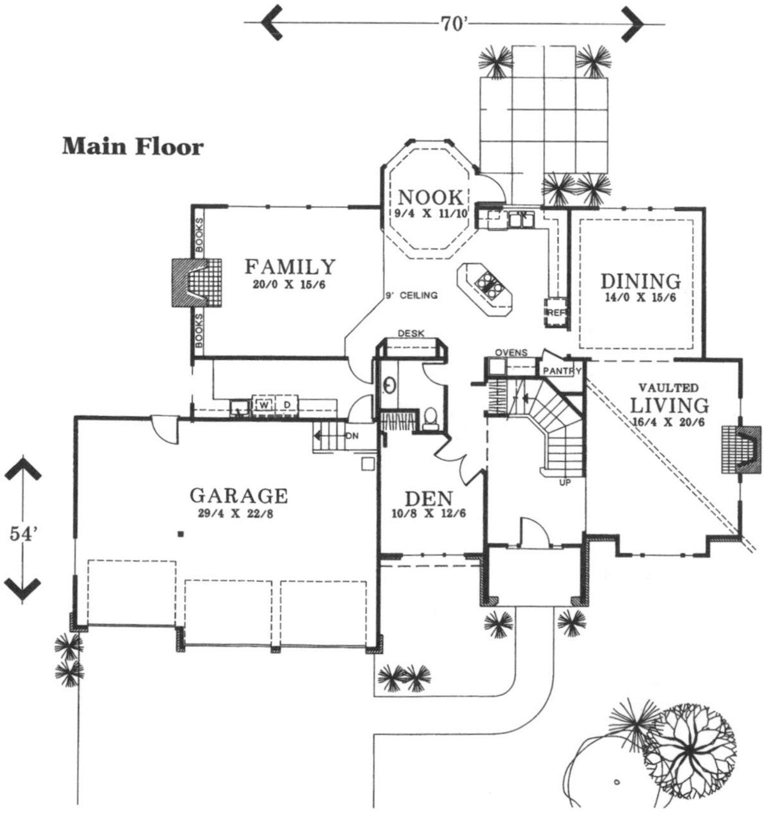

NOOK 9/4 X 11/10

FAMILY 20/0 X 15/6

BOOKS

9' CEILING

DINING 14/0 X 15/6

REF

DESK

OVENS

PANTRY

VAULTED LIVING 16/4 X 20/6

W D

DN

UP

GARAGE 29/4 X 22/8

DEN 10/8 X 12/6

**Upper Floor**

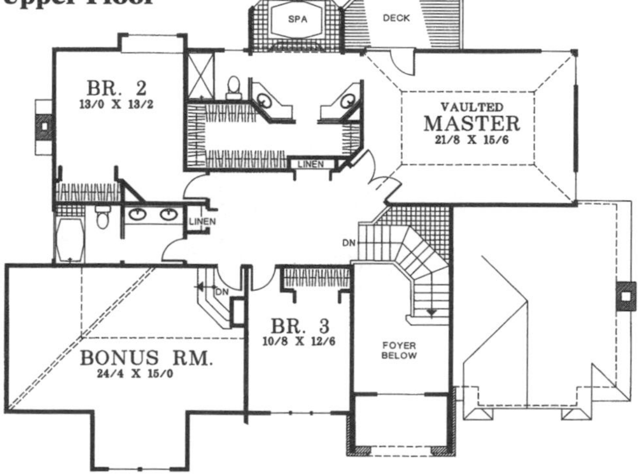

SPA

DECK

BR. 2 13/0 X 13/2

VAULTED MASTER 21/8 X 15/6

LINEN

DN

BONUS RM. 24/4 X 15/0

BR. 3 10/8 X 12/6

FOYER BELOW

| | |
|---|---|
| *Main Floor:* | *1,839 sq. ft.* |
| *Upper Floor:* | *1,365 sq. ft.* |
| *Bonus Room:* | *439 sq. ft.* |
| *Total:* | *3,643 sq. ft.* |

*(Foundation Type: Crawlspace)*

## Design CP9424

# Alamosa

Spectacular is the word for this "Texas" traditional! Designed to sit on a large lot, it features a side-entry garage. Notice the two-story foyer with split stairway and columns framing the openings to the living and dining rooms. The dramatic master suite is found on the main floor. The fireplace serves both the bedroom and the spa area. Three additional bedrooms and two baths are upstairs. The rear bedroom with vaulted ceiling and half-round window would make an ideal library.

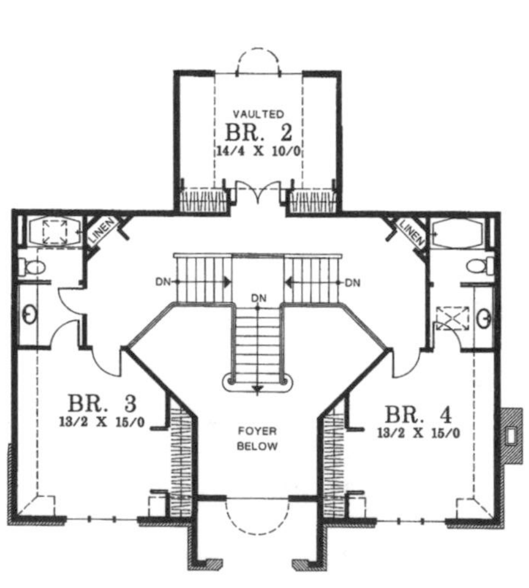


**Second Floor**

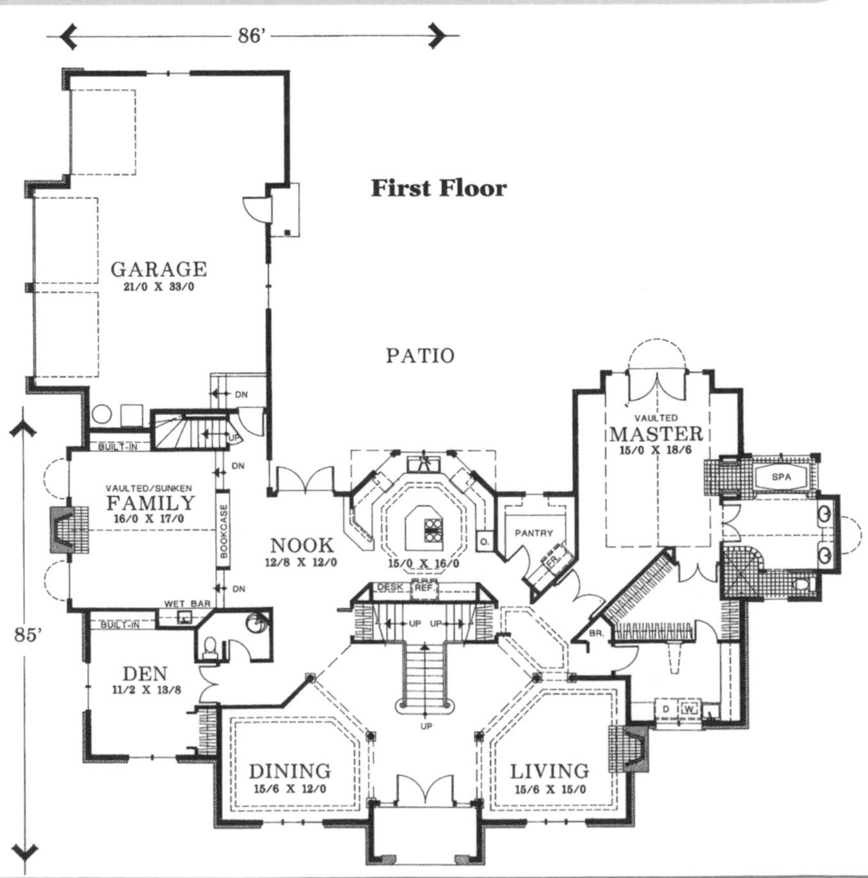


| | |
|---|---|
| *First Floor:* | *2,870 sq. ft.* |
| *Second Floor:* | *1,075 sq. ft.* |
| *Total:* | *3,945 sq. ft.* |

*(Foundation Type: Crawlspace)*

# Silhouette

**Design CP9449**

A soaring entry creates a striking first impression for this two-story contemporary home. Inside, formal areas are kept to the right of the entry foyer. The entire rear of the plan is devoted to casual gatherings, with one open space housing the family room, breakfast nook and L-shaped kitchen. A small den off the foyer is near a full bath; it could serve as a guest room when needed. The upper level contains five bedrooms, including a master suite with double vanity and whirlpool spa.

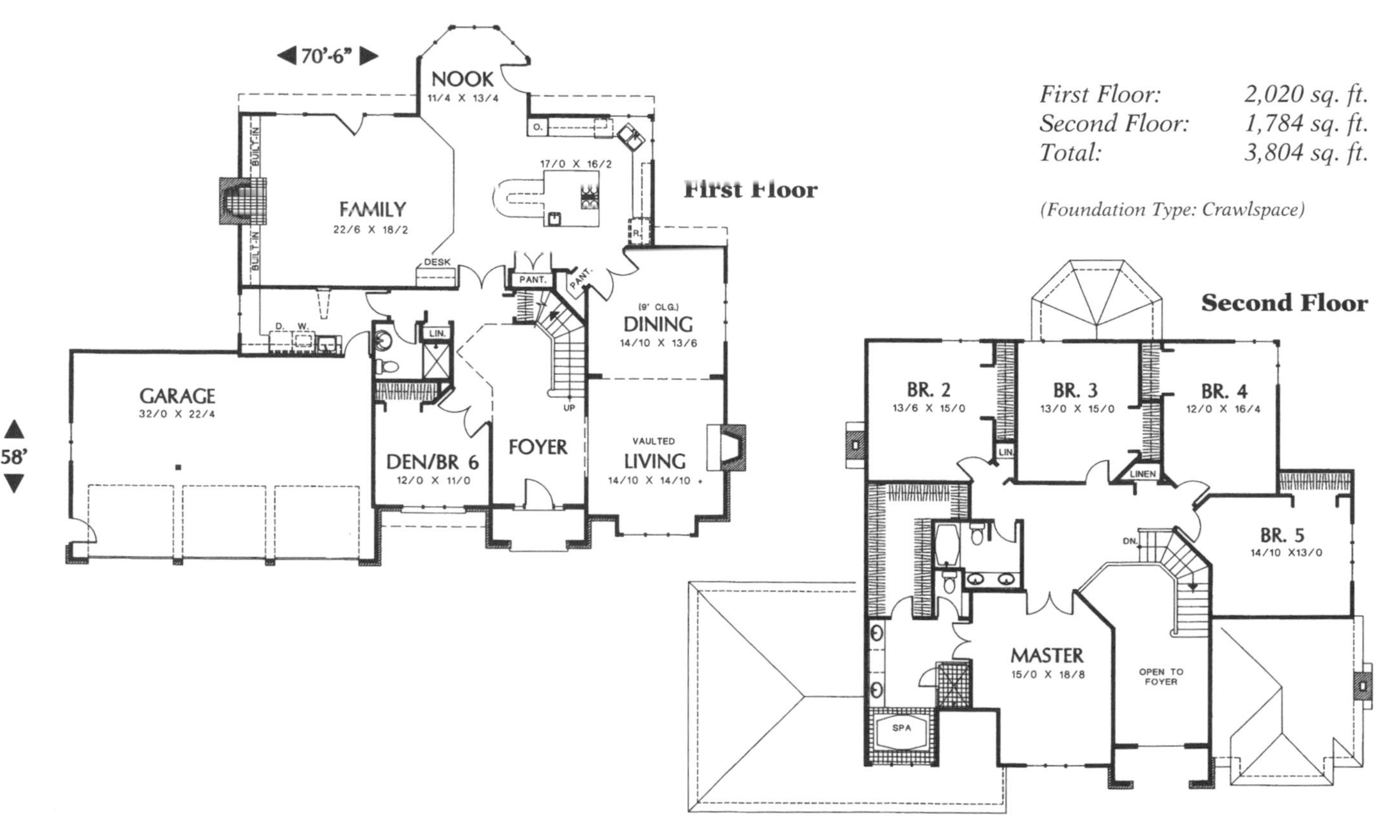


| | |
|---|---|
| *First Floor:* | *2,020 sq. ft.* |
| *Second Floor:* | *1,784 sq. ft.* |
| *Total:* | *3,804 sq. ft.* |

*(Foundation Type: Crawlspace)*

## Design CP9129

# Manhattan

For special living situations, this home offers private living quarters with small kitchen, bedroom, walk-in closet and full bath. A nearby deck allows for outdoor enjoyment. Other outstanding features of the plan include a large sitting area in the master suite, a raised foyer, a bay window in the dining room, a fireplace and media center in the living room and a vaulted ceiling in the breakfast nook. Bedrooms 3 and 4 share a compartmented bath, while Bedroom 2 has its own private bath.

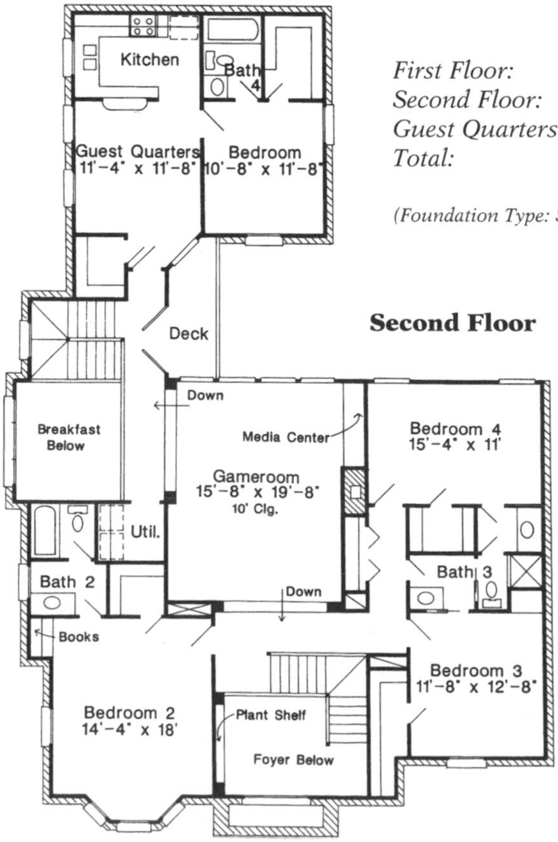

| | |
|---|---|
| *First Floor:* | *2,181 sq. ft.* |
| *Second Floor:* | *1,546 sq. ft.* |
| *Guest Quarters:* | *554 sq. ft.* |
| *Total:* | *4,281 sq. ft.* |

*(Foundation Type: Slab)*

Width 49'
Depth 74'-4"

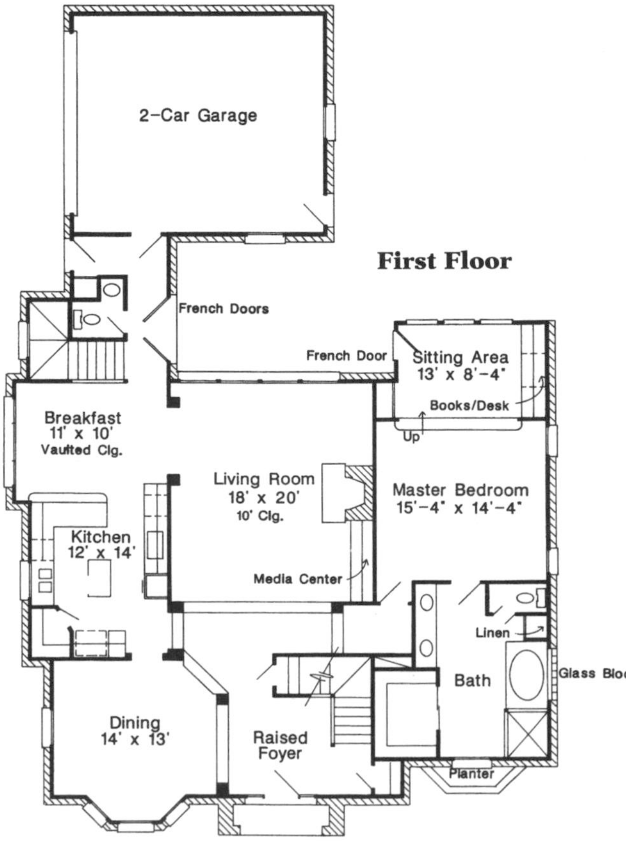

**Second Floor**

Kitchen
Bath 4
Guest Quarters 11'-4" x 11'-8"
Bedroom 10'-8" x 11'-8"
Deck
Down
Breakfast Below
Media Center
Gameroom 15'-8" x 19'-8" 10' Clg.
Bedroom 4 15'-4" x 11'
Util.
Bath 2
Down
Bath 3
Books
Bedroom 3 11'-8" x 12'-8"
Bedroom 2 14'-4" x 18'
Plant Shelf
Foyer Below

**First Floor**

2-Car Garage
French Doors
French Door
Sitting Area 13' x 8'-4"
Books/Desk
Up
Breakfast 11' x 10' Vaulted Clg.
Living Room 18' x 20' 10' Clg.
Master Bedroom 15'-4" x 14'-4"
Kitchen 12' x 14'
Media Center
Linen
Bath
Glass Block
Dining 14' x 13'
Raised Foyer
Planter

# Grosvenor

**Design CP3300**

A dramatic roofline, soaring columns and massive chimneys are some of the magnificent details that accentuate the exterior of this home. The Great Room features a raised hearth, a music alcove and a complete bar, which is accessed by the adjoined study/lounge as well. The kitchen, with cooktop snack bar opens to the family room with fireplace. The master suite is a private retreat found on the second floor. Four bedrooms, with private baths and one with a living room, complete the design.

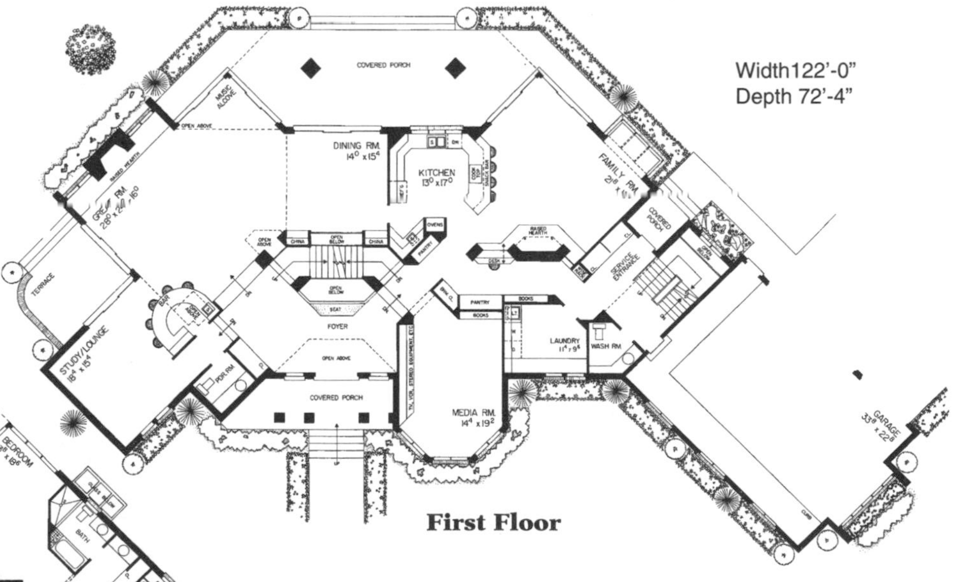

Width 122'-0"
Depth 72'-4"

**Second Floor**

**First Floor**

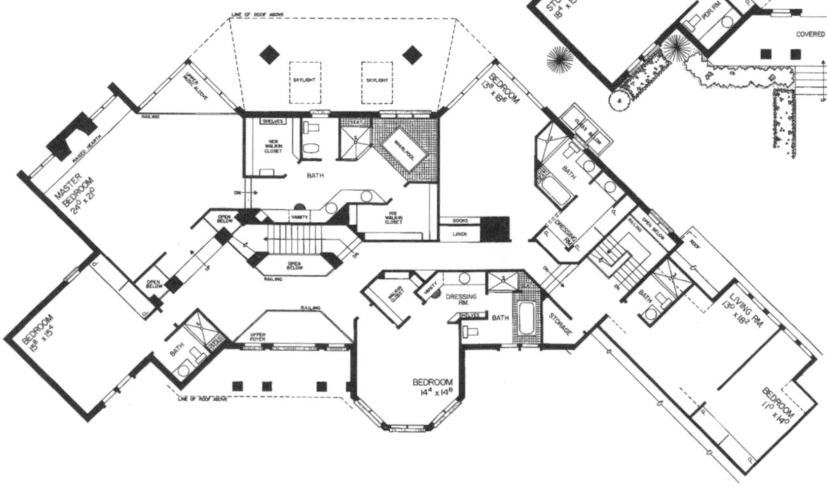

| | |
|---|---|
| *First Floor:* | *3,202 sq. ft.* |
| *Second Floor:* | *3,512 sq. ft.* |
| *Total:* | *6,714 sq. ft.* |

*(Foundation Type: Basement)*

## *Design CP2940* **Alexandra**

Graceful window arches soften the steeply gabled roof of this grand Norman manor. A two-story gathering room is two steps down from the adjacent lounge. The galley-style kitchen, with snack bar and adjacent breakfast room, overlooks the fireplace in the family room. The media room provides space for electronic equipment. The master suite features His and Her baths, a sitting area and a whirlpool. Four additional bedrooms, each with a private bath, join the elegant balcony upstairs.

**Second Floor**

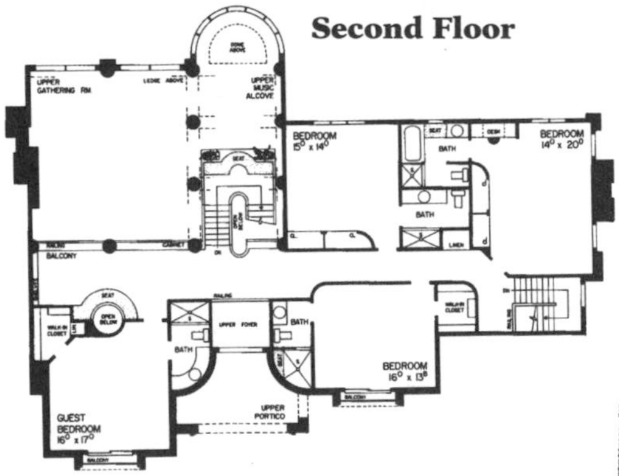

**First Floor**

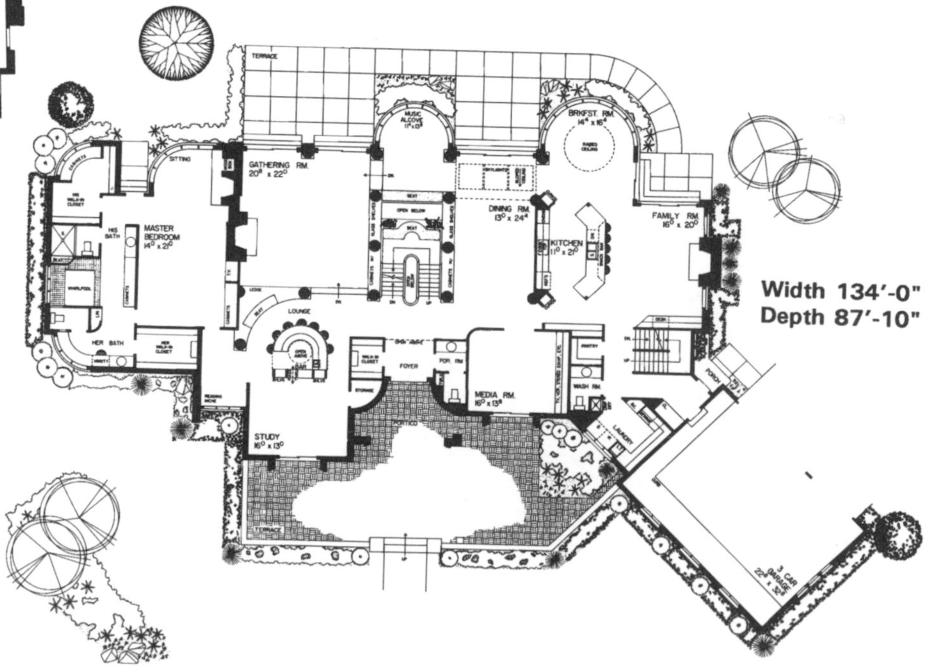

**Width 134'-0"**
**Depth 87'-10"**

| | |
|---|---|
| *First Floor:* | *4,786 sq. ft.* |
| *Second Floor:* | *1,842 sq. ft.* |
| *Total:* | *6,628 sq. ft.* |

*(Foundation Type: Basement)*

# Belaire

**Design CP2968**

A gracious entry, with impressive twin turrets, welcomes all to this stunning manor. The formal dining room and quiet study flank the two-story foyer with semi-circular fanlights. A sunken gathering room features a raised hearth and overlooks the covered porch. An island kitchen adjoins the spacious morning room. The master suite includes an exercise room and spa. The second floor has four bedrooms, three bathrooms and an activities room for entertaining.

**First Floor**

**Second Floor**

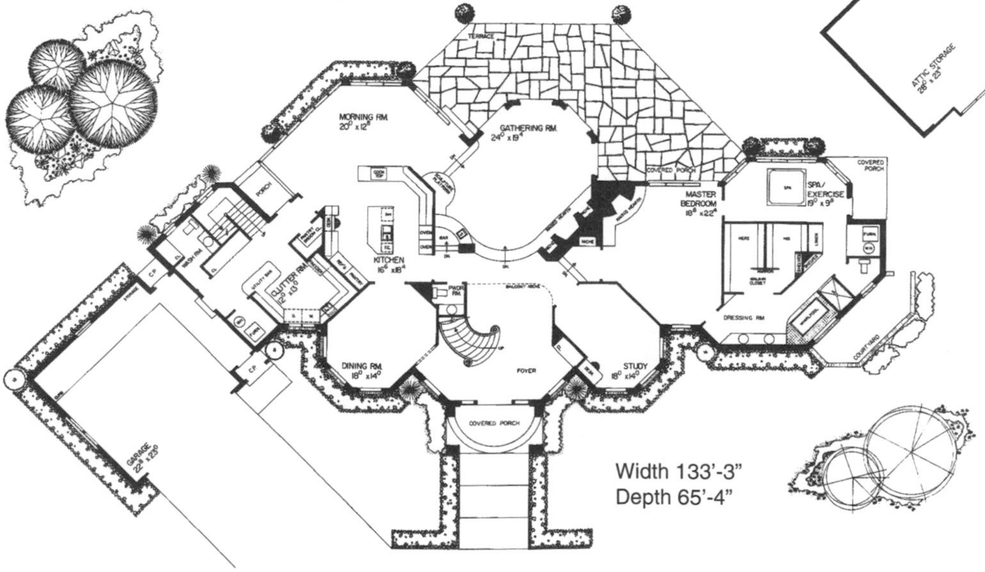

Width 133'-3"
Depth 65'-4"

| | |
|---|---|
| *First Floor:* | *3,736 sq. ft.* |
| *Second Floor:* | *2,264 sq. ft.* |
| *Total:* | *6,000 sq. ft.* |

*(Foundation Type: Slab)*

## Design CP2952 — Harcourt

Semi-circular arches complement the strong linear rooflines and balconies of this exciting contemporary. The first floor is filled with amenities for entertaining and relaxing. The foyer opens to a step-down living room with a dramatic sloped ceiling, fireplace and sliding glass doors that access the front courtyard and terrace. A tavern with built-in wine rack and an adjacent butler's pantry are ideal for entertaining. Each of the four second-floor bedrooms has a private bath and balcony.

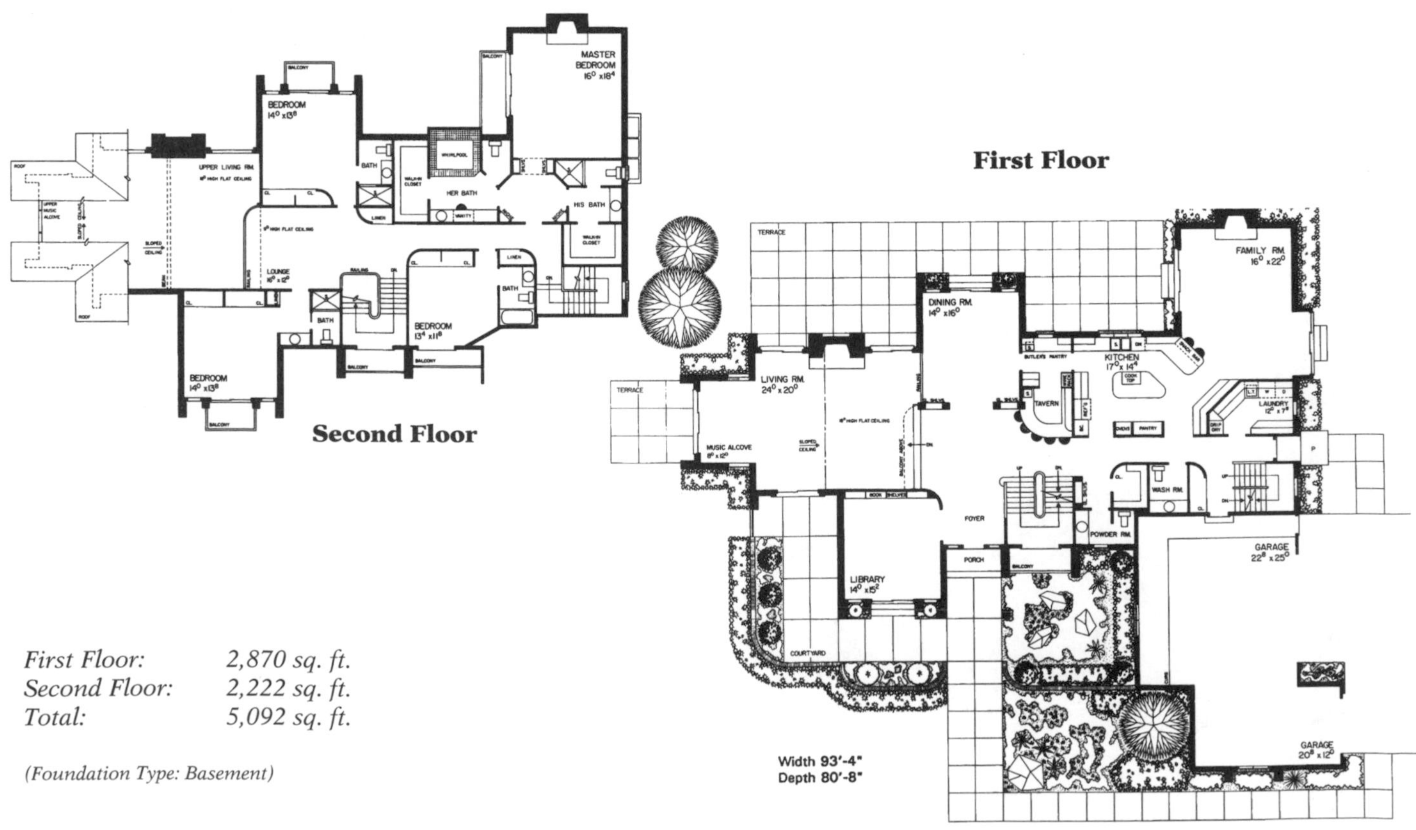


*First Floor:* *2,870 sq. ft.*
*Second Floor:* *2,222 sq. ft.*
*Total:* *5,092 sq. ft.*

*(Foundation Type: Basement)*

# Vancouver **Design CP2956**

Tall windows and two-story arches emphasize the soaring height of this elegant, Northwest contemporary. The foyer and formal dining room adjoin a sunken gathering room, which is warmed by a fireplace. A spacious master suite occupies one wing of the home, with an exercise room, His and Her bathrooms, a whirlpool tub and walk-in closets. The kitchen, with island and separate snack bar, adjoins the family room and breakfast room. Upstairs, there are three additional bedrooms and a quiet study alcove.

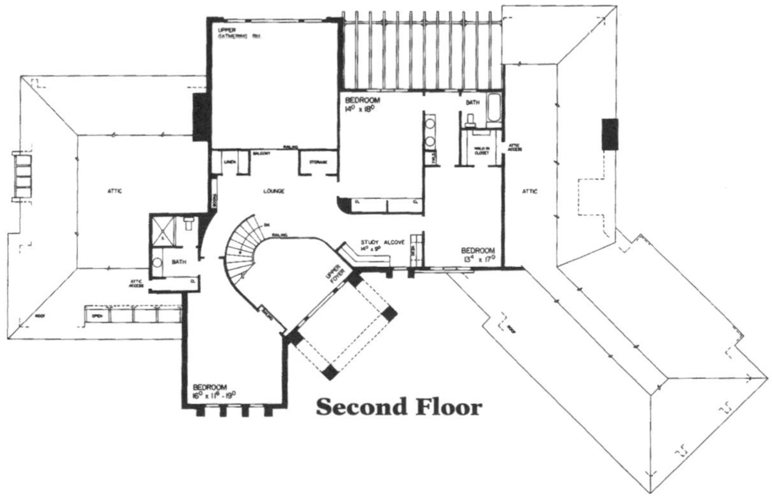

**First Floor**

**Second Floor**

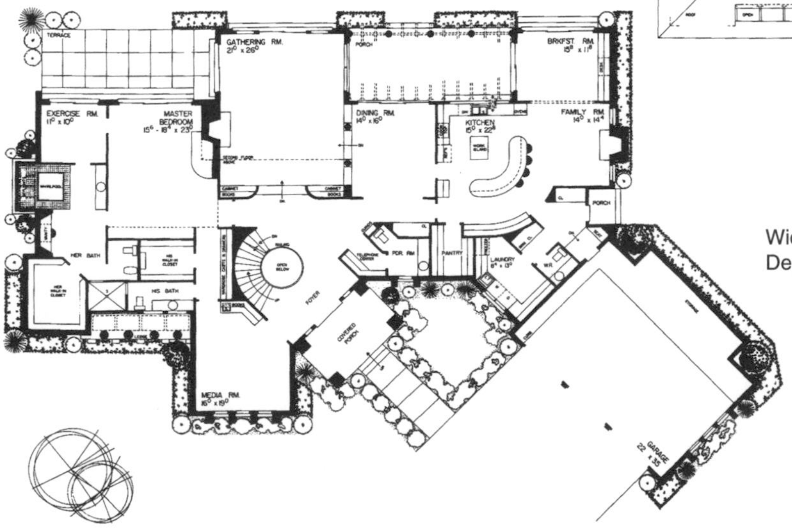

Width 126'-4"
Depth 78'-6"

| | |
|---|---|
| *First Floor:* | *4,222 sq. ft.* |
| *Second Floor:* | *1,726 sq. ft.* |
| *Total:* | *5,948 sq. ft.* |

*(Foundation Type: Basement)*

## Design CP2645

# Laurel

Reminiscent of the Gothic Victorian style of the mid-19th Century, this delightfully detailed, three-story house has a wraparound veranda for summertime relaxing. A grand reception hall welcomes visitors and displays an elegant staircase. The parlor and family room, each with a fireplace, provide excellent living facilities. The second floor has four bedrooms and two baths plus a sewing room or study. The third floor houses an additional bedroom or studio with a half bath, as well as a playroom.

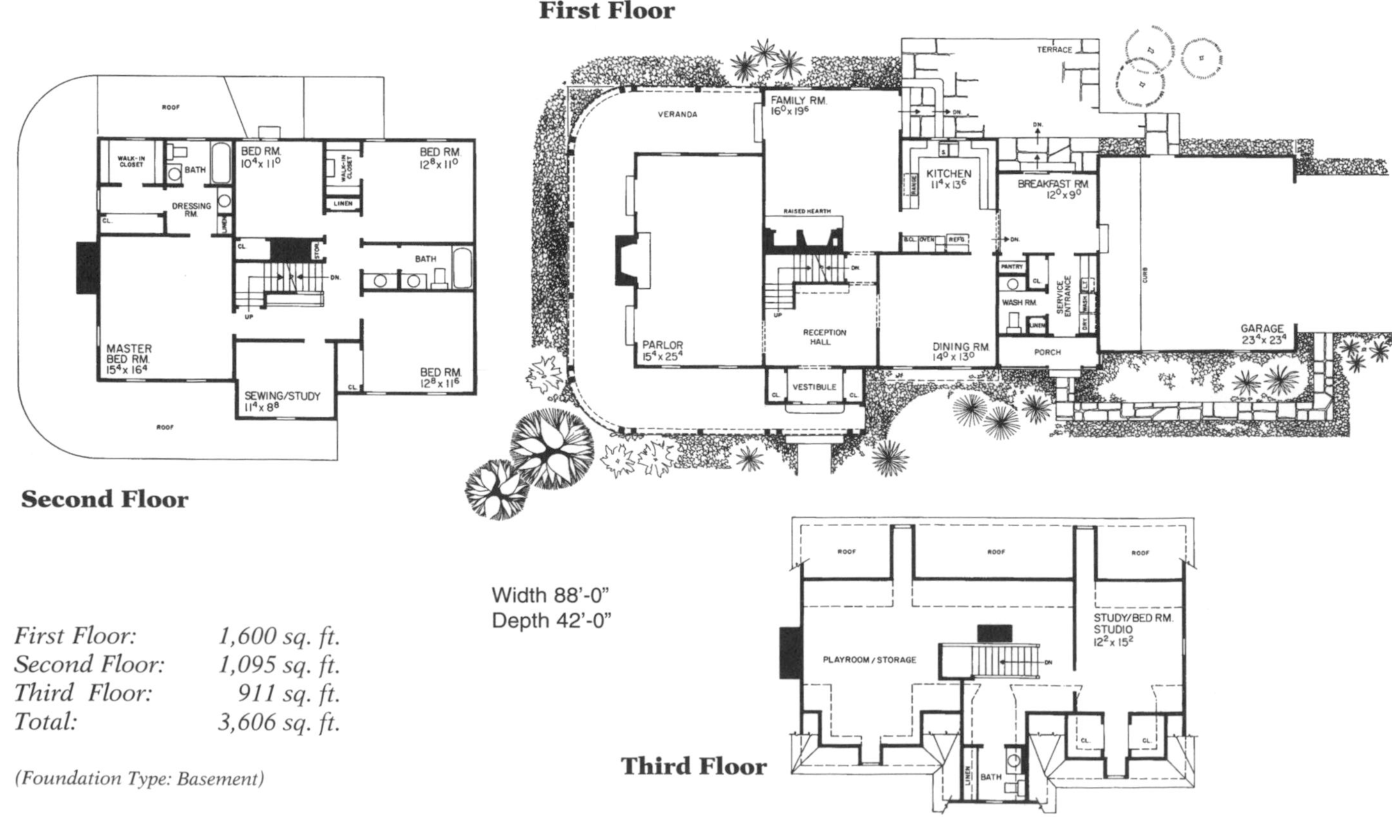


Width 88'-0"
Depth 42'-0"

| | |
|---|---|
| *First Floor:* | *1,600 sq. ft.* |
| *Second Floor:* | *1,095 sq. ft.* |
| *Third Floor:* | *911 sq. ft.* |
| *Total:* | *3,606 sq. ft.* |

*(Foundation Type: Basement)*

# Eileen

**Design CP2829**

Neo-Victorian architecture with a taste of modern styling dominates this home. Detailed with gingerbread woodwork and a handsome double-width chimney, this two-story design is breathtaking. Enter by way of the large, tiled receiving hall and discover a very livable floor plan. The formal living room has a fireplace and access to the covered porch, while the dining room features a bay window. The second floor offers three bedrooms with easy access to two full bathrooms.

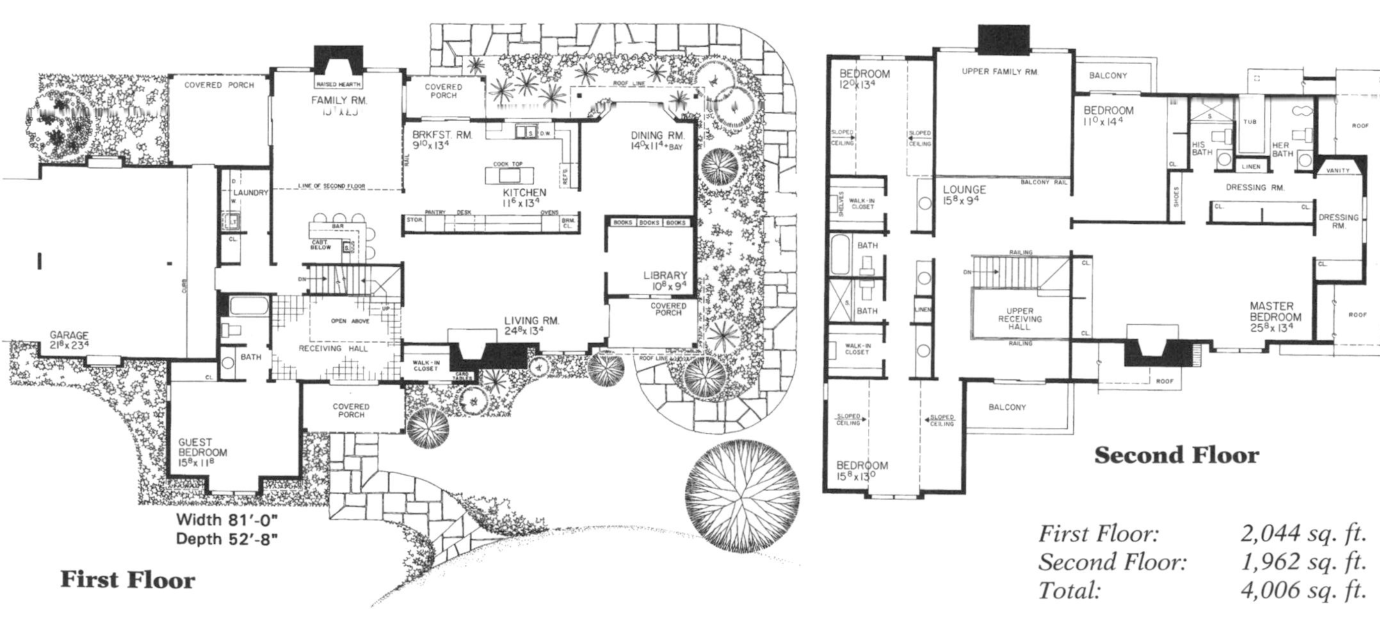


| | |
|---|---|
| *First Floor:* | *2,044 sq. ft.* |
| *Second Floor:* | *1,962 sq. ft.* |
| *Total:* | *4,006 sq. ft.* |

*(Foundation Type: Basement)*

## Design CP9016

# Vaughn

Shingle siding is one of the common elements of the Shingle Style which emerged along the Eastern Seaboard in the late 19th Century. With its cantilevered gable sloping with a gentle curve to the first floor, and a raised turret, this design is representative of this style. Two steps up from the foyer is a mezzanine-level study with curved walls. Overlooking the built-in breakfast booth with a six-foot wide curved picture window is an island kitchen with abundant cabinet space.

| | |
|---|---|
| *First Floor:* | *1,812 sq. ft.* |
| *Second Floor:* | *1,997 sq. ft.* |
| *Total:* | *3,809 sq. ft.* |

*(Foundation Type: Slab)*

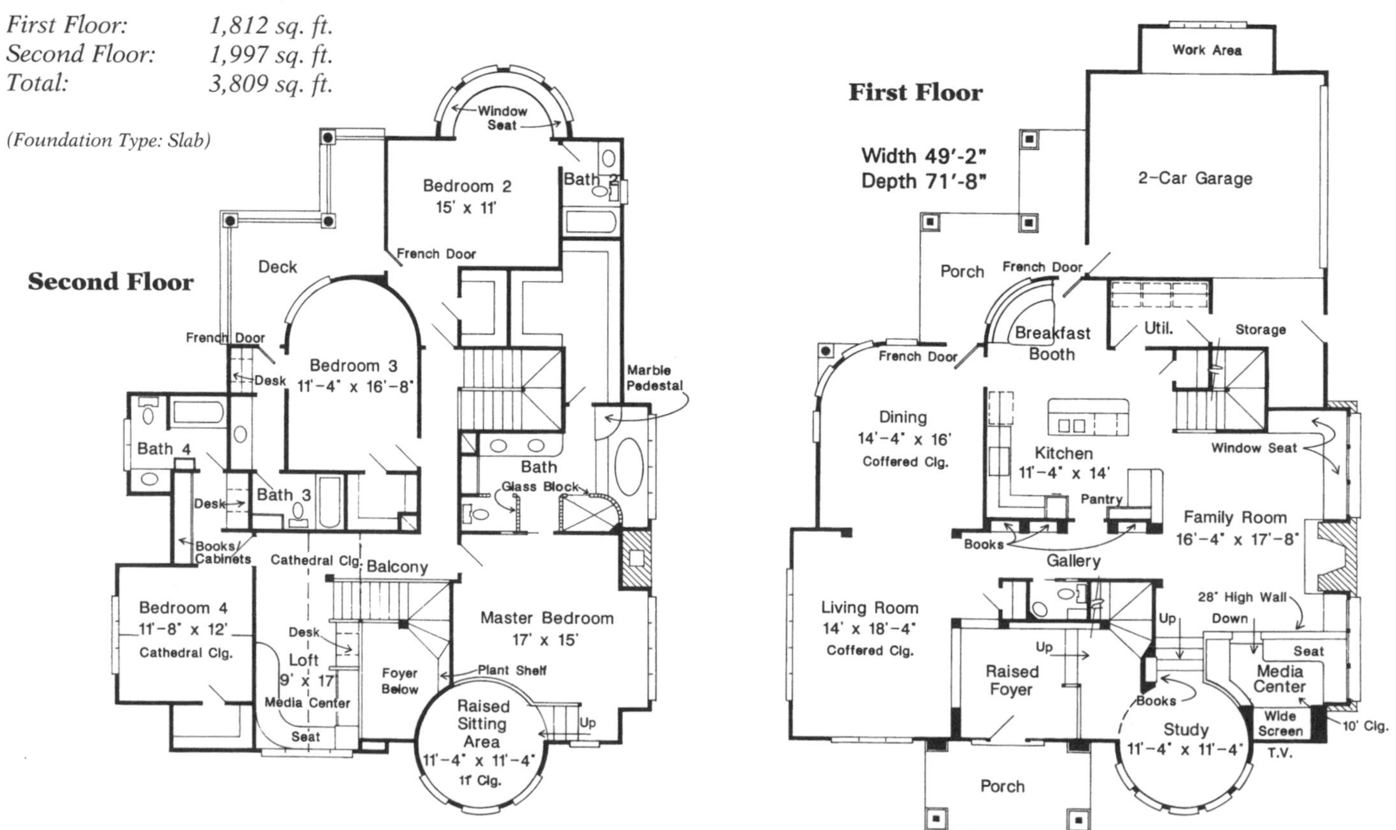

# Randolph

## Design CP9070

Reminiscent of the fashionable summer homes of Newport, Cape Cod, this home typifies the Shingle Style with its shingled surfaces, Palladian window and circular tower. Brick archways in the game room provide a built-in media center and passage to the pub and walk-in wet bar. Windows surround the spacious kitchen. The second floor offers four bedrooms and three baths, as well as a multi-purpose media room. Plans for a three-car detached garage with second-floor living quarters are included.

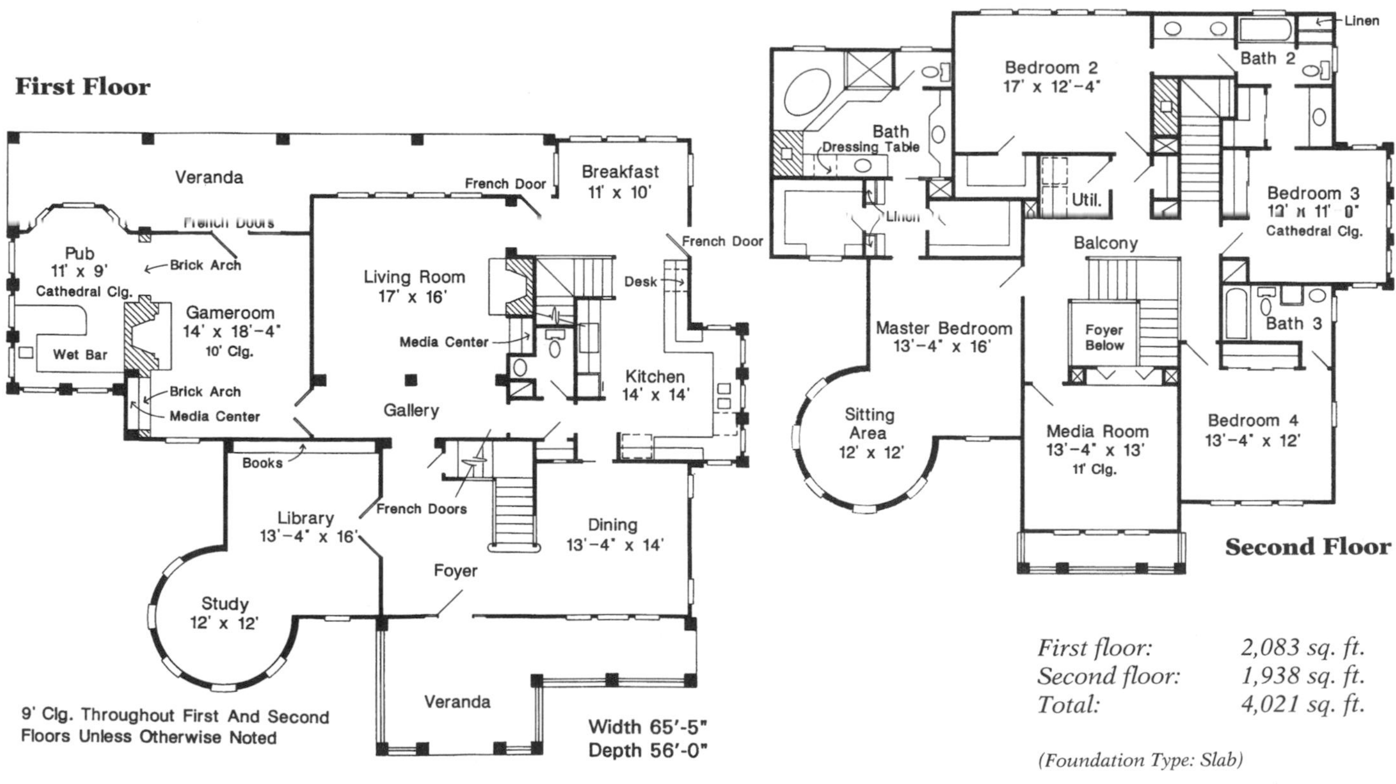


| | |
|---|---|
| *First floor:* | *2,083 sq. ft.* |
| *Second floor:* | *1,938 sq. ft.* |
| *Total:* | *4,021 sq. ft.* |

*(Foundation Type: Slab)*

## Design CP2969 — Nicollet

This delicately detailed exterior with covered porches to the front, side and rear houses an outstanding family-oriented floor plan. Projecting bays provide an extra measure of livability to the living, dining and family rooms, plus two of the bedrooms. The efficient kitchen, with its island cooking station, functions well with the dining and family rooms. Upstairs are three big bedrooms and a fine master bath. A third floor provides a guest suite and huge bulk storage area.

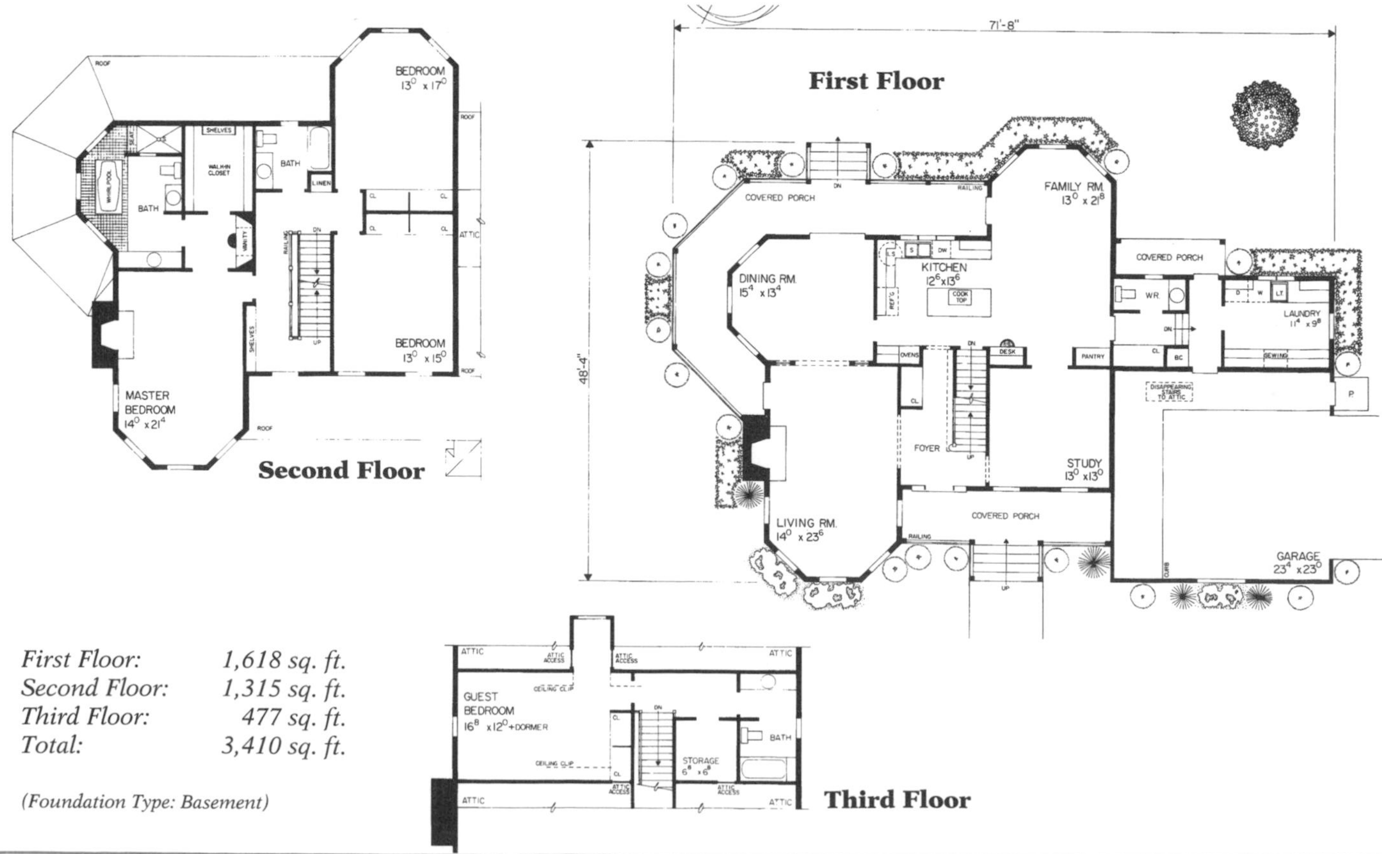


*First Floor:* *1,618 sq. ft.*
*Second Floor:* *1,315 sq. ft.*
*Third Floor:* *477 sq. ft.*
*Total:* *3,410 sq. ft.*

*(Foundation Type: Basement)*

# Cascade

## Design CP9017

Leaded-glass front doors open to a grand foyer with an elegant staircase that leads to the balcony above. The living room features a rounded sitting area and French doors that open to the side veranda. The centrally located kitchen overlooks the family room with a built-in media center, and the breakfast area with two six-foot-wide curved picture windows. Double doors lead from the balcony to the private master bedroom and sitting area with curved walls and leaded-glass windows.

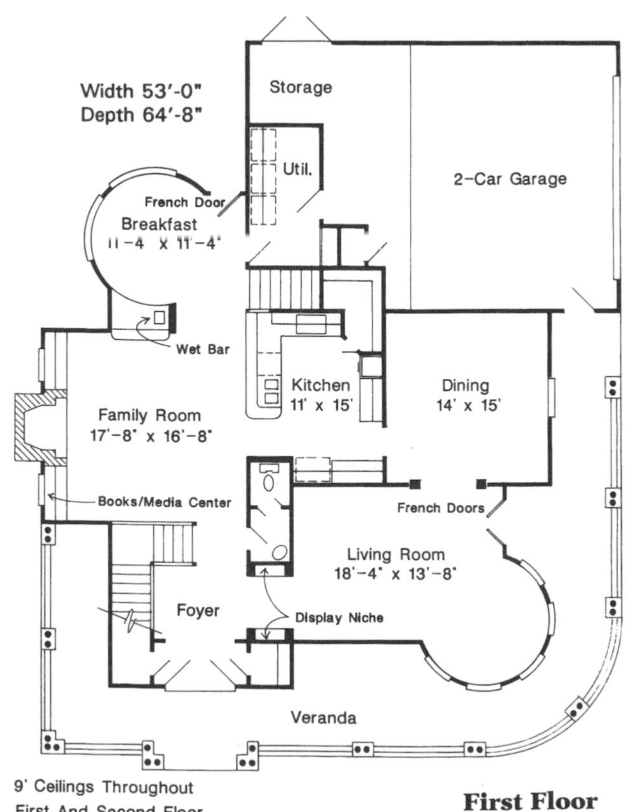


**First Floor**

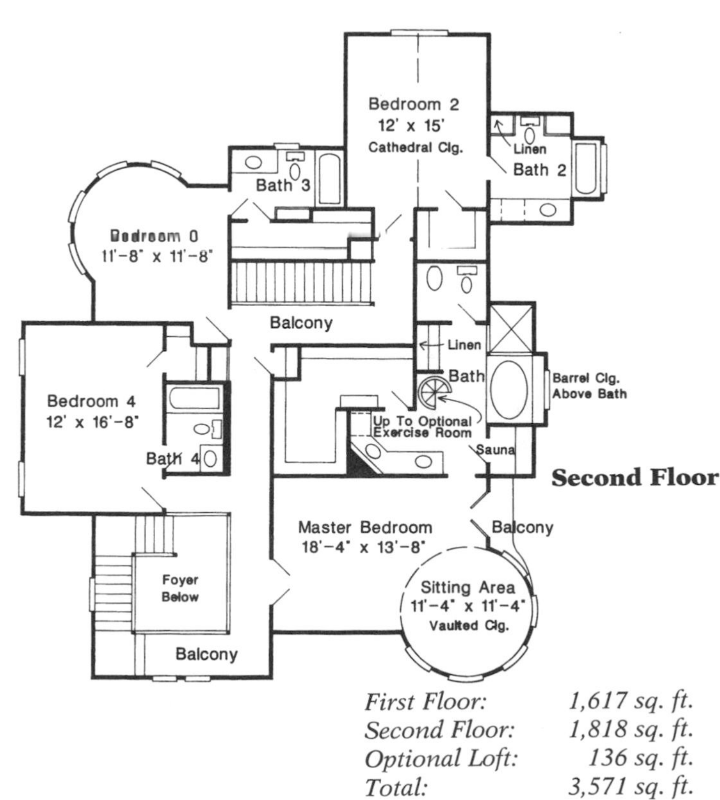


**Second Floor**

| | |
|---|---|
| *First Floor:* | *1,617 sq. ft.* |
| *Second Floor:* | *1,818 sq. ft.* |
| *Optional Loft:* | *136 sq. ft.* |
| *Total:* | *3,571 sq. ft.* |

# Design CP2970 — Aurora

This outstanding Victorian is distinguished by a veranda that covers all four sides of the house. The kitchen is surrounded by the family room, dining area and living room. There are massive fireplaces in both the living and family rooms. The master suite is sited on the second floor, complete with sitting area, dressing rooms and master bath. Two bedrooms and a shared bath complete this floor. The third level provides two additional bedrooms with a bath and plenty of attic storage space.

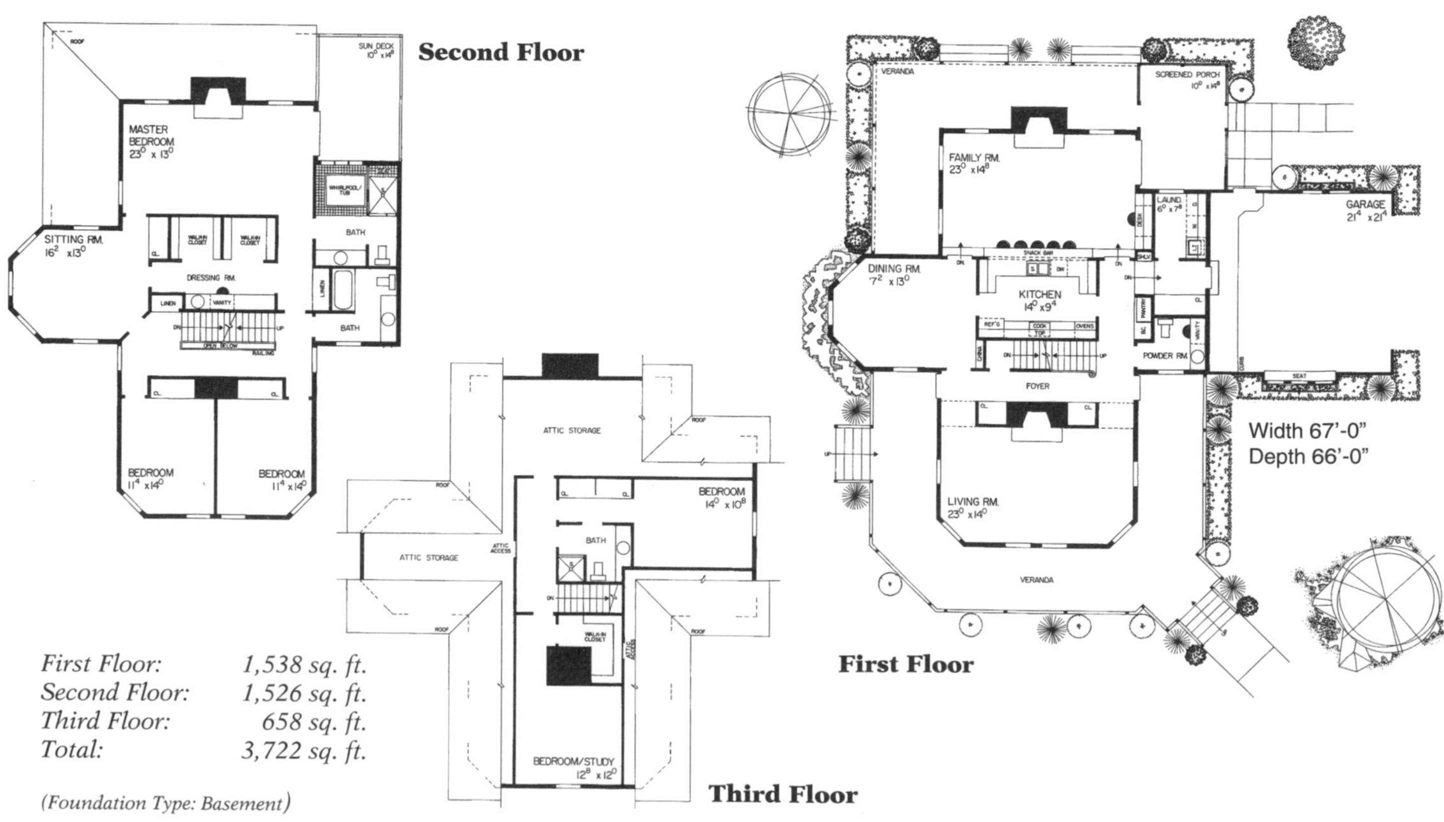


| | |
|---|---|
| *First Floor:* | *1,538 sq. ft.* |
| *Second Floor:* | *1,526 sq. ft.* |
| *Third Floor:* | *658 sq. ft.* |
| *Total:* | *3,722 sq. ft.* |

*(Foundation Type: Basement)*

# Lennox

## Design CP9072

Balance and symmetry, along with elaborate gingerbread detailing, highlight this Queen Anne Style design. Inside, the living room, kitchen and breakfast area are ideal for relaxing or entertaining. The study features built-in bookcases and a walk-in storage area. Rear stairs from the breakfast area lead to the second floor with three large bedrooms. The laundry room is conveniently located here. The master suite features a sitting area and His and Hers baths with walk-in closets.

| | |
|---|---|
| *First Floor:* | *1,920 sq. ft.* |
| *Second Floor:* | *1,898 sq. ft.* |
| *Total:* | *3,818 sq. ft.* |

*(Foundation Type: Slab)*

Width: 53'-6"
Depth: 82'-8"

**First Floor**

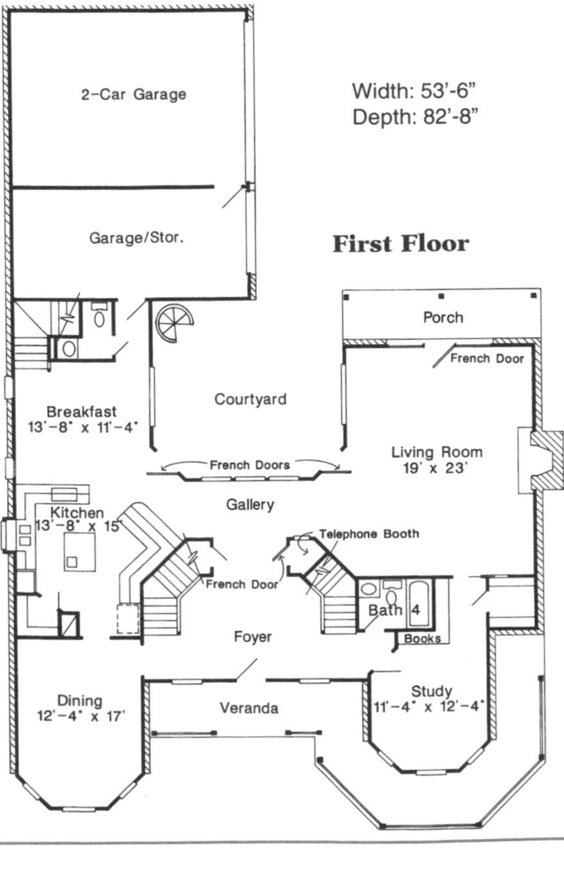

**Second Floor**

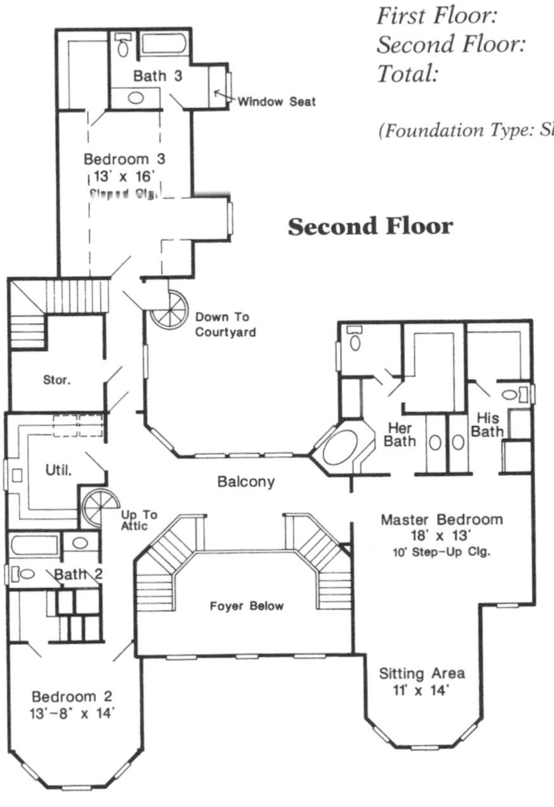

## Design CP3394 — Charlotte

This folk Victorian home is a delightful interpretation with a decorative covered porch that greets the neighborhood. The formal living areas of this plan are set off by a family room with large fireplace. An island kitchen with breakfast nook has easy access to the dining area. The second floor is occupied by a master suite with sitting area and master bath with whirlpool. Two bedrooms share a bath. The third floor is occupied by a guest bedroom with bath and large walk-in closet.

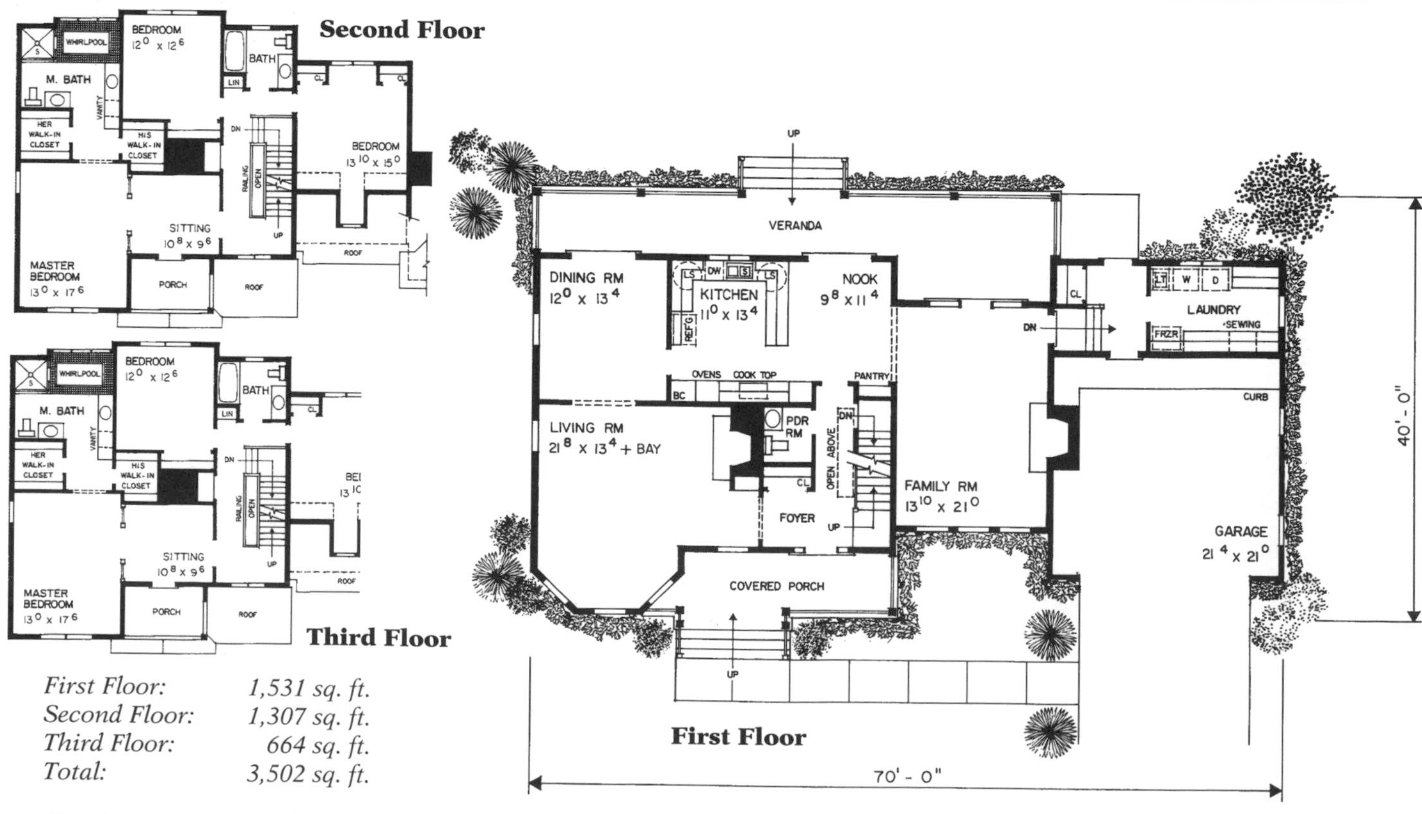


| | |
|---|---|
| *First Floor:* | *1,531 sq. ft.* |
| *Second Floor:* | *1,307 sq. ft.* |
| *Third Floor:* | *664 sq. ft.* |
| *Total:* | *3,502 sq. ft.* |

*(Foundation Type: Basement)*

# Trenton

**Design CP9015**

As authentic as the exterior of this design is, the interior offers all the luxury and elegance that today's homeowners could desire. The formal living and dining rooms are separated by detailed wood columns. Built-in bookcases and cabinets highlight the block-paneled study. The kitchen becomes the focal point of an outstanding family living center which includes a sunken media area, breakfast alcove and a family room with a fireplace. A staircase leads to an optional third floor area.

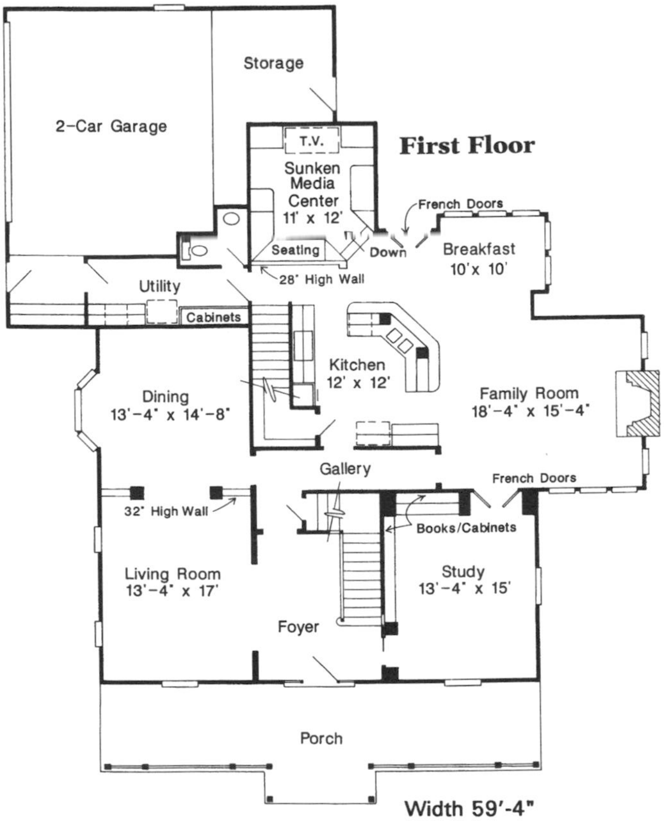

**First Floor**

2-Car Garage
Storage
T.V.
Sunken Media Center 11' x 12'
Seating
Down
French Doors
Breakfast 10'x 10'
28" High Wall
Utility
Cabinets
Kitchen 12' x 12'
Dining 13'-4" x 14'-8"
Family Room 18'-4" x 15'-4"
Gallery
French Doors
32" High Wall
Books/Cabinets
Living Room 13'-4" x 17'
Study 13'-4" x 15'
Foyer
Porch

Width 59'-4"
Depth 72'-8"

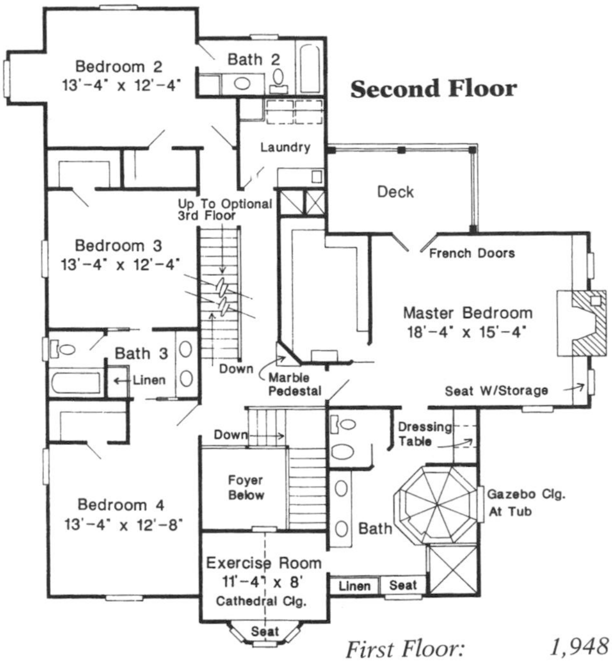

**Second Floor**

Bedroom 2 13'-4" x 12'-4"
Bath 2
Laundry
Deck
Up To Optional 3rd Floor
Bedroom 3 13'-4" x 12'-4"
French Doors
Master Bedroom 18'-4" x 15'-4"
Bath 3
Linen
Down
Marble Pedestal
Seat W/Storage
Down
Dressing Table
Foyer Below
Bedroom 4 13'-4" x 12'-8"
Bath
Gazebo Clg. At Tub
Exercise Room 11'-4" x 8' Cathedral Clg.
Linen
Seat
Seat

| | |
|---|---|
| *First Floor:* | *1,948 sq. ft.* |
| *Second Floor:* | *1,891 sq. ft.* |
| *Total:* | *3,839 sq. ft.* |

*(Foundation Type: Slab)*

## Design CP9071

# Rosebud

This lovely Queen Anne Style design has all the amenities you would expect in such a grand home. The raised foyer overlooks the formal dining room and living area, and provides access to a bay-windowed study and secluded master suite with sitting area and fireplace. Next to the large kitchen and breakfast area is a laundry room and a special home office or hobby room. Upstairs, Bedrooms 2 and 3 each have walk-in closets and separate dressing areas. Plans for a two-car detached garage are included.

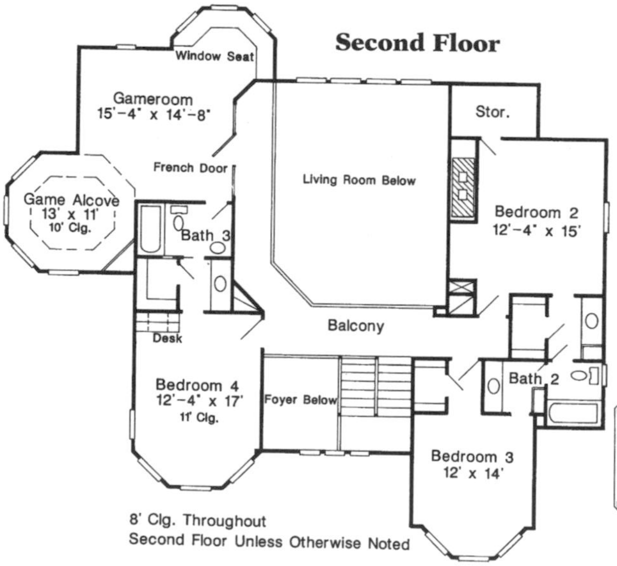

### Second Floor

Window Seat
Gameroom 15'-4" x 14'-8"
Stor.
French Door
Living Room Below
Game Alcove 13' x 11' 10' Clg.
Bedroom 2 12'-4" x 15'
Bath 3
Balcony
Desk
Bath 2
Bedroom 4 12'-4" x 17' 11' Clg.
Foyer Below
Bedroom 3 12' x 14'
8' Clg. Throughout Second Floor Unless Otherwise Noted

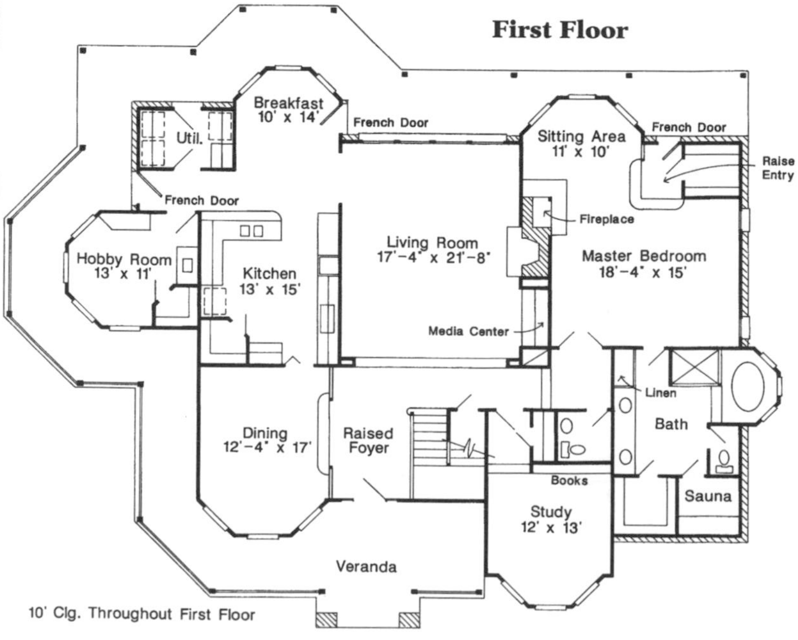

### First Floor

Breakfast 10' x 14'
Util.
French Door
Sitting Area 11' x 10'
French Door
Raise Entry
French Door
Fireplace
Living Room 17'-4" x 21'-8"
Hobby Room 13' x 11'
Kitchen 13' x 15'
Master Bedroom 18'-4" x 15'
Media Center
Linen
Bath
Dining 12'-4" x 17'
Raised Foyer
Books
Sauna
Study 12' x 13'
Veranda
10' Clg. Throughout First Floor

*First Floor:* *2,524 sq. ft.*
*Second Floor:* *1,529 sq. ft.*
*Total:* *4,053 sq. ft.*

Width: 75'-8"
Depth: 62'-4"

*(Foundation Type: Slab)*

# Sedalia

## Design CP9073

All of the essential elements of the Queen Anne Style are present on the exterior of this gracious and inviting home. The living room features built-in bookcases and a media center, and expansive window treatment. The optional garden room can be fully enclosed for all-weather enjoyment, or left open as a covered porch. The island kitchen overlooks a bay-windowed breakfast area. The master suite has a sitting alcove with leaded-glass transom window. An enormous bath showcases an oversized garden tub.

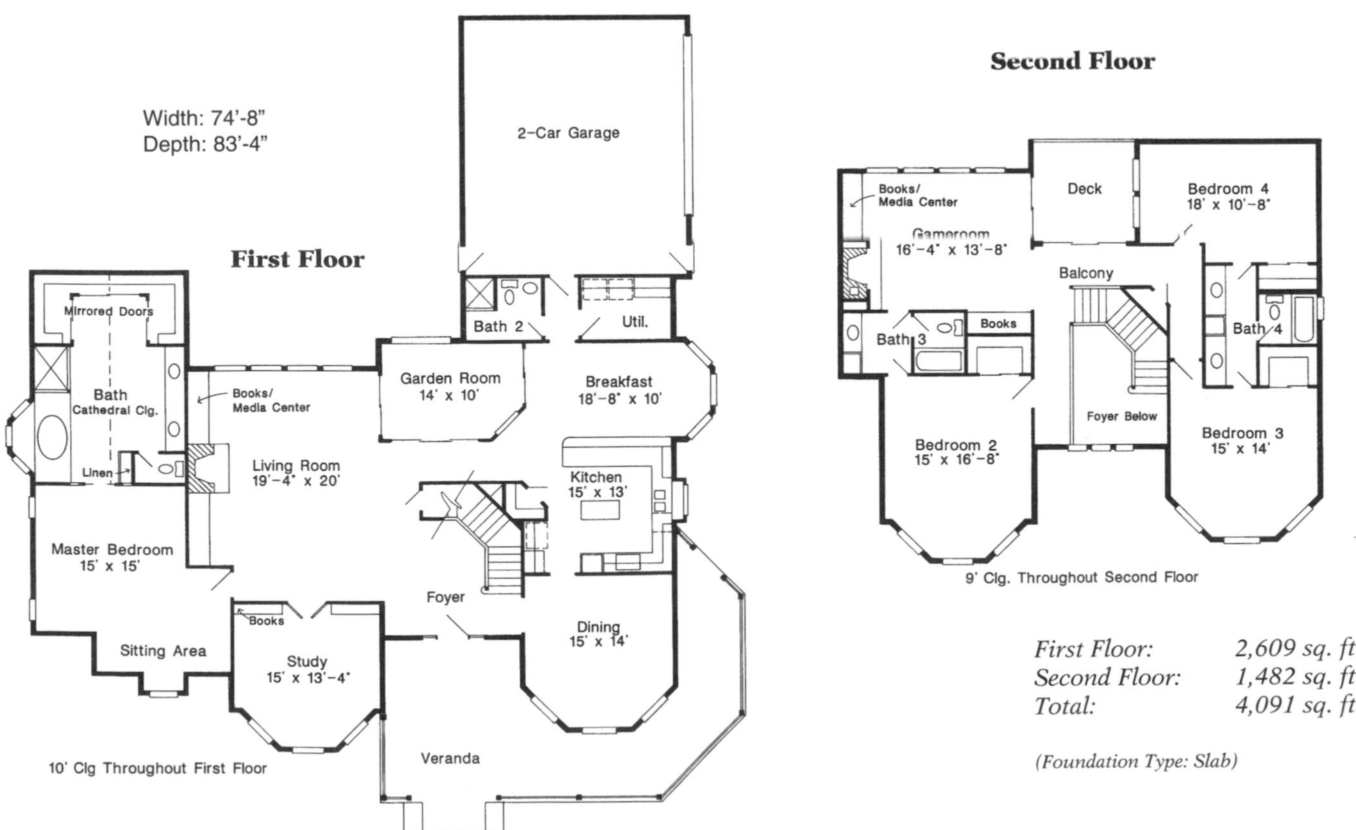


| | |
|---|---|
| *First Floor:* | *2,609 sq. ft.* |
| *Second Floor:* | *1,482 sq. ft.* |
| *Total:* | *4,091 sq. ft.* |

*(Foundation Type: Slab)*

## Design CP2953

# Emily

A magnificent covered porch decorates the facade of this Victorian estate home. The two-story foyer provides a direct view into the Great Room, which has a large central fireplace. A library lined with bookshelves and a dramatic, octagonal-shaped dining room flank the foyer. A luxurious master suite, with sitting room, dressing room and whirlpool, is located on the first floor. Four uniquely designed bedrooms, three full baths and a restful lounge with fireplace are located on the second floor.

**Second Floor**

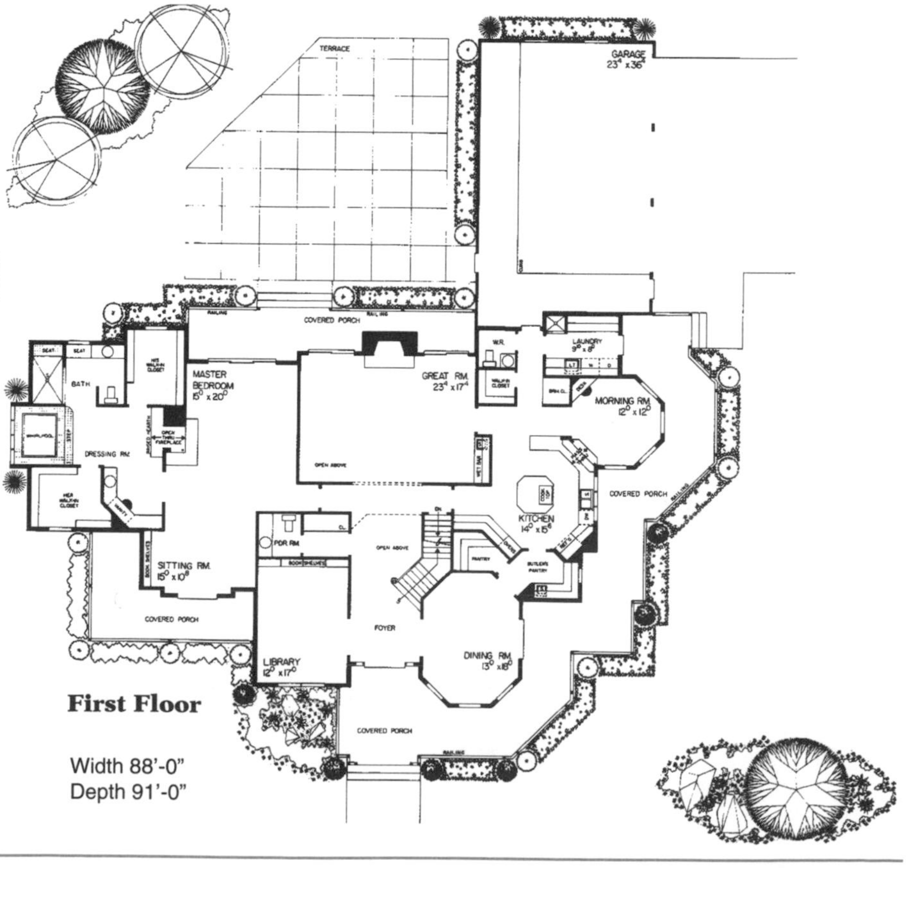

| | |
|---|---|
| *First Floor:* | *2,995 sq. ft.* |
| *Second Floor:* | *1,831 sq. ft.* |
| *Total:* | *4,826 sq. ft.* |

*(Foundation Type: Basement)*

**First Floor**

Width 88'-0"
Depth 91'-0"

# Victoria

**Design CP2954**

The exterior of this enchanting manor displays true Victorian style. Inside, the two-story living room with fireplace and wet bar is located at the rear of the home. The master suite, adjacent to the study, opens to a rear deck. It includes a fireplace, whirlpool bath and dressing rooms. The second floor opens to a large lounge, ideal for study or peaceful relaxation and built with cabinets and bookshelves. Three bedrooms and two full baths complete the second floor.

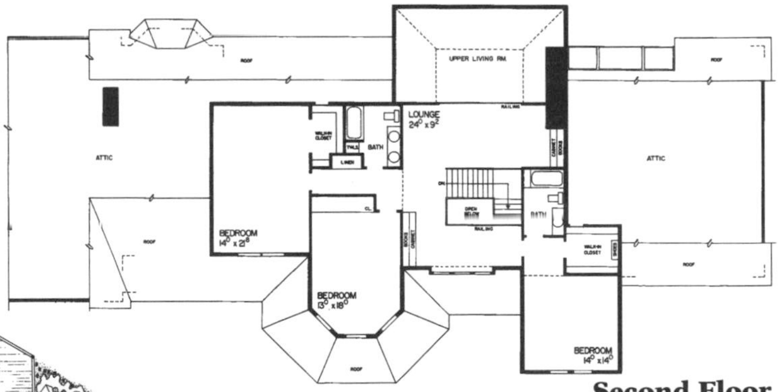

**Second Floor**

**First Floor**

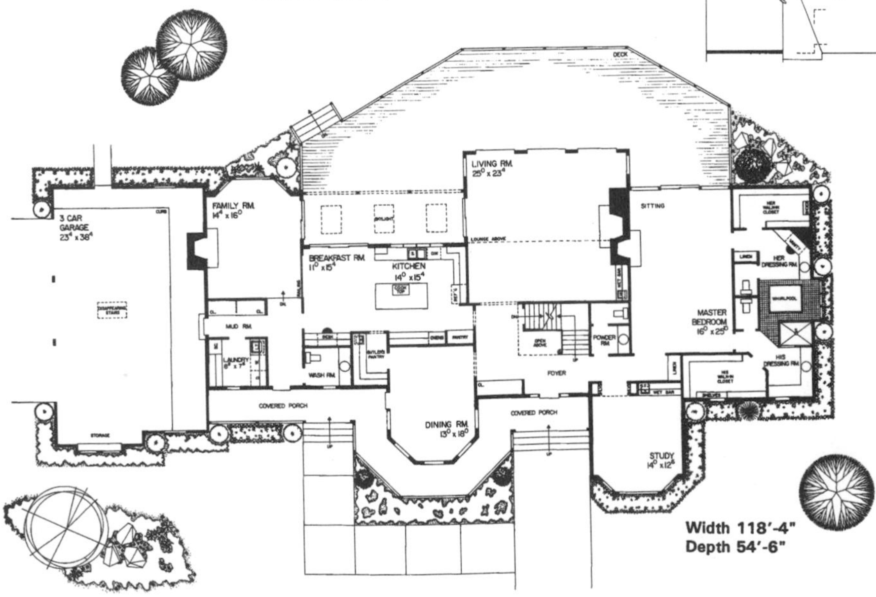

**Width 118′-4″**
**Depth 54′-6″**

| | |
|---|---|
| *First Floor:* | *3,079 sq. ft.* |
| *Second Floor:* | *1,461 sq. ft.* |
| *Total:* | *4,540 sq. ft.* |

*(Foundation Type: Basement)*

## Design CP9013

# Bancroft

This Victorian-inspired home, with its wide veranda, expansive windows and French doors, can take advantage of a site that offers views in every direction. Built-in bookcases and French doors from the living room and the gallery make the study a perfect retreat. The kitchen features a work island, walk-in pantry, and plenty of cabinet space. The spacious master bedroom has French doors opening onto the veranda. A staircase leads to an optional third floor area. A two-car detached garage design is included.

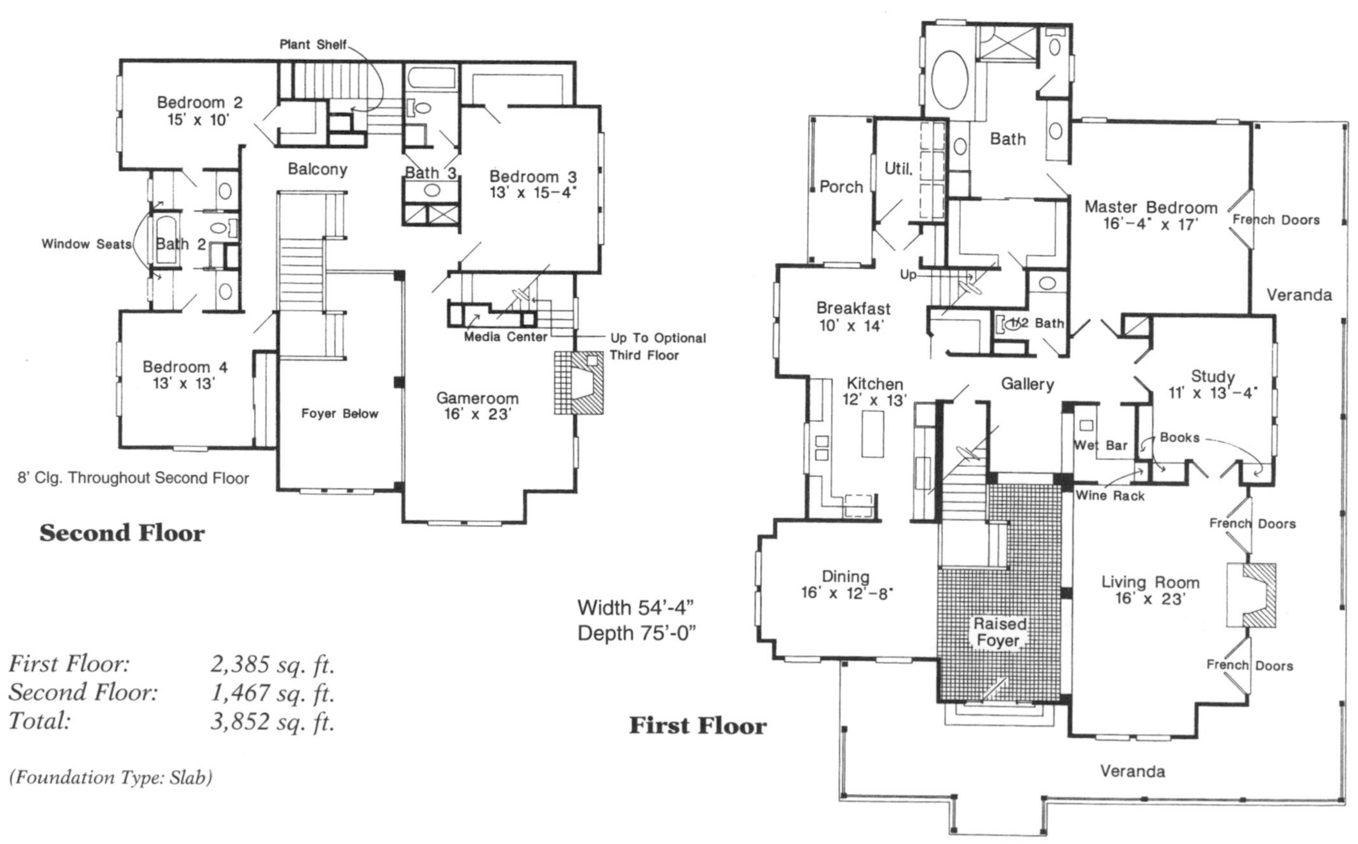


*First Floor:* *2,385 sq. ft.*
*Second Floor:* *1,467 sq. ft.*
*Total:* *3,852 sq. ft.*

*(Foundation Type: Slab)*

# Parnassus Design CP2660

Here is an adaptation of the 18th Century "Single House" so popular in Charleston, SC. In its original form, the house was but a single room wide. This updated version includes an attached kitchen/garage wing. A piazza runs the full length of the home. Fireplaces can be found in the gathering room, parlor, master bedroom and activities room. The second floor provides four large bedrooms, three full baths and a full-length balcony. A guest bedroom with a full bath and a study are found on the third floor.

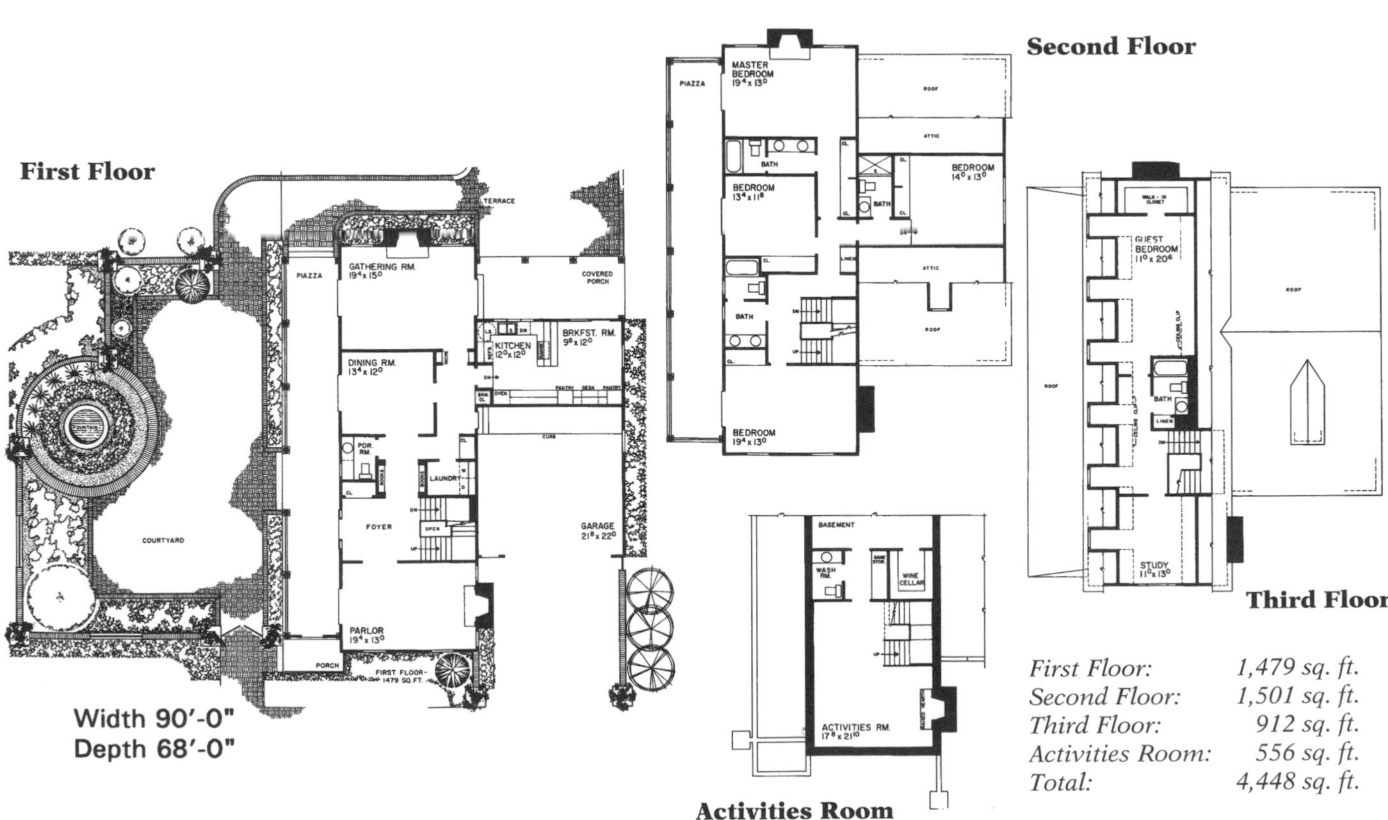

## Design CP2991

# Jesmond

This antebellum Greek Revival manor represents the grace of Southern plantation style. Flanking a wide entry foyer are the formal living and dining rooms, each with a fireplace. Less-formal activities take place in the family room which is conveniently open to the island kitchen. A handy cooktop with snack bar island serves both areas. Separating living areas from the master suite is a quiet study. On the second floor are three bedrooms and three full baths, plus a small sitting room and a storage area.

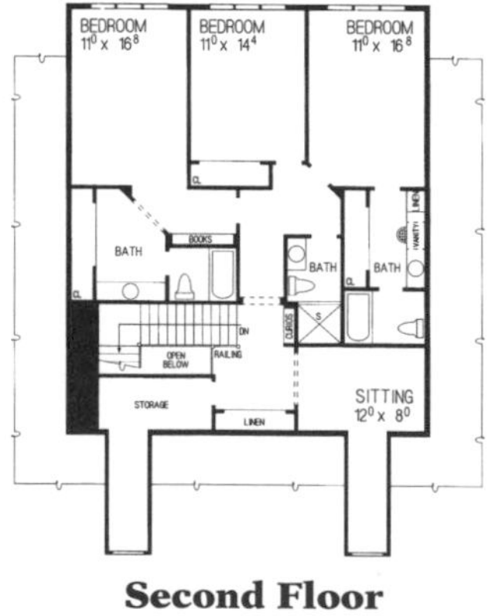


**Second Floor**

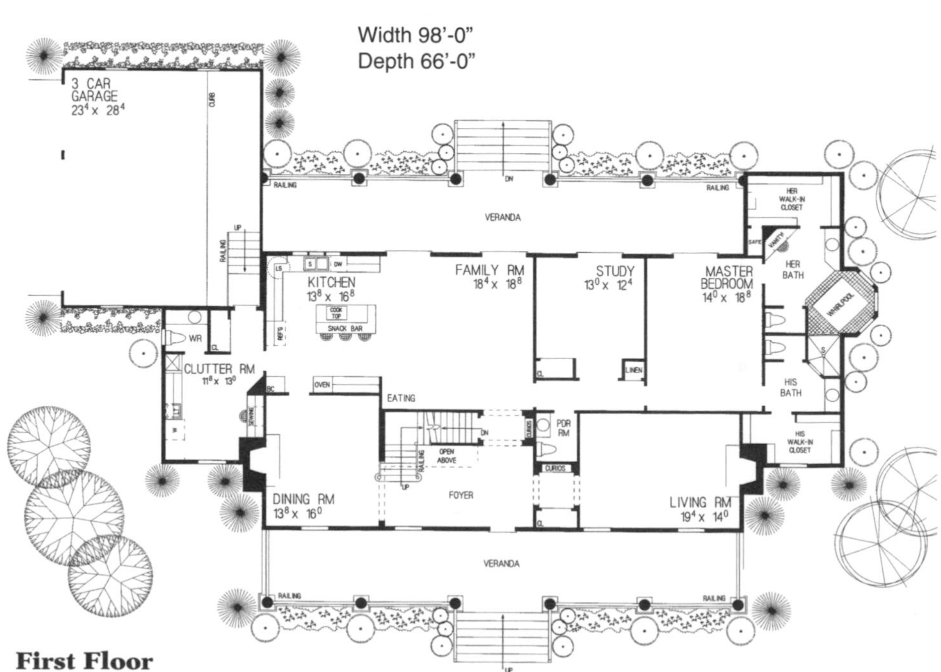


**First Floor**

| | |
|---|---|
| *First Floor:* | *2,658 sq. ft.* |
| *Second Floor:* | *1,429 sq. ft.* |
| *Total:* | *4,087 sq. ft.* |

*(Foundation Type: Basement)*

# Brandon

## Design CP2997

The fine features of this home include five fireplaces. One fireplace warms the master bedroom which has an expansive bath and dressing area, plus access to a private rear terrace. Two additional bedrooms each adjoin a full bath. Large living areas include the living room, dining room and family room with snack bar. A library with fireplace, sloped ceiling and built-in shelves is tucked away in the rear of the home. The exterior of this Georgian manor is just as impressive as the interior.

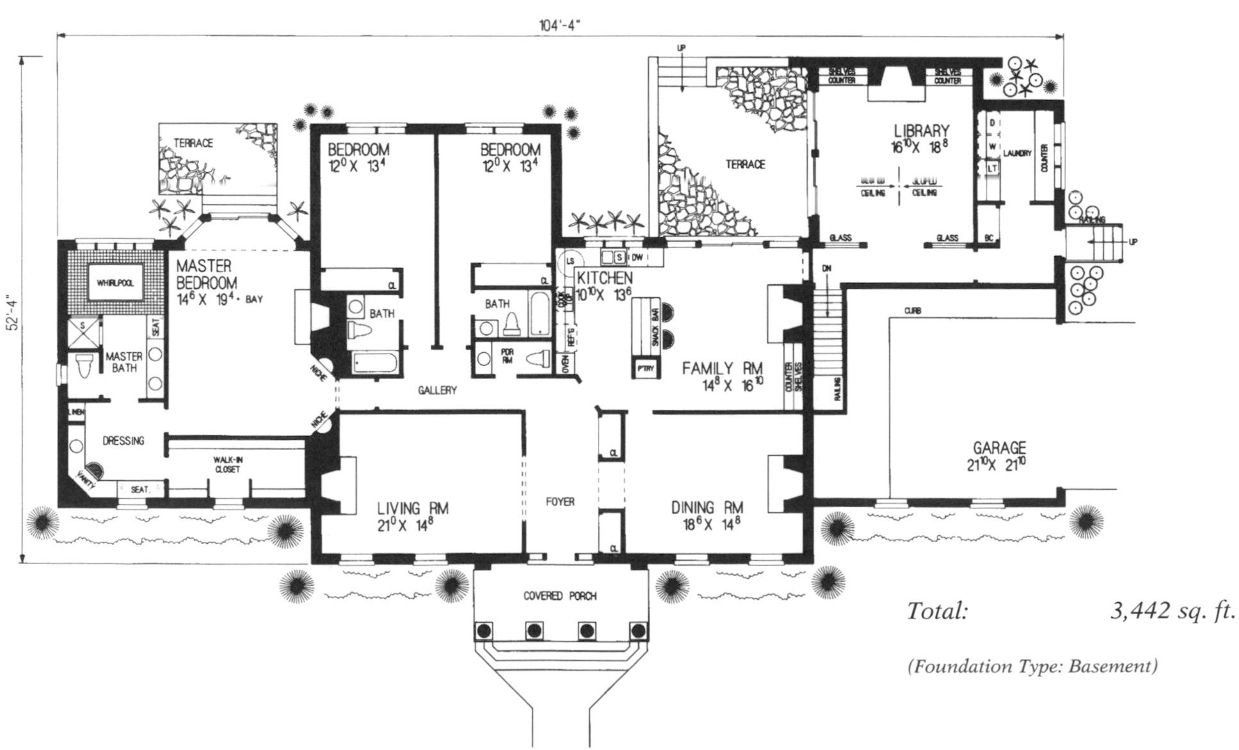


*Total:* *3,442 sq. ft.*

*(Foundation Type: Basement)*

## Design CP2987 **Galahad**

This modern home captures the essence of Andrew Jackson's Hermitage. One wing of the first floor contains a luxurious master suite with a fireplace, His and Hers walk-in closets, a dressing area and a deluxe bath with whirlpool tub. The opposite wing features a country kitchen, laundry, washroom and two-car garage. The family room, dining room and living room, each with a fireplace, are centrally located. On the second floor are three bedrooms (one a guest room) and two baths.

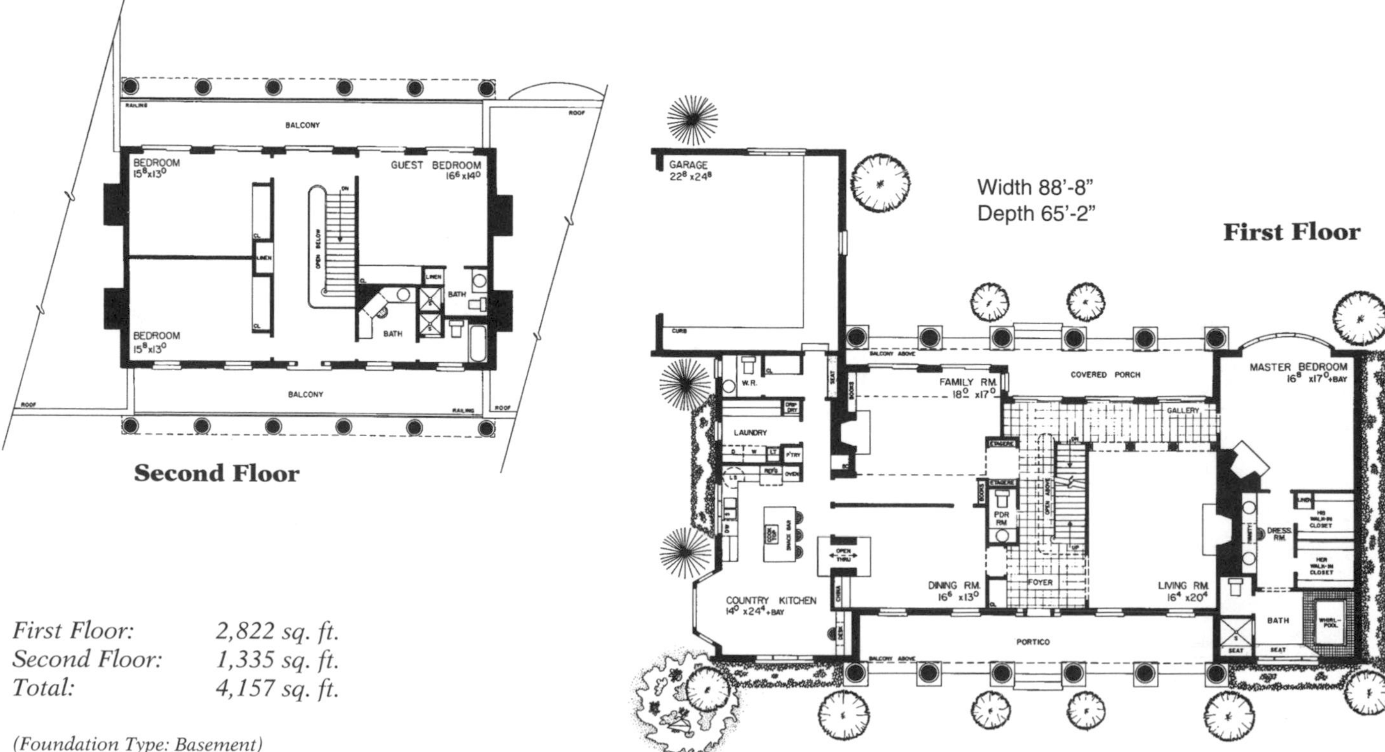


*First Floor:* *2,822 sq. ft.*
*Second Floor:* *1,335 sq. ft.*
*Total:* *4,157 sq. ft.*

*(Foundation Type: Basement)*

# Marbleton

## Design CP3500

A historical facade in the Greek Revival tradition, with sweeping verandas in the front and rear, conceals a livable plan. Massive twin chimneys, a fanlight double-doored entry, a second-floor balcony and symmetrical window treatment enhance the appeal of this clapboard-sided two-story house. Special interior amenities include the rounded stairway, three fireplaces, two pantries, a built-in desk and built-in shelves and bookcases. Four bedrooms on the second floor have access to three full baths.

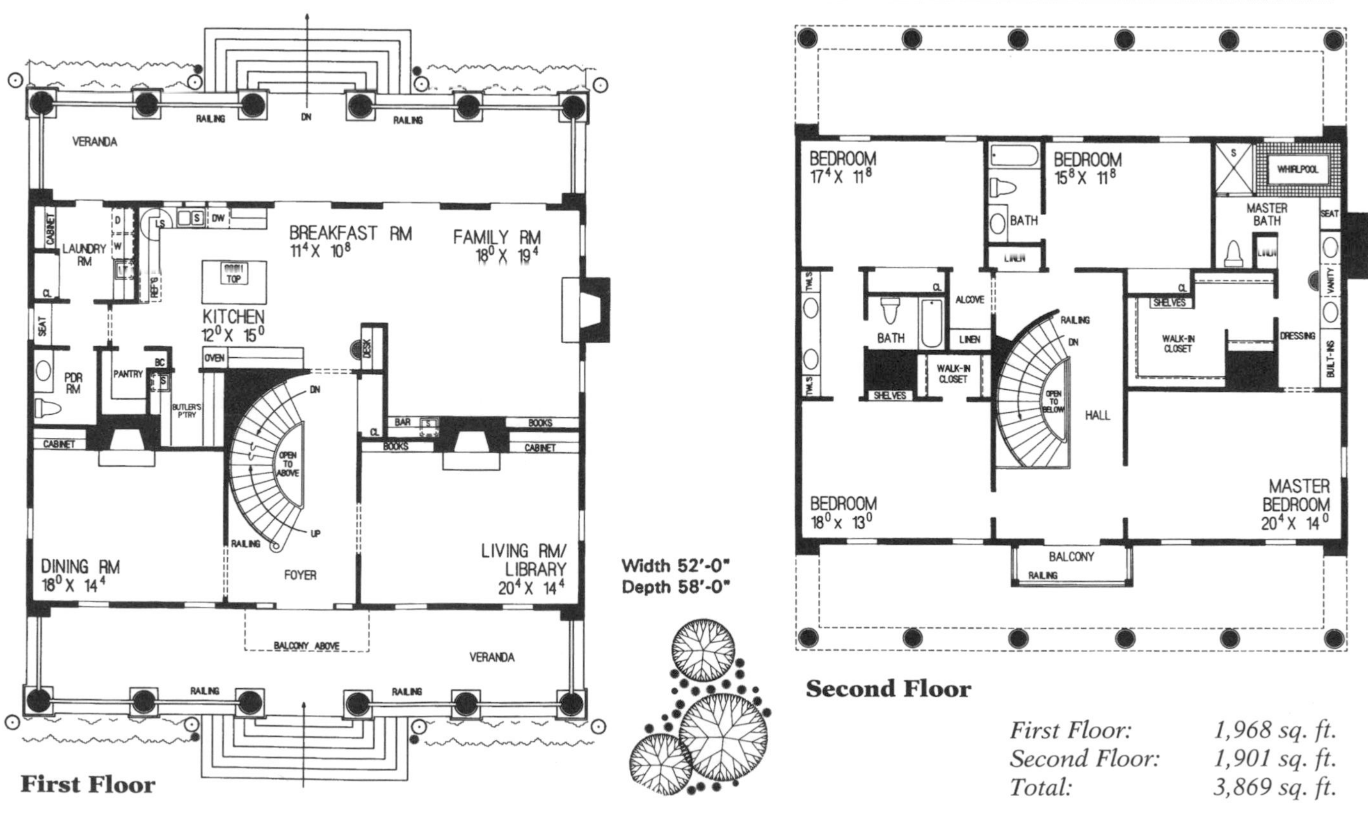


**First Floor**

**Second Floor**

| | |
|---|---|
| *First Floor:* | *1,968 sq. ft.* |
| *Second Floor:* | *1,901 sq. ft.* |
| *Total:* | *3,869 sq. ft.* |

*(Foundation Type: Basement)*

## Design CP2696

# Penhold

This gracious Greek Revival design features a classic white portico with six Doric columns. It is reminiscent of plantation homes built in the South between 1820 and 1860. The interior is no less impressive. The foyer highlights an open staircase to the four-bedroom, three-bath second floor. The formal living and dining rooms are large, and each features a fireplace. The morning room with its wall of windows will be just the place to start the day. Notice the master bedroom with its two fireplaces.

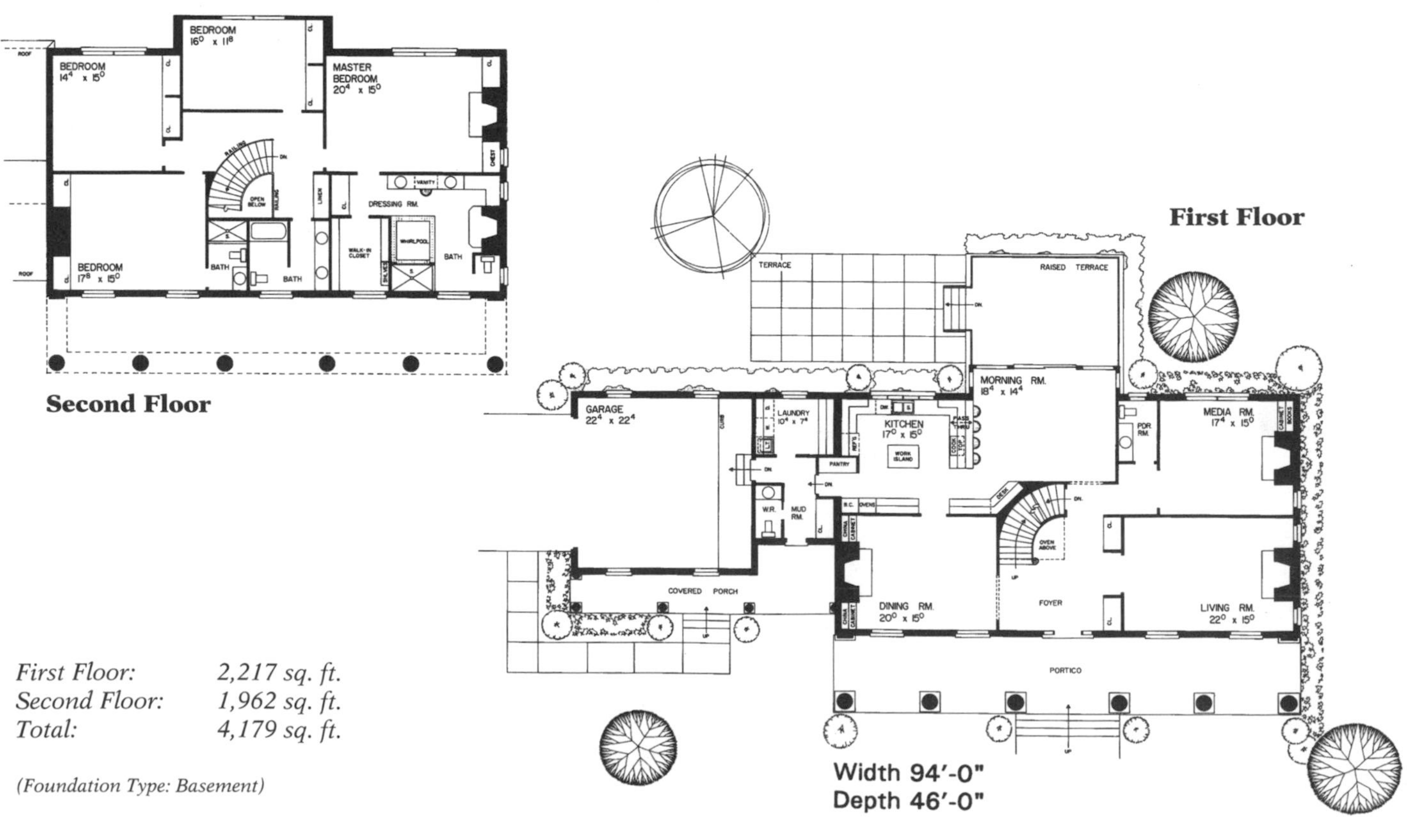


| | |
|---|---|
| *First Floor:* | *2,217 sq. ft.* |
| *Second Floor:* | *1,962 sq. ft.* |
| *Total:* | *4,179 sq. ft.* |

*(Foundation Type: Basement)*

# Sheldon

## Design CP2230

The gracefulness and appeal of this Southern adaptation will be everlasting. The imposing two-story portico is truly dramatic. Notice the authentic detailing of the tapered Doric columns, the balustraded roof deck, the denticulated cornice, the front entrance and the shuttered windows. A spacious entry hall is flanked by the formal living room with fireplace and dining room with built-in china cabinets. The expansive family room features another fireplace. Notice the master suite with His and Hers baths.

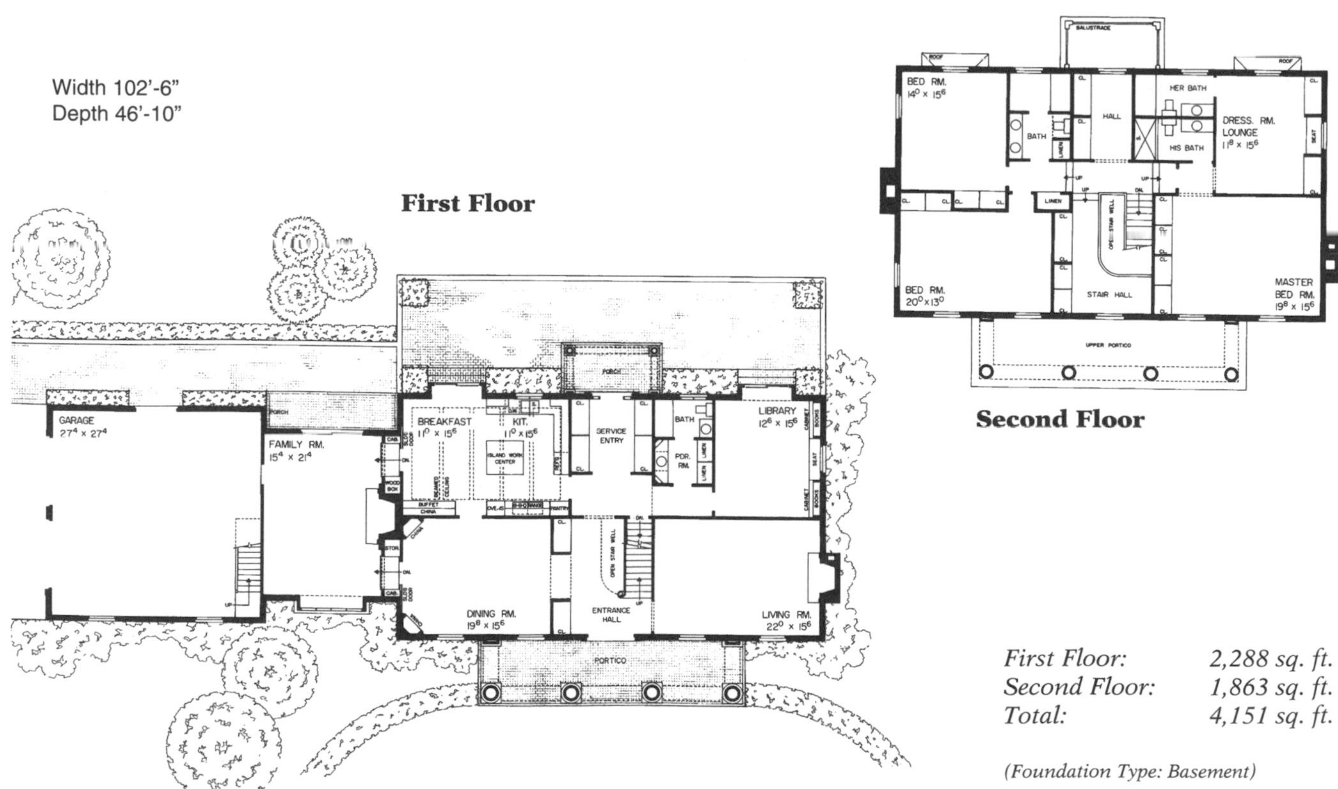


| | |
|---|---|
| *First Floor:* | *2,288 sq. ft.* |
| *Second Floor:* | *1,863 sq. ft.* |
| *Total:* | *4,151 sq. ft.* |

*(Foundation Type: Basement)*

## Design CP3303 **Hawthorne**

With stately columns and one-story wings, this design is a fine representation of 18th Century adaptations. Formal living and dining areas flank the entry and are joined by informal areas in a family room and kitchen with breakfast room. The master bedroom suite includes His and Her dressing areas, a fireplace and whirlpool bath. Upstairs, four family bedrooms with two shared baths and walk-in closets complete the second floor.

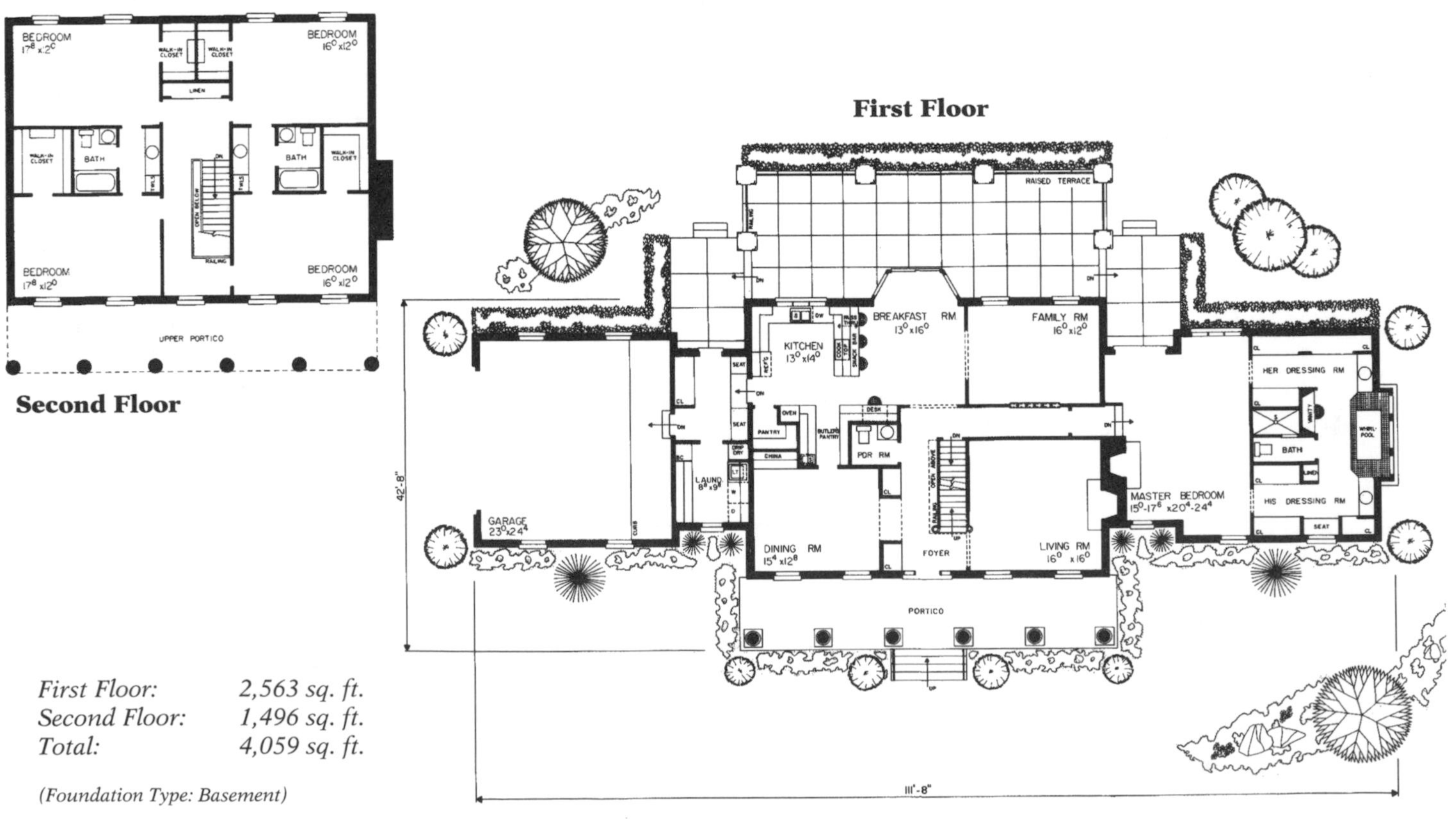


**First Floor**

**Second Floor**

*First Floor:* *2,563 sq. ft.*
*Second Floor:* *1,496 sq. ft.*
*Total:* *4,059 sq. ft.*

*(Foundation Type: Basement)*

# Cristose

**Design CP4505**

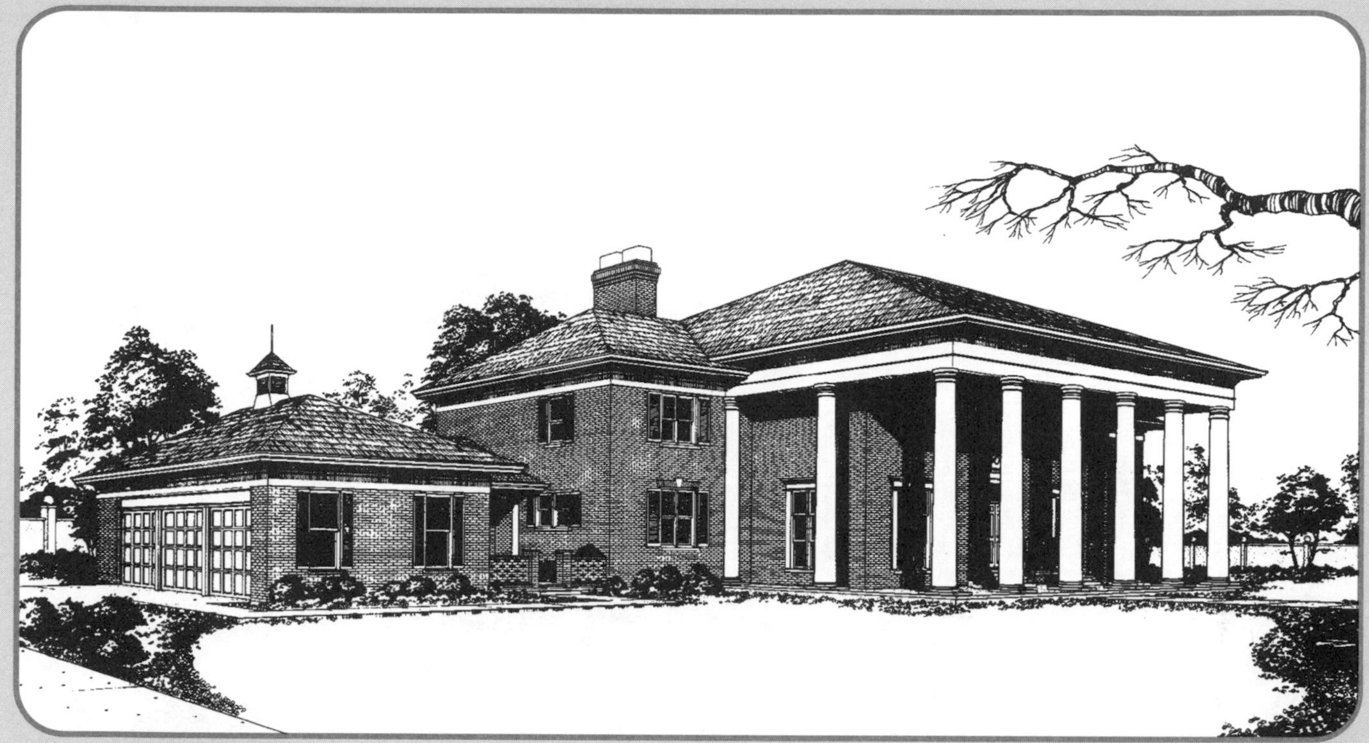

This home recalls the style of the Old South, with gracious columns and a two-story porch. The two-story foyer opens to the living room, family room and dining room. The elegant master suite has an adjoining sitting room with private entrance. The second floor houses six large bedrooms, each with ample closets, three full baths and extra storage space. Located on the basement level are the maid's quarters, a kitchenette and children's playroom.

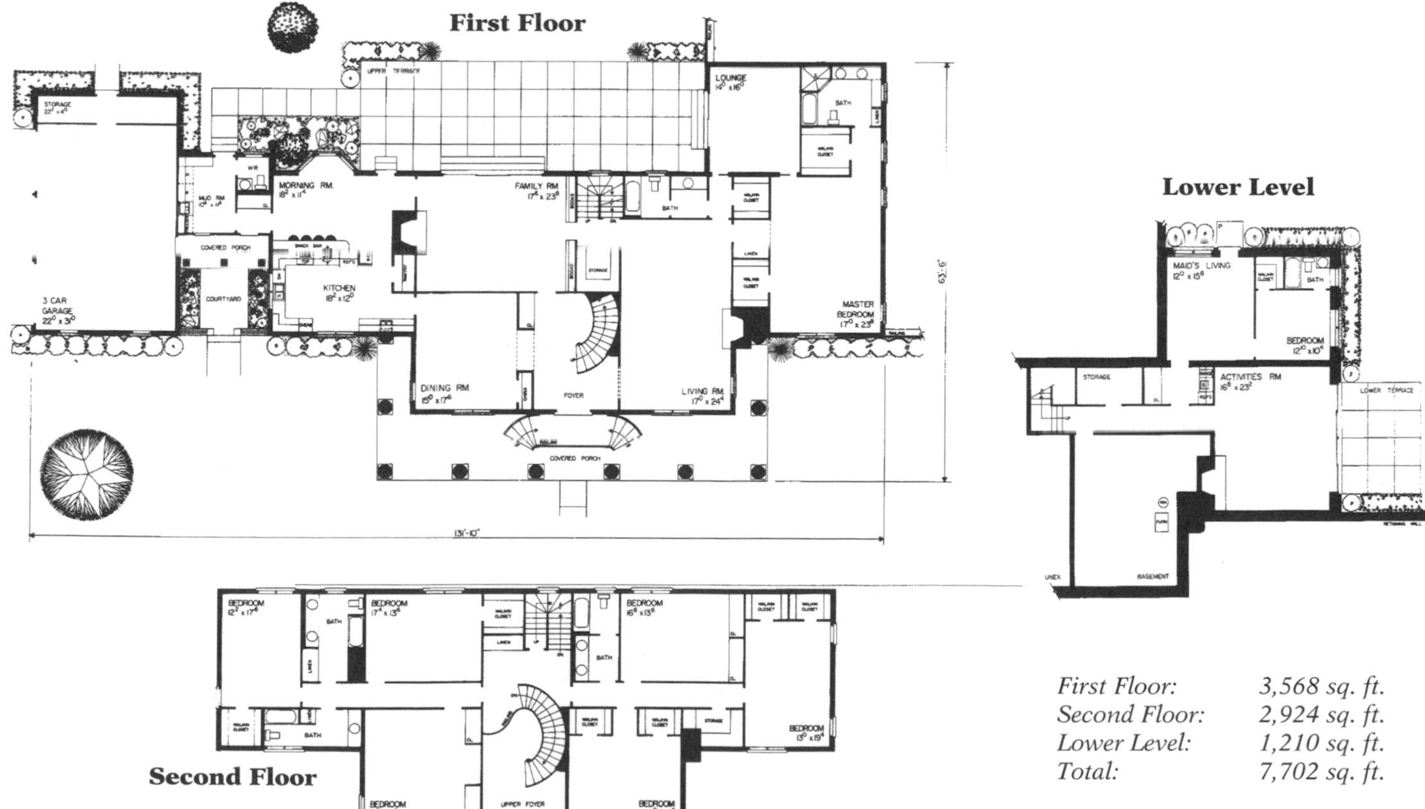


| | |
|---|---|
| *First Floor:* | *3,568 sq. ft.* |
| *Second Floor:* | *2,924 sq. ft.* |
| *Lower Level:* | *1,210 sq. ft.* |
| *Total:* | *7,702 sq. ft.* |

*(Foundation Type: Basement)*

**Design CP2553**

# Garfield

This stately Southern Colonial with massive columns and dramatic pediment gable could hardly be more impressive. Highlighting the first floor, a grand gathering room with fireplace is open to the second floor. The formal living room and study are to the right of the plan. The formal dining room is adjacent to the kitchen and breakfast nook. On the second floor, the master bedroom features a large dressing room. Two family bedrooms with separate vanities share a full bath.

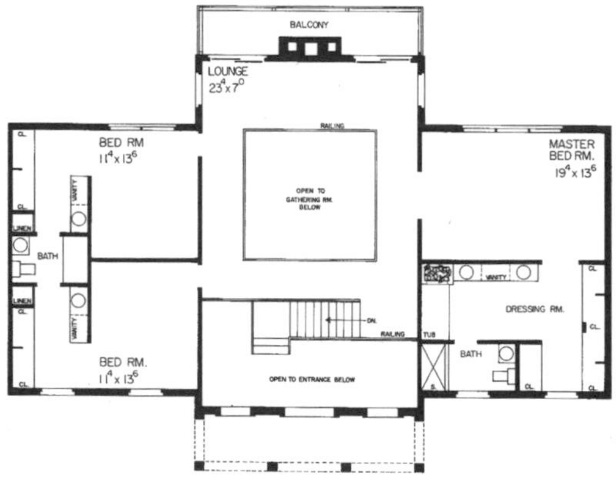

**Second Floor**

**First Floor**

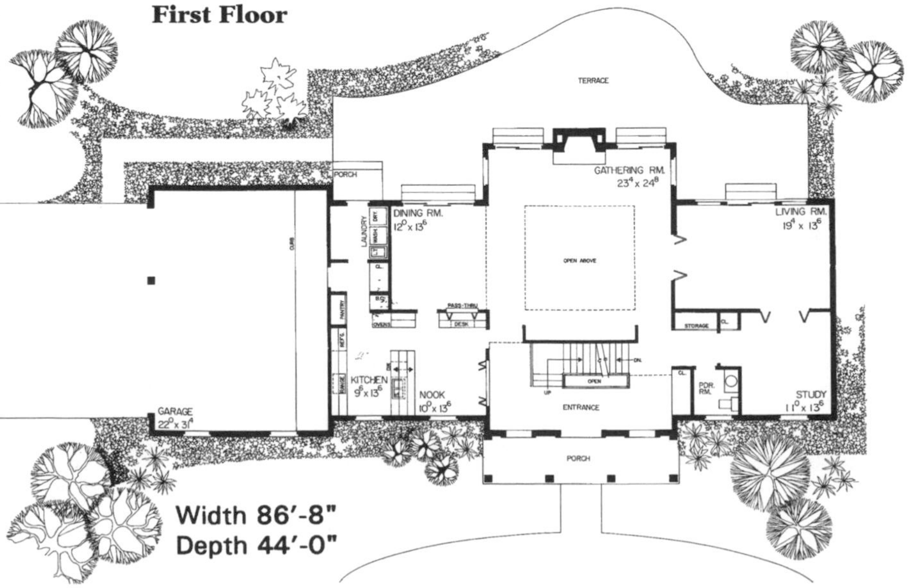

| | |
|---|---|
| *First Floor:* | *2,065 sq. ft.* |
| *Second Floor:* | *1,612 sq. ft.* |
| *Total:* | *3,677 sq. ft.* |

*(Foundation Type: Basement)*

**Width 86'-8"**
**Depth 44'-0"**

# Coronation

## Design CP2693

A stunning example of Georgian symmetry, this one-story features two wings surrounding a central living area with four fireplaces and a central foyer with powder room. Built-ins include bookshelves in the library, a desk in the kitchen, china cabinets in the dining room, and curio shelves in the living room. The combination bedroom/sewing room is adjacent to a full bath and near the clutter room. All three bedrooms feature walk-in closets (His and Hers in the master bedroom).

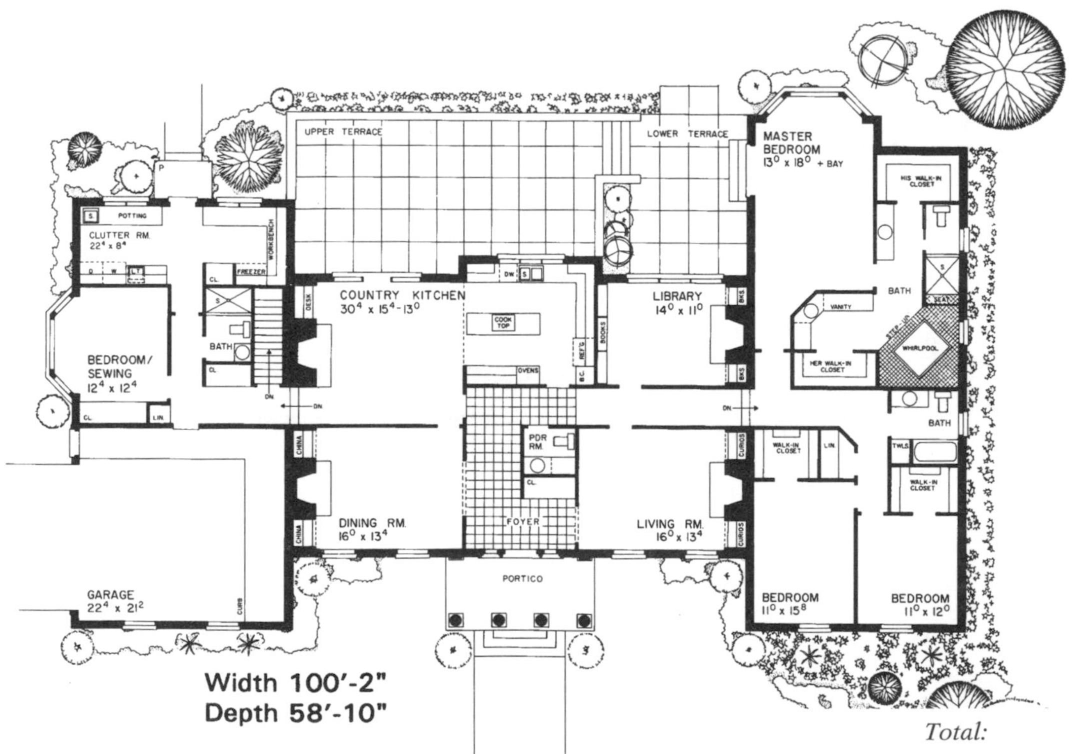


*Total:* *3,462 sq. ft.*

*(Foundation Type: Basement)*

**Design CP2889**

# Lexington

The exterior of this bold, two-story home is graced by four columns. The large receiving hall features two curving staircases, and is flanked by the formal living and dining rooms. The informal gathering room features a massive fireplace and access to the terrace. The kitchen is joined by a breakfast room and service area. Upstairs, the second floor contains a luxurious master bedroom suite with fireplace. Three bedrooms and two baths complete this floor.

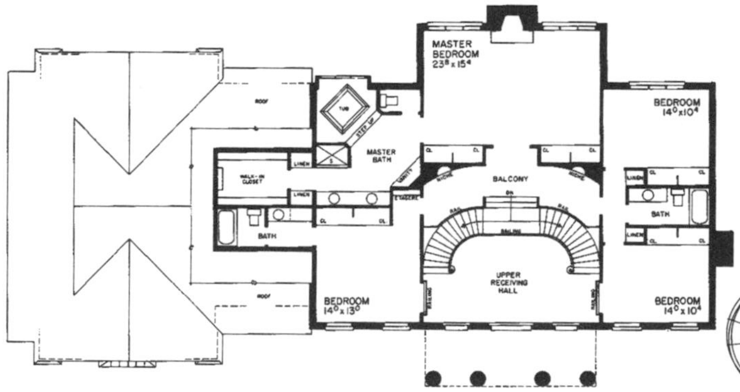

**First Floor**

**Second Floor**

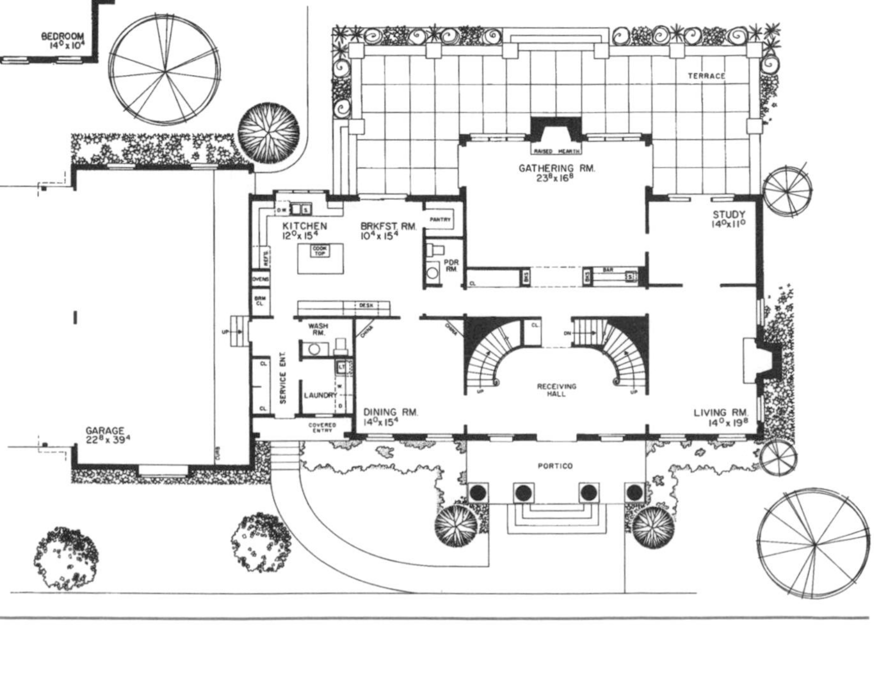

Width 90'-4"
Depth 44'-8"

| | |
|---|---|
| *First Floor:* | *2,349 sq. ft.* |
| *Second Floor:* | *1,918 sq. ft.* |
| *Total:* | *4,267 sq. ft.* |

*(Foundation Type: Basement)*

# Lawrence

**Design CP3337**

The elegant facade of this home is decorated with a columned portico, fanlights and dormers. The gathering room, study and dining room, each with fireplace, provide plenty of room for relaxing and entertaining. A large work area contains a kitchen with breakfast room and snack bar, a laundry room and pantry. The master suite, located upstairs, includes a large exercise room, His and Her closets and a whirlpool bath. The level is complete with three bedrooms, a bath and attic storage.

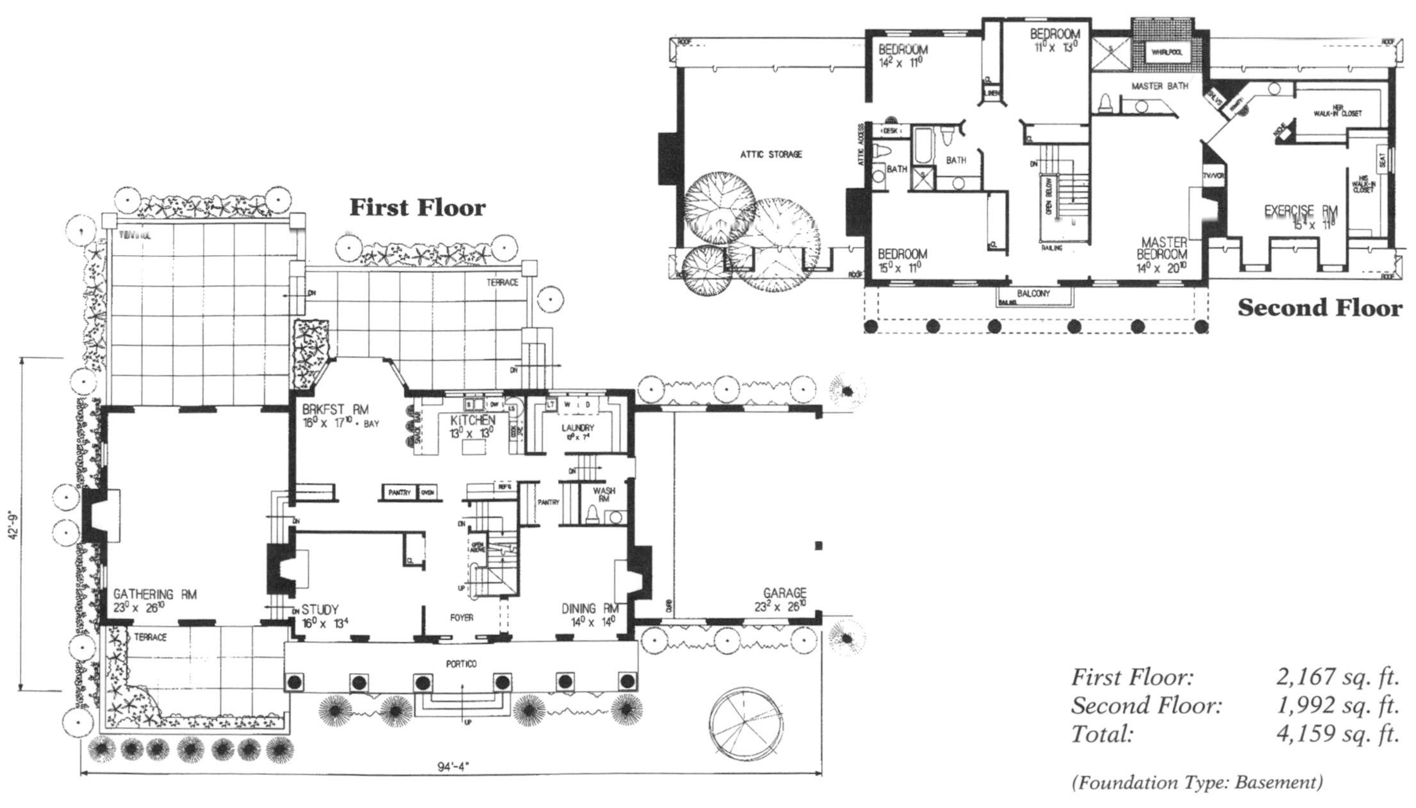


| | |
|---|---|
| *First Floor:* | *2,167 sq. ft.* |
| *Second Floor:* | *1,992 sq. ft.* |
| *Total:* | *4,159 sq. ft.* |

*(Foundation Type: Basement)*

**Design CP3320**

# Lafayette

This home makes a grand impression with its bold columns and brick and wood exterior. The spacious two-story foyer with circular staircase leads to the dining room, media room and two-story gathering room with fireplace. The well-equipped kitchen includes a snack bar for informal meals. A luxurious master suite, found on the main level, includes whirlpool and walk-in closet. Upstairs, four bedrooms with shared baths complete this impressive plan.

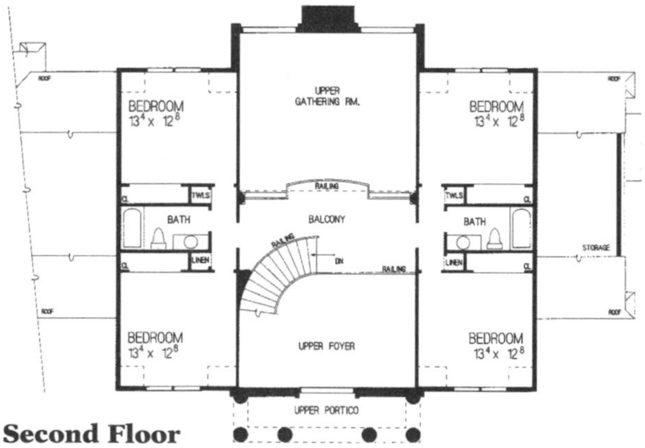

**Second Floor**

**First Floor**

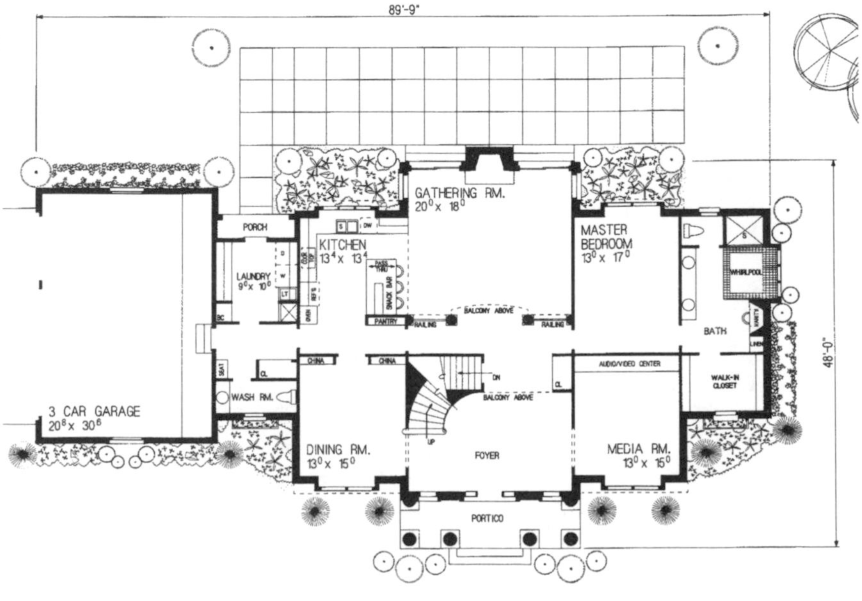

| | |
|---|---|
| *First Floor:* | *2,337 sq. ft.* |
| *Second Floor:* | *1,232 sq. ft.* |
| *Total:* | *3,569 sq. ft.* |

*(Foundation Type: Basement)*

# Rutherford

**Design CP2977**

Both front and rear facades of this elegant brick manor depict classic Georgian symmetry. Fireplaces, built-in shelves and cabinets highlight the living room, dining area, family room and library. The kitchen features a handy work island and pass-through to the dining room. The master suite is located in a private wing and has a lounge/exercise room and an entrance to the atrium. Two bedrooms, with private baths and walk-in closets, are located on the second floor.

**First Floor**

Width 132'-0"
Depth 53'-6"

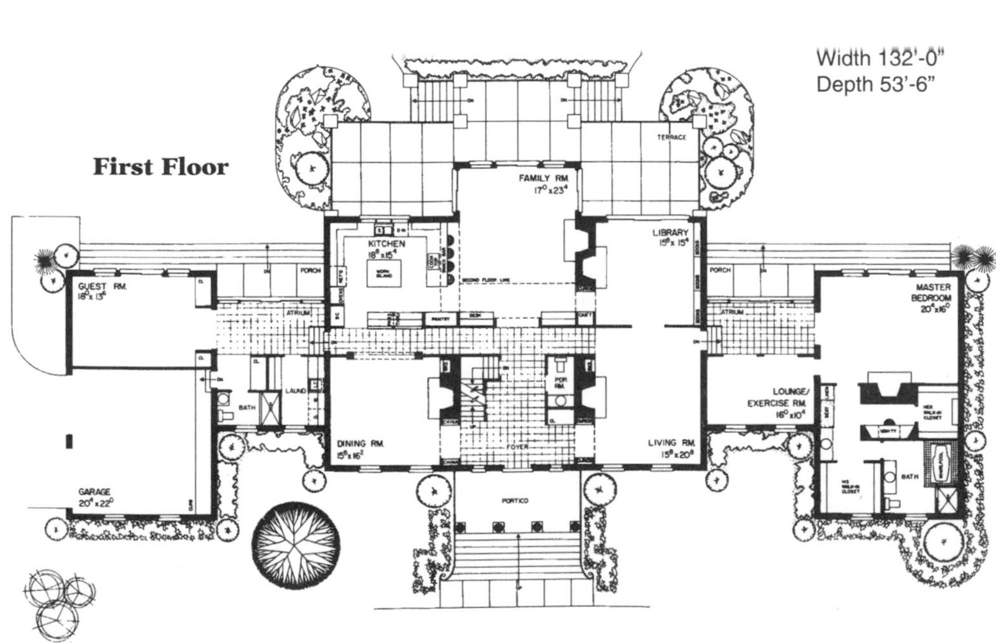


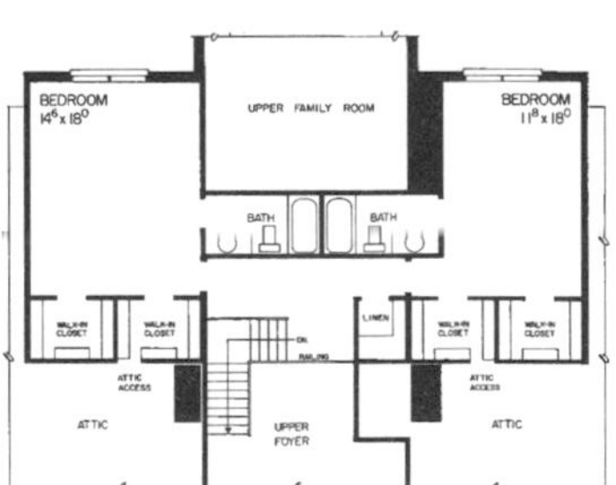


**Second Floor**

| | |
|---|---|
| *First Floor:* | *4,104 sq. ft.* |
| *Second Floor:* | *979 sq. ft.* |
| *Total:* | *5,083 sq. ft.* |

*(Foundation Type: Basement)*

## Design CP2683

# Bedford

This Georgian manor is marked by its brick exterior, massive chimneys and a columned entrance. Inside, the elegant gathering room fills an entire wing. The study and dining room, both with fireplaces, flank the foyer. The kitchen is laid out in an efficient U-shape with a convenient island cooktop. The master suite includes a fireplace and private lounge. Three bedrooms and a bath complete the second-floor living space.

**First Floor**

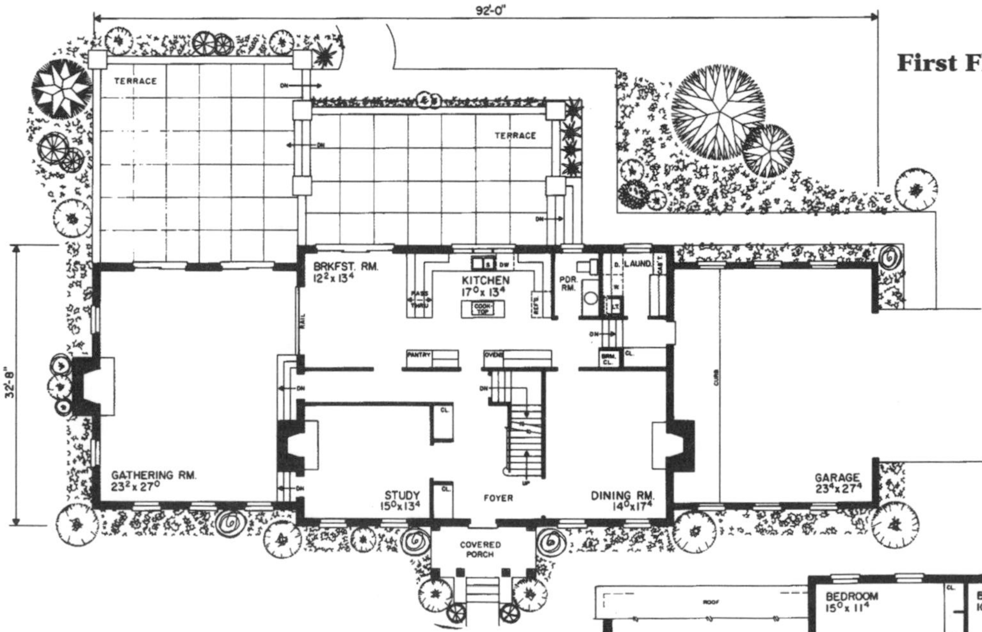

**Second Floor**

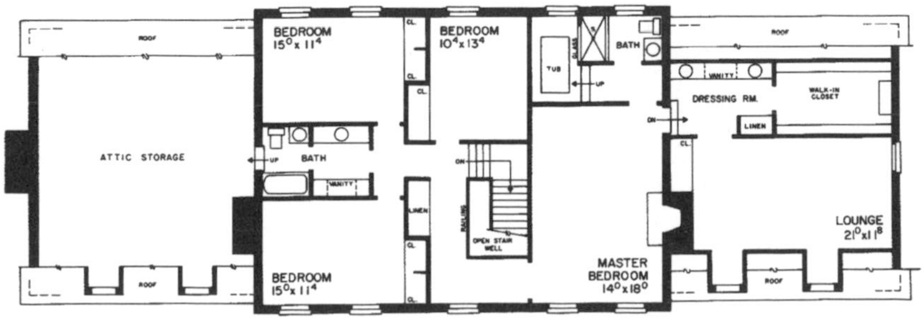

| | |
|---|---|
| *First Floor:* | *2,126 sq. ft.* |
| *Second Floor:* | *1,882 sq. ft.* |
| *Total:* | *4,008 sq. ft.* |

*(Foundation Type: Basement)*

# Memphis

## Design CP4305

Two-story columns dominate the facade of this classic Greek Revival home. The foyer is flanked by the living area and oval dining room. The U-shaped kitchen with snack bar and breakfast room adjoins the family room. The master suite features convenient His and Her baths and three walk-in closets. A spiral staircase leads to the five bedrooms and four baths on the second floor. The lower level has a hobbies/exercise room and an activities room.

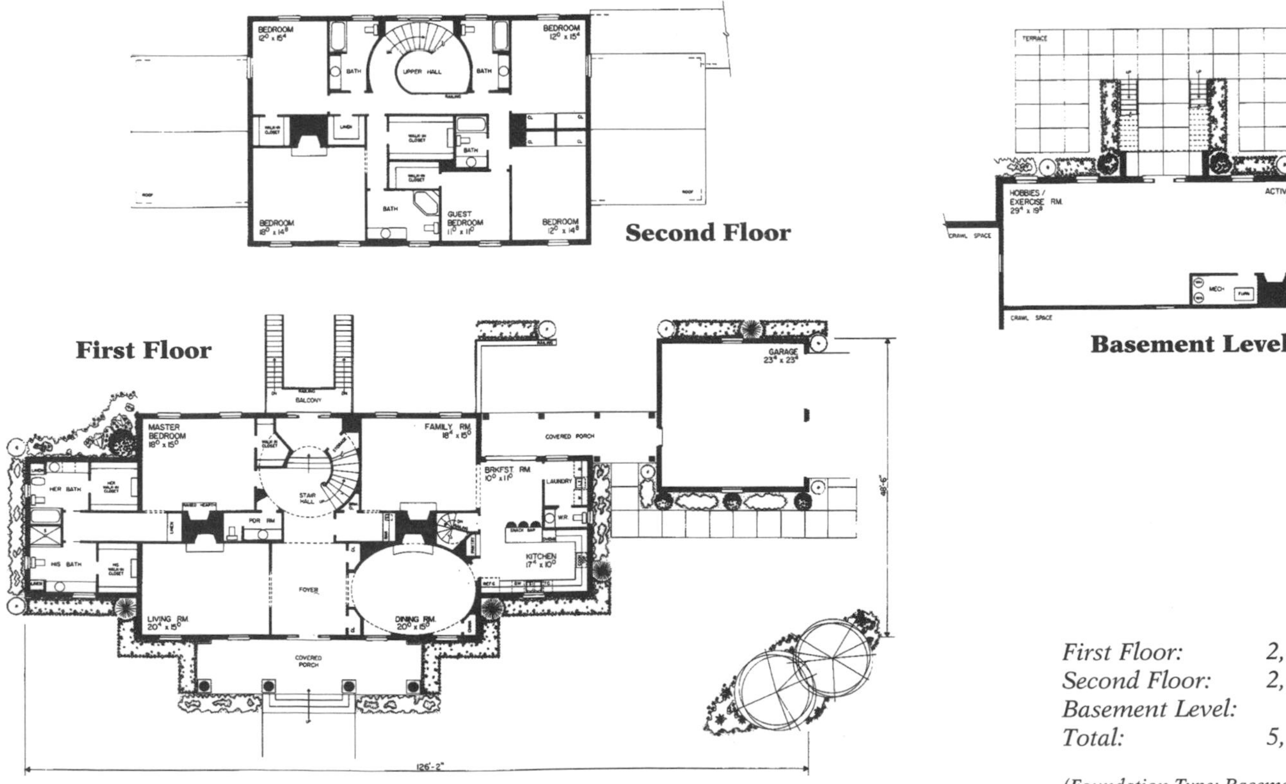


| | |
|---|---|
| *First Floor:* | *2,841 sq. ft.* |
| *Second Floor:* | *2,019 sq. ft.* |
| *Basement Level:* | *860 sq. ft.* |
| *Total:* | *5,720 sq. ft.* |

*(Foundation Type: Basement)*

## Design CP2984

# Whitehall

An echo of Whitehall, built in 1765 in Maryland, resounds in this home. There is no lack of space whether entertaining formally or informally. All are kept cozy with fireplaces in the gathering room, study and family room. An island kitchen with attached breakfast room serves the nearby dining room. Upstairs, a master suite with fireplace, whirlpool and His and Her closets is joined by three bedrooms with private baths.

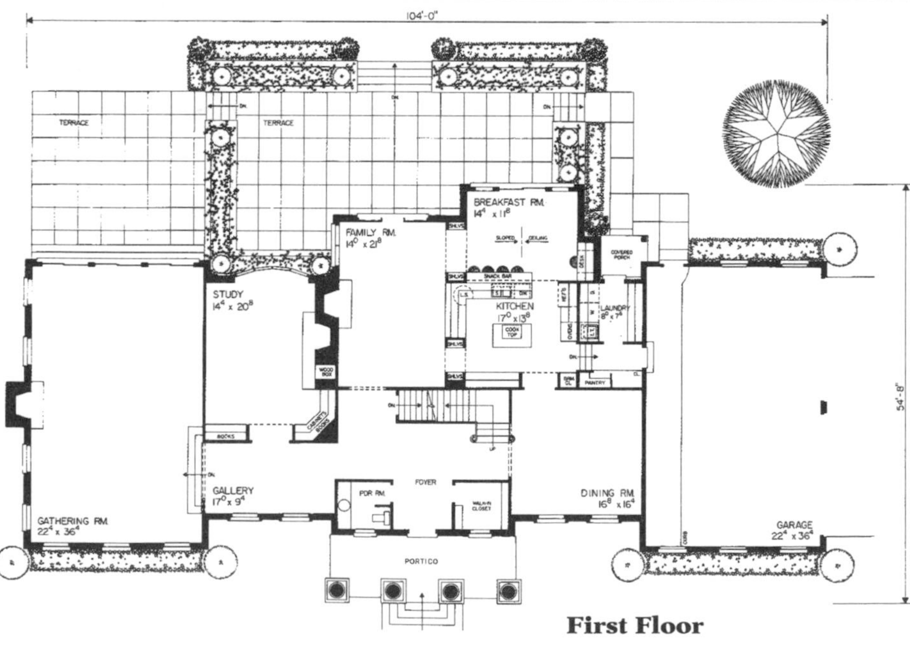


First Floor

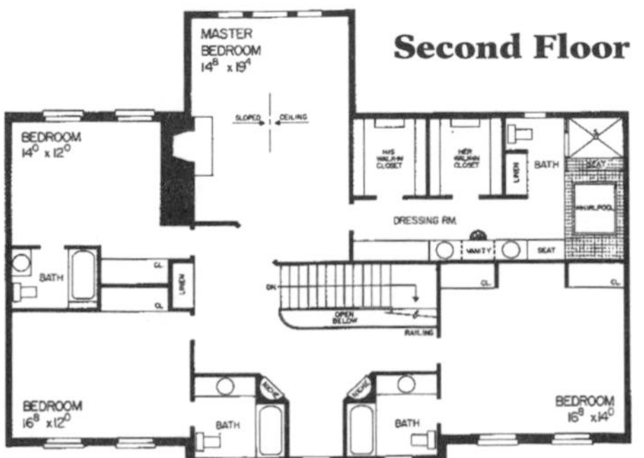


Second Floor

*First Floor:* *3,116 sq. ft.*
*Second Floor:* *1,997 sq. ft.*
*Total:* *5,113 sq. ft.*

*(Foundation Type: Basement)*

# *Franklin* **Design CP4506**

The exterior of this home resembles a Greek Revival but the interior has been designed to fulfill the needs of a modern family. A master suite is joined by two family bedrooms. The family room with fireplace and access to the deck is perfect for entertaining. A kitchen with breakfast nook adjoins the family and dining areas. Upstairs, two bedrooms share a bath. The lower level is occupied by a game room with fireplace and a bedroom with private bath.

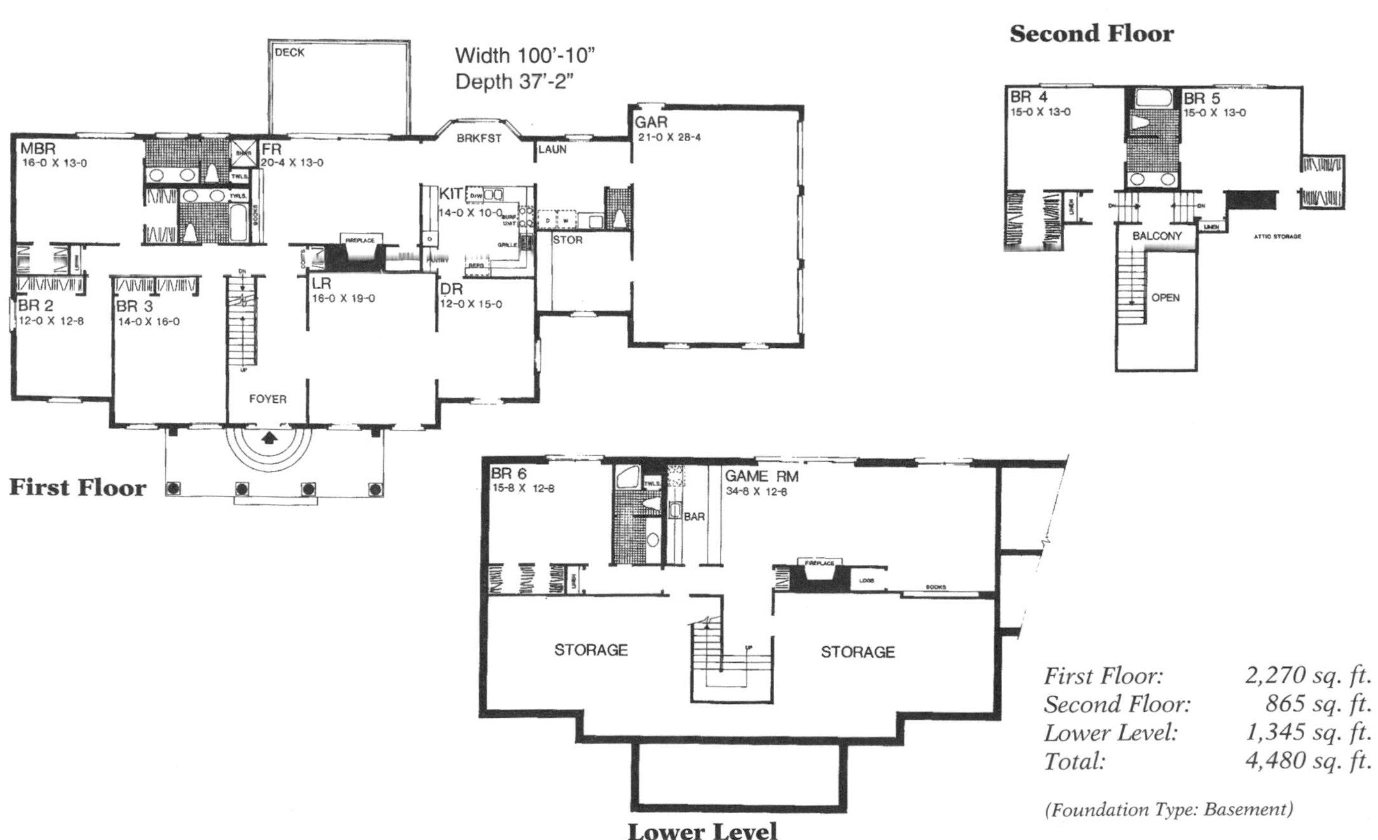


*First Floor:* *2,270 sq. ft.*
*Second Floor:* *865 sq. ft.*
*Lower Level:* *1,345 sq. ft.*
*Total:* *4,480 sq. ft.*

*(Foundation Type: Basement)*

# When You're Ready to Order . . .

## Let Us Show You Our Blueprint Package.

Building a home? Planning a home? Our Blueprint Package contains nearly everything you need to get the job done right, whether you're working on your own or with help from an architect, designer, builder or subcontractors. Each Blueprint Package is the result of many hours of work by licensed architects or professional designers.

## QUALITY

Hundreds of hours of painstaking effort have gone into the development of your blueprint set. Each home has been quality-checked by professionals to insure accuracy and buildability.

## VALUE

Because we sell in volume, you can buy professional-quality blueprints at a fraction of their development cost. With our plans, your dream home design costs only a few hundred dollars, not the thousands of dollars that custom architects charge.

## SERVICE

Once you've chosen your favorite home plan, you'll receive fast efficient service whether you choose to mail your order to us or call us toll free at 1-800-848-2550.

## SATISFACTION

Our years of service to satisfied home plan buyers provide us the experience and knowledge that guarantee your satisfaction with our product and performance.

## ORDER TOLL FREE 1-800-848-2550

After you've studied our Blueprint and Materials List Package on the following page, simply mail the accompanying order form on page 221 or call toll free on our Blueprint Hotline: 1-800-848-2550. We're ready and eager to serve you.

Each set of blueprints is an interrelated collection of floor plans, interior and exterior elevations, dimensions, cross-sections, diagrams and notations showing how your house is to be constructed.

### *Here's what may be included:*

**Frontal Sheet**
An artist's sketch of the exterior of the house, done in two-point perspective. Large ink-line floor plans show all levels of the house and provide a quick overview of your new home's livability.

**Foundation Plan**
In 1/4-inch scale, this sheet shows the complete foundation layout including support walls, excavated and unexcavated areas, if any, and foundation notes. If slab construction, the plan shows footings and details for a monolithic slab. May include a sample plot plan.

**Detailed Floor Plans**
In 1/4-inch scale, these plans show the layout of each floor. All rooms and interior spaces are dimensioned and keys are provided for cross-

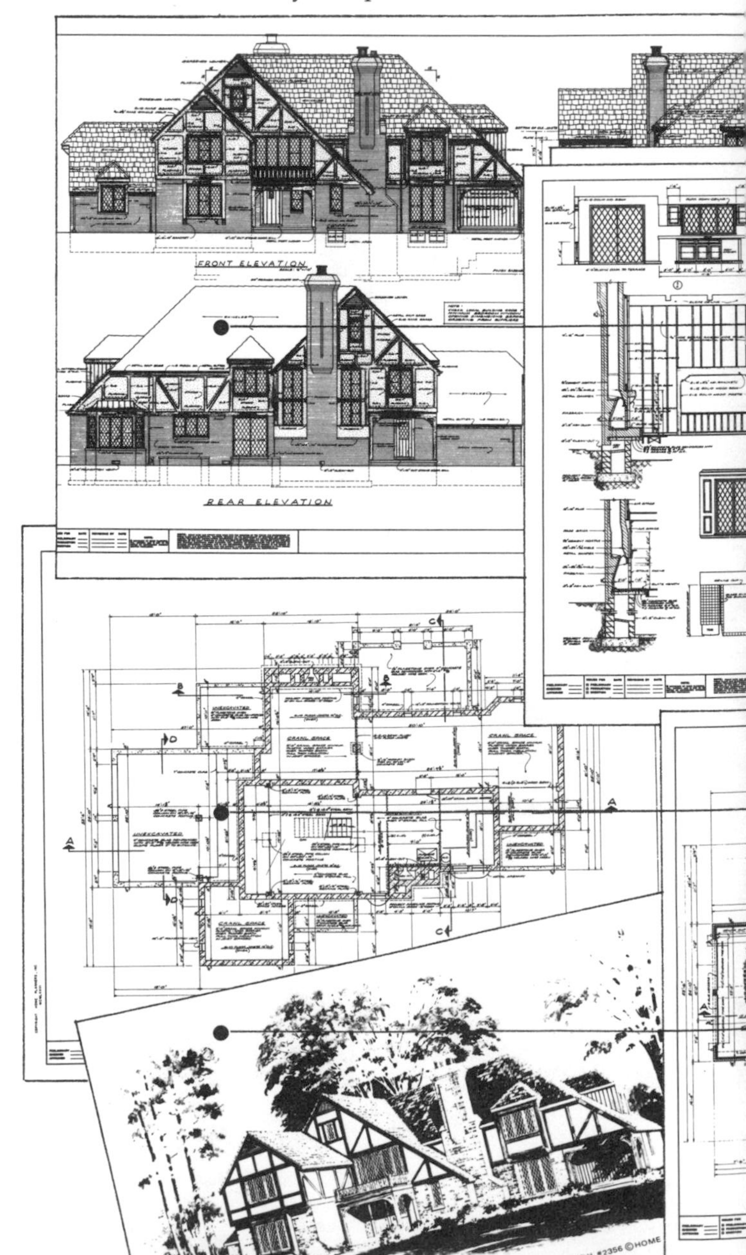

section details given later in the plans. The positions of all electrical outlets and switches are shown.

### House Cross-Sections

Large-scale views, normally drawn at 3/8-inch equals 1 foot, show sections or cut-aways of the foundation, interior walls, exterior walls, floors, stairways and roof details. Additional cross-sections are given to show important changes in floor, ceiling or roof heights or the relationship of one level to another.

### Interior Elevations

These large-scale drawings show the design and placement of kitchen and bathroom cabinets, laundry areas, fireplaces, bookcases and other built-ins. They also provide details that give your home that custom touch.

### Exterior Elevations

Drawings in 1/4-inch scale show the front, rear and sides of your house and give necessary notes on exterior materials and finishes. Particular attention is given to finish items.

## Materials List

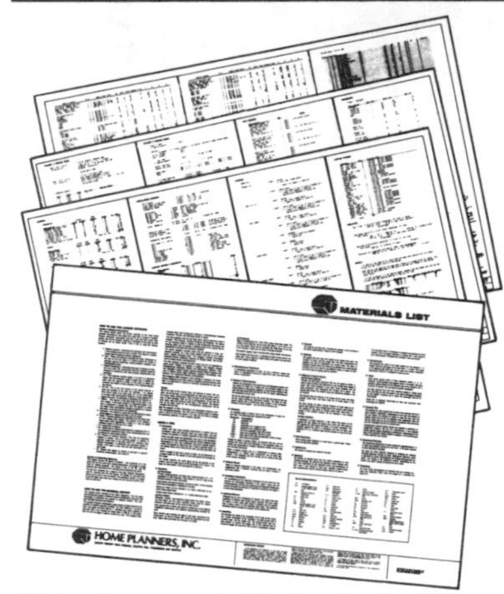


(Note: Because of differing local codes, building methods, and availability of materials, our Materials Lists do not include mechanical materials. To obtain necessary take-offs and recommendations, consult heating, plumbing and electrical contractors. Materials Lists are not sold separately from the Blueprint Package.)

For many of the designs in our portfolio, we offer a customized materials take-off that is invaluable in planning and estimating the cost of your new home. This comprehensive list outlines the quantity, type and size of material needed to build your house (with the exception of mechanical system items). Included are:

- framing lumber
- roofing and sheet metal
- windows and doors
- exterior sheathing material and trim
- masonry, veneer and fireplace materials
- tile and flooring materials
- kitchen and bath cabinetry
- interior drywall and trim
- rough and finish hardware
- many more items

This handy list helps you or your builder cost out materials and serves as a ready reference sheet when you're compiling bids. It also provides a cross-check against the materials specified by your builder and helps coordinate the substitution of items you may need to meet local codes.

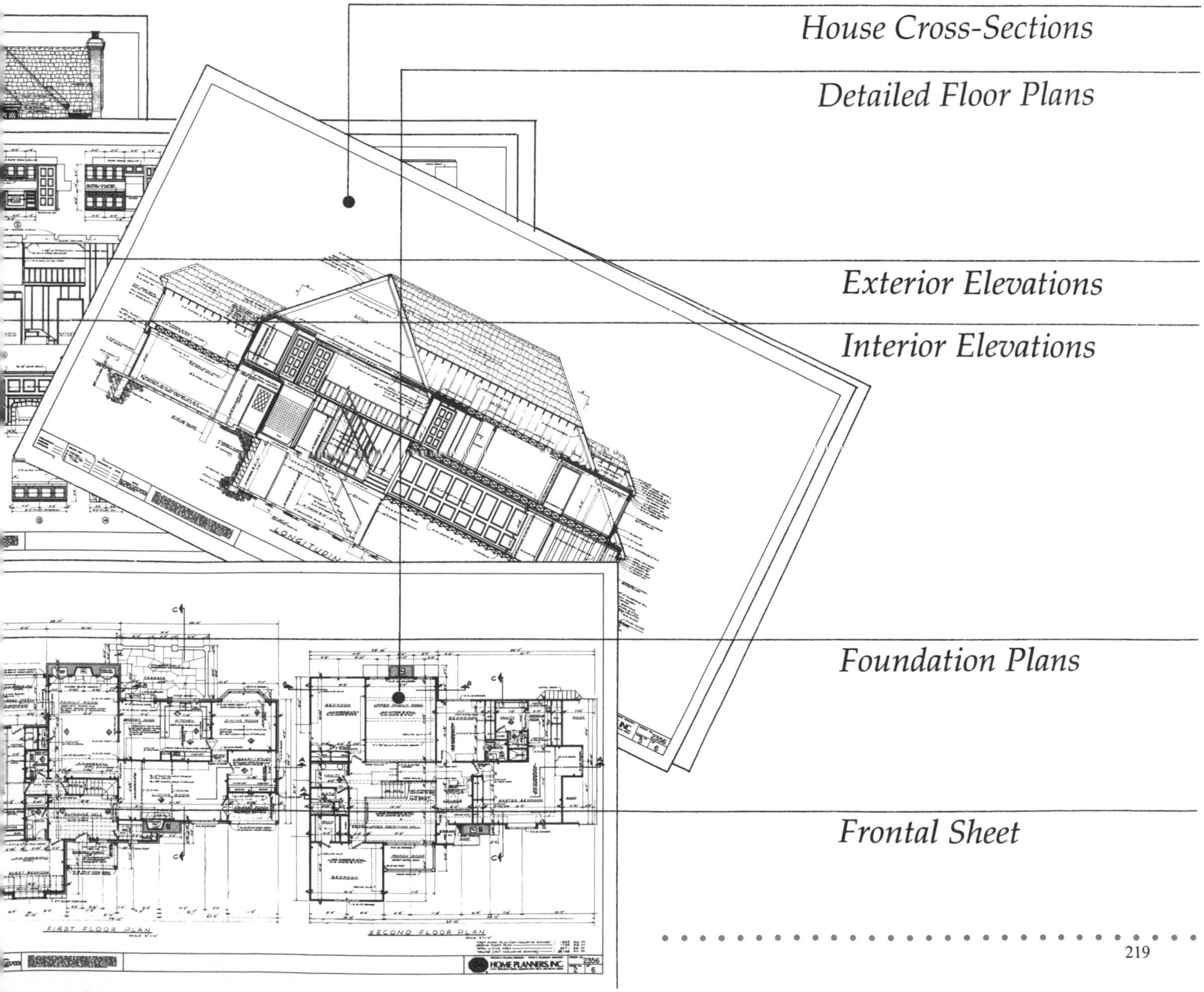

*House Cross-Sections*

*Detailed Floor Plans*

*Exterior Elevations*

*Interior Elevations*

*Foundation Plans*

*Frontal Sheet*

# Price Schedule & Plans Index

These pages contain all the information you need to price your blueprints. In general the larger and more complicated the house, the more it costs to design and thus the higher the price we must charge for the blueprints. Remember, however, that these prices are far less than you would normally pay for the services of a licensed architect or professional designer. Custom home designs and related architectural services often cost thousands of dollars, ranging from 5% to 15% of the cost of construction. By ordering our blueprints you are potentially saving enough money to afford a larger house, or to add those "extra" amenities such as a patio, deck, swimming pool or even an upgraded kitchen or luxurious master suite.

To use the index below, refer to the design number listed in numerical order (a helpful page reference is also given). Note the price index letter and refer to the House Blueprint Price Schedule at right for the cost of one, four or eight sets of blueprints or the cost of a reproducible sepia. Additional prices are shown for identical and reverse blueprint sets, as well as a very useful Materials List to accompany your plans.

### House Blueprint Price Schedule

(Prices guaranteed through December 31, 1994)

| | 1-set Study Package | 4-set Building Package | 8-set Building Package | 1-set Reproducible Sepias |
|---|---|---|---|---|
| Schedule B | $240 | $300 | $360 | $480 |
| Schedule C | $270 | $330 | $390 | $540 |
| Schedule D | $300 | $360 | $420 | $600 |
| Schedule E | $390 | $450 | $510 | $660 |

Additional Identical Blueprints in same order.....$50 per set
Reverse Blueprints (mirror image)........................$50 per set
Materials Lists (for Home Planners' and Alan Mascord's Plans only):

▲ Home Planners' Designs
Schedule B-D..............................................$40
Schedule E....................................................$50

✱ Alan Mascord's Designs...............................$40

To Order: Fill in and send the Order Form on page 221 — or call us **Toll Free 1-800-848-2550**.

# Before You Order . . .

Before completing the coupon at right or calling us on our Toll-Free Blueprint Hotline, you may be interested to learn more about our service and products. Here's some information you will find helpful.

## Quick Turnaround

Every effort is made to begin processing your order the day it is received. However, because each set of blueprints is run in response to your order, it does take 2 to 3 days processing time before an order is shipped. Therefore, please add the necessary processing time to the delivery estimate shown in the Postage and Handling grid at right. Also consult the grid for Commercial Delivery, Post Office Delivery or Overseas Air Mail (including Canada and Mexico).

## Our Exchange Policy

Since blueprints are printed in response to your order, we cannot honor requests for refunds. However, we will exchange your entire first order for an equal number of blueprints at a price of $40 for the first set and $10 for each additional set; $60 total exchange fee for 4 sets; $90 total exchange fee for 8 sets... *plus* the difference in cost if exchanging for a design in a higher price bracket or *less* the difference in cost if exchanging for a design in a lower price bracket. (Sepias are not exchangeable.) All sets from the first order must be returned before the exchange can take place. Please add $8 for postage and handling via ground service; $20 via 2nd Day Air.

## About Reverse Blueprints

If you want to build in reverse of the plan as shown, we will include an extra set of reversed blueprints for an additional fee of $50. Although lettering and dimensions appear backward, reverses will be a useful visual aid if you decide to flop the plan.

## Modifying or Customizing Our Plans

With the wide variety of types and styles of homes offered here, you are likely to find the home that best suits your needs. In addition, our plans can be customized to your taste by your choice of siding, decorative detail, trim, color and other non-structural alterations.

If you do need to make minor modifications to the plans, these can normally be accomplished by your builder without the need for expensive blueprint modifications. However, if you decide to revise the plans significantly, we strongly suggest that you order our reproducible sepias and consult a licensed architect or professional designer to help you redraw the plans to your particular needs.

## Architectural and Engineering Seals

Some cities and states are now requiring that a licensed architect or engineer review and "seal" your blueprints prior to construction. This is often due to local or regional concerns over energy consumption, safety codes, seismic ratings, etc. For this reason, you may find it necessary to consult with a local professional to have your plans reviewed. This can normally be accomplished with minimum delays and for a nominal fee.

## Compliance with Local Codes and Regulations

At the time of creation, our plans are drawn to specifications published by Building Officials Code Administrators (BOCA), the Southern Standard Building Code, or the Uniform Building Code and are designed to meet or exceed national building standards.

Some states, counties and municipalities have their own codes, zoning requirements and building regulations. Before starting construction, consult with local building authorities and make sure you comply with all local ordinances and codes, including obtaining any necessary permits or inspections as building progresses. In some cases, minor modifications to your plans by your builder, local architect or designer may be required to meet local conditions and requirements.

## Foundation and Exterior Wall Changes

Most of our plans are drawn with either a full or partial basement foundation. Depending upon your specific climate or regional building practices, you may wish to convert this basement to a slab or crawlspace. Most professional contractors and builders can easily adapt your plans to alternate foundation types. Likewise, most can easily convert 2x4 wall construction to 2x6, or vice versa.

## About Building Costs

Regional variations in the cost of labor and materials make it impossible for us to estimate the cost of building our houses in different parts of the country. However, you can determine how much houses cost per square foot in your community by consulting local builders and real-estate agents. The figure you derive will help you plan your construction budget. The people best able to determine the true cost of building your house are the general contractors who will bid on the job. So be sure to seek their advice before you commit yourself to any course of action.

# ORDER FORM

HOME PLANS, 3275 West Ina Road
Suite 110, Tucson, Arizona 85741

## THE BASIC BLUEPRINT PACKAGE

Rush me the following (please refer to the Plans Index and Price Schedule in this section):

_____ Set(s) of blueprints for plan number(s) __________. $________

_____ Set(s) of sepias for plan number(s) __________. $________

_____ Additional identical blueprints in same order @ $50 per set. $________

_____ Reverse blueprints (mirror image) @ $50 per set. $________

## IMPORTANT EXTRAS

Rush me the following:

_____ Materials List: Home Planners' Designs @ $40 Schedule B-D; $50 Schedule E; $40 Alan Mascord's Designs. $________

**SUB-TOTAL** $________

**SALES TAX** (Arizona residents add 5% sales tax; Michigan residents add 6% sales tax.) $________

| POSTAGE AND HANDLING | 1-3 sets | 4 or more sets | |
|---|---|---|---|
| COMMERCIAL DELIVERY (Requires street address - No P.O. Boxes) | | | |
| •Regular Service Allow 4-6 days delivery | ❑ $6.00 | ❑ $8.00 | $_____ |
| •2nd Day Air Allow 2-3 days delivery | ❑ $12.00 | ❑ $20.00 | $_____ |
| •Next Day Air Allow 1 day delivery | ❑ $22.00 | ❑ $30.00 | $_____ |
| POST OFFICE DELIVERY If no street address available. Allow 4-6 days delivery | ❑ $8.00 | ❑ $12.00 | $_____ |
| OVERSEAS AIR MAIL DELIVERY | ❑ $30.00 | ❑ $50.00 | $_____ |
| **Note: All delivery times above are from date Blueprint Package is shipped. Allow 2-3 days processing time before shipping.** | | | |

**TOTAL in U.S. Funds** $________

## YOUR ADDRESS (please print)

Name ______________________________

Street ______________________________

City ______________ State ______ Zip ________

Daytime telephone number (_____) ______________

## FOR CREDIT CARD ORDERS ONLY

Please fill in the information below:

Credit card number ______________________

Exp. Date: Month/Year__________

Check one ❑ Visa ❑ MasterCard ❑ Discover Card

Signature ______________________________

Order Form Key: CHPD

Please check appropriate box:
❑ Licensed Builder-Contractor
❑ Home Owner

**ORDER TOLL FREE 1-800-848-2550**

### HOME DECORATING WITH
## PAINT, TILE, WALLCOVERING

Using easy-to-master techniques and everyday materials, this guide focuses on designing and accomplishing today's most stylish options for walls, ceilings, floors and furnishings. Instructions are well illustrated with step-by-step drawings.

**96 pages. $8.95**

### CHOOSING A
## COLOR SCHEME

Learn how to use color with the confidence of a seasoned professional. Photographs demonstrate varied approaches to color, light, pattern and texture and how they make a room look and feel. An invaluable decorating tool.

**96 pages. $8.95**

### PLANNING A PERFECT
## LIVING ROOM

Not only is the living room the showcase of the home, it is also the one place where family members entertain, relax and eat. Learn how to accommodate all of these functions without sacrificing style or comfort.

**96 pages. $8.95**

### DESIGNING AND PLANNING
## BEDROOMS

In order to cater to specific needs, bedrooms require careful planning. This guide is an inspiration to those who dream of the perfect bedroom, but aren't sure how to create it. Guest rooms, studios and more included.

**96 pages. $8.95**

### PLANNING A
## BETTER KITCHEN

From layout design, to choosing appliances, to creating a pleasing atmosphere, no detail of kitchen planning is overlooked. This fully illustrated guide helps homeowners make well-informed decisions in planning the ideal kitchen.

**96 pages. $8.95**

### DESIGNING AND PLANNING
## BATHROOMS

From the planning stage to the decorating stage, this guide is designed to help the homeowner acquire the perfect bathroom. Innovative and dramatic ideas for master baths, fitness bathrooms, powder rooms and more.

**96 pages. $8.95**

# *...for Dream Homes!*

# Home Plan Index